PRIVACY AND EMPLOYMENT LAW

Privacy and Employment Law

JOHN D. R. CRAIG

·HART·
PUBLISHING

OXFORD – PORTLAND OREGON
1999

Hart Publishing
Oxford and Portland, Oregon

Published in North America (US and Canada) by
Hart Publishing c/o
International Specialized Book Services
5804 NE Hassalo Street
Portland, Oregon
97213-3644
USA

Distributed in the Netherlands, Belgium and Luxembourg by
Intersentia, Churchillaan 108
B2900 Schoten
Antwerpen
Belgium

Distributed in Australia and New Zealand by
Federation Press
John St
Leichhardt
NSW 2000

Hart Publishing Ltd is a specialist legal publisher based in Oxford, England.
To order further copies of this book or to request a list of other
publications please write to:

Hart Publishing Ltd, Salter's Boatyard, Oxford OX1 4LB
Telephone: +44 (0)1865 245533 or Fax: +44 (0)1865 794882
e-mail: mail@hartpub.co.uk

British Library Cataloguing in Publication Data
Data Available
ISBN 1 84113–059–1 (cloth)

Typeset by Hope Services (Abingdon) Ltd.
Printed in Great Britain on acid-free paper
by Biddles Ltd, Guildford and Kings Lynn.

Preface

In this Preface, I wish first to address why I chose to spend almost four years researching and writing about the right of privacy in the workplace. The short answer is that the issue is important, raises complex legal issues, and 'someone had to study it so why not me?'. There is much more to it than that, however. My two great loves in law are human rights and labour law. I came to the study of law from a political science and business administration background, which explains in part my attraction to industrial relations and labour law. My interest in the issue of human rights in employment arose from a personal and rather traumatic incident. As a student working for a government agency, I was fired for publishing an article in a university newsletter detailing my personal experiences with, and criticisms of, bureaucracy. My free speech and academic freedom arguments ultimately won back my job, but the experience has remained with me as a reminder of how fragile basic human rights can be in the workplace.

When I decided to pursue doctoral studies at University of Oxford, I knew that my research would combine labour law and human rights issues. I chose to focus on the right of privacy because the controversy surrounding the meaning of privacy and the application of the concept in the employment context provided much fodder for academic analysis. I was also enthusiastic about analysing controversial privacy issues like drug and genetic testing. I should emphasise that I did not approach the topic with a personal agenda to ban drug testing, etc. I feel that I was open-minded, and sceptical in a healthy academic way. My only brush with workplace privacy occurred several years ago when I and several colleagues suspected, but never proved, that a supervisor was reading our inter-office e-mail. This was disconcerting, but was hardly an event justifying several years of doctoral work.

My academic interest in workplace privacy has evolved since January 1996, and through this evolution I have developed stronger, better-defined views. Although it has been enjoyable to pursue an issue which is constantly mentioned in the popular press (and makes for intriguing dinner party conversation), the sheer number of horror stories I have read in the newspapers has made me aware that workplace privacy is not simply a theoretical legal issue, but is a matter of basic human dignity. This fact has been brought home to me on various occasions by the employment experiences of friends—one was drug tested, another was ordered to provide a handwriting sample for a personality assessment, another was required to provide intimate health information irrelevant to the job, while another was told where he could and could not live. I have at times been astonished by the methods of control which employers impose as 'human resource policies'. I am sure that many of these methods reflect bad management practices. I am also certain that many of them should be illegal. The fact that they are not in some jurisdictions is, of course, the reason I undertook this project.

As we approach the next millennium, I believe that we have a unique opportunity to refocus employment regulation in North American and European Union nations; to engage in what I like to refer to as the 'individualisation of labour law'. The essential features of labour law individualisation are: a reduced emphasis on collective labour organisations to promote the welfare of individual employees; the empowerment of individuals through the creation of rights and remedies which are available to job candidates and employees regardless of their organised status; and the transposition of human rights law from the public sphere into the employment relationship, thereby permitting these rights to be asserted by individuals against both employers and collective representatives. Hence, my basic premise is that law can and should provide a foundation of protection, or a 'floor of rights', for all job candidates and employees. In particular, labour law in the twenty-first century should support the inherent dignity of work by recognising and protecting the human right of privacy as part of this 'floor'.

I should add some words about the jurisdictions which I have chosen to consider. Canada is my country, and therefore an obvious choice. It is the best place in the world to live, unless you are a worker whose privacy has been invaded (!). In that case, you would be better off in France, a protective jurisdiction which I chose because it is part of the European Union (thereby permitting me to consider European-level law as well), and presents no linguistic obstacles since I speak French. The United States was the inevitable choice for my third jurisdiction because of its influence on Canadian law, and because its litigious nature has provided me with a wealth of jurisprudence from which to draw.

When I commenced this project, I did not intend to consider the law of the United Kingdom in any detail, since the right of privacy did not exist in UK law. However, the introduction of a Human Rights Act, incorporating the European Convention on Human Rights into domestic law, and the implementation of the European Directive on Data Protection both occurred over the course of my research. I simply could not ignore such exciting, almost revolutionary, developments in UK law. As a result, my project found a new and timely focus: the elaboration of the emerging right of privacy in United Kingdom employment law through an examination of the law of workplace privacy in three other jurisdictions.

This book is a revised, expanded and updated version of my doctoral thesis, 'Legal Principles for the Protection of the Right of Privacy in the Workplace', which I submitted in August 1998 to the Faculty of Law, University of Oxford. Throughout the writing of my thesis and the preparation of this book, it was my good fortune to enjoy tremendous support from family, friends, mentors and colleagues. I would like to take the opportunity here to express my heartfelt gratitude to all, and to single out some for special mention.

First and foremost, I would like to thank my parents for being so wonderful. The same goes for my sister and brother-in-law. Without the love and undying patience of my family, I cannot imagine that this project would ever have been started, let alone completed.

Secondly, I would like to thank two distinguished individuals who have influenced my work, and to whom I dedicate this book: Justice Charles Gonthier of the Supreme Court of Canada, a superb legal thinker and role model, and Professor Peter Darby of Dalhousie Law School, a true great among legal teachers.

I would also like to thank Dr Christopher McCrudden of Lincoln College, University of Oxford, who supervised my doctoral research. In particular, I would like to thank him for allowing me the freedom to engage in academic exploration, while providing the guidance which prevented me from becoming hopelessly lost. Several other academics have provided invaluable support, advice and enlightenment, and I would like to thank them here: Professor Silvana Sciarra of the European University Institute (who sponsored my research visit to Florence, Italy, and permitted me to participate in her European Labour Law seminar), Professor Paul Weiler of Harvard Law School (who sponsored my research visit to Cambridge, Massachusetts), Dr Elaine Bernard of Harvard University's Trade Union Programme, Professor Paul Davies of the London School of Economics, Professor Matthew Finkin of the University of Illinois, Professor Mark Freedland of the University of Oxford, Professor Thomas Kohler of Boston College, Dr Anne Lofaso of the National Labour Relations Board, Washington, DC, Professor Basil Markesinis of the Centre for the Advanced Studies of European and Comparative Law, University of Oxford, Professor Spiro Simitis of J. W. Goethe University, and Professor David Westfall of Harvard Law School.

My friends have provided extraordinary support, and I owe them all a debt of gratitude. I would like to single out for special mention Hazel Oliver, whose contributions to this project were immense.

I also wish to acknowledge the contributions of the Commonwealth Scholarship Commission and the Social Sciences and Humanities Research Council of Canada, both of which provided financial support for my research. I would also like to express my gratitude to Lincoln College, University of Oxford, which served as my base of studies, and more importantly my HOME, from 1993–4 and 1996–8.

Finally, I wish to thank my law firm Osler, Hoskin & Harcourt for supporting the revision of my doctoral thesis into a book, and for providing the resources to make that possible. I am particularly grateful to Sarah Edwards, a summer student with the firm in 1999, for assisting with my final revisions.

I close by expressing the hope that my research, as embodied in this book, will contribute to advancing the law in the United States, France, Canada and the

United Kingdom. I also believe that my comparative analysis can benefit other countries, and assist in efforts to develop international standards through the International Labour Office and other bodies.

DR JOHN D. R. CRAIG

Toronto, Canada
30 June 1999

Table of Contents

List of Abbreviations

ADA	Americans with Disabilities Act
ALI	American Law Institute
AMA	American Medical Association
CNIL	Commission Nationale de l'Informatique et des Libertés
DEC	Drug Evaluation and Classification training
DNA	deoxyribonucleic acid
DPA	Data Protection Act
ECPA	Electronic Communications Privacy Act
EIM	enzyme immunoassay method
EPPA	Employee Polygraph Protection Act
ERA	Employment Rights Act
HGP	Human Genome Project
ILO	International Labour Office
IPCO	Information and Privacy Commissioner of Ontario
MRO	Medical Review Officer
OLRC	Ontario Law Reform Commission
OMB	Office of Management and Budget
OTA	Office of Technology Assessment
PCC	Privacy Commissioner of Canada
PCP	phencyclidine
PCWA	Privacy for Consumers and Workers Act
WSA	Workplace Substance Abuse programme

Table of Statutes and Other Instruments

UNITED STATES

INTERNATIONAL CONVENTIONS AND AGREEMENTS

OTHER

Table of Cases

FRANCE

CANADA

UNITED KINGDOM

EUROPEAN COMMUNITIES

OTHER

1

Introduction

'Workers' rights to privacy should be treated as a fundamental human rights issue.'
Director General of the International Labour Office, 1988

1.1 THE EVOLUTION OF LABOUR AND HUMAN RIGHTS LAW
IN THE UNITED KINGDOM

At the close of the twentieth century and the second millennium, circumstances have brought the issue of human rights in the employment context to the forefront of the legal and policy agendas in the United Kingdom. Foremost among these circumstances is the election in 1997 of the first Labour government in almost 20 years—a government that is receptive to enhancing the rights of workers and to pursuing employment law reform at both the domestic and European levels. In the past, the United Kingdom has been sceptical and even hostile to laws that could interfere in the employment relationship, particularly where such laws were 'imposed' by Europe. Today, this attitude is changing. The incorporation of the European Convention on Human Rights into UK law, and the domestic implementation of the European Directive on Data Protection,[1] are two examples of European-inspired measures which potentially empower workers in their relationships with employers, and limit the controls which employers may assert over workers' lives. I will discuss both of these measures in section 1.2 below, and will return to them again in Chapter 10.

The rethinking of UK employment law is taking place at the end of an era of Conservative rule during which the government was openly opposed to collective labour action. Scepticism about the efficacy of collective solutions to labour problems continues today with the realisation that the labour movement has hardly been a resounding success in promoting the social and economic interests of individual workers. Such scepticism is not UK-centred, of course. The inadequacies of labour law systems which emphasise collective over individual empowerment are all too obvious in jurisdictions like Canada and the United States where, as in the United Kingdom, organised workers account for less than one third of the total workforce. Any jurisdiction which lacks comprehensive legal protection for employees regardless of their organised status not only fails

---

[1] European Directive on Data Protection, Dir. 95/46/EC of the European Parliament and of the Council of 24 Oct. 1995, on the protection of individuals with regard to the processing of personal data and on the free movement of such data [1995] OJ L281/31.

to protect workers from domestic conditions, but is also poorly equipped to resist the late-twentieth century phenomenon of 'social dumping' whereby worker protection is eroded as nations reduce the costs associated with labour to achieve competitive advantages in international trade.

A new movement within labour law is now emerging based on the premise that law can and should provide a foundation of protection, or a 'floor of rights', for all job candidates and employees regardless of their organised status. This movement takes the view that labour law in the twenty-first century should support the inherent dignity of work by protecting and empowering the individual. One important aspect of individual empowerment would involve strengthening human rights law in its application to the employment context. The legal protection of the right of equality through anti-discrimination statutes would be an appropriate model for a more broadly based human rights approach within labour law. Such an approach would not only provide heightened protection to all candidates/employees, but would also achieve certainty—itself an important goal for labour law. As I will demonstrate as this book unfolds, the law of human rights in employment is often an incoherent 'mish-mash'. Employers operating in federal systems, and operating in several nations, may be prevented from adopting unified human resource policies on matters implicating human rights because of conflicts in the laws of different jurisdictions. The identification of legal principles to guide the development of human rights law in all countries will ensure improved protection for candidates/employees, while promoting certainty for employers.

Hence, proposals to reform employment law in the United Kingdom must be considered in the context of increasing governmental enthusiasm for promoting the interests of individual workers through enhanced human rights law, and of rising concern about the challenges posed by the globalisation of labour markets. Against this background, I will consider one particular human right, the right of privacy, and its application in employment. My purpose is to develop legal principles for the protection of workers' private interests. The methodology will be comparative. Although the right of privacy is only now emerging in UK law, it has been a long-standing fixture of human rights law in most other North American and European jurisdictions. Hence, much can be learned from the experiences of those jurisdictions. The workplace privacy laws of three countries, the United States, France and Canada, will be analysed herein. Through this analysis, I will identify regulatory principles that form a 'best practice' model. Then, as a final step, I will employ this model to propose an outline for a new regime of workplace privacy law in the United Kingdom.

1.2 WORKPLACE PRIVACY LAW IN THE UNITED KINGDOM—BACKGROUND

The constitutional law of the United Kingdom does not presently recognise the right to private life, nor does the common law give effect to a tort of invasion of privacy.[2] This state of affairs has been a source of considerable controversy over the past several decades, and various legislative proposals have been advanced to fill the privacy void, yet have failed.[3] Hence, unlike many jurisdictions including the United States, France and Canada, the right of privacy has no historical foundation in British law. This means that there is, in short, no identifiable law of workplace privacy in the United Kingdom, and that management practices such as drug testing, genetic testing, and electronic monitoring are presently unregulated.[4] The only potential source of a right of privacy in the workplace has been the Data Protection Act (DPA),[5] a statute regulating information collection, processing, and storage in the public and private sectors. The DPA does not mention the concept of privacy, regulates only *automated* data, and in practice has been largely irrelevant to employment information practices.[6]

The United Kingdom's lack of workplace privacy regulation is now being challenged by two legal developments: (1) the incorporation of the European Convention on Human Rights (the 'Convention') through the Human Rights Act[7]; and (2) the implementation of the European Directive on Data Protection (the 'Directive') through the new Data Protection Act.[8]

Incorporation of the Convention will effectively create a set of constitutional human rights, and will permit citizens to assert provisions such as the right to private life (as guaranteed by Article 8 of the Convention) before UK courts and tribunals to challenge the actions of public authorities. As a result, the right of privacy will be available to public employees to challenge invasive management practices, as in the United States and Canada.[9] The newly-incorporated right can also be expected to influence the development of the common law and the interpretation of statutes. Hence, as in some American and Canadian jurisdictions, the right of privacy will become relevant to private sector employment through the law of unfair dismissal and the interpretation of the employer's duty of trust and confidence.

Implementation of the Directive will create a legal regime governing both automated and non-automated data, akin to the French model of information

---

[2] See Markesinis (1990d); *Kaye* v. *Robertson* [1990], FSR 62 (CA).

[3] This debate is reflected in the 6 Private Member's Bills on privacy which have been proposed, but rejected, over the past 37 years: Lord Mancroft (1961); Mr Alex Lyon (1967); Mr Brian Walden (1969); Mr William Cash (1987); Mr John Browne (1988); Lord Stoddart (1989). There have also been several governmental and expert reports on the issue, including JUSTICE (British Section) (1970); Committee on Privacy (1972); Committee on Privacy and Related Matters (1990); National Heritage Select Committee (1993); Lord Chancellor's Department/The Scottish Office (1993).

[4] ILO (1993a, 2), 267; (1993, 3), 304. See *Halford* v. *The United Kingdom* [1997] IRLR 47 (ECHR), discussed in greater detail *infra*, section 5.3.2.

[5] Data Protection Act, 1984, c. 35, in force since 1987.

[6] Napier (1992), 11.

[7] The Human Rights Act 1998 received Royal Assent on 9 Nov. 1998. The Act is expected to come into force on 2 Oct. 2000.

[8] The Data Protection Act 1998 received Royal Assent on 16 July 1998. Pursuant to Art. 32 of the Dir., the Act should have come into force by 24 Oct. 1998. Its implementation was delayed in the UK, and it will not be in force until mid-1999.

[9] *Infra*, sections 4.3.3.1, 6.4.1.

privacy which I discuss below in section 5.4.1 of Chapter 5. The Directive is unmistakably a privacy initiative, as it explicitly requires Member States of the European Union 'to protect the right to privacy with respect to the processing of personal data'.[10] This confirms that the right of privacy will soon become an integral part of UK law, including labour law. All information obtained from candidates/employees will be subject to procedural and other safeguards similar to those existing in France. The potential therefore exists for the new Data Protection Act to become as significant to the law governing informational private interests in the workplace as the French Law of 6 January 1978.[11]

These two legal developments will make it possible for a comprehensive body of workplace privacy law to emerge in the United Kingdom. However, the nature and scope of the protection offered by this body of law remains to be determined. One of my key purposes herein will be to provide both general guidance and specific legal principles which may be employed in interpreting the privacy provisions of the Human Rights Act and the Data Protection Act in so far as they apply to employment. To this end, I will move now to Chapter 2, and an analysis of the concept of privacy both generally and in the employment context. This will be followed in later chapters by analyses of the workplace privacy laws of the United States, France and Canada, and of two particularly controversial workplace privacy issues: drug testing and genetic testing. In my final chapter, Chapter 10, I will return to the issue of United Kingdom workplace privacy law, and will explain how this emerging area of law can be developed in a manner consistent with the view that privacy is a fundamental human right.

---

[10]   Art. 1(1).
[11]   *Infra*, section 5.4.1.

2

The Right of Privacy and Competing Interests in the Employment Context

When the right of privacy emerged in the legal systems of Western nations, it was characterised as a 'right to be let alone'—a legal shield which could be asserted by the individual against the prying eyes of the public. In describing the right of privacy, the eminent American commentators, Warren and Brandeis, viewed its role as limiting the scandal-mongering and 'idle gossip' of the press.[1] Privacy thus served to spare individuals from the hurt feelings, embarrassment, and even humiliation associated with public revelations of certain facts deemed to be private. It was, in short, a safeguard of individual spiritual well-being. By the mid-twentieth century, however, the right of privacy had come to be viewed as a fundamental constraint on state power. The connection between totalitarianism and breach of privacy is exemplified by Orwell's classic political novel, *Nineteen Eighty-Four*,[2] where Big Brother's success in maintaining absolute power was achieved through the destruction of citizens' privacy. Although Orwell's fictionalised account was extreme, the privacy-invasive practices of fascist and communist regimes throughout the twentieth century made the threat of Big Brother seem, at times, uncomfortably real. Legal protection of personal privacy in Western nations thus came to have political and ideological significance for society generally, in addition to its importance for the well-being of the individual spirit. In this way, the right of privacy emerged not only as a civil or private right, but also as a constitutional or public right which could be asserted against invasive state activities.

In the past decade, the right of privacy has taken on legal relevance in the employment context, and has been recast by some commentators as an appropriate tool for guiding the regulation of the employment relationship and, in particular, the use by management of certain techniques viewed by workers and others as potentially privacy-invasive. These techniques include what will be referred to as 'testing' (e.g. drug testing, the polygraph, genetic screening, handwriting analysis, etc.) and 'monitoring' (e.g. the monitoring of work

---

[1] Warren and Brandeis (1890), 196.
[2] Orwell (1949).

performance through such means as closed-circuit television cameras, listening devices, etc.). To date, a host of government reports and academic writings have called for the legal protection of worker privacy rights.[3] However, such calls seek to extend the right of privacy beyond its traditional roles in limiting state power and the press. The important issue thus arises whether, and to what extent, the right of privacy should play a role in regulating the employment relationship.

In this chapter, I will consider what is meant by the legal concept of 'privacy', and how that concept may be applied in the workplace. Thus, my objectives in Chapter 2 are to provide a definition of privacy, to identify the interests of job candidates and employees (candidates/employees) which are protected by the right of privacy, and to consider the countervailing interests of employers and the public which may potentially justify limitations of privacy.

2.2 THE PREVALENCE OF PRIVACY-INVASIVE MANAGEMENT PRACTICES

The increasing use of testing and monitoring by employers has resulted in workplace privacy becoming one of the most controversial labour law issues of the 1990s. This controversy has no doubt been fuelled by reports in the popular press concerning the availability of certain sophisticated, yet potentially privacy-invasive, management tools. For example, the use of the following technologies/techniques has been reported in the past several years: computer screen monitoring,[4] chair sensors,[5] bugs and listening devices,[6] motor vehicle on-board sensors,[7] location badges,[8] brain-wave testing,[9] lie detectors,[10] urinalysis drug

---

[3] ILO (1991, 1993a) provides a comprehensive overview of the various governmental reports and academic views.

[4] Also known as 'peeking'. New computer software allows supervisors to call up secretly the screens of employees (*Fortune* (1993)). Employers may now utilise a software tool called 'Little Brother' to monitor the Internet addresses accessed by their employees, and to identify the size and content of any downloaded files. Access to individual sites may also be blocked (*Personal Computer World* (1997)).

[5] These devices, installed in the seat of a chair, measure the amount of time an employee remains seated, and also record movement and shifting on the chair as a gauge of restlessness (*Fortune* (1993)).

[6] It was recently alleged that Northern Telecom had 'bugged' its employees for years, and had used the information obtained to fight union organising campaigns (*ibid.*).

[7] Employer-owned automobiles are being equipped with sensors to measure distance travelled, fuel consumption, deviation from standard routes, length of rest stops and the location of the vehicle at any time (Linowes and Spencer (1990), 601).

[8] Employers may now track employees' movements by requiring them to wear a special badge containing a microchip (*Fortune* (1993)).

[9] Still in its development stages, it is predicted that brain mapping could be employed to assess a prospective candidate's/employee's concentration ability and suitability for certain tasks (Boehmer (1992), 754).

[10] Polygraph testing has long been available to test the honesty of a candidate, and to investigate theft (Linowes and Spencer (1990), 605).

testing,[11] genetic screening and monitoring,[12] personality testing,[13] and voice stress analysis.[14]

The extent to which European Union and North American employers actually use such technologies is unclear, not only because there have been few comprehensive studies on the issue, but also because much of the technology can be used secretly. Moreover, surveys and studies in the field of workplace privacy have largely focused on the situation in the United States. Studies estimate that between six and 20 million American workers, or approximately 10 per cent of the workforce, are presently subject to on-the-job electronic surveillance.[15] In some sectors of the American economy, such as telecommunications, insurance, and banking, it has been estimated that as many as 80 per cent of employees may be subject to telephone- or computer-based monitoring.[16] The growth of employee monitoring and surveillance in the United States over the past decade is demonstrated by the computer industry's 1991 estimate that sales of computer surveillance software would amount to US$175 million, and would continue to grow by 50 per cent each year thereafter.[17] Similar growth is expected in the use by American employers of testing methods, such as drug testing. In fact, the American Management Association reported in 1993 that 98 per cent of Fortune 200 employers were conducting pre-employment and/or employment drug screening.[18] In 1995, seven to ten million American workers were drug tested, with one testing company accounting for 3,760,000 tests.[19]

Studies concerning Canadian employers suggest that the use of testing and monitoring is not as widespread as in the United States, but is nevertheless on the increase. Thus, a 1990 study revealed that 48 per cent of Canadian small business executives favoured some form of drug testing for candidates/employees,[20] while at least 30 large Canadian companies had already implemented such testing. These included Air Canada, Imperial Oil, Toronto-Dominion Bank,

[11] A wide array of sophisticated urine tests have been developed to detect the past consumption of illicit drugs. See *infra*, section 8.4.

[12] The technology is now available to test the genetic make-up of candidates/employees, in order to screen out those who are vulnerable to genetic disease (PCC (1992d), 31; *infra*, section 9.4). *TIME Magazine* (1997) reports that a 1997 study in the United States chronicled 200 subjects who claimed to have been discriminated against as a result of genetic testing.

[13] It is estimated that close to 6,000 American employers use personality testing in screening and hiring candidates (Mello (1995), 662).

[14] A device has been developed which may be installed in a telephone in order to measure stress levels and assess honesty (*ibid.*, 666).

[15] US Representative Pat Williams provided this figure in his opening comments as Chairman, US House of Representatives Committee on Education and Labor (1993). The figure came from a survey in Piller (1993). The OTA estimated the number of workers monitored electronically to be at least six million (Maltby (1993), 67).

[16] Piller (1993), 124–30.

[17] *Fortune* (1993).

[18] American Management Association (1993).

[19] Jacobs (1996), 120. The company was SmithKline Beecham Chemical Laboratories.

[20] This study was conducted by Arthur Anderson & Co., and the results were reported in PCC (1990b).

Canadian National Railways, and Canadian Pacific.[21] In the past eight years, the Ontario Law Reform Commission (OLRC), the Information and Privacy Commissioner of Ontario (IPCO), and the Privacy Commissioner of Canada (PCC) have all identified employment testing and monitoring as matters of serious concern, and have all called for legislative reform to protect privacy in the workplace.[22]

Is the use of privacy-invasive technology primarily a phenomenon of North American management? In its 1993 survey of alcohol and drug testing practices, the International Labour Organisation (ILO) concluded that '[d]rug testing in employment has not been embraced in other industrialized countries with the same enthusiasm or on the same scale as in the United States', but added that some American multinational companies had exported their drug testing policies into other countries like France.[23] A parallel ILO study concerning employee monitoring, with an emphasis on electronic surveillance, also noted that these practices were 'less common' in Europe.[24] There are some limited studies which demonstrate that European Union nations are experiencing a proliferation in the use of potentially invasive technologies, and that the difference in the situations in the European Union and North America is a matter of degree. For example, a study by the Dutch Department of Social Affairs found that the introduction by employers of monitoring systems, such as access cards and the video monitoring of production processes, was increasing rapidly. The study, conducted in 1988, identified 299 monitoring systems in 167 corporate respondents; 114 of these systems had been introduced in 1988 alone.[25] Another study from the Netherlands, this one concerning drug testing, estimated that 20 major companies were testing for alcohol and drug use by employees for safety reasons.[26] Two other studies, one from Sweden and the other from the United Kingdom, each concluded that approximately 10 per cent of private sector employees work in companies that have alcohol or drug testing programmes.[27]

While the problem of workplace privacy may be more pressing in North America than in the European Union, at least judging from the available survey results and studies, the evidence does suggest that the nature of the problem is the same. Essentially, there is a trend in the United States, Canada and the European Union towards the increasing use by employers of testing and monitoring technology. This trend was clearly identified by the ILO in its studies con-

---

[21] OLRC (1992a), 1.

[22] *Ibid.*; IPCO (1993); PCC (1990b).

[23] ILO (1993a, 3), 15, 227.

[24] ILO (1993a, 2), 27.

[25] Dutch Ministry of Social Affairs and Employment (1989). This study is discussed in *ibid.*, 27–8.

[26] Bijl, 'Alcohol and Drugs in the Workplace: Attitudes, Policies and Programmes in the Netherlands', unpublished study discussed in ILO (1993a, 3), 16–17.

[27] *Ibid.*, 17–18. Drug testing in the UK may be on the rise following the recommendation by the Institute of Personnel and Development (1997) that employers should promulgate drug policies including random drug testing. See also Rice and Thomas (1997).

cerning worker privacy.[28] Calls for legal reform in the area of workplace privacy must therefore be viewed not only in the context of the actual use by employers of certain technologies/techniques which raise privacy concerns, but also in light of the proliferation of such technologies/techniques, and the potential for future developments which could fuel this trend. For example, the high cost of testing and monitoring technologies has no doubt discouraged their use in employment, particularly by small and medium-sized employers. However, costs are expected to decrease over time as the technologies are refined. In the case of drug testing, the average cost of testing a subject dropped from US$35 in 1990 to US$15–20 in 1993.[29] AIDS tests, which once cost over US$700 and had to be performed in a laboratory, can now be purchased over-the-counter for US$1–2.[30] Inexpensive testing technology may well become more attractive to employers, particularly where the technology is perceived to further management objectives such as improving worker efficiency or ensuring workplace safety.

Given that the use by employers of potentially privacy-invasive technology is on the increase in both North America and the European Union, one can predict that the conflict and controversy surrounding the issue will become magnified. One preliminary question must be addressed in any discussion of privacy-related employment matters: where should the authority lie to determine whether, and to what extent, employers may adopt policies and practices which have the potential to infringe candidates'/employees' privacy? Should it be a matter solely within management prerogative? Should it be left to negotiations between management and collective labour representatives, in those firms where such negotiations are possible? Or does the law, in one or more of its forms, have a role to play in the area? Before proceeding to consider these questions in Chapter 3, I will first offer a working definition of 'privacy', and will explain the role of the concept in the employment context from the perspectives of candidates/employees, employers, and the public.

2.3.1 Definitional Uncertainty and the Functional Approach

The intensity and complexity of life, attendant upon advancing civilization, have rendered necessary some retreat from the world, and man, under the refining influence of culture, has become more sensitive to publicity, so that solitude and privacy have become more essential to the individual; but modern enterprise and invention have, through invasions of privacy, subjected him to mental pain and distress, far greater than could be inflicted by mere bodily injury.[31]

---

[28] ILO (1993s, 2, 3).
[29] *Ibid.* (3), 20.
[30] *Ibid.*, 47–8.
[31] Warren and Brandeis (1890), 196.

So wrote Warren and Brandeis in their groundbreaking 1890 *Harvard Law Review* article, advocating the recognition at common law of a general right of privacy. Referring to the right specifically as the 'right to be let alone',[32] Warren and Brandeis argued that privacy was central to the enjoyment of life, but was coming under attack in modern society. The common law, according to the two writers, should respond through the judicial recognition of a tort remedy for invasions of privacy, since such invasions offend the human spirit.[33]

Warren and Brandeis were the first common law[34] scholars to recognise that the importance of privacy to the individual and society should be fostered through legal privacy protection, and they were thus the first to advocate the judicial recognition of a general privacy right. However, the concept of 'private life', as distinct from 'public life', and the role of that conceptual distinction in liberal-democratic societies, have been part of political and philosophical debate for centuries.[35] This debate has sought to distinguish between the areas of life where governmental, or public, intervention is justified, and a private area immune from such intervention. However, the law will remain relevant even to this private sphere of life, since there may arise a need to shield by law that which is private from public encroachment. Thus, the common law has developed a considerable body of protection against *tangible* intrusions by others on the person (e.g. battery) and property (e.g. trespass). Certainly, as at 1890, notions of private life were not foreign to the common law. However, Warren and Brandeis argued that legal protection should be extended to *intangible* qualities of life—dignity, thoughts, sentiments and emotions—which were at risk because of technological developments. For example, developments in printing technology, production methods and instantaneous photography were identified by Warren and Brandeis as threatening 'to make good the prediction that "what is whispered in the closet shall be proclaimed from the housetops"'.[36] They thus argued that common law remedies for intrusions upon private life should expand beyond their traditional roots in tangible bodily and property interests, in order to protect the more sweeping and intangible concept of 'invi-

---

[32] Warren and Brandeis (1890), 195.

[33] *Ibid.*, 197.

[34] A remedy for invasion of privacy had already been recognised under the French Civil Code, as was acknowledged by Warren and Brandeis (*ibid.*, 214). See *infra*, section 5.2.

[35] Konvitz (1966), 274, suggests that '[t]o mark off the limits of the public and private realms is an activity that began with man himself and is one that will never end'. Consider, for example, the work of Bentham (1789). Bentham distinguished between 'the whole business of legislation' and 'private ethics', defining the latter as determining, 'how each man may dispose himself to pursue the course most conducive to his own happiness, by means of such motives as offer of themselves' (282 and 293). Mill (1859) questioned whether it was possible to distinguish the private from the public. He wrote that '[t]here is no recognized principle by which the propriety or impropriety of government interference is customarily tested' since people generally support state interference where they perceive an evil to be remedied. Mill then advanced the self-protection principle, and argued that '[t]he only part of the conduct of any one, for which he is amenable to society is that which concerns others. In the part which merely concerns himself, his independence is, of right, absolute. Over himself, over his own body and mind, the individual is sovereign' (77–9).

[36] Warren and Brandeis (1890), 195. See also Gormly (1992), 1350–2.

olate personality', under which the dignity and emotional well-being of the individual would be paramount.

This evolution in thinking about the relationship between private life and the common law during the past century has resulted in a vigorous academic debate over the justifications for protecting private personality, or privacy. One hundred years after Warren and Brandeis, there is a consensus that privacy is essential to life in all societies, and particularly modern ones.[37] That privacy has emerged as an important societal value is demonstrated by the inclusion of the right against arbitrary interference with privacy in Article 12 of the Universal Declaration of Human Rights, and Article 17 of the International Covenant on Civil and Political Rights. The right of privacy appears in Article 11 of the American Convention on Human Rights,[38] Article 8 of the European Convention on Human Rights, and is a fundamental right protected by the legal order of the European Union.[39] Privacy also enjoys the status of a constitutional right in three of the countries considered in this book: the United States,[40] France,[41] and Canada.[42] The fact that privacy has only recently emerged within United Kingdom law must therefore be considered an anomaly.

Despite the general recognition of privacy as a human right, the academic literature evinces controversy over its nature and scope. This is largely a function of the fact that privacy has been pitched from its inception as a broad right protecting certain personal interests, deemed 'private'. Many commentators have sought to bring greater specificity to the concept of privacy, yet it would seem that for every commentator there is a different definition of privacy and at least five reasons why every other definition is inadequate.[43] Consider the following examples, all of which are variations on the 'right to be let alone':

(1) Privacy is the legally recognised freedom or power of an individual to determine the extent to which another individual may (a) obtain or make use of his ideas, writings, names, likeness or other indicia of identity, or (b) obtain or reveal information about him or those for whom he is personally responsible, or (c) intrude physically or in more subtle ways into his life sphere and his chosen activities.[44]

---

[37] Westin (1967b) examined several modern and pre-industrial societies, and concluded that, '[n]eeds for individual and group privacy and resulting social norms are present in virtually every society' (at 13). Moreover, 'the achievement of privacy for individuals, families and groups in modern society has become a matter of freedom rather than the product of necessity' (at 21–2). For a different perspective, see Thomson (1975), 295–315.

[38] See also Art. V of the American Declaration of the Rights and Duties of Man.

[39] *Commission* v. *Germany*, [1992] ECR I–2575 (ECJ), para. 23; *X* v. *Commission* [1992] ECR II–2195 (ECJ), para. 17.

[40] See the Fourth Amendment of the United States Bill of Rights; *infra*, sect. 4.3.3.1.

[41] See *infra*, sect. 5.2.

[42] See ss. 7 and 8 of the Canadian Charter of Rights and Freedoms; *infra*, sect. 6.3.

[43] Gormly (1992), 1353; Parent (1983).

[44] Beaney (1966b), 254.

(2) Privacy is the claim of individuals, groups, or institutions to determine for themselves when, how and to what extent information about themselves is to be communicated to others.[45]

(3) Privacy is a complex of three independent and irreducible elements: secrecy (the extent to which an individual is known), anonymity (the extent to which an individual is the subject of attention) and solitude (the extent to which others have physical access to an individual).[46]

(4) Privacy concerns personal information regarding aspects of life which reasonable members of society would respect as being such that an individual is ordinarily entitled to keep them to himself, whether or not they relate to his mind or body, to his home, to his family, to other personal relationships, or to correspondence or documents.[47]

(5) Privacy is control over when and by whom the various parts of us can be sensed by others.[48]

Such definitional diversity perhaps reflects the futility of attempting to devise a 'perfect' privacy definition. Any such effort would require some means of distinguishing between public and private aspects of life, yet that distinction is circumstantial. Thus, any definition of privacy must have a considerable level of generality. Some have viewed this as a stumbling block to the legal protection of privacy. For example, Brittan has argued against the recognition of the tort of invasion of privacy at common law because 'neither in its common law nor in its statutory form does [privacy] provide a logical or workable criterion'.[49] The Younger Committee echoed this view in recommending against the introduction of the tort in the United Kingdom:

> the kinds of privacy to which importance is attached and the intrusions against which protection is sought differ so widely from one individual to another and from one category to the next that it has not so far been found easy to fit the concept tidily into a single legal framework, so as to give it reasonably comprehensive recognition and protection through the civil and criminal law.[50]

This conclusion seems suspect given that civil protection of private life has emerged in the American[51] and New Zealand[52] common law, in the Quebec,[53]

---

[45] Westin (1967b), 7. This definition was adopted in Ontario Commission on Information and Individual Privacy (1980). In a similar vein, Lusky (1972), 709, defines privacy as a 'condition enjoyed by one who can control the communication of information about himself'.

[46] Gavison (1980), 433–4.

[47] Committee on Privacy and Related Matters (1990), 49.

[48] Parker (1974), 283–4, 290.

[49] Brittan (1963), 267. See also Shils (1966), 281.

[50] Committee on Privacy (1972), 5.

[51] ALI (1972b), 376–403.

[52] *Bradley* v. *Wingnut Films Ltd.* [1993] 1 NZLR 415 (HC); *Tucker* v. *News Media Ownership Ltd.* [1986] 2 NZLR 716 (HC).

[53] Invasion of privacy was first recognised as a general delict within art. 1053 of the Quebec Civil Code in *Robbins* v. *CBC* (1957), 12 DLR (2d) 35 (Que. SC). This view has subsequently been codified, with privacy being elevated to the status of a right. See s. 5 of Quebec's Charter of Human Rights and Freedoms, RSQ 1977, c. 12, and chap. 3 of the Civil Code, SQ 1991, c. 64.

French[54] and German[55] civil law, and has found expression in numerous privacy statutes.[56] Clearly, the lack of a precise, exhaustive definition of privacy has not been a bar to its legal protection in a variety of contexts. Indeed, the 1990 Report of the UK's Calcutt Committee repudiated the views of the Younger Committee on the issue of defining privacy:

> We accept that there is little possibility of producing a precise or exhaustive definition of privacy or, for that matter, public interest. We have taken this into account when examining proposals for additional remedies, whether statutory or non-statutory. Nevertheless, many other legal concepts, such as defamation or negligence, are workable though incapable of precise or exhaustive definition. The courts have been able to develop a detailed case law, as they have done on privacy in other countries.[57]

Although the Calcutt Committee did not recommend the introduction of a privacy tort, preferring other options such as media self-regulation, the Committee stressed that it was possible to define privacy adequately, and that '[o]ur grounds for recommending against a new tort do not, therefore, include difficulties of definition'.[58]

If a workable (as opposed to ideal) legal definition of privacy is to be developed, various considerations should be kept in mind. First, while it is understandable that legal philosophers have turned their minds to the pursuit of definitional perfection, the standard by which to assess the adequacy of any privacy formulation should be legal certainty and not legal perfection. On this point, consideration of the legal principle of 'vagueness' is helpful. Uncertainty may arise from a legal concept in two situations: (1) the concept is so vague that no clear meaning can be ascribed to it in any circumstance (i.e. perfect vagueness), and (2) the concept has a certain core meaning, but has uncertain boundaries (i.e. core-periphery vagueness).[59] The former type of uncertainty, which is quite rare, renders a concept legally useless. More common is core-periphery vagueness. In fact, virtually all legal concepts suffer from some peripheral uncertainty, since human language is not itself an exact tool.[60] Keeping this in mind,

---

[54] A remedy for invasion of privacy had been recognised in France even before Warren and Brandeis's 1890 article (Warren and Brandeis (1890), 214). See *infra*, sect. 5.2.

[55] *Schacht*, BGHZ 13, 334 (1954).

[56] See, e.g., New Zealand's Privacy Act (1993, No. 28), or the four Canadian provincial privacy statutes: British Columbia (*Privacy Act*, RSBC 1979, c. 336), Manitoba (Privacy Act, RSM 1987, c. P125), Newfoundland (Privacy Act, RSN 1990, c. P–22), and Saskatchewan (Privacy Act, RSS 1978, c. P–24).

[57] Committee on Privacy and Related Matters (1990), 49. See also Lord Chancellor's Department/The Scottish Office (1993).

[58] Committee (1990), 48–9.

[59] Hart (1958), 67, writes that for every legal concept, 'there must be a core of settled meaning [and] a penumbra of debatable cases'; Marmor (1992), 124–35; Waldron (1994), 516–26.

[60] The approach to vagueness and uncertainty offered here is heavily influenced by two decisions of Justice Gonthier of the Supreme Court of Canada: R. v. *Nova Scotia Pharmaceutical Society* [1992] 2 SCR 606, and *Ontario* v. *Canadian Pacific* [1995] 2 SCR 1031. These decisions canvas the literature and jurisprudence on the issue of vagueness from the USA and Europe, and adopt the following test for vagueness: a concept is legally vague if it fails to provide a basis for legal debate. Clearly, the concept of 'privacy' provides fertile ground for legal debate, and on that standard, passes muster easily.

it is hardly surprising that the concept of 'privacy', and in particular its scope, is the subject of legal debate. Marmor has written that the legal concepts we employ generally have a core meaning, which is identifiable by reference to 'standard examples' explaining the applications of the concept.[61] On this basis, privacy is not perfectly vague because there is general agreement that the right of privacy protects certain personal interests (i.e. standard examples), them-selves capable of identification and definition. These include such interests as bodily integrity, intimate communications, the home and information concern-ing one's health, political views or sexual orientation. It thus becomes possible to offer legal protection for 'privacy', as defined by reference to specific private interests at the core of the concept, even if it is not possible to identify exhaus-tively all the peripheral interests which may also find protection. Such an approach does indeed offer sufficient legal certainty, at least with regard to the interests at the core of the right of privacy.

While vagueness analysis dispenses with the argument that privacy is too uncertain to be given legal effect, privacy should not be limited in perpetuity to the legally recognised interests forming its core in 1999. Certainly, such an approach would reduce (or perhaps even eliminate) controversy, but would merely represent a 'snapshot' of the scope of privacy as it has evolved to the pre-sent day.[62] One must recognise that privacy is a dynamic and evolving concept, and that interests presently at its periphery may one day achieve the status of core privacy interests. Hence, any definition of privacy must take this factor into account. It may well be preferable, then, to adopt a general privacy principle, in order to accommodate the varied contexts in which privacy concerns will arise, the diverse circumstances in which the private interests of an individual may be compromised, and the evolution in our understanding of what interests should be considered private.[63] Of course, such a flexible and general principle would not be applied *in abstracto*. On the contrary, assistance may be drawn from an analysis (albeit a *critical* analysis) of privacy jurisprudence and academic com-mentary from jurisdictions such as the United States, France, and Canada.

Although the theoretical contest of the definition of privacy is of value in fur-thering our understanding of what is, admittedly, a difficult concept,[64] it should not be allowed to cloud the issue of how best to implement legal privacy pro-tection in a particular context, for example the employment setting. Certainly, privacy theory has advanced sufficiently for us to be confident of the concept's core meaning, and of our success in giving legal effect to this core. It is notable that the problem of defining privacy has been most influential in scuttling legal

---

[61]   Marmor (1992), 134.

[62]   Gavison (1980), 460–1, writes of the 'poverty of reductionism', arguing that defining privacy with reference to extant case law could result in incoherence, because conflicting, judicial decisions, and is too narrow an approach because the data base underlying the definition would be limited to litigated cases.

[63]   Hart (1994), 130–1.

[64]   Waldron (1994), 532–3.

reform in the United Kingdom,[65] whereas the right of privacy has been implemented in the United States, France and Canada by establishing general privacy principles, and allowing them to be developed and refined over time. This approach is certainly more pragmatic than one requiring the precise identification of all interests protected by the right of privacy as a precondition to its legal recognition.

Given my conclusions on the issue of legal certainty, I am of the view that it is justifiable to premise the legal protection of privacy on a pragmatic privacy principle, encapsulated in the following proposition: *a person's private interests should be legally protected from encroachment by others*. While this proposition might seem simplistic, it is deceptively so. In a particular context, the crux of the matter will be to identify the interests which are at stake, and which find protection within the general privacy principle. This form of analysis may be labelled a functional approach, because it recognises that the role of the right of privacy is to protect certain aspects of life from public scrutiny, and that the true challenge is to identify those aspects which are relevant in a particular context, such as employment.

2.3.2 Identifying the Private Interests at Stake in the Workplace Context

One might consider the identification of private interests protected by the right of privacy, which is the first step in applying the functional approach, to be as daunting a task as the achievement of a satisfactory definition of privacy itself (hence the deceptive simplicity of the general privacy principle stated above). Fortunately, the interest-identification process is aided by an initial focus on the concept of 'zones' of privacy. To illustrate, in the Supreme Court of Canada's decision in *R. v. Dyment*, the Court sought to define the right of privacy for the purposes of section 8 of the Canadian Charter. Justice LaForest wrote that the first challenge was 'to find some means of identifying those situations where we should be most alert to privacy considerations'.[66] To this end, he adopted a zonal approach, and identified three privacy zones: territorial, personal/corporeal and informational.[67] Territorial privacy refers to places, such as the home, which are typically considered to be private. Personal, or 'corporeal', privacy is concerned with the human body. Finally, informational privacy was described by Justice LaForest as follows:

> This notion of privacy derives from the assumption that all information about a person is in a fundamental way his own, for him to communicate or retain for himself as he sees fit. In modern society, especially, retention of information about oneself is extremely important. We may, for one reason or another, wish or be compelled to

---

[65] *Infra*, sect. 10.2.

[66] *R. v. Dyment* [1988] 2 SCR 417, 428.

[67] Justice LaForest adopted this formulation of privacy from Task Force established by the Department of Communications/Department of Justice (1972), 12–14.

reveal such information, but situations abound where the reasonable expectations of the individual that the information shall remain confidential to the persons to whom, and restricted to the purposes for which it is divulged, must be protected.[68]

A fourth zone of privacy, related to a person's 'material' possessions, could also be identified. This would protect items such as clothing, handbags, purses, wallets, etc. from intrusion.[69] Justice LaForest did not identify a distinct 'material' zone of privacy, and for my purposes herein, it will be assimilated with the personal zone.

A zonal approach is valuable because it identifies the general categories of personal interests protected by the right of privacy. In a given case, once the relevant general category is identified, then greater specificity will be achieved by focusing on the particular private interest falling within that category. An interest may be considered private in two distinct ways. First, as Benn has argued, certain 'objects' are by their very nature to be considered private:

> 'Private rooms', 'private affairs', 'private correspondence' belong to the category of objects of privacy rights. These are legal, moral or conventional norms that constitute reasons not to try to share or participate in such objects without the permission of the specified holder of the privacy right.
>   The use of 'private' in such a context invokes a rule or convention. It does not describe a state of affairs; rather, it signals the sort of behaviour that is appropriate to its object.[70]

According to Benn, the 'subject' of privacy (i.e. the individual asserting privacy) must be able to point to some 'object' falling within a zone of privacy in order to succeed in her claim.[71] Whether or not an object can be considered private will depend on the traditions, social norms and laws of the society in question. This is exactly the approach taken by the Court of Appeal for California when assessing privacy claims under California's constitutional privacy right. The Court has adopted a zonal approach, but has also recognised the need to achieve greater specificity by determining whether a particular interest falls within a privacy zone and is therefore eligible for protection. Such eligibility, according to the Court, depends on '[w]hether established social norms safeguard a particular type of information, or protect a specific personal decision from public or private intervention'.[72] The common law, statutes and constitutional jurisprudence will all be of assistance in identifying the social norms relevant to the particular interests over which the right of privacy is claimed.[73]

---

[68] *Supra*, n. 66, 429–30.

[69] Canadian arbitration cases concerning workplace searches have distinguished between body searches and searches of workers' belongings. While both attract privacy, the former has been considered a more serious intrusion. See *infra*, sect. 6.5.1.

[70] Benn (1978), 602.

[71] *Ibid.*

[72] *Hill* v. *National College Athletic Association*, 216 Cal. Rptr. 2d 834 (Cal. CA, 1994), 856.

[73] *Ibid.*

Secondly, interests may take on a private nature by reason of certain circumstances, even if traditions or norms do not generally recognise the interest as having an inherently private element. This is particularly important in the case of employment, where a privacy right may arise even though employees are situated on property, and/or are using property, owned by the employer. An example will illustrate how this is possible. Although one would not generally attach the label 'private' to communications made during on-duty time by employees over employer-owned equipment, if the employer permits employees to make personal telephone calls or send personal e-mails on office systems, or if employees engage in such activities with the employer's knowledge and tolerance, then this may create an expectation on the part of employees that those communications are private. In other words, representations, promises or other circumstances may create a privacy expectation relating to an interest, and this expectation may be relied upon in advancing the right of privacy.

By focusing on zones of privacy, and the particular private interests falling within those zones, we can see that worker interests in all three zones have been legally recognised and protected. This demonstrates that the right of privacy does indeed have force in the employment context.

The territorial zone of privacy is perhaps the least problematic in the context of the workplace, although it may initially seem counter-intuitive that an employee could enjoy a privacy right over a 'place' within the workplace.[74] However, because privacy is a personal right, as opposed to a right in property, and as noted above can be premised on an individual's expectation of privacy, it is possible for an employee to have a private interest of a territorial nature within a place in which he possesses no property rights. For example, in a decision of the European Court of Human Rights, *Halford* v. *United Kingdom*, it was held that the employee enjoyed privacy with regard to her office and the telephone line in her office because she was given permission to engage in matters unrelated to work while in her own office.[75] Similarly, the United States Supreme Court held in *O'Connor* v. *Ortega* that an employee may have a privacy interest in his office, which could be infringed by an unauthorised employer search.[76] Private interests have also been identified by the American courts in employee lockers,[77] and in employee vehicles parked on the employer's premises.[78] One would also expect employees to have private interests in relation to washrooms and changing rooms.[79]

[74] An employee could also assert territorial privacy away from the workplace, perhaps in relation to a house or motel room. See *Sowards* v. *Norbar*, 605 NE 2d 468 (Ohio CA, 1992), where the employer searched a motel room which it provided to an employee. The employee was successful in an action for invasion of privacy. He had a reasonable expectation of privacy in the room, even though his employer had paid for it.

[75] See *Halford* v. *The United Kingdom* [1997] IRLR 47 (ECHR).

[76] 107 S Ct. 1492 (1989).

[77] *K-Mart Corp.* v. *Trotti*, 677 .. 2d 632 (Tex. CA, 1984).

[78] *Terrel* v. *Rowsay*, 647 NE 2d 663 (Ind. CA, 1995).

[79] In their testimony before the US House of Representatives Committee on Education and Labor (1993), the American Nurses Association described the employer practice of placing videocameras

More controversial in light of technological developments are employer policies which impact upon the personal zone of privacy. In this regard, the various forms of testing to which candidates/employees may be subjected are problematic. Because drug testing is generally carried out through blood and urine analysis, it requires a subject either to offer up a body fluid, or accept to certain adverse consequences (denial of employment, discipline, etc.). There are long-recognised private interests in body fluids. Similar comments could be made about genetic testing as well, since it must be performed on body tissue taken from the subject. Polygraph and personality testing also constitute profound intrusions into the personal zone of privacy. Such tests are directed at the human mind and thought, which are core interests protected by personal privacy.[80]

Personal private interests may also be implicated by the searching[81] and surveillance of employees. Typically, managerial observation of work performance, whether conducted personally or through electronic means such as television cameras, has not been viewed as an invasion of privacy *per se*. However, some forms of employer observation may impact directly upon important private interests. For example, as part of urinalysis drug testing, it is sometimes necessary for the act of urination to be observed by the tester, to ensure that there has been no tampering with the urine sample.[82] Obviously, there are private interests in certain bodily functions which may be invaded by such observation.

Interests in the informational zone of privacy are also threatened by a host of management practices. In fact, challenges to polygraph, personality and drug testing have often relied not only on their impact on corporeal interests, but also on the private information which can be obtained. In *Long Beach City Employees Association* v. *Long Beach*, the Court found the practice of subjecting employees to polygraph testing to be an invasion of privacy contrary to the California Constitution, in part because the questions asked during the test were 'intimate', 'embarrassing', and 'outrageous'.[83] Similar criticisms have been levelled at the personality testing of candidates, since such tests may query respondents on matters irrelevant to job performance, such as sexual orientation, religion and family life.[84]

Drug, genetic and other forms of medical testing present different problems related to informational privacy, since such tests require the subject to provide a biological sample containing the raw data sufficient to identify a host of physical

---

in changing rooms and washrooms. In one case, scenes of nurses changing clothes were broadcast on an in-house cable channel—the result of wires being crossed. See also PCWA, s. 9(b), discussed *infra*, sect. 4.3.4.4.

[80] *Long Beach City Employees Association* v. *Long Beach*, 719 P 2d 660 (Cal. SC, 1986), 672.

[81] *Supra*, nn. 69, 74.

[82] Oscapella (1992), 332–3.

[83] *Supra*, n. 80, 664–5. The questions which troubled the Court included: 'Ever been arrested for any reason?'; 'Any history of epilepsy?'; 'Ever been treated by or consulted a psychiatrist for any reason?'; 'Ever experimented with any type of drugs?'.

[84] Mello (1994), 664.

qualities about the subject.[85] In the case of urinalysis, an employer may obtain information not only about drug use, but also about pregnancy and conditions such as arthritis, epilepsy and diabetes.[86] With genetic testing as a means of screening candidates looming on the horizon, one can only imagine the kinds of information which could be obtained by employers.[87] At the very least, considerable details about a person's health, both present and future, could be revealed to an employer through a genetic test. That employer could then use this information to exclude candidates who are genetically prone to certain conditions or diseases.

The electronic surveillance of employees also threatens informational private interests. Although the monitoring of job performance, perhaps through 'peeking' on to a computer screen,[88] does not necessarily impact upon private informational interests, such interests may be implicated where the monitoring captures private information. This may occur directly, for example where an employer plants microphones around the workplace to obtain information to fight a union organising campaign.[89] It may also occur indirectly, where job performance monitoring also captures private information. France's CNIL has warned that pervasive electronic monitoring of employees' activities and communications will almost certainly result in the acquisition of information unrelated to work, and thereby offend the right of privacy.[90] American courts have reached the same conclusion in relation to the monitoring of employees' telephone calls, reasoning that while employers are entitled to monitor business calls, and also personal calls to the extent necessary to identify them as such, they may not monitor personal calls *per se*.[91]

In summary, while it was not my intention to provide an exhaustive review of the interests implicated by each and every privacy invasive management policy or practice, I was able to demonstrate that certain management actions may impact upon candidates'/employees' private interests falling within all three zones of personal privacy.

2.3.3 Placing Value on the Private Interests of Workers

My discussion above identified the private interests which may be implicated by management policies and practices. However, because interests premised on

---

[85] Weir (1994), 455. Gerhart (1995a), 10, reports that Belgian law now prohibits the surreptitious testing of blood samples for AIDS and HIV because of certain employers' practices of secretly testing employees for the disease.

[86] Stille (1986), 1–2; Feldthusen (1988), 94.

[87] *Infra*, sect. 9.4.

[88] *Supra*, n. 4.

[89] *Supra*, n. 6.

[90] CNIL (1995k), 113–19.

[91] *Watkins* v. *L. M. Berry*, 704 F 2d 577 (11th Circ., 1983), interpreting Electronic Communications Privacy Act, 18 USC, ss. 2510–2521 (1993), an amendment to Title III of the Omnibus Crime Control and Safe Streets Act (1986), Pub. L. No. 90–351, 82 Stat. 212 (1988). The case is discussed *infra*, sect. 4.3.4.4.

intangible and abstract human rights may seem ethereal when viewed in light of the practical and even quantifiable interests of employers (a matter taken up below in section 2.3.4), there is a danger that they may be seen as trifling, or not sufficiently significant to attract legal protection. Historically, the right of privacy has been open to accusations of triviality and pettiness[92]; there is no reason to believe that it will avoid such accusations in the employment context.[93] By moving beyond the interests protected by the right of privacy to consider the justifications for that protection, I hope to develop a better appreciation of the true value of privacy to both the individual worker and society as a whole.

Four justifications may be identified for recognising a personal right of privacy in individuals, and each is premised on the promotion of a distinct social value: (1) autonomy; (2) dignity and well-being; (3) healthy relationships; and (4) pluralism.[94] As I will demonstrate below, each has force in the employment context.

2.3.3.1 Autonomy

Privacy is often linked to the concept of autonomy, meaning the ability of an individual to choose freely and independently his goals or relations.[95] According to Raz, a person lives autonomously when he lives in 'a certain environment, an environment which respects the conditions of independence and furnishes him an adequate range of options'.[96] In society generally, certain social norms and pressures have a conforming influence, operating to diminish individual autonomy by reducing the options available for individual action. Privacy insulates the individual from external social pressure by providing a realm of retreat.[97] Privacy allows individuals to explore all the options available, while resisting pressures to conform merely 'for the sake of'. The private life and the independent life are so linked as to be practically synonymous.[98]

Employment has a potentially profound impact on individual autonomy, as the very nature of the employment contract is to subordinate the independence of the employee to the interests and objectives of the employer.[99] This is not nec-

---

[92]   Kalven Jr. (1966); Bloustein (1968b); Westin (1973c), 28.

[93]   The IPCO (1993) canvassed the views of 'stakeholders': employee organisations, employers and government. Several employers responded that from their point of view, workplace privacy was an insignificant matter, and that the IPCO was wasting his time, and public money, on the study (at 14).

[94]   This is not to suggest that there are only four justifications underlying the right of privacy. There may, or may not, be others. In any event, these four in particular have force in the employment context.

[95]   Raz (1986), 369–72. See also: Shils (1956), 21–2; Benn (1978), 605; Eichbaum (1979).

[96]   Raz (1986), 391.

[97]   Gavison (1980), 448–50.

[98]   But note that one can act autonomously but not privately. E.g., one can choose to give a speech in public. The important point is that *the decision to act* in a particular way is made privately and therefore independently. Whether the act itself is private or public is secondary.

[99]   Employer control over an employee is the essence of the employment relationship. The ALI (1958a), 12, defines a 'servant' as a person, 'employed by a master to perform service in his affairs

essarily problematic since the economic rewards for the employee can be great, thereby increasing the options available (and hence promoting individual autonomy and independence) during off-duty hours. Employment may be viewed as a trade-off: a reduction in autonomy during work hours in return for an increase in autonomy during non-work hours. Given the importance of autonomy, it should be presumed as a general proposition that employees consent to this trade-off on the condition that there is a sufficient link between the controls placed on their independence by the employer, and job performance.[100] Therefore, management policies which lack that link impact upon the private interests of workers, and should be viewed as serious and unacceptable reductions of their autonomy.

Worker autonomy may be affected in two ways. First, a management policy may threaten to penalise candidates/employees for activities occurring outside the workplace which bear only a slight, or perhaps no, relationship to legitimate management interests. Drug testing, for example, has been criticised because employers may refuse to hire, or may discipline, individuals for their use of drugs away from the workplace, although it is controversial whether employers have a legitimate interest in asserting control over off-site drug use. Other efforts by employers to regulate their employees' private lives have led to numerous court challenges. Examples include discipline for political and recreational activities, and discipline related to intimate co-worker relationships formed during non-work hours. [101] Typically, courts have been concerned about the privacy impact of such employer actions, and have placed the onus on the employer to demonstrate a nexus between the impugned employee conduct and the employer's operations.[102]

Secondly, the problem of employer control over workers' private lives becomes more complex as on-duty and off-duty time blurs. This point was made eloquently by Justice Blackmun in *O'Connor* v. *Ortega*:

> [T]he reality of work in modern times, whether done by public or private employees, reveals why a public employees' expectation of privacy in the workplace should be carefully safeguarded and not lightly set-aside. It is, unfortunately, all too true that the workplace has become another home for most working Americans. Many employees spend the better part of their days and much of their evenings at work . . . Consequently, an employees' private life must intersect with the workplace, for example, when the employee takes advantage of work or lunch breaks to make personal telephone calls, to attend to personal business, or to receive personal visitors in the office. As a result, the tidy distinctions . . . between the workplace and professional

whose physical conduct in the performance of the service is controlled or is subject to the right to control by the master'. The French definition of 'employee' is based on a similar concept of 'subordination': Lyon-Caen (1992b), 115.

[100] Savatier (1990a), 51, concludes that a worker who enters into an employment contract consents to subordination only to the extent necessary for the, '*exécution de la prestation de travail; dans la reste de sa vie il demeure libre*'.

[101] Wilcots (1995).

[102] *Ibid.*, 6.

affairs, on the one hand, and personal possessions and private activities, on the other, do not exist in reality.[103]

It is surely unreasonable for employers to expect every minute of their employees' working day to be dedicated solely to employment matters. Private matters (e.g. telephoning a sick spouse or child, arranging a medical appointment, etc.) are bound to come up at the office. For this reason, pervasive employer monitoring of employee movements, conversations and telephone calls impacts directly upon the autonomy of workers. Such monitoring limits the range of options available to employees, not simply because it actively discourages activities unrelated to work, but also because it places a chill on what employees will say or do even during their personal time (i.e. lunch hours, coffee breaks, etc.). The practice of e-mail monitoring illustrates this point. The use of inter-office electronic message systems is now widespread, and employees routinely use such systems for both work-related and personal matters. Several cases have arisen in the United States concerning the surreptitious monitoring by employers of e-mail.[104] Employees who are aware that their messages may be accessed and read by supervisors will no doubt feel constrained in their use of e-mail. They may be less candid, or may choose not to send personal messages at all, even if the employer has no stated policy against the personal use of e-mail.[105]

If an individual is to act autonomously and independently, then he must be able to resist external controls and pressures. Such controls may flow from state action (the state–citizen relationship) or social norms (the society–individual relationship). However, the employment relationship is also a powerful source of control over individual autonomy and independence. Therefore, any management practice which exerts control over the private interests of candidates/employees is cause for serious concern, and should be scrutinised closely.

2.3.3.2 Dignity and Well-being

Some commentators, most notably Jourard, have linked privacy to individual dignity, health and well-being.[106] Jourard argues that privacy is crucial not only because it allows individuals to escape social pressures for the purpose of autonomous decision-making, but also because it affords to everyone an environment where they 'can simply *be*, rather than be *respectable*'.[107] The ability to retreat from society ensures that individuals have outlets for self-expression,

---

[103] *Supra*, note 76.

[104] *Shoars* v. *Epson America Inc.*, No. BC 007036 (Cal. Sup. Ct., 1994); No. B073243 (Cal. CA, 1994); *Bourke* v. *Nissan Motor Corp.*, No. YC 003979 (Cal. Sup. Ct., 1994); *Washington Federation of State Employees & Ron Collins* v. *Department of Labor and Industry, State of Washington*, No. 90–2–02130–8 (Wash. Sup. Ct., 1993); *Cameron* v. *Mentor Graphics*, No. 716361 (Cal. Sup. Ct., 1993). *USA Today* (1996), 1, reported that a survey of American managers found that 75% believe they have a right to view their employees' e-mail.

[105] Telephone monitoring presents the same problem. See *Watkins* v. *L.M. Berry, supra*, n. 91.

[106] Jourard (1966).

[107] *Ibid.*, 310 (emphasis in original text).

can explore alternative ways of life and are able to resist conformist pressures. The mental well-being of individuals, according to Jourard, is preserved and promoted by the protection of private life. Denial of privacy is not simply upsetting to the victim, or offensive to the victim's dignity; it can lead to pain, stress, anxiety, hopelessness and malaise.[108] Westin has reached a similar conclusion, observing that '[t]he numerous instances of suicides and nervous breakdowns resulting from' invasions of privacy are a reminder of the critical social need to respect private life.[109]

All forms of management practices implicating private interests may adversely affect the dignity and well-being of candidates/employees. Pervasive monitoring and surveillance, in particular, may be cause for concern. A University of Wisconsin/Communications Workers of America study of stress-related complaints among telephone operators revealed that monitored employees had significantly more complaints relating to headaches, back pain, severe fatigue, shoulder soreness, extreme anxiety and stiff or sore wrists.[110] The ILO, in a 1993 Report, referred to stress in the workplace as a 'world-wide epidemic', and stated that '[a]s the use of computers spreads throughout the world, workers in many countries are being subjected to new pressures, including electronic eavesdropping by superiors . . . '[111]

Anecdotal evidence confirms that individuals may suffer humiliation and distress from invasive management practices. A reservation agent employed by Southwest Airlines, testifying before the United States House of Representatives Sub-committee on Labor–Management Relations, expressed her concerns over her employer's telephone monitoring policies:

> Although the constant fear that you are being monitored adds to the already great pressure of the job, secret monitoring raises other serious concerns as well. It raises the matter of worker dignity. We are all adults who take are [*sic*] jobs very seriously. Nonetheless, we are spied on and secretly listened to. It is just not right. Imagine if every conversation you had during your entire workday could be recorded without your knowledge. How would your staff feel if every telephone conversation they had was secretly taped and then used to discipline them? . . . What would it do to their self-esteem?[112]

In a similar vein, a candidate subjected to a urinalysis drug test provided the following account of the experience:

> I was not informed of the test until I was walking down the hall towards the bathroom with the attendant. I thought no problem. I have had urine tests before and I do not take any type of drugs besides occasional aspirin. I was led into a very small room with a toilet, sink and a desk. I was given a container in which to urinate by the attendant.

---

[108] *Ibid.*, 309.
[109] Westin (1967b), 33–4.
[110] Smith (1990). See also Ditecco (1987); Smith (1986).
[111] ILO (1993b).
[112] Statement of Rachel Hernandez before United States House of Representatives Committee on Education and Labor (1993).

I waited for her to turn her back before pulling down my pants, but she told me she had to watch everything I did. I pulled down my pants, put the container in place—as she bent down to watch—gave her a sample and even then she did not look away. I had to use the toilet paper as she watched and then pulled up my pants. This may sound vulgar—and that is exactly what it is . . . I am a forty year old mother of three and nothing I have ever done in my life equals or deserves the humiliation, degradation and mortification that I felt.[113]

Because employer monitoring and testing practices often challenge the dignity of candidates/employees, and subject them to added stress, they implicate one of the key justifications underlying the legal protection of personal privacy, namely the promotion of individual well-being.

2.3.3.3 *Healthy Relationships*

Fried has argued that privacy is inherent in the notions of respect, love, friendship and trust, and that close human relationships are only possible if individuals enjoy and accord to each other a certain measure of privacy.[114] The view that privacy is not only essential to individual autonomy and mental well-being, but is also a condition of healthy, trusting relationships, is premised on the individual's right to control private information, and to determine who should have access to that information, and in what circumstances. Relationships of trust are possible only if the sharing of private information concerning attitudes, interests and details about a host of subjects is voluntary. Surveillance, testing and other privacy intrusions destroy the voluntariness and exclusivity of that sharing, undermine trust, and create conflict in relationships.[115]

The employment relationship is, for many people, one of the most important in their lives. Thus, employment transcends its contractual nature, and operates as a social relationship based on trust, loyalty, respect and good faith. This has been recognised by economists, psychologists, sociologists and management theorists, who appear unanimous in the view that trust is essential to the success of any human relationship, including those operating within business organisations.[116] Labour law in many countries recognises the importance of trust in employment by implying a duty of good faith and fair dealing into the employment contract.[117] The imposition of policies impacting upon workers' private interests risks alienating those same employees, who may feel that their dignity

---

[113] Anonymous employee, quoted in Siegel (1987), 706.

[114] Fried (1968a), 477.

[115] Any reader of Orwell (1949) will appreciate the argument that constant surveillance prevents the development of close, trusting relationships.

[116] Blau (1964), 99; Golembiewski (1975), 131–3; Hirsch (1978), 78; Lewis (1985), 968; Hosmer (1995), 379.

[117] This is certainly the case in France (*infra*, chapter 5, text at nn. 33 and 34), and in some American states. See California, *infra*, sect. 4.3.4.3. Canadian law only requires *employees* to perform the employment contract in good faith (*infra*, sect. 6.2), whereas UK law imposes upon both employees and employers a mutual duty of trust and confidence (*infra*, sect. 10.3.1).

is being attacked by an employer who does not trust them to do their jobs. This in turn creates a breakdown in the employment relationship, adversely affects employee loyalty and motivation, and may well undermine worker productivity.[118] As one labour group has observed:

> It seems trite to say that a happy worker is likely a productive worker; that a worker who is accorded respect is likely to return it . . . On the other hand, a worker who must produce in an atmosphere of distrust and lack of consideration seems more likely to treat her or his employer in kind.[119]

The fact that the labour movement strongly opposes many forms of testing and monitoring, including drug testing and electronic surveillance, because of their impact on the privacy rights of workers demonstrates that privacy issues have the potential to become serious sources of conflict between management and employees.[120]

2.3.3.4 Pluralism

Privacy acts as a shield against conformist pressures, and thereby fosters the development of new ideas, attitudes, beliefs and lifestyles. Privacy thus breeds diversity, which is essential to any pluralistic, democratic society.[121] To a certain extent, then, the democratic justification for privacy is similar to that for freedom of expression, since both the free formulation of viewpoints and their free expression are necessary to democratic political debate and the right to vote.[122] I would go further, and suggest that the protection of private life should be viewed as a precondition to freedom of expression.[123] After all, freedom of expression would lose much of its value if everyone simply conformed to social norms, and thus had nothing unique, creative or controversial to express.

Given the importance of pluralism to democratic society, any diminution in the privacy of individuals, whether or not in their capacity as workers, is a serious matter. Certainly, management efforts to control the off-duty lifestyles of workers, perhaps through non-fraternisation or anti-drug use policies, promotes conformity, as opposed to diversity, in society. Moreover, pluralism plays an important role in the workplace, where innovation is so critical to the success of any organisation. Innovation occurs through 'industrial pluralism': the fostering of new ideas and new approaches. Management policies implicating the private interests of workers, such as monitoring and testing, may be at odds with the promotion of creative thinking, since they can contribute to a stifling and oppressive work environment. Innovation, which requires an open and dynamic workplace, is unlikely to flourish where an employer implements

---

[118] Maltby (1993), 68.
[119] IPCO (1993), 11.
[120] ILO (1993a, 3), 22–7; Weir (1994), 451; Charlton (1994); Canadian Labour Congress (1990).
[121] Westin (1966a), 1019.
[122] Gavison (1980), 455.
[123] Paton-Simpson (1995), 233–4.

policies which diminish the autonomy of employees, subject them to indignities and are antithetical to trust and respect in the employment relationship.

2.3.4 The Interests of Employers and the Public which may Justify Limiting Worker Privacy

If voyeurism or prurience lay behind employer policies infringing upon worker private interests, then the legal response to workplace privacy issues would be relatively straightforward. However, employers have been able to support policies such as psychological testing or performance monitoring by relying on several credible justifications. Consider, for example, the problem of pilfering by employees. Estimates of the annual drain on the American economy caused by employee theft range in the hundreds of billions of dollars.[124] It is for this reason that some retail employers have taken anti-theft measures such as installing video cameras and/or implementing mandatory search policies. In doing so, such employers may rely not only on their own interest in maximising profits by minimising losses due to theft, but may also point to a public interest—protecting the public from higher prices which result when the cost of stolen goods is passed on to consumers.

New technology allows managers to exert greater control over their workforce, with resulting (or, at least, perceived) economic benefits. In a highly competitive economy, companies succeed by continually improving service quality and efficiency, while reducing expenses and waste. Similarly, and particularly in times of fiscal restraint, governments seek to improve public sector efficiency in order to limit spending and control levels of taxation. Hence, motor vehicle onboard sensors[125] may have business appeal. Not only do they assist an employer in co-ordinating the movements of its automobile fleet, but they also allow for the detection of waste: an employee spending too much time on coffee breaks, or driving too slowly, or taking personal side-trips. From the employer's point-of-view, this is a win-win situation because service efficiency is improved while waste (i.e. wasted time, wasted fuel, etc.) is reduced.

The management-related justifications which have been advanced by employers in response to privacy claims tend to fall into the following five categories: (i) improving economic conditions; (ii) protecting the health and safety of workers, consumers and the public; (iii) deterring and controlling employee abuse of the employment relationship; and (iv) complying with state-imposed regulatory requirements. Furthermore, (v) employers have been able to point to public interest considerations in support of certain invasive practices.

---

[124] Boehmer (1992), 744
[125] *Supra*, n. 7.

2.3.4.1 *Improving Economic Conditions*

Employers have an obvious concern about the job performance of their workers, since the efficiency and profitability of an enterprise is directly linked to the
ability of staff to carry out their assigned tasks. Job performance may be negatively affected by certain conduct on the part of an employee which undermines
her ability to carry out tasks, by an employee's lack of skills or experience or by
inherent flaws in the employee's physical or psychological make-up. These
scenarios are all relevant in justifying certain privacy-invasive management
practices under the economic rationale.

In the case of employee conduct undermining job performance, employers
may find that an employee's job performance is suffering because of the inter-
mingling of private and work life. Consider off-duty drug and alcohol use.[126]
Employers may conclude that there is a link between substance abuse outside
the workplace and tardiness, absenteeism, inferior job performance and
accidents.[127] They may then justify the drug testing of candidates/employees by
relying on the desirability, from a productivity perspective, of a drug-free workforce.

Similarly, employers may be concerned about intimate relationships formed
by employees during off-duty hours, because of the potential conflict which such
relationships can introduce to the work environment, with resulting harm to
service and productivity.[128] Consider the case of *Somers* v. *Westours*,[129] where
the plaintiffs were both employees of a motel. After they began an intimate relationship, complaints were made against them for lateness, absenteeism and
inappropriate workplace conduct, including drunkenness. The employer
ordered them to cease their relationship; they refused, and their employment
was terminated. The court upheld the dismissal as a reasonable exercise of the
employer's business judgement, since the employees were fired not for their relationship, but for their inability to perform their jobs as a result of the relationship. The *Somers* case illustrates that employers may wish to promulgate
non-fraternisation policies to ensure that the work of employees does not suffer
from distractions related to their intimate associations.

While performance monitoring may also be justified under the same economic rationale advanced in support of drug testing and non-fraternisation
policies, the primary purpose of such monitoring is not to ensure the separation
of private and work life. Instead, video cameras, computer 'peeking'[130] and
other such technologies assist the employer in identifying job performance
weaknesses, and in training and coaching employees. In the telemarketing
industry, for example, it is commonplace for employers to monitor secretly the

---

[126] *On-duty* drug and alcohol use is obviously a matter of serious concern to employers as well.
[127] This matter will be considered *infra*, in Chap. 8.
[128] Kelly (1994), 74.
[129] 1 Individ. Empl. Rts. Case (BNA) 1479 (Alaska Sup. Ct., 1986).
[130] *Supra*, n. 4.

business telephone calls of employees, for the purpose of assisting employees in improving their sales techniques.[131] MCI, an American telecommunications company, claims that:

> Our customer service professionals who handle in-bound calls from M.C.I. customers constitute the front-line testing ground for the sincerity of M.C.I.'s commitment to customer service. These employees understand that telephone monitoring is a key practical ingredient of their training and evaluation and are told about monitoring well before sitting down for their first call. These programs are designed and implemented to directly benefit them as well as the company in guiding and improving their work.[132]

Finally, certain privacy-invasive management practices find their justification under the economic rationale because they identify inherent flaws in a candidate's/employee's psychological or physical make-up which could prevent the individual from carrying out assigned tasks in the manner preferred by the employer. Personality testing, for example, has as its primary objective the determination of whether there is a 'fit' between a subject and a particular job. Thousands of employers use psychological screening, handwriting analysis and other such testing methods to determine whether candidates/employees possess interpersonal skills, integrity, honesty and other positive personal characteristics.[133] In *McKenna* v. *Fargo*,[134] the Court rejected a challenge to an employer's personality testing practices by applicants for a firefighting job, since the test in question measured the ability of the subject to cope with stress, which the court characterised as an essential qualification for firefighters.

It has been suggested that genetic testing could be used to screen candidates/employees for undesirable physical traits which might impede job performance.[135] In his 1992 Report concerning genetic testing, the Privacy Commissioner of Canada observed that genetic screening could be employed in the workplace to identify 'less productive' or 'defective' employees or applicants,[136] and, in particular, to screen-out persons prone to physical conditions such as high blood pressure and depression, which might negatively impact upon productivity.[137]

2.3.4.2 Protecting the Health and Safety of Workers, Consumers, and the Public

Safety concerns are often advanced by employers to justify privacy-invasive management practices. Under health and safety legislation, employers are under

---

[131] *Ibid.*

[132] Testimony of John Gerdelman, Senior Vice-President, Consumer Markets, MCI Communications Corporation, before the US House of Representatives Committee on Education and Labor (1993).

[133] Mello (1995), 662.

[134] 451 F Supp. 1355 (NJ Dist. Ct., 1978).

[135] This matter will be considered *infra*, in Chap. 9.

[136] PCC (1992c), 16.

[137] *Ibid.*, 17.

a general duty to provide a safe workplace, and to protect the health of employees. Moreover, employers may be vicariously liable for the actions of their employees which jeopardize the safety of consumers and the general public. For these reasons, employers have a clear interest in monitoring the activities and job performance of workers.[138] This is particularly the case in what are considered 'high risk' enterprises such as hospitals, railways, airlines, and power generating plants where, given the dangers involved, one can appreciate the rationale behind more extensive (and therefore potentially more intrusive) supervision and monitoring practices.

Since, as noted above, substance abuse may be linked to diminished job performance and an increase in workplace accidents, safety concerns have been advanced to justify drug and alcohol testing programmes in a number of industries. Tribunals in the United States, France and Canada have all upheld employer testing policies where the workers subject to the policies were engaged in tasks having a significant safety component.[139] Thus, the concept of a 'safety employee' has emerged in the drug testing jurisprudence. Safety concerns have also played an important role in the debate in the health care industry about the adoption of HIV and AIDS testing policies.[140] This is because HIV-infected health care professionals who perform invasive or close-contact procedures may contaminate patients.[141] In other safety-sensitive industries, it has been suggested that employers may be concerned about the HIV status of workers because of the dementia and deterioration of the central nervous system which can accompany AIDS.[142]

2.3.4.3 *Deterring and Controlling Employee Abuse of the Employment Relationship*

In 1989, it was estimated that employees in the United States 'stole' US$170 billion of employers' time through absenteeism and the simple failure to perform while in the workplace.[143] Abuse of long-distance telephone calls,

---

[138] Feldthusen (1988), 88. See, e.g., Occupational Health and Safety Act, RSO 1990, c. O–1, s. 25; Health and Safety in Employment Act (New Zealand, 1992), s. 6(a).

[139] See *infra*, sects. 4.3.4.3, 5.3.1 and 6.5.1.

[140] Mello (1994); OLRC (1992a), 62–71; In an Italian constitutional decision, a law forbidding employers from inquiring about an employee's HIV status, or conducting HIV tests, was struck down because it failed to provide for compulsory HIV tests where employee activity is potentially dangerous to third parties (Judgment No. 2430, Cass. (Italy), [1991] Foro It. I (Constitutional Court)). See Romei and Sciarra (1995).

[141] In *Leckelt* v. *Board of Commissioners of Hospital District No. 1*, 909 F 2d 820 (5th Circ., 1990), the court upheld the decision by the respondent hospital to terminate the employment of the appellant nurse, after he refused to disclose the results of an HIV test which had been requested by the hospital. The appellant was a known homosexual, and had previously failed to disclose that he was a carrier of hepatitis and syphilis. Moreover, his room mate had died of an AIDS-related illness, making it possible that he had been exposed to HIV. Given these facts, and given the court's view that hospitals have the right to test employees who have a high medical risk of carrying infectious diseases, the termination of the appellant's employment was held to be justifiable.

[142] PCC (1989a), 21.

[143] Boehmer (1992), 744.

photocopying, laser printing, automobiles, sick days, etc. must add countless billions more to the financial drain, thus increasing costs for the employer, impacting upon profitability and inflating consumer prices. Employee abuse goes further, however. In many industries, most notably the retail and hospitality sectors, employee theft is a serious problem. The American Society for Industrial Security has argued that:

> The consensus among security professionals in this country appears to be that the majority of crimes against business involve—directly and indirectly—dishonest insiders. Annual losses to the private sector from business crimes exceed $50 billion. The cost of those crimes is ultimately borne by the public in the form of higher prices for goods and services, as well as higher taxes.
>
> . . .
>
> Thus, employers have both a right and an obligation to safeguard the workplace from dishonest insiders. Monitoring has proven to be an effective tool toward that end.[144]

Surveillance and search policies have been justified by employers on the basis of deterring employee abuse and identifying those responsible for the abuse.[145] Some courts have agreed that it is legitimate for employers to adopt anti-abuse policies and practices, even if they are privacy-invasive. In *Chenkin* v. *Bellevue*,[146] for example, the Court accepted the employer's argument that its employee search policy was justified because of the serious theft problem it was experiencing.

Employers have also relied on the abuse deterrence rationale to support workplace drug testing, on the theory that in a drug-free workplace, employees will not engage in theft to support a drug problem.[147] An employer may also be concerned about the possibility that drug-using workers could commit the illegal activity of drug trafficking while in the workplace.

2.3.4.4 Complying with State-imposed Regulatory Requirements

Some jurisdictions have adopted legislation requiring or authorising employers to implement policies of a privacy-invasive nature. In a survey of national policies, the ILO remarked upon laws which oblige or permit employers to engage in alcohol, drug and other forms of employee testing.[148] Clearly, in cases where the employer has no choice but to adopt a privacy-invasive policy, the employer's interest in complying with the law will be sufficient to support the policy. The real issue is the validity of the law in question. Of course, if an employer's policy extends beyond the legal requirements, then it must be supported by other interests in so far as it exceeds the parameters of the relevant

---

[144] *Security Management* (1992), 93.
[145] Hoekstra (1996).
[146] 479 F Supp. 207 (SD NY, 1979).
[147] PCC (1990b), 6.
[148] ILO (1993a, 3), 28–30.

legislation. However, in situations where the law permits an employer to implement a particular policy, but leaves the ultimate decision to the employer, it is difficult to conclude that the existence of authorising legislation constitutes, in itself, an interest sufficient to support a privacy-invasive policy. The better view is that where the employer has a choice, and chooses a privacy-invasive policy, then the policy must be supported by a distinct employer interest (as noted above) or a public interest (as discussed below).

2.3.4.5 *Promoting the Public Interest*

The concept of 'public interest' is somewhat nebulous, and whether or not something is in the public interest can be controversial. In the case of workplace privacy issues, candidates/employees and employers can generally point to certain interests (which we might call 'public interests') to reinforce their own individual interests and objectives. To illustrate, the public clearly has an interest in employers succeeding in improving productivity and reducing workplace theft. This interest is largely economic, since consumers and taxpayers generally benefit when enterprises are able to reduce their operating expenses. In the case of employer promotion of health and safety, however, public interests range from the economic (e.g. reducing public costs associated with accidents), to the social (e.g. avoiding injuries to individuals which could prevent them from being happy, successful members of society), to the environmental (e.g. protecting the natural environment from oil and chemical spills).[149] Nevertheless, one must keep in mind that there is also a strong public interest in protecting the privacy of candidates/employees. Where the interest advanced by an individual, for example the interest in not being subjected to a humiliating search, has the legal status of a human right, then that fact alone engages the public interest. This demonstrates that the public interest cuts both ways, and can often be seen to support both candidate/employee and employer interests.

Public-interest considerations are particularly significant to the workplace privacy debate where they are unconnected to any employment interests which could legitimately be asserted by labour or management, yet stand as justifications in their own right for a particular privacy-invasive employment practice. On this point, it is relevant to the issue of workplace drug testing that public policy for over a decade has been coloured by the so-called 'war on drugs'. Drug possession and use are not only contrary to criminal law in many jurisdictions, but also impact negatively on the social and economic fabric of a society. Some nations have responded to the drug challenge by imposing severe criminal sanctions for drug possession, use and trafficking. State action has extended beyond the criminal law, however, toward a more pro-active policy of promoting drug testing as a means of deterring and identifying drug use generally. In the United

---

[149] In *Hennessey* v. *Coastal Eagle Point Oil Co.*, 609 A 2d 11 (NJ CA, 1992), 23, the employer justified discharging an employee who tested positive for drug use in part because 'the safety-sensitive nature of Hennessey's employment raises the potential for enormous public injury'.

States, the 1986 President's Commission on Organized Crime recommended that all employers screen candidates/employees for drugs as a means of combating drug use in society at large.[150] President Reagan responded by issuing an Executive Order with the stated aim of achieving drug-free workplaces, which required all federal agencies to adopt drug testing programmes for employees in 'sensitive positions'.[151] This itself resulted in the United States Department of Transportation issuing regulations requiring all employers to drug test employees holding commercial drivers' licences.[152] One American state, Georgia, has even provided workers compensation premium refunds to employers who undertake pre-employment, random and post-accident drug-testing.[153]

Although the Canadian government has not been as enthusiastic about drug testing, its National Drug Strategy did propose random alcohol and drug testing for federal transportation workers including pilots and truck drivers.[154] Similarly, in 1994 the New Zealand government proposed the introduction of legislation authorising employers in some industries to engage in drug testing.[155] Although such legislation has not yet appeared, the government's proposal is indicative of its support for private-sector drug testing.

State promotion of drug testing in private-sector workplaces, and its implementation of drug testing plans in the public sector and in regulated industries, has naturally impacted upon the attitudes of private employers towards drug testing. As Feldthusen observes, '[t]he private sector does not wish to become a safe haven for drug use', and has co-operated with the government's 'war on drugs' out of 'a sense of civic duty'.[156] This has led some private-sector employers to rely on the public policy against drug use to justify their own drug testing policies, and the dismissal of those who test positive.[157]

---

[150] President's Commission on Organized Crime (1986).

[151] Executive Order 12,564, 51 Fed. Reg. 32,889–32,893 (17 Sept. 1986).

[152] The Omnibus Transportation Employee Testing Act of 1991 (Pub. L. No. 102–143, 105 Stat. 952, 953) directed the Secretary of Transportation to promulgate regulations requiring employers of transportation workers performing safety-sensitive functions to establish alcohol and drug testing programmes for their employees. See Controlled Substances and Alcohol Use and Testing, 49 CFR para. 382 ff. See also Allison and Stehlut (1995).

[153] Bill 811, State of Georgia (1 July 1993).

[154] This proposal was ultimately abandoned (PCC (1992–3d), 35). However, Canadian Forces personnel were subjected to drug testing between 1990 and 1995. In 1995, however, the Department of National Defence suspended its programme of random testing (PCC (1990b), 52–55; PCC (1994–5e), 16–17).

[155] Shaw (1995), 56. As in Canada (prior to 1995), members of the New Zealand military have been subject to random drug testing (57).

[156] Feldthusen (1988), 93. Shaw (1995), 25, argues that President Reagan's 1986 Executive Order (*supra*, n. 151) 'has helped create and sustain a climate of strong community and judicial support for employee drug-testing programmes'.

[157] In *Exxon Shipping Co. v. Exxon Seamen's Union*, 993 F 2d 357 (3d Circ., 1993), the employee was dismissed for testing positive for marijuana use after his ship ran aground, although in all probability the drug was consumed during off-duty hours and could not have affected his job performance. An arbitrator ordered the employee's reinstatement, but this was overturned by the 3rd Circuit Court. It was held that the employer did not have to prove that the employee had used, or had been under the influence of, drugs while on the job. Instead, the employer could rely on a public policy of protecting the public and environment from the operation of vessels by drug users

One can conclude that in the case of drug testing, employers have relied not only on management-related justifications for invasive policies, but have also sought support from public policy, advanced vigorously by some governments for the past decade, of deterring drug use generally. Employers have thus been drafted as generals in the 'war on drugs'. It would be a mistake, of course, to think that employers do not benefit from participation in this 'war'. While there may be tangible benefits, for example the workers compensation premium refunds offered to employers in the State of Georgia, there are also intangible benefits, in particular the goodwill flowing from an image of being a good corporate citizen who is working alongside the government to combat a serious social ill.

2.3.4.6 Conclusion

In the above discussion, I was able to identify a variety of employer and public interests which may be advanced to justify management policies impacting upon private interests, and to demonstrate that these 'competing' interests form a complex array of managerial, economic and public policy considerations. The discussion also underlined the fact that discrete workplace privacy issues may implicate different interests, or the same interests but for different reasons or to a different degree. For example, while a hospital's HIV-testing policy would find support primarily under a public safety rationale, a retail store's drug testing plan could be supported by a combination of economic, safety and abuse-deterrence considerations. Both policies would clearly engage important private interests falling within the personal and informational zones.

2.4 CONCLUSIONS

In this chapter, I provided the essential foundation for the development of legal principles to govern the regulation of workplace privacy issues by defining the concept of 'privacy', analysing the private interests of candidates/employees, and identifying the competing interests of employers and the public. The following conclusions flow from the discussion:

(1) While the use by management of privacy-invasive testing and monitoring practices is presently more common in North America than in the European Union, there is a trend in all industrialised nations toward the increased use of such practices;

(2) Within each of the 'zones' of privacy (personal, territorial and informational), it is possible to identify a range of private interests which may be

(360–4). The Court identified this public policy as flowing from the US Coast Guard's own testing regulations, which stipulate that an individual who tests positive for drugs should be 'denied employment as a crew member'. Interestingly, the crewman in *Exxon* had passed the Coast Guard's drug test, but had failed Exxon's own, stricter test.

threatened by certain management policies and practices. This fact demonstrates that the right of privacy has relevance in the employment context;

(3) The values promoted by the right of privacy, namely autonomy, dignity and well-being, healthy relationships and pluralism, are directly at stake in the workplace. This underscores the significance of candidates'/employees' private interests.

(4) Employer interests which may potentially justify limitations on private interests generally fall into five categories: (i) improving economic conditions; (ii) protecting the health and safety of workers, consumers, and the public; (iii) deterring and controlling employee abuse of the employment relationship; (iv) complying with state-imposed regulatory requirements; and (v) advancing the public interest.

I also developed and advanced a functional approach to the right of privacy, which focuses not on exhaustively defining the right, but rather on identifying the private interests protected by the right which are implicated in a particular context. I will revisit the functional approach in Chapters 8 and 9, where I will discuss the issues of employment drug testing and genetic testing in detail. In Chapter 3 I will consider how workplace privacy issues can be addressed under competing theories of labour law.

3

Labour Law and the Right of Privacy

3.1 INTRODUCTION

In Chapter 2, I established that certain management practices may infringe upon private interests at the core of the right of privacy, and then identified various competing employer and public interests. The question arises how labour law should respond to these interests. Not surprisingly, this is a controversial matter. In Chapter 3, I will consider workplace privacy from the perspective of management and organisation theory, and will then proceed to assess the approaches of three competing labour law schools: collective *laissez-faire*, market individualism and 'floor of rights'.

3.2 MANAGEMENT AND ORGANISATION THEORY AS A STARTING POINT

Although one of my central premises is that the use of privacy-invasive technologies/practices by employers raises serious legal concerns, the issue has also been approached from the perspective of management and organisation theory. In fact, workplace privacy issues such as drug testing and performance monitoring have received considerable attention in the recent human resource and industrial psychology literature.[1] Before I proceed to consider workplace privacy within labour law, an assessment of this literature is necessary because, in the absence of legal regulation or regulation through collective agreements, privacy issues will fall within the prerogative of management.[2] Hence, management and organisation theory takes on some importance in understanding the considerations influencing employers when facing matters of workplace privacy.

Vetting job applicants, selecting employees from applicant pools, supervising employees, co-ordinating work efforts—from the time of the very first workplace, these have all been considered functions within the realm of management prerogative. Management theorists have long recognised the link between

---

[1] See: Harris (1992); Aiello and Svec (1993); Carayon (1993); Bates and Holton (1995); Zigarelli (1995).

[2] In *United Steelworkers* v. *Warrior and Gulf Navigation Co.*, 363 US 574 (1960), 583, Justice Douglas stated the principle of management prerogative as follows: 'Management hires and fires, pays and promotes, supervises and plans. All these are part of its function, and absent a collective bargaining agreement, it may be exercised freely except as limited by public law and by the willingness of employees to work under the particular unilaterally-imposed conditions.'

promoting workforce productivity and increasing firm profitability. However, the question of how management functions should be carried out in order to optimise worker productivity (and thereby maximise profitability) has been a subject of controversy amongst commentators in the fields of organisation and management theory.

Following the industrial revolution, as the assembly line production method and its division of labour necessitated greater job specialisation, there arose a significant management interest in controlling the workplace in order to co-ordinate the disparate efforts of individual workers. The primary aspiration of 'scientific management', spearheaded by the American engineer Frederick W. Taylor, was to convert management from an art of personal style to, as its name suggests, a science. Taylor pioneered the idea of the scientific study of jobs, urging the development and implementation of systematic methods for selecting, training, and supervising employees. This, so Taylor argued, would ensure that employees performed their work exactly according to goals determined by scientific analysis.[3] Scientific management thus gave rise to the very first management practices with the potential to invade privacy: psychological testing of job candidates,[4] and mechanical aids in supervising workers such as punch-clocks and keystroke counters. Inevitably, technological advances have seen the rise of more sophisticated means of controlling workers and measuring their job performance. In fact, the present-day use of chair sensors, location badges and urinalysis drug tests[5] is consistent with the principles underlying scientific management.

The classical school of human resource management, inspired by the demands of the industrial revolution and the teachings of scientific management, viewed the workplace as a quasi-machine, with individual workers as replaceable component parts[6] (hence the expression 'cog in the wheel'). The classical workplace is a rigidly hierarchical organisation, with workers being assigned well-defined tasks and subjected to clear job-performance expectations. Because of hierarchy and specialisation, the most prized management values in such a workplace are *control* and *co-ordination*. Managers are expected to know what is going on at all times, and must be able to determine whether workers are complying with the rules and meeting performance requirements.

In the past, the predominance of a management ethos premised on 'control' gave rise to pervasive employer interference in the off-duty lives of employees. Finkin refers to this as 'quasi parental corporate control', through which rules were imposed by employers in areas such as dating, association, recreation and religion.[7] Employer efforts of this kind were often regarded with suspicion by

---

[3] Cascio and Thacker (1994), 37–8.

[4] In 1913, Hugo Munsterberg described the use of psychological testing to select street-car operators and ships' officers. See Moskowitz (1977).

[5] *Supra*, see nn. 5, 7, 11, Chap. 2.

[6] Ackoff (1994), 7–8.

[7] Finkin (1996b), 251.

employees, who viewed strict regulation of their off-duty lives as paternalistic and demeaning.[8] Beginning around 1920,[9] the classical emphasis on control was challenged by the human relations movement, which viewed the workplace as a complex social system in which productivity is directly related to the quality of the human relationships within the system. Workers, therefore, should not be seen as isolated individuals co-ordinated through managerial control. Instead, they are members of a common social system, held together by a sense of affiliation and belonging, and hence capable of working together co-operatively.[10] The human relations movement gave rise to the behavioural school of human resource management, which advances *cohesion* and *motivation* as predominant values. Such values are to be pursued not through job specialisation and rigid control, but rather through methods which motivate workers and reinforce their sense of belonging within the organisation. These might include participative decision-making, information sharing and the encouragement of personal development.[11]

Certainly, many of the assumptions of the classical school of management—in particular the equating of human workers with machine components—have been discredited by modern human resource theorists.[12] The view that organisations exist, at least in part, to serve the social and emotional aspirations of their stakeholders is hardly controversial. However, the values promoted by classicism, in particular control and co-ordination, are of obvious importance even in those organisations which best exemplify the principles of the human relations movement. The recognition that classical values remain relevant has given rise to the 'competing values' theory of management, in which any management decision impacting upon human resources (which would include a considerable majority of such decisions) must be assessed within the framework of an economic cost-benefit analysis.[13] What are the potential benefits of a course of action in terms of control and co-ordination? Are these benefits outweighed by the potential costs in terms of cohesion, motivation and morale?

The recent literature approaching testing and monitoring as issues of human resource management theory has applied the competing values framework for the purpose of identifying optimal economic solutions. Not surprisingly, commentators are divided on the result of the value competition. Hence, some have applauded the reduction in worker absenteeism which may be achieved where employers adopt drug testing plans, and weed out drug users from applicant pools. In the case of computer-based performance monitoring, proponents argue that the technology can be used to enhance control over the production

---

[8] *Ibid.*, 251–3.

[9] The human relations movement is generally considered to have arisen out of the famous Hawthorne experiments in Chicago in 1923. See Pennock (1930).

[10] O'Neill (1993).

[11] *Ibid.*

[12] For a competing viewpoint, see Friedman (1970).

[13] O'Neill (1993); Quinn (1983).

process, assist in planning future workloads and target training programmes.[14] Other commentators have emphasised the costs of testing and monitoring, and in particular the danger that the assertion of control through new technology could undermine trust in the working relationship, create a worker perception of unfairness and heighten stress in the workplace.[15] Still others have observed that the increasing use of testing and monitoring technologies represents a shift in emphasis from employee development to employee discipline[16] and marks a return to the depersonalised 'sweatshop' atmosphere of nineteenth-century industry.[17]

The inability of the competing values school to provide clear guidance on privacy issues follows from the fact that human personalities, perceptions and emotions are at issue. These are complex matters which do not lend themselves to quantification for the purposes of an economic cost-benefit analysis. This point is illustrated by the fact that a management decision concerning the adoption of testing and/or monitoring technology does not necessarily present a stark choice between the competing values of classicism (i.e. control) and behaviouralism (i.e. motivation). In fact, the monitoring of job performance may assist managers in providing constructive feedback to employees, and may promote the employer's dual interests in controlling job performance, while motivating employees to improve their work. Employees may find the objective statistics generated by technological monitoring systems to be a more reliable basis for evaluating their performance than the subjective observations of managers. Similarly, drug testing might conceivably create the perception among workers of improved safety. This could promote cohesion, by making some employees feel secure in the work environment, and confident that management is concerned about their well-being. In short, given the complexity of approaching workplace privacy matters within the competing values framework, it is understandable that no management consensus has yet emerged on the merits of monitoring and testing.

Certain practical issues demonstrate the potential inadequacies of management theory in effectively responding to workplace privacy issues. First, management theory is just that—theory. Hence, even if management policies such as drug testing and performance monitoring implicate important human relations values, there is surely no guarantee that, in practice, managers will be aware of the need to take into account such values in their decision-making. After all, despite the rise of behaviouralism in the 1920s, there was no rush on the part of employers to incorporate human relations considerations into their decision-making. A much greater impetus for attitudinal and organisational change has been the emergence of collective labour action, particularly after the Second

---

[14] Bates and Holton (1995), 269.
[15] Nussbaum (1986).
[16] Aiello (1993).
[17] Irving (1986).

World War.[18] In the context of the often conflictual labour–management relationship, managers may simply respond to the worker interests asserted (or which they anticipate will be asserted) by unions, as opposed to pro-actively incorporating human relations considerations into the decision-making process. This means that the ability and willingness of unions to express worker interests, such as privacy, is significant. The decline of unionisation in recent decades in countries like the United States[19] and the United Kingdom[20] could well result in a parallel decline in employer respect for the human relations interests of workers.

This leads to the further difficulty that management theory is distinctly unitarist in nature, and therefore assumes a broad managerial prerogative.[21] It thus fails to take into account the influence of unions (or works councils[22]) in the decision-making process, and the limitations on managerial prerogative resulting from collective negotiations/participation. In many industries, 'management' decisions reflect not only the values and objectives of the employer, but also the competing values and objectives of collective labour.[23] Of course, the participation of labour representatives does not necessarily guarantee a greater emphasis on human relations interests. Unions, like management, may prefer to approach issues from an economic perspective (although, obviously, the economic aspirations of unions are different from those of employers). Thus, even if a union appreciates that human relations interests are implicated by a management proposal or decision, it may bargain away those interests in exchange for higher salaries, improved benefits or other economic concessions. This is not to say that unions will necessarily be insensitive to privacy concerns flowing from testing and monitoring policies. This is simply to suggest that unions may pursue tangible economic gains for their members, as opposed to intangible human relations benefits such as privacy protection.[24]

---

[18] Cascio and Thacker (1994), 38; Ackoff (1994), 12–13. Deakin and Morris (1995), 50, observe that participative decision-making is more a product of unionisation than of the adoption of employee-oriented human resource management models.

[19] Weiler (1990a), 9.

[20] Deakin and Morris (1995), 42–5.

[21] Fox (1974), 249: unitarist thinking emphasises 'the need for a unified structure of authority, leadership, and loyalty, with full managerial prerogative legitimized by all members of the organization'.

[22] Consider the extensive role of French works councils in relation to workplace privacy (*infra*, sect. 5.5).

[23] The pluralist perspective on labour relations is a response to unitarism. Pluralists view the enterprise as a collection of groups and individuals each with their own interests and aspirations. Conflict is inevitable. Therefore, according to Fox (1974), 260–1, '[m]anagement is seen as making its decisions within a set of constraints which include employees, consumers, suppliers, government, the law, the local community, and sources of finance'.

[24] Lyon-Caen (1992b), 14, reports that French collective agreements '*ne contiennent pratiquement rien sur le sujet [des libertés publiques et l'emploi] et cette remarque à elle seule est importante, manifestent un certain désintérêt des interlocuteurs sociaux, relativement à la protection des libertés personnelles*'.

Finally, even if managers are aware that important human relations interests are implicated by a decision, these interests will only be controlling if they are deemed to have some relevance to the economic welfare of the firm. This results from the fact that human resource management theory views the promotion of human interests (i.e. dignity, autonomy, etc.) not as an end in itself, but as a *means* to an end—namely enhanced profitability. If profit is the goal of the firm, then managers will choose the means which they believe best achieves that goal. This may well result in behavioural values being subordinated to classical values, if the cost-benefit analysis ultimately favours control over cohesion or motivation.[25] Where a relevant human interest is also an individual human right (for example, a *privacy right*), then the application of cost-benefit analysis could result in that interest being trumped by the economic goals of the firm. In the case of privacy, this would mean that the private interests of workers would be limited whenever an employer could identify an economic interest (such as those discussed in section 2.3.4.1 of Chapter 2) that it perceived to be promoted by the limitation. While the subordination of individual rights to competing interests is not in itself unusual, the subordination of certain individual rights to *economic* goals (a potential and perhaps inevitable result of the economic emphasis of cost-benefit analysis) is cause for concern in societies, like those of North America and the European Union, where those rights are also important constitutional and societal values. In fact, this phenomenon of economic subordination contributed to the enactment of anti-discrimination legislation. Societies with such legislation were not willing to tolerate the denial of employment opportunities to members of certain groups, even in circumstances where refusing to hire (or firing) members of those groups might well follow from an economic cost-benefit analysis.[26]

Certainly, classicism, behaviouralism and the competing values school all contribute to the way we think about workplace privacy problems, and provide a framework within which managers can work towards identifying the optimal economic solutions for their organisations. However, given the theoretical and practical difficulties inherent to human resource management, its relevance to a legal analysis of workplace privacy is limited.

---

[25] Royal Commission on Trade Unions and Employers Associations (1965–8), para. 18; Weiler (1990a), 33–4.

[26] 'Economically rational' discrimination is discussed by Epstein (1992b), 59–76. As a simple illustration, consider a situation where customers refuse to be served by a black employee. An employer's perception of economic realities could result in the employee being reassigned or fired. An employer might also rely on an economic justification to refuse to hire (or fire) women of childbearing years, because of the costs to the employer associated with pregnancy. For examples of cases where employers have relied (unsuccessfully) on economic arguments to justify the termination of a pregnant employee see: *Dekker* v. *VJV*, [1991] IRLR 31 (ECJ), and *Webb* v. *EMO Air Cargo*, [1994] E.C.R. I-3567.

3.3 COMPETING APPROACHES WITHIN LABOUR LAW

While it is possible to define labour law simply as a system of legal rules governing the employment relationship,[27] this descriptive formulation ignores the fact that labour law has for decades been a controversial, yet critical, element of social policy in Western nations.[28] Any discussion of workplace privacy as a legal issue must begin with an appreciation of the important socio-economic functions of labour law.

State intervention in, and regulation of, the employment contract have traditionally been linked to two distinct aspects of public policy.[29] The first may be labelled 'worker protection' or 'industrial justice', and includes measures to protect individual workers from the economic might of their employers, and to promote a higher quality of life for workers. Minimum wage laws, health and safety standards, and anti-discrimination requirements fall into this category. The second, 'industrial stability', is the policy aspect promoting economic growth through the preservation of industrial harmony, and the limitation and management of industrial conflicts. Typically, this includes laws imposing certainty in the collective negotiation process: laws governing the certification of bargaining units, strike votes, employer interference in union activities, etc. In other words, it might well be said that the extensive regulation of the employment relationship is the state's response both to the economic power imbalance between employers and workers, and to the potential industrial instability flowing from labour's collective response to this power imbalance, unionisation.[30] Labour law is, then, the mechanism through which the state has endeavoured to balance the competing interests of employees, employers and the public.

Although there is general agreement on the two public policy aspects of extant labour law—industrial justice and industrial stability—there is considerable debate over the extent to which the state should pursue these two aspects through legal regulation, if at all. As with any labour law issue, solutions to workplace privacy issues will differ depending on the approach to labour law which is adopted. I will consider three competing approaches below: collective *laissez-faire*, market individualism and 'floor of rights'.

---

[27] In North America, labour law is often characterised as governing *collective* relations between management and labour, in contrast to employment law, which deals with the relationship between an employer and the *individual* employee. See Arthurs *et al.* (1993), 32. The term 'labour law' is used here in a broader (and more European) sense, to describe the set of laws governing all facets of employment.

[28] Davies and Freedland (1993), in particular 653–5; Deakin and Morris (1995), 1.

[29] At least in modern times. State regulation and intervention in the employment contract have a long history in both the United Kingdom and North America, as documented by Mason (1925). Often, of course, such regulation has run counter to the interests of employees.

[30] Kade (1988).

3.3.1 Collective *Laissez-faire*

The underlying premise of collective *laissez-faire* is that freedom of contract, in so far as it applies to the relationship between labour and management, should be respected to the fullest extent possible. Hence, the concept of 'voluntarism' captures the essence of *laissez-faire* thought: the employment relationship is a voluntary association entered into freely by two parties, employee and employer, and therefore should be regulated by agreements entered into between those parties, or between their collective representatives, unions and employers' associations.

Legal abstentionism is closely related to collective *laissez-faire*, as it implies a minimum of both judicial and legislative intervention in the individual employment relationship, and relies instead on regulation by autonomous collective organisations.[31] Kahn-Freund's abstentionist analysis is perhaps the most influential. Writing about United Kingdom labour law in 1958, he stated that the main characteristics of the labour movement were 'its aversion to legislative intervention, its disinclination to rely on legal sanctions, its almost passionate belief in the autonomy of industrial forces'.[32] He further noted that this attitude was shared by employers, employers' associations and the civil service, and was therefore the defining force in UK labour policy. This attitude, which supported a policy of collective *laissez-faire*, resulted in the state distancing itself from industrial relations, except where legislation was necessary as a 'stop-gap' due to the failure of collective bargaining (a situation arising, according to Kahn-Freund, from cases of 'disequilibrium of social forces'[33]). Legislative 'stop-gaps' include statutes concerning hours of work, safety and health, minimum wages and social security.[34] These comprehensive yet limited laws were originally justified by Kahn-Freund on industrial justice grounds, as he argued that they were a product of 'the growing insight into the need for protecting the health of the nation and therefore for the regulation of the working conditions of all employees'.[35] However, he later expressed a view consistent with industrial stability, arguing that such measures were needed to limit conflict in the workplace and reduce the incidence of strikes.[36]

What, then, is the explanation for the legal abstentionism which Kahn-Freund identified in the UK's approach to labour law? First, the labour movement developed a distrust of political and judicial processes during the nineteenth and twentieth centuries as a result of interventions which ran counter to workers' interests. This resulted in a 'tendency to keep the legislature and the

---

[31] Lewis (1979), 208.

[32] Kahn-Freund (1959a), 224.

[33] *Ibid.*, 225.

[34] *Ibid.*, 245.

[35] *Ibid.*, 247.

[36] Lewis (1979), 214, commenting on Kahn-Freund's views as expressed in Britain's Royal Commission on Trade Unions and Employers Associations (1965–8), particularly para. 528.

courts out of the mainstream of labour relations'.[37] Secondly, the British tradition of individualism, including a strong commitment to the individual's freedom to contract, discouraged legislative intervention to control both a worker's right to sell her labour and an employer's right to purchase that labour as he saw fit.[38] These forces meant that the preference for extra-legal approaches to labour relations continued in the United Kingdom throughout the twentieth century, even though unions had achieved considerable political influence, and legislators would have been more sympathetic to the demands of workers.

Although Kahn-Freund was writing about the state of the UK's labour law system, he was not merely describing the *status quo*. In fact, he very much believed in the merits of voluntarism and collective *laissez-faire*, primarily because he viewed them as expressions of his pluralist philosophy.[39] Indeed, Kahn-Freund conceptualised the employment relationship as one of conflicting interests in which workers, and their representative unions, find themselves in permanent opposition to employers. The state's role in the face of constant conflict is, generally, to remain neutral and to allow the parties themselves to reach agreements. However, Kahn-Freund did see a legitimate (though again limited) role for the state in equalising the bargaining strength of labour and management. Hence, he wrote that the 'main purpose of labour law [was] to redress any disequilibrium of power'.[40] This goal was to be accomplished largely through procedural regulations which Kahn-Freund likened to the 'Queensberry' rules.[41] Such regulations do 'not settle wages, hours or other conditions of employment', but instead constitute 'rules for their settlement' and 'for the enforcement of terms' of collective agreements.[42]

The general theory of legal abstentionism thus considers the primary concern of labour law to be the preservation and promotion of a balance of power between management and labour. Hence, regulations promoting industrial stability, which are often procedural rules governing the mechanics of collective bargaining, should be the focus of labour law. The content of collective agreements should be left to the parties, although there will be limited exceptions where the legislature is entitled to limit the exercise of the managerial prerogative. Such exceptions will arise only where the matter at issue cannot be addressed effectively by collective bargaining.[43] In those cases, legislation functions as a 'stop-gap'. In essence, then, labour law should be governed by a form of subsidiarity: the state should only legislate in areas which cannot be addressed effectively by collective negotiations.

[37] Lewis (1999), 232; see also Flanders (1974), 353–4.
[38] Kahn-Freund (1959a), 225, 253–9.
[39] *Supra*, n. 23.
[40] Kahn-Freund (1972c), 1.
[41] Kahn-Freund (1969b), 302.
[42] Kahn-Freund (1983e), 60.
[43] In fact, Kahn-Freund (1969b), 303, opined that 'the greatest defect of the law is the absence of any attempt to create a body of regulatory norms to provide the parties with a clear ruling where collective bargaining fails to give it'.

While legal abstentionism has had its greatest influence on the labour law of the United Kingdom, the principles associated with it—collective *laissez-faire* and voluntarism—continue to have force in other Western labour law systems. Thus, Wellington has observed that early American labour relations were characterised by worker distrust of the judiciary and legislature, which then gave rise to an abstentionist mood similar to that prevailing in the United Kingdom, and an emphasis on collective bargaining and freedom of contract to determine employment terms.[44] Weiler has made a similar point about early Canadian labour relations.[45] The North American brand of legal abstentionism was nevertheless tempered by legislative action to prevent exploitation in situations where the bargaining power of employers outweighed that of labour. Thus, 'law has tended to reject freedom of contract in those classes of cases where experience suggests its retention too often will result in unfairness between the parties'.[46] Labour law in North America reflects the tension between collective *laissez-faire* and legislative amelioration of bargaining inequality. Thus, labour relations statutes create the framework through which collective bargaining must occur, and are largely procedural in nature.[47] Such statutes promote collective bargaining, but as a general rule do not dictate the outcome of that bargaining. This is evinced by the 'Preamble' to the Canada Labour Code:

> Whereas there is a long tradition in Canada of labour legislation and policy designed for the promotion of the common well-being through the encouragement of free collective bargaining and the constructive settlement of disputes;
>
> And whereas Canadian workers, trade unions and employers recognize and support freedom of association and free collective bargaining as the bases of effective industrial relations for the determination of good working conditions and sound labour-management relations . . . [48]

In short, the labour law systems of both Canada and the United States are marked by substantial legislative control over the collective bargaining process,[49] yet there remains a strong reliance on the principle of freedom of contract to determine the substance of collective agreements.[50] Similarly, European

---

[44] Wellington (1968), 13–26.

[45] Weiler (1990a), 161.

[46] Wellington (1968), 32.

[47] There is an obvious comparative issue resulting from the presence in North America of labour legislation promoting collective bargaining, and the relative lack of similar legislation in the UK Kahn-Freund (1959a), 228–9, explains this difference in approach by noting that American unions have not been as averse as their British counterparts to appealing to state intervention. In Kahn-Freund (1969b), 302, he opined that UK trade unions (unlike their counterparts in other advanced industrial countries) attained considerable bargaining strength long before their members had obtained the franchise. This resulted in unions relying on industrial rather than on political pressure, and on collective negotiations rather than on legislation.

[48] RSC 1985, c. L–2. For a recent discussion of collective *laissez-faire* in Canada, see *Royal Oak Mines* v. *Canada* [1996] 1 SCR 369, particularly 445–55 (*per* Justice Major, dissenting).

[49] Canada Labour Code, *supra* n. 48; National Labour Relations Act, 29 USC (1982).

[50] Stone(a) (1981), 1514–16. Prominent American labour law commentators shared Kahn-Freund's pluralistic view. See Cox (1947), 1; Wellington (1968).

labour law systems such as those of France and Germany have placed great reliance on collective participation and bargaining as a source of employment standards,[51] and in recent times have moved away from centralised regulation of employment to decentralised negotiation as a means of achieving greater economic flexibility.[52] It thus seems clear that any argument advocating legal protection for individuals in their capacity as workers, such as measures enforcing the right of privacy in the workplace, must overcome the collective *laissez-faire* tradition underlying Western labour law systems.

Relating this to the issue of workplace privacy, the collective *laissez-faire* school would generally resist legal intervention in preference to solutions flowing from collective bargaining, on the basis that legal intervention to control the substance of the employment relationship constitutes interference in the autonomy of management and labour. However, even Kahn-Freund's notion of legal abstentionism does not preclude state intervention in exceptional circumstances, namely where either industrial stability or industrial justice (or perhaps both) is at stake, and a *laissez-faire* reliance on employers' and workers' representatives is unlikely to achieve justice or preserve stability.[53] Hence, judicial or legislative action to vindicate the private interests of workers could be justified if it could be shown that industrial justice demands such action and/or industrial stability could be jeopardized by inaction (because privacy issues left unaddressed are potential sources of conflict between workers and management) *and* it could further be shown that a policy of collective *laissez-faire* either cannot, or will not, prevent injustice and/or instability.

As I demonstrated in Chapter 2, the right of privacy has considerable force in the employment context. Therefore, the public policy aspect of labour law concerned with industrial justice would support legal intervention to protect workers from at least some forms of invasion of privacy. Moreover, in Chapter 2 I also established the potential of workplace privacy issues to create conflict between workers and managers, thus demonstrating that industrial stability is at stake. The question, from a collective *laissez-faire* perspective, is whether the challenges posed by privacy are best addressed within an environment stressing freedom of contract or through legal intervention. One answer is that union membership and collective bargaining coverage are unlikely to ever reach levels approaching 100 per cent,[54] while the decline in unionisation in some countries may be accompanied by a commensurate decline in employer respect for human relations values (of which privacy is one). Moreover, collective bargaining is unlikely to address the situation of job candidates. Hence, collective bargaining cannot provide a comprehensive response to workplace privacy issues, and legal

---

[51] See France, *infra*, sect. 5.5.

[52] Chouraquai (1993), 144.

[53] Wellington (1968), 32, makes a similar point.

[54] According to ILO (1997–8d), trade union membership is: United Kingdom (25.6%, 1994), United States (12.7%, 1995), France (6.1%, 1995), Canada (31.0%, 1993) (243, Table 3.1); collective bargaining coverage is: United Kingdom (?/%, 1995), United States (11.2%, 1995), France (90.0%, 1995), Canada (37.0%, 1996) (248, Table 3.2).

'stop-gaps' are required to afford protection to candidates and non-unionised employees.

However, even assuming a situation in which collective representation can address the needs of all candidates/employees, a strong argument can be mounted that the protection of privacy rights in the employment context is simply not an appropriate subject for collective bargaining. The inclusion of issues implicating the right of privacy in collective bargaining, as one matter among many to be settled by the parties, opens up the possibility that such rights will be traded away in return for economic or other gains. Hence, the deficiency noted earlier in section 3.2 of this Chapter *vis-à-vis* human resource management theory has equal force in relation to collective *laissez-faire*—in the context of collective bargaining, individual interests may be subordinated to economic goals. Where that interest is also of a human rights quality (as in the case of privacy), such economic subordination (or even its potential) is problematic. In short, industrial justice and stability objectives in relation to the right of privacy may only be pursued comprehensively through legal regulation. For this reason, an approach to privacy premised on collective *laissez-faire* would not necessarily preclude the enactment of legal standards.

3.3.2 Market Individualism

The past two decades have seen a new emphasis in the labour law of Western nations. Many governments, facing high unemployment and spiralling debt, have come to view deregulation of labour markets as a means of reducing the costs of labour, and thereby promoting job creation and economic development.[55] This governmental retreat from labour markets is not premised on a theory of industrial pluralism or voluntarism, as is the case with collective *laissez-faire* thought, but instead is based on a scepticism about the collective representation of workers and a desire to minimise state interference with the market. Hence, this school of labour law may be termed, 'market individualism'. Market individualism has been advocated most vociferously by commentators associated with the 'law and economics' school.[56] These writers are openly hostile to a fundamental premise of modern labour law (a premise even accepted by legal abstentionists), namely the view that legal intervention can be justified where it seeks to preserve and promote the public policy of industrial justice. They argue that the assumed power imbalance between workers and

---

[55] Deakin and Wilkinson (1991a), 8. This deregulation trend was felt most strongly in the UK during the 1980s and 1990s, but was also apparent in other European and North American labour systems. In terms of North America, see: England (1995), 558–9, 609; Glasbeek (1993b), 233–8. In relation to France, see Lyon-Caen (1993c), 3–5. Note that French 'deregulation' was achieved through an increase in statutory rules in order to promote 'flexibility' and regulate diverse forms of employment.

[56] For an American perspective, see Epstein (1983a). For a British perspective, consider Hayek (1980).

employers, which underlies industrial justice regulations, is either seriously exaggerated or fallacious, and that, in pursuing such policies, the state actually creates a power imbalance favouring workers, while imposing rigidities on the labour market which result in a drag on the economy.

One of the most important works in the area of market individualism is Epstein's *Forbidden Grounds*,[57] an economic analysis of anti-discrimination laws in which the author advocates their repeal (at least in their application to private employers). Because Epstein is concerned with the role of a human right, equality in the labour market, his analysis foreshadows an economic treatment of workplace privacy. It is therefore instructive to draw on it here.

Epstein argues that the anti-discrimination principle constitutes 'a powerful brake against . . . freedom of contract and the concomitant but limited role of the state'.[58] In championing freedom of contract (in a manner evoking collective *laissez-faire*), he proceeds to establish that the benefits of anti-discrimination law are largely symbolic,[59] while the economic costs are considerable. Such costs include direct expenditures associated with state enforcement, employer compliance and litigation costs,[60] as well as certain indirect economic burdens. This latter category would include costs incurred when firms act to avoid accusations of discrimination—the hiring of less-qualified candidates from protected categories (i.e. women or Blacks), the adoption and administration of quota systems for the members of those categories, and the elimination of employment tests which, though valuable, may be attacked as discriminatory.[61] Epstein even suggests that discrimination may have productivity advantages, since it allows the employer to avoid hiring, or to dismiss, workers who do not 'fit in', and thereby contributes to workplace harmony and worker motivation.[62] He then proceeds to explain why the market, and not legislative intervention, would better address the discrimination faced by women and members of racial minority groups. In his view, an ideal social policy would allow these individuals to offer their labour to whomever they choose at whatever wages they wish, and 'competitive pressures will do the rest'.[63] Hence, if individuals suffer discrimination, they should be able to lower the cost of their labour in order to overcome the reluctance of employers to hire them.[64] Discrimination, according to Epstein, is combated by making anti-discrimination profitable, as opposed to making discrimination illegal.

---

[57] Epstein (1992b).
[58] *Ibid.*, 4; see also 147.
[59] *Ibid.*, 497.
[60] *Ibid.*, 166, 174, 181.
[61] *Ibid.*, 178–9, 236–41.
[62] *Ibid.*, 65–8. Epstein's argument here is an interesting twist on the management theory of behaviouralism, since he argues that discrimination against women, ethnic minorities, etc. may have important motivational advantages. Epstein suggests that a homogeneous workplace may be a more supportive environment for some workers.
[63] *Ibid.*, 265.
[64] *Ibid.*, 40–5, 263.

In a similar vein, market individualists would hold to the view that any legal intervention to regulate the use of privacy-invasive employer practices would: (i) rigidify the labour market by preventing or limiting the use of management techniques which may contribute to increasing productivity and efficiency; (ii) impose costs associated with enforcement and compliance, such as litigation expenses; and (iii) ultimately be unnecessary, since the labour market itself has the ability to control any abuse by managers of such technology.

This third point requires some elaboration. In the context of drug testing, Weiler has explained the argument that labour market forces will impose limitations on employers. To paraphrase the argument which he presents:

> If an employee is subjected by her employer to a mandatory random drug testing program, she is free to take another job with another employer. Hence, the first employer loses the benefits of her skills and services, plus the investment it has made in her training. The firm might also suffer damage to its reputation which could hamper its ability to recruit, retain and motivate its workforce.[65]

This form of argument effectively equates individual workers with consumers. Hence, the consumer withdraws his business in order to effect change in a retailer, while the employee withdraws his services in order to effect change in an employer. In reliance on this reasoning, proponents of an economic model of labour law would reject state regulation in preference to the 'natural' regulation of the labour market. Thus, if workers oppose privacy-invasive policies, and withdraw their services as a result, then employers who adopt such policies will suffer, while employers who do not will benefit. Ultimately, the labour market will determine whether or not the policy should be implemented.

There are several reasons for finding this economic reasoning to be inadequate.[66] The market argument assumes that employees are able to move freely from one job to another in a series of relatively low-cost transactions. However, the notion that workers will leave their jobs in protest over management policies seems suspect in economies where rates of unemployment can range from 8 per cent to 12 per cent (or even higher), and jobs in many fields may therefore be scarce. The simple logic of neo-classical supply and demand suggests that where supply outstrips demand, as is the case during periods of unemployment, economic power rests with the demand side. What incentive would an employer have to change or eliminate a drug testing policy if, for every worker who left in protest, another was available for immediate hire? Moreover, several additional factors impede job-switching: financial obligations (e.g. mortgages and other bank loans), the difficulties of relocation (e.g. moving house, switching children to new schools), contractual limitations such as confidentiality and restraint of

---

[65] Weiler (1990a), 17. I must emphasise that this is an argument that Weiler advances for discussion (and refutation) purposes.

[66] *Ibid.*, 282–3.

trade clauses, the social stigma of unemployment,[67] and perhaps even the loss of statutory benefits.[68] Recent studies have concluded that a significant number of employment relationships are long-term, and that firms deliberately structure employment to encourage employee longevity. Techniques include progressive wage structures and benefits linked to years of service, both of which reward an employee financially for remaining with the employer in the long term. Resignation may be a costly affair for an employee if it results in the loss of seniority-linked benefits.[69]

Market individualists like Epstein would respond that individuals in a competitive labour market who wish to enjoy privacy in the workplace should reduce the price of their labour, thus making it profitable for employers to adopt privacy-friendly policies which would permit them to take advantage of cheaper labour. However, it is unjust to expect employees who wish to enjoy the right of privacy to internalise the costs of the right in order to benefit from it. Such an approach creates a powerful financial incentive for employees to forego their privacy in return for higher wages. In any event, market individualism would set up a distasteful competition between those who are willing to sacrifice their privacy for economic benefits, and those who are prepared to lose out economically in defence of their private interests.

A further point is of fundamental significance. If labour law were merely concerned with ensuring the most economically profitable mechanisms for managing employer–employee relations, then it might well be justifiable to consider, and even place reliance upon, the labour market to determine employment standards. However, what is being purchased and sold in the labour market is the work of human beings. For this reason, labour law aspires to protect interests beyond the economic objectives of employers; in particular, as I argued above, it has traditionally been within the purview of labour law to impose standards linked to industrial justice objectives, in recognition of the human aspect of the labour market. Weiler refers to this phenomenon as a 'protective ethical stance of the law',[70] and notes that it operates within both the labour and consumer markets. Hence, while labour law might restrict the drug testing of employees, consumer law (or in some cases criminal law) restricts the sale and use of narcotics. The law thus intervenes in the contractual freedom of parties, whether employer–employee or retailer–consumer, in order to achieve social policy goals. Even in an era of deregulation, the social policy aspect of labour law has

[67] Singer (1980), 619–21, considers similar points in establishing the ways in which individuals and communities rely on employment, and are therefore profoundly affected when that employment is withdrawn.

[68] In UK law, benefits related to unfair dismissal and redundancy are linked to a 2-year qualifying period. An employee who leaves a job for another before completing the qualifying period will lose access to those benefits and will have to complete the qualifying period in the new job in order to gain access. See Employment Rights Act, 1996, ch. 18, ss. 108(1), 155).

[69] Kim (1996), 712.

[70] Weiler (1990a), 21, 282–3.

hardly disappeared, as is evinced by the continuing existence of a range of regulations such as minimum wage laws, health and safety statutes, etc.

It is surely notable that at no point in Epstein's argument against anti-discrimination law does he confront the fact that the right of equality and the value of human dignity which it embodies are at stake. This demonstrates the manner in which market individualism places economic concerns over human relations interests, reduces human labour to the status of a commodity like any other, and thereby focuses the labour law analysis on economic costs while ignoring issues of human suffering and dignity.[71] As a result, it presents a world view in which economic efficiency and freedom of contract are the only relevant values. Social values embodied in the right of privacy, such as those I discussed in section 2.3.3 of Chapter 2 (autonomy, dignity and well-being, healthy relationships, and pluralism), have no place in an economic approach to employment.

3.3.3 'Floor of Rights'

So far, we have seen that judicial and legislative intervention in limited circumstances may be justified under a collective *laissez-faire* approach to labour law, while market individualists would surely frown on such intervention (and particularly any intervention premised on industrial justice objectives) as uneconomical and unnecessary. A third school, which is largely a response to the deregulatory, anti-law tendencies of market individualism and the decline of unionisation, advocates the legislative enactment of a 'floor of rights' which would be guaranteed to all candidates/employees regardless of their employer, occupation, participation in a union, etc. This approach seeks to take certain matters of employment out of the realm of private regulation, and thereby guarantee a basic standard of protection on those matters to all individuals.[72] Such an approach is hardly new, as a legislated floor of worker protection in areas such as health and safety has existed for decades. Pay equity legislation, guaranteeing to all employees the right to equal pay for work of equal value, is a more recent example. What is new, however, is the view that the implementation of a *comprehensive* set of basic rights should become a focus of labour law. The 'floor of rights' school thus moves considerably beyond the 'stop-gap' approach of legal abstentionists to legislated employment standards. This is not surprising, however, when one recalls that the decline in union influence over the past decades in many countries, coupled with the impact of market individualists, have converted the 'gaps' resulting from collective bargaining into veritable 'chasms'.

---

[71] Crain (1992), 563–4; Verkerke (1992), 2084–6; Dowd (1993).

[72] Glasbeek (1993b), 259–62. Glasbeek does not use the label, 'floor of rights', but instead calls for 'Treating the Labour Market as a Whole', in order to guarantee worker protection to all regardless of their unionised status.

Deakin and Wilkinson have been advocates of the 'floor of rights'. They note that the premise of deregulation is that greater flexibility and economic opportunity for individuals may be achieved by adopting policies which reduce the impact of collective institutions and mechanisms on the market.[73] However (and ironically), deregulation of labour markets threatens to leave many candidates/employees in a vulnerable position because it exacerbates pre-existing weaknesses of the welfare state, such as 'the incomplete coverage of protective legislation [and] the inability of regulation to cope with underlying inequalities between groups based on their labour market position',[74] while at the same time failing to address the inherent deficiencies of the unregulated market, such as limits upon information and the abuse of economic power.[75] Deakin and Wilkinson thus argue for the re-regulation of labour markets and, to this end, urge the adoption of universal minimum employment rights and standards which would establish a 'general floor to the labour market'.[76] This would include both a floor of rights in relation to wages and job security and the harmonisation of basic terms and conditions across the labour market.[77]

The floor of rights school clearly has its roots in a strong commitment to industrial justice. Its reliance on legislation extends considerably beyond what would traditionally be tolerated by legal abstentionists. However, in light of deregulation and the decline of unionisation, the floor of rights approach may be the only means of achieving industrial justice objectives in a comprehensive manner. Indeed, in the absence of a legislated floor, companies may strive for a competitive advantage by limiting the rights and benefits of their workers, thus reducing labour costs. A floor of rights ensures that human relations interests are not sacrificed at the altar of competition.

In a similar vein, a floor of rights approach has advantages in the context of international trade liberalisation and economic integration. There is a danger that firms in a liberalised international market will attempt to secure a competitive advantage through the reduction of the social costs associated with labour. This phenomenon of worker protection erosion, or 'social dumping', could distort trade patterns if it were permitted (or even encouraged) under the labour law regimes of some trading partners, but not of others. One solution which avoids worker protection erosion, and its resulting trade distortions, is a floor

---

[73] Deakin and Wilkinson (1991a), 34.

[74] *Ibid.*

[75] *Ibid.*, 36.

[76] *Ibid.*, 35–6; see also Muckenberger and Deakin (1989). An interesting American view is provided by Fried (1984b), particularly 1040. Unlike Deakin and Wilkinson, who view the floor of rights as a means of softening the impact of deregulation, but who do not necessarily endorse that deregulation, Fried advocates the direct imposition of specific minimal terms and standards *in conjunction with* the deregulation of collective labour law, in order to achieve greater economic flexibility.

[77] *Ibid.*, 36. Deakin and Wilkinson extend their analysis to include the harmonisation of social security, and a realignment of the tax and benefit structure, thus demonstrating that the floor of rights approach can extend beyond the traditional purview of labour law. However, in the context of workplace privacy, it is unnecessary to consider the broader ramifications of 'floor of rights'.

of rights common to all trading partners.[78] This is exemplified by Article 119 of the Treaty of Rome, which implements the principle of equal pay for equal work in the Member States of the European Union. Its adoption prevented the distortion of competition between Member States arising from differences in the application of the principle of equal pay for men and women, and in particular prevented firms in Member States from achieving a competitive advantage by relying on cheap female labour.[79] The labour accord signed in relation to the North American Free Trade Agreement, under which the signatories commit to the protection of certain fundamental labour rights, is another example.[80]

Advocates of a floor of rights also argue that positive economic benefits may flow from legislated employment standards. Wilkinson has observed that by preventing firms from competing on the basis of reduced labour costs, such standards impede the use of undervalued labour to compensate for managerial, organisational and other inadequacies, such as obsolete equipment.[81] Moreover, deregulation of labour markets, and a reduced emphasis on industrial justice, may well demoralise large segments of the workforce, with resulting productivity losses. A floor of rights, re-affirming a societal commitment to industrial justice, would provide a remedy.[82]

Recent calls for the adoption of social rights as a means of guaranteeing a minimum standard of worker protection within the Member States of the European Union are an important manifestation of floor-of-rights thinking.[83] Thus, Rodriguez-Pinero and Casas have called for a European Union 'Social Constitution' with specific application to labour law because:

> in the specific field of labour law, the constitutional operation of a declaration of fundamental social rights is essential in order to guarantee the maintenance and future course of the European social model . . . the enshrinement of social rights would form the foundation of the Union's social policy and law, the 'unitary basis for a European labour law'.[84]

Because the floor-of-rights approach would require in this case the creation of new labour-specific rights, it naturally provokes debate about what should and should not be included in the catalogue of rights to be recognized as part of the legislated 'floor'.[85] A consensus on this basic issue has not yet been achieved, and may not be for some time. However, the inclusion within a 'floor of rights'

---

[78] Deakin and Wilkinson (1994b), 301–7.
[79] Deakin and Morris (1995), 485–6.
[80] North American Agreement on Labour Co-operation, 13 Sept. 1993, Can.–Mex.–US, 32 ILM 1499 (1993); see Adams and Singh (1997).
[81] Wilkinson (1994), 3; Deakin and Wilkinson (1994b), 294.
[82] Deakin and Wilkinson (1991a), 33.
[83] Sciarra (1996); Lenaerts (1991).
[84] Rodriguez-Pinero and Casas (1997), 27.
[85] See Lenaerts (1991). Rodriguez-Pinero and Casas (1997), 36, refer to the legislative enactment of social rights as 'phase two' in the protection of social rights; 'phase one' involves the identification of these rights. A separate, difficult issue is whether employer rights, such as the 'right to lock out', should be incorporated into the legislated floor.

of workplace privacy protection is bound to be less controversial because the right of privacy already exists in the legal systems of most North American and European Union countries. It is therefore possible, as I demonstrated in Chapter 2, to identify certain private interests protected by the right, and to implement a 'floor' of employment standards to ensure that these interests are respected by employers.

3.4 CONCLUSIONS

I began this chapter with an examination of workplace privacy issues as they have been dealt with by management and organisation theorists, and I then proceeded to consider these same issues from three competing labour law perspectives: collective *laissez-faire*, market individualism and 'floor of rights'. I offer the following conclusions:

(1) While management and organisation theory contributes to the way we think about workplace privacy problems, its function is to assist managers in identifying economic solutions. Within the various competing schools of management theory, human relations interests (such as privacy) are always at risk of being subordinated to economic objectives. The fact that an individual right may be infringed in such a manner is cause for concern in nations which have a tradition of protecting human rights.

(2) The collective *laissez-faire* approach to labour law discourages both judicial and legislative interference with freedom of contract, except in cases where collective representation is unlikely to yield industrial justice or industrial stability. The declining influence of workers' representatives, coupled with the fact that collective representation is not available to all workers and cannot address the needs of job candidates, justifies state action to preserve and promote justice and stability. Because workplace privacy issues implicate both justice and stability, the collective *laissez-faire* approach could well tolerate judicial and legislative action to protect candidates/employees from privacy-invasive management practices.

(3) In contrast, market individualism teaches that state interference in the labour market should be avoided. Instead, freedom of contract should be respected in order to promote economic growth and flexibility. Thus, legislative intervention on behalf of worker privacy would almost certainly be opposed. However, market individualism is suspect because it is premised on questionable assumptions about the labour market, and fails to take into account human relations values such as dignity and autonomy (i.e. the very values underlying the right of privacy).

(4) The 'floor-of-rights' approach is primarily an industrial justice response to the deregulatory influence of market individualism, and calls for the legislative enactment of basic rights and standards for the benefit of all

candidates/employees. Advocates of a floor of rights argue that legislated employment standards prevent employers from competing on the basis of undervalued labour, and also postulate that certain positive economic benefits flow from guaranteed employment rights. The legal regulation of privacy-invasive management practices would be consistent with the floor of rights theory of labour law.

The fact that two influential labour law schools, collective *laissez-faire* and 'floor of rights', would support the implementation of legal standards for the protection of worker privacy evinces the existence of a sound theoretical base for workplace privacy *laws*. Such laws would be consistent with the industrial justice and stability objectives of labour law—yet another reason for looking to law as opposed to management theory for solutions to issues such as employment drug testing, electronic surveillance, etc. However, the substance of any such legal regulation remains to be considered. My task in the next three chapters, Chapters 4, 5 and 6, will be to assess the extant laws of workplace privacy in the United States, France, and Canada respectively. The mode of analysis I adopt will be comparative, examining the similarities, differences, strengths, and weaknesses of the law in the three countries. This analysis will form the bases of Chapters 7, 8 and 9, in which I will advance a set of workplace privacy principles, and apply them to the issues of employment drug and genetic testing. Finally, in Chapter 10, I will employ these principles in a normative fashion to elaborate upon the development of workplace privacy law in the United Kingdom.

4

Privacy in the Workplace in the United States

Having established that the right of privacy has force in the employment context, and that legal intervention to protect private interests may be justified within the collective *laissez-faire* and 'floor-of-rights' schools of labour law, I will now consider the extant workplace privacy laws in three jurisdictions: the United States, France and Canada. The purpose of this comparative analysis will be to identify the similarities and differences in, and the strengths and weaknesses of, the legal approaches to workplace privacy in the three countries. In this chapter, I will focus on the law of the United States. First, however, it is necessary to address the comparative law challenges presented by an analysis of this nature.

4.2 COMPARATIVE LABOUR LAW AND THE RIGHT OF PRIVACY

Labour law is the expression of a constant social, political and economic debate concerning the appropriate balance between the often-conflicting interests of employees, employers and the public. At the same time, the labour law issues faced in one jurisdiction are rarely unique. Other jurisdictions have probably been grappling with the same issues, and some may have proposed, or even implemented, legal reforms. For this reason, labour law lends itself to comparative analysis. However, the potential pitfalls of such an analysis are considerable, and a brief overview may prove helpful to the discussions which follow.

4.2.1 The Comparative Approach and Individual Labour Law

In Kahn-Freund's seminal writing on the use of comparative approaches within labour law, he argued that an effective comparison had to take into account not merely the extant law in the various jurisdictions under consideration but, more importantly, the socio-political factors which form the background against which that law has developed. Hence, a meaningful comparative analysis must consider the 'power structure' which has influenced and formed the law or, more particularly, factors such as the constitutional framework, the distribution of powers between the judicial and legislative branches of the state, political conventions and traditions, and the role and influence of interest groups (in particular, unions). The potential success of transplanting an aspect of one country's labour law into another is, according to Kahn-Freund, largely determined by the extent to which the power structures of the two countries are similar.[1] However, he drew a distinction between two aspects of labour law: (1) individual labour law, imposing standards within the employment relationship on matters such as health and safety, anti-discrimination, etc.; and (2) collective labour law, concerning matters of unions, collective bargaining, strikes, etc.[2] He wrote:

> In my opinion the first element—individual labour law—lends itself to transplantation very much more easily than the second element—that is collective labour law. Standards of protection and rules on substantive terms of employment can be imitated—rules on collective bargaining, on the closed shop, on trade unions, on strikes, can not.[3]

Kahn-Freund added that the transplantation of a particular employment standard is most likely to succeed where it is done between countries which have reached similar stages of economic development.[4]

The view that individual labour law lends itself more easily to comparative analysis and transplantation has been justified on the basis that while the structures, institutions and traditions of collective labour law tend to be strongly influenced by the complexities of a particular nation's historical, political, economic and social conditions, individual labour law generally addresses problems of a universal nature—universal in the sense that such problems affect all workplaces in all countries.[5] This largely explains the focus of the ILO on promulgating recommendations and conventions concerning matters of individual employment law.[6] If one thinks about labour law in terms of 'substance' (i.e. the substantive rules governing the employment relationship) and 'style' (i.e. the manner in which those rules are given effect),[7] collective labour law tends to be markedly different from country to country in both areas because it is a reflection of unique power structures. This necessarily hampers comparative work. However, dramatic differences in the substance of individual employment standards are quite rare in developed countries, and the style of implementation generally entails legal intervention that removes the matter at issue from the

---

[1] Kahn-Freund (1974d), 18–20. See also Stein (1977); Whelan (1984); Blanpain (1993).

[2] See Mason (1925) and Kade (1988), nn. 31 and 32 in Chap. 3 above. Laws promoting 'worker protection' or 'industrial justice' generally fall into the category of individual labour law (or, in North America, employment law), whereas labour laws concerned with 'industrial stability' are often collective in nature.

[3] Kahn-Freund (1974d), 21.

[4] *Ibid.*, 23.

[5] Whelan (1984), 1449.

[6] Kahn-Freund (1974d), 21; Whelan (1984).

[7] Markesinis (1994b).

realm of the employment contract (or management prerogative), and imposes upon the parties either a minimum standard or a result from which they may not deviate.[8] If one country wishes to adopt an employment standard from another country, what is generally required is the transplantation of the new standard through legislation.

The protection of worker privacy lends itself to a meaningful comparative analysis because the issue concerns the development of standards for the protection of individual private interests, a matter squarely within individual employment law. Moreover, there are two basic similarities between the United States, France and Canada which make it appropriate to compare their respective approaches to workplace privacy: (1) all three already recognise the right of privacy as an aspect of their constitutional and private laws (including their labour laws); and (2) all three are industrialised liberal-democracies at a similar stage of economic development. There are nevertheless some important differences between the three legal systems. France is a civilian jurisdiction, the United States is a common law jurisdiction and Canada is mixed in the sense that the Province of Quebec, representing approximately one-third of the Canadian population, is civilian, while the other nine provinces are common law.[9] Furthermore, France's approach to labour law since the Second World War has tended to be more interventionist than those of the two North American jurisdictions, where collective *laissez-faire* and legal abstentionism have been more influential. While such differences could prove problematic in a comparative analysis of a collective labour law issue, they should be less so in the substantive analysis herein, which concerns a matter of individual employment law and human rights law. Nevertheless, differences in the legal traditions and institutions of the three jurisdictions may provide insights into matters of national style or, in other words, the legal methods and institutions prevailing in each of the three countries for protecting the private interests of candidates/employees.

In Chapter 10, I will advance the principles identified from American, French and Canadian law as a guide to developing the law of workplace privacy in the United Kingdom. Although the issue of 'transplanting' such principles into UK law will be considered in more detail in section 10.2 below, I observe here that the United Kingdom's legal, political and economic systems are sufficiently similar to those of the other three countries that a comparative approach to individual employment and human rights law is eminently feasible.

---

[8] Willborn *et al.* (1993), 3, refer to two branches of individual employment law: (1) immutable rules that the parties cannot change by agreement, and (2) default rules that state the applicable rules unless the parties agree to alter (generally, to improve upon) them.

[9] The USA is not entirely common law, since the state of Louisiana is a civilian jurisdiction.

4.3 WORKPLACE PRIVACY LAW IN THE UNITED STATES

4.3.1 Introduction

One commentator has referred to the law of workplace privacy in the United States as 'a mess . . . rife with silences, doctrinal gaps, and inconsistencies'.[10] This is in some measure a product of the American federal system, which confers upon the national government a broad and paramount jurisdiction over employment matters, yet permits state legislation in the absence of national measures. This gives rise to a veritable 'checquerboard' of judicial and legislative approaches to employment privacy law in the 51 jurisdictions forming the United States, since there is as yet little federal legislation on the issue.

The predominant factor directing the development of American employment law is a deeply embedded attachment to *laissez-faire* economic theory and the corresponding principle that private parties should be free to contract as they wish.[11] The judicial and legislative branches of American government have often been unwilling to interfere in the employment relationship because of its private character. In practice, this has meant that worker protection initiatives have been the exception rather than the rule, and that American labour law remains abstentionist in nature.

At the same time, tension has arisen between *laissez-faire* thinking and a competing set of powerful American values such as individual dignity, autonomy and fairness, flowing from the constitutional order and, in particular, the Bill of Rights. The United States is often considered to be a rights-conscious society, with a long legal tradition of empowering individuals in their relations with socially and economically advantaged actors.[12] In some cases, in some of the American jurisdictions, this tradition has manifested itself in worker protection initiatives of a human rights nature which apply to both private and public employment. Such initiatives are not necessarily inconsistent with collective *laissez-faire* since, as I observed in section 3.3.1 of Chapter 3, industrial justice considerations will support substantive labour laws of a worker protection nature. The most notable example is racial anti-discrimination law. The United States' history of racial discrimination gave rise to a powerful movement for equal rights and legal reform, which eventually led to the enactment of Title VII in 1964.[13] By prohibiting racial discrimination in the private workplace, this legislation effectively recognised that the denial of human rights within the private sector is an appropriate subject of concern and intervention on the part of the state. This marked a shift in emphasis away from freedom of contract and legal abstentionism toward greater governmental involvement in the field of worker

---

[10] Finkin (1995a), xxi. See also Decker (1987a), xxii, 2.
[11] Orren (1991), 68–82, 102–3; Wheeler (1994), 12–13.
[12] Berle (1952), 942–6. See also, Finkin (1996b), 254; Gerhart (1995b), 177.
[13] Civil Rights Act of 1964 (Title VII), 42 USCA, ss. 2000e–1–2002–17 (1982).

protection, while at the same time lending credibility to human rights arguments related to other employment matters. Hence, national statutes prohibiting age and disability discrimination were subsequently enacted,[14] and Congress has recently debated a proposal for national worker privacy legislation.[15] Various state measures have also sought to transpose human rights protection into the private sector workplace.[16] The United States is, today, fertile ground for new human rights initiatives in employment law. However, the schizophrenic nature of American legal culture, with its dual emphasis on fostering private economic freedom, while protecting rights-values of public concern, has produced legal diversity. This in turn has prevented the emergence of a unifying and coherent approach to workplace privacy.

I do not intend the following discussion to be an exhaustive enumeration of workplace privacy law in the United States, as this has been accomplished by several other writers.[17] Instead, I will assess critically the dominant themes and recent developments in American law.

4.3.2 Background—the Employment-at-will Doctrine and Worker Protection

American labour law has been influenced by each of the competing approaches to employment regulation discussed in Chapter 3: collective *laissez-faire*, market individualism and 'floor of rights'. This is evident in the case of workplace privacy—some legislators and judges have refused to intervene, others have sought to at least provide a minimum set of standards for some issues, while others have brought the full force of human rights law to the defence of candidates'/employees' private interests. American workplace privacy law is, therefore, a muddle. This should not be surprising, given the forces which have traditionally shaped American labour law. As I observed above, freedom of contract has been a paramount, but not always dominant, factor. Closely related to freedom of contract is the employment-at-will doctrine, which dictates that either party may terminate the employment contract without notice and without explanation. Employment-at-will is a general 'default' rule in the private sector,[18] meaning that unless the parties themselves contract for notice periods, substantive limitations on dismissal, grievance procedures, etc., then the employment contract may be terminated at any time by either party.[19] In theory, this rule ensures that employers may respond flexibly to economic

---

[14] Age Discrimination in Employment Act of 1967, 29 USCA, ss. 621–634 (1982); Americans with Disabilities Act of 1990, 42 USCA, ss. 12101–12213 (1992).

[15] Privacy for Consumers and Workers Act, (S.984, 103d Cong., 1st Session) which was introduced before the US Congress on 30 June 1993. This is discussed *infra*, sect. 4.3.4.4.

[16] With regard to workplace privacy legislation, see *infra*, section 4.3.4.4.

[17] See Decker (1994b); Finkin (1995a).

[18] Montana is the only state which has provided a statutory right against wrongful dismissal. See Mont. Code Ann. s. 39–2–901 to 914 (1989).

[19] Willborn *et al.* (1993), 6.

circumstances and human resource problems by dismissing employees quickly and easily, while at the same time protecting workers from being bound by oppressive contractual terms (a matter no doubt of some concern in the United States following the slavery experience). However, in practice, employment-at-will reinforces the economic inequality inherent to the employment relationship by creating an uncertain climate for employees due to the threat of unexpected and arbitrary dismissal.[20] Of course, under the theory of freedom of contract, employees may bargain for job security. Protection against wrongful dismissal is, in fact, a key feature of virtually all collective agreements in the United States. However, similar contractual protection in the non-organised private sector (accounting for approximately 80 per cent of American workers[21]) is rare. Prospective employees generally accept the employment contract as drafted by management, and such contracts naturally incorporate the employment-at-will doctrine. Even if the employee disapproves, she may be reluctant to demand job security guarantees, fearing that the employer will suspect some problem which might necessitate her future reliance on such guarantees.[22]

Where the employment-at-will doctrine governs, an employer may dismiss an employee for any reason or no reason, and the employee has no legal recourse to seek reinstatement or compensation. This scenario is the ultimate in legal abstentionism. It renders employees highly vulnerable to human rights infringements in the workplace—employees may be dismissed as a result of a human rights abuse, or may be dismissed even for complaining about the potential for an abuse, and the law offers no redress. There are numerous disturbing examples in the field of workplace privacy where the courts have been unwilling to provide a remedy for a dismissal resulting from a privacy-invasive management practice. Consider the Texas case of *Brunner* v. *Al Attar*,[23] where the employee worked as a volunteer during off-duty hours at a shelter for AIDS patients. The employer ordered her to cease the volunteer work and when she refused, terminated her employment. Although the employer's actions constituted an attempt to control the employee's private life in a manner entirely divorced from legitimate management concerns, the Texas Court of Appeal gave effect to the employment-at-will doctrine and refused to provide a remedy. It is important to note, however, that Texas has vehemently adhered to the employment-at-will doctrine.[24] As discussed below in section 4.3.4, private sector employees in several other states may have recourse to various common law, statutory and even constitutional remedies.

In the following discussion, I will analyse American workplace privacy law as it applies in the public and private sectors. With regard to the public sector, I

---

[20] Feinman (1976), 120–2.
[21] ILO (1997–8d), 248, Table 3.2.
[22] Willborn *et al.* (1993), 7.
[23] 786 SW 2d 784 (Texas CA, 1990). See also *Scroghan* v. *Kraftco*, 551 SW 2d 811 (Ky. CA, 1977) (employee fired after refusing to give up night school courses in law).
[24] *Jennings* v. *Minco Technology Labs, Inc.*, 765 SW 2d 497 (Texas CA, 1989).

will consider constitutional privacy law and the federal law of information privacy. I will then assess three distinct sources of workplace privacy in the private sector: public policy/wrongful dismissal privacy, common law tort privacy and statutory privacy. California's constitutional right of privacy will be treated separately because of its unique application to both the public and private sectors.

4.3.3 Workplace Privacy Protection in the Public Sector Workplace

Government employees in the United States have considerable advantages in the area of worker protection for three reasons.[25] First, the extent of unionisation in the American public sector is considerably higher than in the private sector, meaning that more public employees enjoy the benefits of collective representation and have the advantage of collective agreements which provide for job security through protections against unfair dismissal.[26] Secondly, public sector workers may assert constitutional rights, including the right of privacy. In theory, public employees who believe that their human rights are threatened by employer practices may launch a constitutional court challenge. The same holds for public sector job candidates, since any rights-infringing act by a state body is subject to constitutional limits.[27] Thirdly, public sector employees enjoy certain statutory protections not generally available in the private sector, such as laws on information privacy.

4.3.3.1 The Constitutional Right of Privacy in the United States

The 'constitutional law' of the United States includes provisions of (and decisions interpreting) the federal and state constitutions. In the case of the right of privacy, both the federal Bill of Rights and 11 state constitutions confer privacy protection upon citizens.[28] In this chapter, I will focus on the federal privacy right.[29] I will consider California's constitutional privacy right in section 4.3.4.3, as it uniquely applies to both public and private actors.

The word 'privacy' does not appear in the United States Constitution, yet this has not prevented the concept from attaining constitutional status. To trace the

---

[25] Gerhart (1995b), 178.

[26] Approximately one-third of public sector employees are unionised, versus 10% of private sector employees: United States Bureau of the Census (1995), 443; ILO (1997–8d), 243, Table 3.1.

[27] Only the rights enumerated in California's State Constitution are available to private sector employees.

[28] The states which explicitly protect a right of privacy are Alaska, Arizona, California, Florida, Hawaii, Illinois, Louisiana, Montana, Rhode Island, South Carolina and Washington (Finkin (1995a), 35). Several other states have recognised the right of privacy as an implied right. See Feyler (1986).

[29] State constitutions may, in theory, provide greater privacy protection to individuals than the federal Bill of Rights: Barker (1992), 1133–4. See the discussion below concerning California (*infra*, sect. 4.3.4.3).

origin of the right of privacy in American legal discourse, one must look to Warren and Brandeis's seminal 1890 article.[30] Although the two authors did not mention constitutional privacy protection, as they were primarily concerned with the common law, it is important to keep in mind that they borrowed the concept of 'the right to be let alone' from Judge Cooley, himself a respected commentator in both tort and constitutional law fields.[31] Twenty years before Warren and Brandeis had written of tort privacy, Cooley had linked the Fourth Amendment of the Constitution (outlawing unreasonable search and seizure) to privacy, characterising it as guaranteeing 'to the citizen immunity in his home against the prying eyes of government'.[32]

The interplay between constitutional privacy protection and the common law of privacy has continued to influence American jurisprudence throughout this century. In the first significant American decision to recognise the common law tort of invasion of privacy, *Pavesich* v. *New England Life Insurance Co.*,[33] constitutional principles were crucial. Justice Cobb, for the Georgia Supreme Court, linked privacy to the principles of personal security and liberty which form the basis of both the Bill of Rights and the common law. He then identified the right of privacy as flowing both from natural law, and from the constitutional guarantee in the Fourteenth Amendment that no person shall be deprived of liberty except by due process of law.[34] He further observed that the Fourth Amendment is a constitutional expression of the 'ancient right' to privacy over the home, and concluded that '[t]he liberty of privacy exists, has been recognized by law, and is entitled to continual recognition'.[35] Subsequently, in *Olmstead* v. *United States*,[36] Justice Brandeis's dissenting view of the Fourth Amendment as a personal privacy right linked to human dignity repeated his and Warren's earlier theory of the common law tort (the very view which had been adopted by Justice Cobb in *Pavesich*). This stood in sharp relief to the position of the Supreme Court majority that an infringement of the Fourth Amendment could only occur through an actual trespass by state officials onto a defendant's private property. Forty years later, in *Katz* v. *United States*, this narrow, property-centred conception of the Fourth Amendment was repudiated by the United States Supreme Court in favour of the broader position advocated by Justice Brandeis.[37] The result, then, is that the interpretation of the Fourth Amendment has evolved to protect not merely private property rights, but also

---

[30] Warren and Brandeis (1890), see nn. 31–7, Chap. 2 above.
[31] See Cooley (1868a); Cooley (1888b).
[32] Cooley (1868a), 299.
[33] 50 SE 68 (Ga. CA, 1905).
[34] *Ibid.*, 70–1.
[35] *Ibid.*, 71–2.
[36] 277 US 438 (1927).
[37] 389 US 347 (1967). The Court also rehabilitated Justice Murphy's dissenting position from *Goldstein* v. *United States*, 316 US 114 (1942), where he argued that the Fourth Amendment should be interpreted to protect the very same interests underlying the common law tort of privacy.

a whole range of private interests falling in the personal, territorial and informational zones.[38]

In more recent times, the United States Supreme Court has broadened its conception of constitutional privacy to include private interests extending beyond the Fourth Amendment. In the *Roe* v. *Wade* decision on abortion, for example, the Court 'recognized that a right of personal privacy, or a guarantee of certain areas or zones of privacy, does exist under the Constitution', and thought that the right found protection in the concept of liberty guaranteed by the Fourteenth Amendment.[39] In other cases, the right of privacy was linked to the First Amendment,[40] the Fourth and Fifth Amendments together,[41] and the Ninth Amendment.[42] In *Griswold* v. *Connecticut*, the Court declared that the right of privacy actually flowed from the 'penumbras' of all these rights.[43]

Leaving aside the confusion about the actual source of constitutional privacy in the United States, it is at least clear that protection extends to personal, territorial and informational private interests through the Fourth Amendment, and to certain privacy interests considered 'fundamental' or 'implicit in the concept of ordered liberty'.[44] These interests include matters related to marriage, procreation, contraception, abortion, child-rearing and education.[45] The power of the state to regulate such matters is limited by the right of privacy on the theory that the state must respect decisions taken by individuals in areas related to bodily integrity and family relationships.[46]

4.3.3.2 Workplace Privacy Constitutional Jurisprudence

The American constitutional conception of privacy clearly protects 'zones' of privacy, along with particular private interests falling within those zones. In this manner, it reflects the functional approach to the right of privacy that I advocated in section 2.3.1 of Chapter 2. How does this play out in the public employment context? A review of workplace privacy constitutional challenges reveals that public employees rarely encounter difficulties in establishing that the private interest at issue is constitutionally protected. Thus, privacy has been

---

[38] State efforts to 'seize' private information about a person may implicate the Fourth Amendment. See Decker (1994b), 89.

[39] 410 US 113 (1973), 152–4.

[40] *Stanley* v. *Georgia*, 394 US 557 (1969).

[41] *Terry* v. *Ohio*, 392 US 1 (1968), and *Katz, supra*, n. 37. The Fourteenth Amendment stipulates that, 'No State shall . . . deprive any person of life, liberty, or property, without due process of law', while the Fifth Amendment protects individuals against self-incrimination.

[42] The lower court in *Roe* v. *Wade, supra*, n. 39, thought that privacy was one of the rights contemplated by the Ninth Amendment: 'the enumeration in the Constitution, of certain rights, shall not be construed to deny or disparage others retained by the people'.

[43] 381 US 479 (1965).

[44] *Roe* v. *Wade, supra*, n. 39, 152.

[45] *Ibid.*; Decker (1994b), 107–8.

[46] Although these matters are unlikely to be regulated by state employer practices, their fundamental nature has meant that courts have adopted a strict scrutiny analytical standard (Barker (1992), 1115).

implicated in constitutional cases involving workplace drug testing,[47] office searches and searches of employees' private property,[48] employer efforts to control off-duty affiliations with political organisations, and political activities,[49] interrogations concerning sexual habits and conduct[50] and grooming policies.[51]

What is most revealing about constitutional workplace privacy jurisprudence is the manner in which abstentionist and deferential thinking has influenced the analysis, and effectively diminished the level of protection afforded to public employees. Thus, the Court has adopted a 'reasonableness' balancing test in which the individual's protected private interest is weighed against the state's justification for infringing upon the interest. This analysis has been coloured by the articulation of deferential principles which inevitably diminish the weight of the privacy claim. These include: (1) the government should be accorded 'wide latitude . . . in the dispatch of its own affairs'[52]; (2) '[t]he operational realities of the workplace may make some employees' expectations of privacy unreasonable'[53]; (3) there is a 'common sense realization that government offices could not function if every employment decision became a constitutional matter'[54]; (4) 'the privacy interests of government employees in their place of work . . . while not insubstantial, are far less than those found at home or in some other contexts'[55]; and (5) the nature of employment naturally reduces expectations of privacy: '[o]rdinarily, an employee consents to significant restrictions in his freedom of movement where necessary for his employment, and few are free to come and go as they please during working hours'.[56] A common element in the

---

[47] *National Treasury Employees Union* v. *Von Raab*, 489 US 656 (1989); *Skinner* v. *Railway Labor Executives Association*, 109 S. Ct. 1402 (1989) (both argued under the Fourth Amendment).

[48] *O'Connor, supra*, n. 76, Chap. 2 above (argued under the Fourth Amendment).

[49] *Elrod* v. *Burns*, 427 US 347 (1976) (argued under the freedom of association branch of the First Amendment).

[50] *Richardson* v. *Hampton*, 345 F. Supp. 600 (DDC, 1972) (argued under the First Amendment); *Duckworth* v. *Sayad*, 670 SW 2d 88 (Mo. CA, 1984) (argued under the Ninth Amendment).

[51] *Kelley* v. *Johnson*, 425 US 238 (1976); *Nalley* v. *Douglas County*, 489 F. Supp. 1228 (Ga. ND, 1980) (both argued under the First Amendment).

[52] *Kelley*, n. 51 above, 247. In *Kelley*, the majority concluded that a regulation limiting the length of a policeman's hair was a reasonable limit on the First and Fourteenth Amendments, while the dissent characterised the regulation as an irrational effort to regulate off-duty appearance (see in particular 256, n. 7).

[53] *O'Connor*, see n. 76, Chap. 2 above, 717. In *O'Connor*, the Court decided that while workplace searches triggered the Fourth Amendment, it was not necessary for a public employer to obtain a warrant prior to the search, or even to have probable cause for conducting the search. Hence, searches related to investigations of work-related misconduct are to be assessed according to a reasonableness balancing test. The four-judge dissent preferred to maintain the warrant and probable cause requirements in the case of investigatory searches of employees' offices, lockers, personal effects, etc.

[54] *Ibid.*, 722. See also *Von Raab, supra*, n. 47, 666.

[55] *O'Connor, ibid.*, 726.

[56] *Skinner, supra*, n. 47, 624. In *Skinner*, the Court upheld regulations permitting the administration of blood and urinalysis drug testing to all railway workers who might be connected to a railroad accident, even absent any probable cause or suspicion for believing that the job performance of those workers (or any particular worker) had been influenced by drug use. The two-judge dissent characterised the policy as an affront to privacy due to the lack of even an individual suspicion requirement.

Court's constitutional workplace privacy jurisprudence is the view that employment is a separate and unique context in which the Constitution operates less rigorously to restrain the state. The Court has clearly been concerned that imposing strict constitutional limitations on privacy-invasive practices will hamper the day-to-day operations of the public sector workplace, and thereby create inefficiencies.[57] In this sense, its jurisprudence combines abstentionist thinking with the efficiency analysis of market individualists. It is also notable that the workplace privacy cases have attracted strong dissents, in which the minority has expressed grave doubts about relying on efficiency concerns and reduced expectations of privacy in the employment context.[58] Hence, while an abstentionist position has prevailed to date in the United States Supreme Court, it has been challenged by a more interventionist approach to employment law. This reflects the schizophrenic nature of American labour and human rights law, as I discussed in section 4.3.1 above.

An analysis of one United States Supreme Court decision will highlight the relevant aspects of its constitutional workplace privacy jurisprudence. *National Treasury Employees Union* v. *Von Raab*[59] concerned the constitutionality of a United States Customs Service programme imposing drug testing on all employees applying for transfer or promotion to positions involving interdiction of illegal drugs, or requiring carriage of a firearm.[60] A positive drug test would result in denial of transfer or promotion, and possible dismissal from the Service. The case resulted in an acrimonious split between majority and dissent. The majority, *per* Justice Kennedy, rejected the traditional requirement that governmental searches and seizures should be conditioned on the existence of a warrant, or at least some individualised probable cause or reasonable suspicion. Justice Kennedy thought that such conditions would unduly hamper the enforcement of the Service's no-drug-use policy. In his view, the objective of the testing programme was to eliminate drug users from the Service in order to promote public safety and national security. He characterised this as a substantial state objective since the employees targeted by the testing programme are part of the 'first line of defense against one of the greatest problems affecting the health and welfare of our population' (i.e. drug smuggling and drug use).[61] Such employees, particularly those carrying firearms, must be closely monitored to ensure that their perception and judgement are not hampered by drugs. Moreover, drug users in the Customs Service may be vulnerable to blackmail, threats or bribes, and cannot be trusted with the drug contraband seized by the Service.[62] Justice Kennedy then turned to the privacy interests at stake. Although the collection of urine for drug testing could be a substantial threat to privacy in some

---

[57] In *O'Connor*, the court emphasised the government's interest in 'the efficient operation of the workplace' (see n. 76, Chap. 2 above, 720–1).

[58] *Infra*, n. 65.

[59] *Supra*, n. 47.

[60] Drug testing was also imposed upon employees handling 'classified materials'. See *infra*, n. 70.

[61] *Supra*, n. 47, 668.

[62] *Ibid.*, 669–72.

contexts, he doubted that the Customs Service was one of them. In reliance on the principle that 'operational realities' in the public sector workplace may reduce the standard of constitutional protection available to employees, he observed that those who enforce drug laws, or who carry firearms, have a lower expectation of privacy in relation to their own drug use: '[u]nlike most private citizens or government employees in general, employees involved in drug interdiction reasonably should expect effective inquiry into their fitness and probity'.[63] The reasonableness balance thus favoured the Customs Service's interests over those of its employees.

The *Von Raab* decision may be criticised on three bases. First, in assessing the weight to be accorded to the objectives underlying the drug-testing policy, the Court failed to apply a rigorous analysis, and instead relied on highly speculative and anecdotal evidence concerning the potential problems posed to the Customs Service by drug use. In fact, there was no evidence that drug use had been a problem in the Service prior to the implementation of the testing programme,[64] nor that any bribery, blackmail or threats had ever been directed at Customs Officers because they used drugs. It was the lack of evidence supporting the stated objectives of public safety and national security which concerned Justice Scalia, dissenting with three others. He accused the majority of engaging in empty rhetoric, and challenged readers of the majority opinion to 'search in vain for real evidence of a real problem that will be solved by urine testing of Customs Service employees'.[65]

Secondly, the Court inexplicably devalued the private interests at stake. The majority simply concluded that Customs Officers charged with the task of enforcing American drug import laws have a reduced expectation of privacy vis-à-vis their own drug use. Even if this were so, it says nothing about the actual weight to be accorded to their private interests in the balancing exercise. In fact, the Court appears to have minimised the intrusion on employees' privacy not by considering the private interests at stake, but by referring to the substantial state objective underlying the drug testing policy. The Court thus 'double-counted' the government's objective in the balancing process by holding both that the state's objectives were substantial, and that the private interests were insubstantial *because* the state's interests were substantial.[66] Since the majority failed entirely to identify the corporeal and informational private interests at stake, or the autonomy, dignity, trust and pluralism justifications underlying those interests, one is left with no idea of the true weight to be assigned to those interests relative to the objectives attached to the drug testing programme. It may well be that the weight of those interests, even in the Customs context, would never-

---

[63] *Ibid.*, 672.

[64] The Commissioner of the United States Customs Service believed it to be 'largely drug free' (*ibid.*, 683). See Note (1989c), 270.

[65] *Von Raab, supra*, n. 47, 681. Justice Scalia concluded that the drug testing programme was purely symbolic, and designed to set an example for the American people (at 687).

[66] Note (1989c), 277.

theless still outweigh the feeble justifications advanced in support of the impugned drug testing policy. In fact, Justice Scalia thought that the employees' private interests were quite significant, referring to drug testing as 'a type of search particularly destructive of privacy and offensive to personal dignity'.[67]

Thirdly, the Court argued against individualising the drug testing programme as a means of limiting its impact on privacy. Hence, the Court rejected both the warrant requirement and a condition of reasonable suspicion in advance of testing, and endorsed universal pre-employment drug testing without cause. The result of this, however, is that thousands of Customs employees who are innocent of any wrongdoing will be subject to invasive drug testing in order to identify a few drug users.[68] The Court's reasoning on this point was, essentially, that the governmental interest is so substantial, and the private interests at stake so reduced in value, that individualising the drug testing plan through a warrant or suspicion condition is unnecessary. Since this finding depends on the Court's inadequate assessment of the state and private interests at stake, it is suspect. The better view would surely be that given the very minor extent of known drug use within the Customs Service, and the important corporeal and informational private interests at stake, an individualised suspicion requirement in advance of drug testing would not impose an unreasonable burden on the ability of the Service to meet its no-drug-use objective.[69]

Another matter of individualisation was raised by Justice Scalia, who criticised the Court for endorsing the application of the drug testing policy not only to employees involved in drug interdiction, but also to those carrying firearms or having access to 'sensitive' documents.[70] In his view 'the Court exposes vast numbers of public employees to [the] needless indignity' of drug testing.[71] He observed, correctly, that the Court's rationale of public safety justifying drug testing for those possessing firearms could be extended to any employee whose work, if influenced by drugs, might endanger the public. Thus, all public employees operating motor vehicles could be subjected to drug testing.[72] Similarly, the security rationale justifying drug testing for those with access to 'sensitive information' would also permit drug testing of every public employee with a security clearance.[73] The implications of *Von Raab* are therefore dramatically broad, as the Court provided the government with a mandate to

---

[67] *Von Raab, supra,* n. 47, 680.

[68] In the first year of Customs Service drug testing, 3,600 employees were tested with only 5 positive results (*ibid.,* 683–4).

[69] Justice Scalia took the view that when a Customs Officer's drug use became a problem to the Service, this would be apparent through supervision. Therefore, he preferred to maintain the reasonable suspicion requirement (*ibid.,* 682–3).

[70] The majority did express concerns in relation to the category of employees handling 'classified materials', as the positions covered included such things as 'animal caretaker', 'baggage clerk' and 'electric equipment repairer'. There was thus a 'question whether the Service has defined this category of employees more broadly than necessary', and the matter was remitted to the lower courts for consideration (*ibid.,* 678).

[71] *Ibid.,* 687.

[72] *Ibid.,* 685.

[73] *Ibid.,* 686.

impose workplace drug-testing whenever the possibility exists that a drug-using employee might endanger safety through the impaired operation of equipment, or compromise security as a result of being bribed, threatened or blackmailed. In all likelihood, most public sector drug testing policies could survive constitutional scrutiny under such a lax standard.[74]

4.3.3.3 Conclusions—Constitutional Workplace Privacy in the United States

In its constitutional workplace privacy jurisprudence to date, the Supreme Court of the United States has applied a deferential level of analysis. The Court has treated employment as a special constitutional context, in which the judicial application of the right of privacy must be sensitive to 'operational realities', and must avoid imposing inefficiencies.[75] The Court is clearly hesitant to second-guess decisions taken by the state in its role as employer. Given this abstentionist background, it should really be no surprise that the Court has been deferential to state objectives underlying invasive management practices, while devaluing public employees' private interests. Hence, the jurisprudence to date indicates that constitutional privacy protection will be available to public employees only in the most egregious situations.

It is significant that much of the Supreme Court's workplace privacy jurisprudence to date has concerned drug testing—an issue of uniquely pressing concern to the government and people of the United States.[76] It may be that the so-called 'war on drugs' has clouded the reasoning of the majority of the Supreme Court. In fact, the dissenters in the drug testing cases of *Von Raab* and *Skinner* believed this to be the case.[77] One might therefore hesitate to draw general conclusions from the drug testing cases. Nevertheless, the basic Fourth Amendment approach to workplace privacy had been developed prior to *Von Raab* and *Skinner* in the office search case of *O'Connor* v. *Ortega*.[78] There, similar deferential principles were asserted by the majority position upholding certain types of warrantless and suspicionless searches.

4.3.3.4 Information Privacy Law

The American federal government has enacted information privacy legislation, the Privacy Act,[79] which is available *in theory* to protect federal public (but not

---

[74] Note (1989c), 269.

[75] The Court's concern with inefficient use of resources explains its departure from the warrant requirement under the Fourth Amendment for workplace searches and seizures (*Von Raab, supra*, n. 47, 666).

[76] *Supra*, sect. 2.3.4.5; *infra*, sect. 8.2.

[77] *Von Raab, supra*, n. 47, 686–7, *per* Justice Scalia (accusing the court of upholding a symbolic drug testing policy); *Skinner, supra*, n. 47, 654, *per* Justice Marshall (stating that the Court had been 'swept away with society's obsession with stopping the scourge of illegal drugs').

[78] 107 S Ct. 1492 (1989).

[79] Privacy Act (1974), 5 USC s. 552(a) (1988); see also *Freedom of Information Act* (1966), 5 USC s. 552(a) (1988).

private[80]) sector employees from privacy-invasive information-gathering and disclosure practices.[81] The Act stipulates that federal agencies may maintain in records[82] (including personnel files) only information about a subject which is relevant and necessary to accomplish a purpose of the agency (section 552(e)(1)), and must collect information directly from subjects whenever practicable (section 552(e)(2)). The Act further imposes a duty on agencies to maintain records with accuracy, relevancy, timeliness and completeness (section 552(e)(5)), and grants to subjects the right to access their files and demand rectification of errors (section 552(d)(1) and (2)). Finally, agencies are generally prohibited from disclosing information about subjects to third parties without the subject's prior written consent (section 552(b)) and must implement administrative, technical, and physical safeguards to ensure the security and confidentiality of records (section 552(e)(10)).

Although the Privacy Act grants important information privacy rights to federal public employees,[83] it has had only a minimal impact in the workplace, in stark contrast to the French and Canadian information privacy laws I discuss in Chapters 5 and 6 respectively.[84] Employment was not a focus of the Privacy Act at the time of its enactment in 1974, as it was largely a response to the public desire for open and honest government in the wake of the Watergate scandal.[85] Since 1974, the regime has suffered from enforcement problems, as there is no independent administrative body to oversee the Act, or receive, investigate and adjudicate complaints.[86] The Office of Management and Budget (OMB), a section of the Executive Office of the President, has been given the responsibility for developing guidelines and regulations for the use of agencies. However, it has dedicated virtually no resources to this function.[87] The only significant contribution by the OMB to workplace privacy came in 1987, when it issued guidelines on the Privacy Act implications of systems to monitor employees' use of telecommunications systems.[88]

The telecommunications guidelines concern the recording of long-distance telephone numbers for the purpose of determining the employees responsible for particular calls. Typically, at the end of a particular period, a list of calls is circulated in the workplace, and employees are asked to check off personal calls,

---

[80] Pincus (1995), 58, reports that private sector employers were originally included in the Privacy Act, but this was amended because Congress did not believe that the benefits outweighed the costs to business.

[81] Several states have enacted information privacy laws applicable to their own public sectors. Moreover, 14 grant to private sector employees the right to access their personnel files (ILO (1991a, 1), 152).

[82] 'Record' is defined as any item or collection of information about an individual which permits his identification (s. 552(a)(4)).

[83] Fast (1993), 439–41.

[84] *Infra*, sects. 5.4.1 and 6.4.2.

[85] Bennett (1992), 72; Michael (1994), 88.

[86] A temporary committee was created which reported in 1977. See Privacy Protection Study Commission (1977), 26–30.

[87] Bennett (1992), 176.

[88] OMB (1987); Flaherty (1989), 329–30.

for which they are then billed. The guidelines 'recommend strongly' that agencies comply with the Privacy Act when implementing and operating a 'telephone accounting' (or 'call detail') system, if the information recorded by the system permits the identification of the employee/caller.[89] Hence, employees should be notified that such systems exist, and should be able to access (and rectify) their personal records. Moreover, the guidelines emphasise that all systems must have legitimate purposes, such as providing the information necessary to bill employees for their personal calls, and must not be used for surveillance or harassment. Examples of proper and improper information disclosures are also given: it would be proper to disclose system records to supervisors for the purpose of identifying the employee responsible for a particular call, but improper to disclose records to identify whistleblowers or to satisfy someone's curiosity.[90] The guidelines do not have the force of law, and are quite general. They also do not appear to have made much of an impact on agencies. In fact, when they were circulated to over 100 agencies for comments, only four responded.[91]

The American model of information privacy is one of 'voluntary compliance and self-help',[92] meaning that agencies are expected to comply with the Privacy Act through their own internal initiatives, while individuals may assert their statutory rights in the courts. The lack of a privacy-dedicated agency to publicise the Act and develop its provisions in relation to employment has meant that the legislation is much less significant to workplace privacy issues than the French and Canadian equivalents. As I will demonstrate below, both France and Canada have established active and independent administrative commissions which have committed resources to information privacy in employment, and have developed employment-specific privacy principles within the framework of general information privacy provisions. The United States' approach is nevertheless consistent with the essentially abstentionist character of its legal culture.[93]

4.3.4 Workplace Privacy Protection in the Private Sector Workplace

Because the American law of workplace privacy is influenced by the constitutional conception of privacy, one would expect to see the inadequacies discussed above replicated and even exacerbated in the law as it applies to the private sector. This will be apparent in my discussion below.

---

[89] OMB (1987); Flaherty (1989), 12991.
[90] *Ibid.*, 12990.
[91] *Ibid.*
[92] Bennett (1992), 170.
[93] *Ibid.*, 198–9.

4.3.4.1 *Dismissal in Contravention of Public Policy*

Although employment-at-will is the general default rule in American employment law, courts in some states have nevertheless developed a common law exception to the at-will rule, namely a tort of wrongful discharge in contravention of public policy, which limits the contractual right of the employer to discharge an employee at any time.[94] The determination of what constitutes 'public policy' has generated controversy in the United States, and has led to diversity in the law.[95] Courts in some states, such as Texas[96] and New York,[97] have refused to adopt the public policy exception, reasoning that it would be inappropriate for the judiciary to limit contractual rights. In essence, these courts have held to the view that employment is a private relationship beyond public concern, and therefore immune to public interference. Other state courts have identified the socio-economic ramifications of employment dismissal, thereby embracing the public policy exception. Hence, the Illinois Supreme Court justified adopting the exception by noting that 'the employer and employee do not stand on equal footing' and that 'unchecked employer power . . . has been seen to present a threat to the public policy carefully considered and adopted by society as a whole'.[98] Nevertheless, certain courts have limited public policy to narrow situations where clearly identifiable state interests are offended by dismissal. These situations generally involve the interest of the state in ensuring the integrity of its laws, as would arise when an employee has been dismissed for refusing to commit an illegal act, for disclosing that the employer has committed an illegal act (i.e. whistleblowing), for exercising a statutory right such as filing a workers' compensation claim or for performing a public obligation such as jury duty.[99] This approach is consistent with a narrow reading of public interest. A competing and broader view is that the 'public interest' may also be threatened where employees' human rights are infringed. Thus, where the interest of the individual which is threatened by an employment decision has the status of a human right, then that fact alone engages the public interest. A third group of state courts have taken this view, and have adopted a much broader conception of public policy which includes situations where dismissal has occurred in contravention of an employees' constitutional rights, including privacy. These include Alaska, California, Connecticut, Illinois, Maryland,

---

[94] Willborn *et al.* (1993), 79. Some courts have viewed the public policy exception as a matter of contract law. See *Luedtke* v. *Nabors Alaska Drilling, Inc.*, 768 P 2d 1123 (Alaska SC, 1989), and California's approach, *infra*, secti. 4.3.4.3.

[95] See, generally, Kim (1996).

[96] *Supra*, n. 23.

[97] *Murphy* v. *American Home Products Corp.* 448 NE 2d 86 (NYCA, 1983), 87–90. New York has also rejected the implied contractual duty of good faith, for much the same reason. See Willborn *et al.* (1993), 132.

[98] *Palmateer* v. *International Harvester Co.*, 421 NE 2d 876 (Ill. SC, 1981), 878.

[99] Willborn *et al.* (1993), 79–80. See, for example, *Kelsay* v. *Motorola, Inc.*, 384 NE 2d 353 (Ill. CA, 1979) (workers' compensation claim); *Nees* v. *Hocks*, 536 P 2d 512 (Or. CA, 1975) (jury duty).

Massachusetts, Michigan, New Jersey, Pennsylvania, West Virginia and Wisconsin.[100]

The 1989 decision of the Alaska Supreme Court in *Luedtke* v. *Nabors Alaska Drilling Inc.*[101] demonstrates that the public policy exception may afford a remedy to an employee who has been dismissed as a result of an invasion of privacy. The case concerned the termination of two oil rig workers who refused to submit to drug testing without cause. In considering their claim for damages for wrongful dismissal in contravention of public policy, the court considered it relevant that both the federal Constitution and Alaska's state Constitution protect the right of privacy, and that the common law affords protection against tortious invasions of privacy. Hence, the court reasoned that 'there is a sphere of activity in every person's life that is closed to scrutiny by others', and thereby concluded that public policy in Alaska permitted employees to withhold 'private' information from employers.[102] In the case of workplace drug testing, the court observed that a balancing was required between the public policy supporting employee privacy, and the public policy supporting health and safety in the workplace (the suggested rationale for the impugned drug testing programme). In conducting this analysis, the court thought that the workplace privacy jurisprudence related to the Fourth Amendment of the Constitution would be relevant. Since the *Luedtke* decision pre-dated the *Von Raab* and *Skinner* decisions of the United States Supreme Court, it is of only limited relevance in the application of public policy to privacy issues. However, the Alaska Supreme Court concluded that the public policy balance favoured drug testing oil rig employees, with the caveat that two procedural protections must be instituted to safeguard privacy: (1) the drug testing must be conducted at a time reasonably contemporaneous with the employee's work time, to ensure that the employer is not regulating off-duty activity *per se*, but only off-duty activity which threatens job performance; and (2) employees must receive reasonable notice of the adoption of a drug-testing plan, in order to provide them with an opportunity to contest it, resign, negotiate the conditions of testing or 'prepare for the test so that [they] will not fail it'.[103] This procedural finding was later followed in the New Jersey case of *Hennessey* v. *Coastal Eagle Point Oil Co.*, where the State Supreme Court added that 'employers may conduct only those tests necessary to determine the presence of drugs in the urine, and are under an obligation not to disclose information obtained as a result of testing'.[104]

---

[100] Willborn *et al.* (1993), 132; *Novosel* v. *Nationwide Ins. Co.*, 731 F 2d 894 (Pa. SC 1983); *Palmateer, supra*, n.98, 878 (Illinois). In the case of privacy, see: *Luedtke, supra*, n. 94 (Alaska); *Semore* v. *Pool*, 266 Cal. Rptr. 280 (Cal. CA, 1990); *Cort* v. *Bristol-Myers Co.*, 431 NE 2d 908 (Mass. CA, 1982); *Hennessey, supra*, n. 149, Chap. 2 (New Jersey); *Twigg* v. *Hercules Corp.*, 406 SE 2d 52 (W. Va. CA, 1990).

[101] *Luedtke, supra*, n. 94.

[102] *Ibid.*, 1132–3, 1135.

[103] *Ibid.*, 1136–7.

[104] *Supra*, n. 149, Chap. 2, 23.

Although the public policy doctrine holds out some hope for privacy protection in the American workplace, it is inadequate for several reasons. First, in so far as the public policy exception transposes constitutional privacy principles into the private sector, it will simply replicate the flaws discussed above in relation to the United States Supreme Court's existing workplace privacy jurisprudence. Moreover, the deference applied by courts in assessing public sector employers' objectives, and the lack of rigour in valuing the private interests of employees, are likely to be exacerbated when courts apply the privacy balancing test in private sector disputes. The public/private distinction continues to influence judicial thinking, even in states which have agreed that public policy favours protecting the right of privacy.[105] Hence, if one detects deferential thinking in the public sector cases, one is likely to find it with even greater force in relation to the private sector.

Secondly, a right of privacy situated within the law of dismissal is problematic because employees are only in a position to assert the right as part of a wrongful dismissal claim. Loss of employment as a precondition to asserting a workplace privacy right is a high price which most workers cannot afford to pay.[106] Moreover, dismissal law offers job candidates no protection from invasive employer hiring practices. Thus, the right of privacy which has been adopted by some American states as an aspect of the public policy doctrine has little relevance as a source of employment regulation for both actual and prospective employees.

Finally, the development of workplace privacy law as an aspect of public policy in the United States has been a slow process, not unlike most matters dealt with under the common law. The law also remains highly controversial, and therefore in a state of flux. One can expect the law to continue to develop in an *ad hoc* and incremental matter, meaning that both employers and employees will obtain little guidance from the jurisprudence in the short to medium term. The law will remain reactive, although a more comprehensive and proactive regulatory framework may be needed to address the complexities of workplace privacy issues like genetic testing or performance monitoring.

4.3.4.2 *The Common Law Tort of Invasion of Privacy*

In section 4.3.3.1 above, I observed that the common law tort of invasion of privacy is an established aspect of American law, and is premised on the same principles of human dignity, bodily integrity and security of the person which underlie the constitutional conception of privacy. At first glance, the common law tort could be a powerful legal weapon in combating privacy-invasive management practices. Unlike the public policy right of privacy discussed above, the tort right is distinct from the law of employment dismissal, meaning that it

---

[105] See, e.g., the opinion of Chief Justice Matthews (concurring in the result) in *Luedtke, supra,* n. 94, 1139.

[106] See *supra,* sect. 3.3.2.

would be available to job candidates, actual employees and dismissed employees. Moreover, the tort right is generally accepted throughout the United States.[107] In theory, it is available to challenge employer intrusions upon privacy such as electronic monitoring of telephone calls and e-mail, video surveillance, searches of employees' belongings, polygraph, drug and genetic testing, psychological profiling, demands for personal information and the disclosure of personal information to third parties.[108]

In reality, the judicial approach to the privacy tort in the employment context evinces considerable deference to privacy-invasive management practices. After reviewing the case law, one leading commentator concluded that the tort is largely an 'irrelevance' in protecting employees from systematically invasive action.[109] This is primarily because courts have linked privacy protection in the workplace to the concept of a 'reasonable expectation of privacy', and have then significantly devalued employees' expectations. The extent of privacy that employees are reasonably entitled to expect is largely dependent on the amount of privacy their employers are willing to tolerate. Hence, established employer policies on matters such as drug testing, psychological testing and performance monitoring have, merely by reason of their existence, been taken to reduce employees' expectations of privacy. This approach adopts the view that the employer is entitled to establish working conditions, and that candidates who accept employment knowing those conditions, or employees who submit to those conditions, have consented to them and are not entitled to expect anything better. The existence of this 'consent' precludes a subsequent complaint of invasion of privacy. In *Luedtke*, for example, the Alaska Supreme Court rejected the claim that an invasion of privacy had occurred in the case of one complainant who had 'voluntarily' surrendered a urine sample for testing.[110] This view of consent tends to place candidates/employees in an impossible situation, since their submission to a privacy-invasive practice may be regarded as consent, while their refusal to submit (with the probable consequence of losing job opportunities) means that no invasion of privacy has actually occurred. An example of this 'no-win' situation arose in the Texas case of *Jennings* v. *Minco Tech. Labs*,[111] where the complainant objected to her employer's drug-testing plan and challenged it as a tortious invasion of privacy. The court rejected the claim because the drug-testing plan ensured that no test would be performed without the consent of the subject. There could be no test, and therefore no invasion of privacy, if the employee refused; and there could be no invasion of privacy if the employee consented to the test. It did not trouble the court that

---

[107] New York is one exception, as it has limited invasion of privacy to matters concerning appropriation of personality (NY Civ. Rights Law, s. 51 (1992)). Because New York has rejected the public policy right of privacy (*supra*, n. 97), employees in that State are uniquely deprived of privacy protection.

[108] Pincus (1995), 61; Cavico (1993), 1271–8.

[109] Finkin (1996b), 240. See also, King (1994), 460–1.

[110] *Supra*, n. 94, 1137.

[111] *Supra*, n. 24, Chap. 47.

refusing consent would result in dismissal. Under the law of contract, the court reasoned, the fact that one party faces economic loss by refusing consent in no way affects the validity of that consent. The court saw nothing unique in the employment context which would necessitate a departure from the normal laws of contract: '[t]here cannot be one law of contracts for the rich and another for the poor'.[112]

I would emphasise here a key difference between tort privacy and public policy privacy, in that the defence of consent plays a diminished role where privacy is being asserted in the public interest. Tort privacy is concerned exclusively with the relationship between the parties and, in particular, with the duty owed by one to the other. The actions, reactions, perceptions and understandings of the parties form the factual background against which to determine whether a claim lies by one against the other.[113] Courts, which are already reluctant to interfere in private relationships, may be doubly reluctant to interfere where the actions of Party A appear to have been accepted by Party B, particularly if Party A has relied on that acceptance in some way. This explains the importance of consent in tortious workplace privacy law. Public policy privacy differs because the key concern is not to sort out the differences between the parties, but to ensure that the public interest is advanced. Consent diminishes in importance because, quite simply, it may not be in the public interest for consent to operate as a defence where human rights are concerned.[114]

Because the common law privacy to which employees are entitled is often determined by reference to the policies and practices adopted by management and made known to employees, employers may be advised that they can insulate themselves from future privacy claims by publicising potentially privacy-invasive policies and practices well in advance of their implementation.[115] Existing case law would support this defensive approach to privacy claims: a publicised policy can establish a 'business practice' which precludes a reasonable expectation of privacy; alternatively, the fact that employees continue to work under a particular policy supports a finding of consent.[116] However, it is surely problematic that the right of privacy in the workplace can be so circumstantial, and premised on such shifting ground. It would be absurd to permit an employer to avoid the limitations of anti-discrimination legislation by advising employees in advance that they could be subject to discrimination. It is equally absurd to think that an employer could place video cameras and microphones throughout the workplace, record every movement and conversation of employees, yet claim that this did not deny the right of privacy in some respects because the employees had been informed about it in advance, and therefore had no

---

[112] *Ibid.*, 502.
[113] Issacharoff (1990), 617.
[114] This surely explains why in *Luedtke, supra*, n. 94, the plaintiffs were unable to make out a claim for tortious invasion of privacy due to consent, but were nevertheless permitted to raise public policy privacy.
[115] For example, see Guffey and West (1996), 745.
[116] Finkin (1996b), 226.

expectation of privacy. The better view must be that the right to respect for private life creates substantive limitations on the actions and policies of management, which all persons are entitled to expect and enjoy regardless of advance warnings or pre-existing policies.[117]

In three other important ways, American tort privacy is inadequate. The first two are related to the concept of a 'reasonable expectation of privacy'. First, because systematic invasions of privacy resulting from established employer practices and policies are generally held not to infringe privacy, employees' reasonable expectations of privacy act as a block against only *outrageous* conduct. In fact, many courts have adopted a 'highly offensive' test in assessing privacy claims.[118] Thus, an employee subjected to an invasive search in an anomalous situation may succeed in her privacy claim, whereas an employee who is searched pursuant to an established employer policy will probably not.[119] Similarly, employees who are monitored surreptitiously by video-cameras in the staff washroom or lunchroom are likely have a tort privacy claim, although they probably would not if management disclosed in advance that the monitoring would take place.[120] In practice, this means that the common law tort operates very narrowly in the workplace context.

Secondly, the law has held that although job candidates may claim against employers for invasion of privacy, they have a lower expectation of privacy on the theory that by putting themselves forward for employment consideration, they necessarily consent to a probing inquiry by the employer into their fitness for the job. Moreover, the argument has been advanced that candidates do not have roots in the company, and are therefore not entitled to expect the same level of protection as actual employees.[121] This reduced protection for job applicants ignores the fact that they as a group are particularly vulnerable to privacy invasions, since the hiring process is by its nature searching and intrusive, yet protections flowing from collective representation or public policy are not available.

Finally, as with constitutional and public policy privacy, courts have tended to be deferential to employer justifications when applying the common law tort in the workplace context. Some have concluded that once a legitimate business objective has been established, the right of privacy must give way. Courts have therefore been unwilling to second-guess the means chosen to achieve legitimate objectives, even when the ramifications for employee privacy are excessive, or a non-invasive alternative exists. In *Seldana* v. *Kelsey-Hayes*,[122] the employer investigated the plaintiff's work-related injury (which it was legitimately enti-

---

[117] Craig and Oliver (1998), 56.

[118] ALI (1972).

[119] See *K-Mart Corp.*, n. 77, Chap. 2 above.

[120] See *Speer* v. *Ohio Department of Rehabilitation & Correction*, 624 NE 2d 251 (Ohio CA, 1993).

[121] This is the sort of argument which equates actual employment with property rights in a job, and grants greater legal protection to those who possess such rights. See Willborn *et al.* (1993), 193.

[122] 443 NW 2d 382 (Mich. CA, 1989).

tled to do) by placing him under constant surveillance even in his own home. While the majority opinion found in favour of the employer, the lone dissenter, Justice Holbrook, thought that the employer's intrusion into the plaintiff's home was a clear invasion of privacy. He wrote, '[e]ven if the purpose for conducting an investigation into private matters is legitimate, the defendant is not entitled to carte blanche investigate without regard to the degree and nature of the intrusion'.[123]

In short, the application of the tort of invasion of privacy in the employment context has tended to repeat and even magnify the inadequacies of both constitutional and public policy privacy. In a sense, this is consistent with the general nature of American labour and employment law. Thus, judicial deference to employer objectives reflects an abstentionist approach to labour law, while the traditional notion of employment as a contractual relationship of equals (with the law ignoring the unequal economic power of the parties) is evident in rules concerning consent and reduced protection for job candidates.

4.3.4.3 *The Constitutional Right of Privacy in the State of California*

The state of California merits special attention because Article I of its own Constitution uniquely guarantees the right of privacy in both the public and private sectors.[124] In theory, then, the constitutional right is available to all Californian employees, regardless of the nature of their employment, and to all job candidates. The question thus arises whether residents of California enjoy superior workplace privacy protection relative to their counterparts elsewhere in the United States.[125]

The first decision of the California Court of Appeal (Third District) applying the constitutional right of privacy in the private sector workplace promised little to candidates/employees. In *Wilkinson* v. *Times Mirror Corp.*, the court rejected a claim by job applicants that the defendant's drug-testing policy contravened the constitutional right of privacy. The defendant was a private publishing company which had a policy of drug testing all of its employees, including copy editors and legal writers. There was obviously no health or safety interest justifying the testing plan—the employer's motivation was economic and highly speculative. Although the Court agreed that the applicants could assert the constitutional right, it chose to define the scope of that right

---

[123] *Ibid.*, 385. See also *Cort, supra*, n. 100, where the employer was permitted to ask non-job-related questions about family and personal finances as part of its legitimate process of inquiry.

[124] In 1972, California voters amended by referendum Art. I, sect. 1 of the state Constitution to include the right of privacy as an 'inalienable right'. In *Wilkinson* v. *Times Mirror Corp.*, 264 Cal. Rptr. 194 (Cal. CA, 1989), the court concluded that the provision applies to invasions of privacy by both government and business. Prior to this, the California Court of Appeal had already recognised an implied covenant of good faith and fair dealing which required employers to respect worker privacy (*Rulon-Miller* v. *IBM*, 208 Cal. Rptr. 524 (Cal. CA 1984)). See generally Kelso (1992).

[125] One California court concluded that the constitutional right of privacy was adopted in that state to fill a perceived gap in federal coverage: *American Academy of Pediatrics* v. *Van de Kamp*, 263 Cal. Rptr. 46 (Cal. CA, 1989), 49.

pursuant to the United States Supreme Court's own privacy jurisprudence, and in particular the *Von Raab* and *Skinner* decisions.[126] This inevitably duplicated the inadequacies of those rulings, such as the 'reasonableness' balancing test, and perhaps explains the court's deference to the very weak justification advanced by the employer. The court further adopted the consent argument from tort privacy, holding that since the applicants had refused to consent to the drug testing, they had suffered no actionable invasion of privacy even though they had been denied the opportunity of employment.[127] Finally, the court stated that 'the most important factor' was that the plaintiffs were all job applicants who had a reduced expectation of privacy in the hiring process.[128] The end-result was that the Court combined the deferential elements of constitutional, public policy and tort workplace privacy law to uphold a drug testing plan premised on the flimsiest of rationales.

One year later, in the drug-testing case of *Luck* v. *Southern Pacific Transportation Co.*,[129] the Court of Appeal (First District) adopted a stricter test for invasions of privacy by private employers, holding that the constitutional right of privacy requires that any incursion upon individual privacy must be justified by a 'compelling interest' test. This new standard 'places a heavier burden on [a defendant] than would a Fourth Amendment privacy analysis',[130] or a common law privacy analysis, both of which focus on a lower 'reasonableness' test. Hence, the court believed that the Californian Constitution mandated a more rigorous approach than had been adopted in *Von Raab* and *Skinner*. On this basis, the court entered into an extensive analysis of the plaintiff-employee's actual job, to determine whether the railway which employed her had a compelling interest in subjecting her to drug testing and in penalising her refusal to comply. The employer advanced several justifications including safety, deterring drug use, efficiency, competence, creating a drug-free work environment, enforcing rules against drug use and ensuring public confidence in the integrity of the railway industry. However, the court concluded that only safety could conceivably meet the compelling interest test. After examining the plaintiff's work functions, the court held that it was contrary to Article I of the state Constitution to subject her to drug testing because 'Luck's job did not have sufficient safety aspects to constitute a safety interest that might be balanced against the intrusion of her privacy rights'.[131]

Confusingly, the court then concluded that this constitutional breach was insufficient to form the basis for a tort damage award for wrongful dismissal in contravention of public policy, because: (1) the right of privacy is a private right, and not a public right, and therefore cannot be a legitimate matter of 'public

---

[126] *Wilkinson, supra,* n. 124, 200–1.
[127] *Ibid.,* 204.
[128] *Ibid.,* 203.
[129] 267 Cal. Rptr. 618 (Cal. CA, 1990).
[130] *Ibid.,* 629.
[131] *Ibid.,* 631–2.

policy'; (2) a public policy claim must be a matter on which reasonable people can have little disagreement, yet drug testing is controversial and no reasonable consensus has emerged; and (3) the public policy was not sufficiently established at the time the employer instituted its drug testing policy in 1985, since the constitutional ramifications of drug testing were first recognised in 1989 in *Skinner* and *Von Raab*. Thus, Luck was limited to contract damages on the theory that the employer had breached its implied duty of good faith by dismissing her for refusing to provide a urine sample for testing. She could recover neither tort damages for emotional distress nor punitive damages. This demonstrates the important distinction between remedies in tort and contract, and that employees may be better off suing in tort (and in particular, under the public policy exception).[132] More importantly, it is a highly peculiar result.[133] The court's finding that the employer breached an 'inalienable right' protective of human dignit,[134] and its application of the 'compelling interest' test both indicate the seriousness it attached to Luck's claim. How can one reconcile this with the court's holding that an infringement of the right of privacy is not an issue raising public policy? A matter of *human* dignity is, by definition, a *public* concern.[135] In fact, a careful reading of the court's judgment reveals that its primary reason for rejecting tort remedies was its sympathy with the employer's position. Hence, the court reasoned that the employer should not be subject to higher tort damages since it did not know that drug testing was unconstitutional when it instituted the testing programme. Apparently, many other 'reasonable' people made this same mistake, according to the court. However, this highly deferential view ignores the fact that the employer had no reasonable justification for invading the employee's privacy, and dismissed her when she asserted her constitutionally guaranteed human right. The fact that many other employers have invaded their employees' privacy in a similarly unjustifiable manner is, one would think, an argument for a broader range of damages to deter future constitutional infringements. The dissent noted that the Court's approach on the damages issue constitutes 'a return to an era of masters and servants [inconsistent with] modern notions of employer-employee relations'.[136]

A further improvement on the low standard set in *Wilkinson* v. *Times Mirror Corp.* came in the 1993 case of *Soroka* v. *Dayton Hudson Corp.*,[137] where job applicants filed a class action, alleging that the psychological screening imposed by the defendant employer was an invasion of privacy contrary to the Californian Constitution. In particular, the plaintiffs objected to questions concerning religion and sexual orientation. The employer argued that the 'compelling interest' test should not apply in the case of job candidates, but the Court

---

[132] Although the issue of remedies is indeed significant, it will not be pursued further herein. It is important to note, however, that damages for workplace privacy depend on the cause of action.

[133] The dissent referred to the majority position as 'bizarre' (*supra*, n. 129, 639).

[134] *Ibid.*, 626.

[135] *Supra*, sect. 2.3.4.5; Kim (1996), 725.

[136] *Supra*, n. 129, 639–40.

[137] 1 Cal. Rptr. 2d 77 (Cal. CA, 1991).

of Appeal (First District) disagreed, concluding that 'no distinction should be made between the privacy rights of job applicants and employees'.[138] While the court thought that the employer had a compelling interest in hiring emotionally stable persons, it found that the impugned questions were insufficiently linked to this interest, and were therefore an unconstitutional threat to privacy.[139]

Californian law is therefore in a state of flux in its application of the state Constitution's privacy guarantee to the private sector workplace. While the initial position of the state Court of Appeal demonstrated little sensitivity to privacy as a constitutionally protected human right, and instead replicated the inadequacies of federal constitutional, public policy, and tort privacy, later cases generated important advances. Thus, the 'compelling interest' test holds out greater protection to private sector employees than would be available under any other cause of action, and the traditional distinctions drawn in the United States between public and private sector employees, and actual employees and job candidates, no longer have relevance in California. Nevertheless, the approach of the California Court of Appeal (First District) on the remedy issue reflects the enduring influence of abstentionist thinking in labour and employment law, and the tension which exists in the United States between the emerging field of human rights in employment and the more traditional view of employment as a private relationship governed by contract principles.

4.3.4.4 Statutory Protection

A stunning array of statutory provisions have emerged at the state and federal levels, perhaps in response to the inadequate constitutional and common law protections afforded workers in the field of workplace privacy. I simply cannot discuss these in detail here. However, few workplace privacy issues remain untouched. Those regulated in some American jurisdictions include drug testing,[140] genetic testing,[141] HIV testing,[142] psychological testing,[143] poly-

---

[138] 1 Cal. Rptr. 2d 77 (Cal. CA, 1991), 83–4, 86.

[139] *Ibid.*, 87.

[140] The federal government's initiatives encouraging drug testing are discussed *supra*, in sect. 2.3.4.5. Finkin (1995a), 165–6, writes that 14 states have legislated in the area of employment drug testing. The legislation is diverse, with some states restricting drug testing, and others focusing on providing procedural protections. An example of the former is Montana's legislation (Mont. Code Ann., s. 39–2–304(1)–(5) (1988)), which prohibits pre-employment drug testing unless the job involves hazardous work environments or primary responsibility in security, public safety or fiduciary positions. An example of the latter is Minnesota's law (Minn. Stat. ss. 181–950–957 (1988)), which requires employers to develop official written policies for drug testing and bring these to the attention of employees and applicants. The law also requires second-test confirmation, and stipulates that all test results remain confidential, except in certain limited circumstances.

[141] See New Jersey (1981, NJ Stat. Ann., s. 10:5–5(y) (West Supp. 1991)); New York (1992, NY Civ. Rights Law, s. 48 (Supp. 1992)); Wisconsin (Wis. Act of 5 Mar. 1992 (1991 Wis. Laws 117)); Oregon (Or. Rev. Stat., s. 659.227 (Supp. 1990)). Oregon also prohibits psychological testing and brain-wave testing.

[142] See Cal. Health and Safety Code, s. 120980(F) (West, 1997); Ky. Rev. Stat. Ann., s. 207.150(1) (Banks-Baldwin, 1996); Wis. Stat. Ann., s. 103.15 (West, 1996).

[143] Md. Ann. Code art. 100, s. 95a (1985).

graphs,[144] electronic surveillance[145] and employer control of off-duty activities.[146] When examining privacy legislation, it is apparent that the protection afforded to employees varies markedly from state to state, a phenomenon which exacerbates the complexity already existing in the application of constitutional and common law privacy protection. Multi-state employers, in particular, may find this legislative diversity daunting.[147] Although the federal government has the constitutional power to legislate uniform workplace privacy standards, as it did in the case of anti-discrimination law, this has occurred only in relation to polygraph testing.[148] Other federal laws have an incidental impact upon workplace privacy: legislation prohibiting racial and disability discrimination (impacting upon drug, genetic, and medical testing in employment),[149] and the Electronic Communications Privacy Act (ECPA)[150] (which regulates the interception of conversations,[151] telephone calls[152] and possibly e-mail,[153] and the use or communication of any information obtained through such interceptions).

Although one should hesitate to generalise about the statutory protection of worker privacy in the United States, it is hardly surprising that deference to employer interests tends to colour legislation, reflecting yet again the influence of abstentionist and market-oriented thinking in American labour and employment law. Hence, despite the notorious inaccuracy of the lie detector, the federal Employee Polygraph Protection Act (EPPA) permits its limited use in the case of workers involved in certain security functions, and as part of an 'ongoing investigation involving economic loss or injury to the employer's business' such as theft, embezzlement or industrial espionage.[154] In the latter investigative context, the legislation limits the use of the polygraph to cases where the employer already has a reasonable suspicion of wrongdoing, and prohibits the

---

[144] 27 states and the federal government have regulated the use of polygraphs and other lie detectors by employers. See, in particular, Employee Polygraph Protection Act, 29 USC ss. 2001–2009 (1990), and Finkin (1995a), 165–6.

[145] Connecticut forbids the surveillance of employees by sound or closed circuit television in 'areas designated for their health, personal comfort, or for safeguarding their possessions such as restrooms, locker rooms, or lounges' (Conn. Gen. Stat. s. 31–48(b) (1993)). See also Michigan Comp. Laws, s. 750. 539d (1993); NY Labor Law, s. 201–d2 (1993 Supp.).

[146] See Colorado Rev. Stat. 24–34–402.5 (1993 Cum. Supp.): 'It is a discriminatory or unfair employment practice for an employer to terminate the employment of any employee due to that employee's engaging in any lawful activity off the premises of the employer during non-working hours'.

[147] Pincus (1995), 54–5.

[148] *Supra*, n. 144.

[149] Civil Rights Act, see n. 13, Chap. 4; Americans with Disabilities Act of 1990, see n. 14, Chap. 4; Gostin (1991); Stone (1991b); Boehmer (1992), 777–8. The role of anti-discrimination law in protecting privacy is discussed *infra*, sect. 6.5.2.2.

[150] See n. 91, Chap. 2.

[151] The Act prohibits the use of 'any electronic, mechanical or other device to intercept any oral communication' (*ibid.*, s. 2511(1)(b)).

[152] *Watkins*, see n. 91, Chap. 2.

[153] Baumhart (1992).

[154] See n. 144, Chap. 4; Finkin (1995s), 55; Note (1988b); *Long Beach City Employees Ass'n* v. *City of Long Beach*. see n. 28, Chap. 2, 667. Note that Iowa prohibits absolutely the use of polygraphs in employment (Iowa Code Ann., s. 730.4 (West 1988)).

employer from acting solely on the basis of test results. Nevertheless, it is surely significant that federal law permits an employer to utilize polygraph testing to protect its own economic interests.

In a similar vein, the ECPA contains an exception which permits employers and others to monitor certain communications 'in the ordinary course of business'.[155] This has focused the judicial analysis on what constitutes ordinary business practice, as opposed to what constitutes an acceptable limitation on privacy.[156] It is notable, however, that courts have adopted a restrictive interpretation of monitoring 'in the ordinary course of business'. Thus, it has been held that personal telephone calls may only be monitored, 'to the extent necessary to guard against unauthorized use of the telephone or to determine whether a call is personal or not'.[157] This means that an employer may listen in to an employee's personal telephone call to determine its nature, but once it is ascertained that the call is personal, the employer must cease the monitoring.

Personal telephone calls and other communications may be monitored, however, 'where one of the parties to the communication has given prior consent to such interception'.[158] This raises two dangers. First, communications between the employer and an employee may be monitored and recorded if the *employer* consents, regardless of the knowledge or wishes of the employee. Secondly, in relation to communications not involving the employer, there is the potential that the approach to consent from tort privacy could be adopted in interpreting the Act, and that prior notification to employees of a general monitoring policy could later form the basis for a finding of implied consent. To date, however, courts have been reluctant to imply consent unless employees are informed in detail about the nature of monitoring to which they will be subject. Hence, an employer may only avail itself of the consent defence if the monitored employee has been notified in advance that all his telephone conversations may be subject to monitoring, and has been informed of the manner of monitoring.[159] Although this is a relatively rigorous standard for consent, it nevertheless permits the ECPA to be circumvented by employers through full disclosure in advance of actual monitoring.[160] Presumably, the theory behind this reasoning is that employees who object to monitoring have the option of resigning. Given the fact that this 'option' is not realistic in many circumstances, the ECPA effectively provides only as much privacy to employees as their employers are willing to tolerate. Thus, the substantive limitations on employer eavesdropping provided by the ECPA are easily avoided, although the procedural safeguards of prior notification and full disclosure remain available to employees.

---

[155] See n. 91, Chap. 2, s. 2510(5)(a)(i).
[156] Boehmer (1992), 793.
[157] *Watkins*, n. 91, Chap. 2.
[158] See n. 91, Chap. 2, s. 2511(2)(d).
[159] *Williams v. Poulos*, 11 F 3d 217 (1st Circ., 1993), 281–2, relying on *Griggs-Ryan v. Smith*, 904 F 2d 112 (1st Circ., 1990); *Deal v. Spears*, 980 F 2d 1153 (8th Circ., 1992), 1157.
[160] Gantt (1995), 357–8.

Both the EPPA and the ECPA demonstrate a further problem with workplace privacy legislation in the United States. The legislation tends to be 'device specific', regulating only one or a few technologies which have similar functions and a similar impact upon the right of privacy. While employers might cease or limit their use of the regulated technologies, they may be able to accomplish the same results with different, unregulated methods. The polygraph legislation, for example, is generally credited with leading to the increased use of personality tests to measure honesty.[161] Although such tests are regarded as highly unreliable, they remain unregulated in most of the American jurisdictions.

The most ambitious federal legislative initiative to protect the right of privacy in the workplace is the proposed Privacy for Consumers and Workers Act (PCWA),[162] which was introduced before the House of Representatives on 28 April 1993. Its purpose is '[t]o prevent abuses of electronic monitoring in the workplace', through the regulation of the collection, storage, analysis and reporting of information concerning an employee's activities by any method other than direct observation by another person. All methods of electronic monitoring, including computer performance monitoring, video surveillance, telephone monitoring and call detail systems, would be subject to the Bill.[163] Moreover, all public and private sector employers would be regulated, and some protection would be provided to job candidates.

The problem of consent, which plagues American workplace privacy law, including the ECPA, would be avoided under the Bill through the imposition of substantive limitations on employer monitoring practices. Highlights include: (1) an employer may only monitor an employee secretly if the employer has a reasonable suspicion that the employee has engaged in illegal activity or wilful gross misconduct which adversely affects the employer's interests or the interests of other employees, and the employer executes prior to the monitoring a statement stipulating in detail the justification for the monitoring (section 5(c)(1) and (2)); (2) an employer may not engage in random or periodic monitoring of an employee with five years' seniority (section 5(b)(2)); (3) an employer may not intentionally collect personal information about an employee through electronic monitoring, and must limit its use of electronic monitoring to the work of the employee (although incidental collections of personal information are permissible) (section 9(a)(1)); (4) routine electronic monitoring in bathrooms, locker rooms and dressing rooms is impermissible (section 9(b)); and (5) an employer may not base employment decisions exclusively on information obtained by electronic monitoring (section 8(b)).[164] In essence, the Bill sets a general standard that electronic monitoring should occur only with the knowledge of employees, and should be strictly limited to matters of job performance. It would not be possible to contract out of the Bill's substantive protections

---

[161] Boehmer (1992), 812.
[162] See n. 13, Chap. 4.
[163] *Ibid.*, s. 1(A).
[164] The Bill also includes protection for employees' First Amendment rights (s. 9(c)).

(section 16(c)), nor could an employer avoid the limitations of the Bill by obtaining employees' consent to broader electronic monitoring.

The Bill also contains certain procedural protections, including: (1) prior notification to all employees of electronic monitoring (section 3(a)), and notification to all job candidates 'at the first personal interview' of existing forms of electronic monitoring to which they may be subject (section 4(c)(1)); and (2) a right of access permitting employees to review information obtained about them through electronic monitoring (section 7(a)). The Bill further provides that information obtained through electronic monitoring should remain confidential, and should only be disclosed to the employee-subject, or to officers and employees of the employer who have a legitimate need for the information in the performance of their duties (section 9(a)).

The proposed PCWA was clearly an attempt to create a floor of rights for American workers in the area of workplace electronic monitoring. In fact, the Bill is surprisingly interventionist, and is certainly at odds with the abstentionist, *laissez-faire* tradition underlying American labour and employment law. The failure of Congress to pass the Bill is largely due to business opposition and the concern that new regulation in the area of electronic monitoring would be costly and inefficient,[165] while perhaps stifling beneficial uses of technology.[166] Given the influence of abstentionist and market individualist thinking in the United States, the prospects for passage of the Bill in the near future are minimal.[167]

4.4 CONCLUSIONS

My examination of workplace privacy law in the United States has revealed the split personality of American labour and employment law. On the one hand, a full range of private interests are eligible for legal protection, and at least some judges and legislators have begun to take privacy seriously as a matter of human rights law. However, the law remains deferential in assessing the justifications advanced by employers for invasive management practices, and downgrades the value of candidates'/employees' private interests through principles such as 'a reasonable expectation of privacy', 'ordinary' business practices and consent. American workplace privacy law is a product of both legal abstentionism and

---

[165] See Chairman Pat Williams, see n. 15, Chap. 2; See also Statement of James I. Royer, FMC Corp., and Statement of Suzanne Sheuerman, Sernior Vice-President, Household International Inc., Testimony Before the US House of Representatives Committee on Education and Labor (1993); King (1994), 472–3; the federal Bill was modelled on a Massachusetts proposal, which was itself withdrawn after encountering vigorous opposition from business interests (Note (1990d), 1908).

[166] See Statement of John Gerdelman, Senior Vice-President, MCI Communications Corp., testimony Before the United States House of Representatives Committee on Education and Labor (1993), defending the use of telephone monitoring and criticising the Bill for failing to recognise its benefits.

[167] The 1993 version of the Bill died without a congressional vote, and no subsequent efforts have been made to resurrect it. See Gerhart(b) (1995), 205.

market individualism. Nevertheless, the emergence of a more protective 'floor of rights' approach to workplace privacy can be seen in extant American law, and in particular the constitutional law of California. In fact, a trend can be identified which holds out some promise for the future. Courts and legislators in the United States have begun to reject the legal distinction between public and private sector employees, and between employees and candidates, in favour of a more comprehensive approach. There is also an indication that courts are becoming increasingly sceptical of justifications premised on employer economic interests, and are favouring only 'compelling' interests such as public safety. Procedural protections are also finding their way into the workplace privacy jurisprudence. Optimism must be muted, however, by the realisation that the United States Supreme Court, in its constitutional workplace privacy jurisprudence, has set a highly deferential example for other courts. The inadequacies and incoherence of American workplace privacy law will be overcome only through a federal legislative solution which provides substantive and procedural protections to all candidates/employees in a manner consistent with the 'floor of rights' approach discussed in section 3.3.3 of Chapter 3. In the short to medium term, this seems unlikely.

5

Privacy in the Workplace in France

In contrast to the American situation, the law of workplace privacy in France is considerably more coherent. This is partly attributable to France's unitary governmental system. French labour law is determined centrally, thus avoiding conflicts between, and diversity among, national and subsidiary jurisdictions. It is therefore possible to speak of *one* French law relevant to employment—a fact which simplifies the analysis herein. Moreover, the protection of human rights in French employment law is substantially more extensive than in the United States, with the Labour Code stipulating the basic principle that employers and labour organisations such as unions and works councils must respect the individual and collective freedoms of employees.[1] While this reflects the historical importance of rights and liberties in French law,[2] similar traditions in the United States have not yet produced comprehensive protection of human rights in employment. French legal culture, particularly as it has developed since the Second World War, deviates from that of the United States in several important ways, which together account for the difference in approach.

The French experience during the Second World War provides the context in which subsequent human rights initiatives must be considered. France, like much of continental Europe, experienced first-hand the human rights violations and atrocities of fascism. This has left an indelible mark on the political and legal cultures of all Western European states, underscoring the need to be vigilant in protecting rights and freedoms.[3] Prior to the Second World War, French law viewed the employment contract as creating a 'permanent link of subordination', thus permitting paternalistic control to be asserted by employers as a matter of course.[4] This situation underscored the dangers of private sources of power, like the employment contract, and ensured that the public/private distinction would not present artificial obstacles to modern human rights protection in employment. Since the War, the legal view of workers has been revised;

[1] Discussed *infra*, sect. 5.3.1.

[2] Consider the Declaration of the Rights of Man and the Citizen (1789), incorporated into the present Constitution of 1958.

[3] The European Convention on Human Rights was an initiative undertaken in response to the events of the Second World War. Authors writing about German law have emphasised the Nazi era in explaining why the right of privacy is so well protected today (see Weiss and Geck (1995), 75; Markesinis (1994a), 64). The commitment to human rights in nations like France and Italy is similarly rooted in the legacy of fascism.

[4] Ray and Rojot (1996), 62; Rojot (1992), 137.

workers are no longer 'subordinates', but instead are 'citizens' within the enterprise, retaining the rights and freedoms which they enjoy outside the enterprise,[5] and enjoying certain labour-specific rights. Hence, the preamble to the Constitution of 1946 (later incorporated into the present Constitution of 1958) guarantees to all workers the right to join a trade union, the right to strike, the right to participate in determining working conditions and the right of equality with regard to an individual's origins, opinions or beliefs.

Furthermore, France's political culture has been receptive to state regulation of economic relationships and more favourable to legislative intervention to address social injustice.[6] This explains in part the electoral success of the French Left (a combination of Socialist, Communist and 'Radical' political parties), whose influence over the development of law has been substantial. These parties have, not surprisingly, been sympathetic to the interests of workers,[7] and unimpressed with the market-based arguments which have influenced the development of American labour law. In general, industrial relations have been more extensively regulated in France than in the United States and Canada, and even recent pressures to deregulate have been resisted in favour of 're-regulation' to provide greater flexibility within the labour market.[8]

Finally, employee interests have been expressed in France through a strong system of collective representation.[9] French unions in particular have been politically influential, taking advantage of ties with the Left. In the past, the French labour movement was accused of engaging in 'relatively fruitless oppositionism',[10] but in recent decades the state has sought to foster a co-operative industrial climate by involving unions as 'social partners' in economic planning. The role of unions in the formation of economic and social policy has been formalised—as social partners, unions play a role in managing the social security system, and participate in the constitutionally-mandated Economic and Social Council which advises the government.[11] Furthermore, even where employees have no union representation, the law requires there to be elected workers' representatives ('*délégués du personnel*') or works councils ('*comités d'entreprise*') in all firms with 11 or more employees.[12] The influence of collective labour rep-

---

[5] Lyon-Caen (1993c), 50–51; Savatier (1990a), 49–50.
[6] Flaherty (1989), 170.
[7] Several of the most important legislative measures protecting the human rights of French workers were implemented during the terms of Socialist President Francois Mitterand (1981–96).
[8] Lyon-Caen (1990a), 3–4.
[9] Although only 6% of French non-agricultural workers are members of unions, 90% of French workers are covered by collective agreements (ILO (1997–8d), 243, 248, Tables 3.1 & 3.2).
[10] Dickson (1994), 189.
[11] *Ibid.*, 189–90.
[12] Workers' representatives exist in firms with 11 to 50 employees (Art. L.421–1 of the Labour Code), while works councils must be organised in all firms with more than 50 employees, or in smaller organisations by agreement (Art. L.431–1 of the Labour Code). French law requires that workers' representatives be permitted to offer opinions on work rules, while works councils must be consulted on all issues of working conditions (as discussed *infra*, sect. 5.5). Note that only representative unions have the capacity to negotiate and conclude collective agreements with legal effect (Trowers (1995), 86–7).

resentatives has ensured that the rights and interests of workers have remained high on France's political and legal agendas.

France thus stands in contrast to the United States, which has never experienced fascist oppression, has no electorally successful socialist political party, has a relatively weak labour movement and still adheres to the public/private distinction in human rights law. The American conception of liberty in the workplace is exemplified by the employment-at-will doctrine, which has been justified as liberating employees from management control by permitting them to leave their employment at any time without penalty. The freedom of the American worker within the employment relationship has, perhaps paradoxically, appeared time and again as an argument against the extension of human rights into the workplace—workers do not require enhanced protection since they are free to resign if they do not like management policies and practices. The French conception of employment as economic and social subordination has had the opposite effect, with state intervention being viewed as essential to free employees from management control, and to promote their 'citizenship' within the enterprise. Thus, the United States is clearly an abstentionist jurisdiction in the field of human rights in employment, while France must be considered 'interventionist'.

5.2 BACKGROUND—THE RIGHT OF PRIVACY IN FRENCH LAW

The written Constitution of France differs from those of countries like the United States and Canada in that it does not include an enumerated list of guaranteed human rights. Instead, the Preamble merely refers to 'the attachment of the French people' to the human rights defined in the Declaration of the Rights of Man and the Citizen (1789), and the Preamble to the Constitution of 1946. There has been some controversy in France over the justiciability of these rights, as they are rather vague and are cited in the Preamble as opposed to the main body of the Constitution. Moreover, there is certainly no mention of the right of privacy in the 1789 Declaration or the 1946 Preamble.[13] Despite the apparent lack of justiciable constitutional human rights in the French Constitution, the Conseil Constitutionnel has created for itself a role as protector of civil liberties, and has defined a set of fundamental human rights principles which may be applied in determining the constitutional validity of legislation. Principles of freedom of association, freedom of education, equality and privacy have all been characterised by the Conseil as fundamental to the French constitutional order.[14]

---

[13] As noted *supra*, in sect. 5.1, the 1946 Preamble does refer to various rights, including a right of all workers to be free from discrimination on the basis of origins, opinions and beliefs. These could be construed in a limited sense as protecting aspects of private life.

[14] Dadomo (1997), 152–6. See Decision of 13 Aug. 1993 [1993] RDCC 224.

Citizens cannot apply to the Conseil Constitutionnel to challenge the constitutionality of legislation or state action. In fact, the Conseil's jurisdiction is limited to considering legislation prior to its proclamation, and may only be invoked by the President, the Prime Minister, the Presidents of the National Assembly and the Senate, or by 60 elected members of either of these parliamentary chambers. In practice, this means that the decisions of the Conseil concerning human rights are relatively rare, and that the influence of constitutional human rights principles in the development of French law has been minor in comparison to the United States. This has not impeded the recognition of the right of privacy, however. In fact, a legal action for invasion of privacy in France predates the American tort of invasion of privacy. Warren and Brandeis even referred to French privacy law in support of their argument that privacy should be protected by the common law.[15]

Several authors have recounted the development of the civil law delict of invasion of privacy in French law.[16] What is most notable is that judges first fashioned a remedy for an intrusion upon private life in 1858. Since then, the right to private life has become a fundamental aspect of the civil law, eventually being incorporated into the French Civil Code in 1970 as Article 9.[17] As is typical of the civil law, the French notion of privacy is premised on a single principle, namely that individuals should be protected from interference by others with respect to the private aspects of their lives. This principle has then been applied by courts in a variety of contexts, and it is therefore possible to identify various private interests which attract legal protection in the personal, territorial, and informational zones.[18] There is a general recognition that an exhaustive definition of privacy is neither possible nor advisable[19]; hence the French have avoided the definitional controversies characterising the British privacy debate,[20] and efforts at categorisation as have occurred in the United States.[21] Privacy in France will continue to develop through the application of a basic principle to unique fact situations. French law is therefore able to protect a diverse range of private interests, while continuing to evolve—a feature which ensures its relevance even in the face of new, privacy-invasive technologies.

In addition to the civil law recognition of the right of privacy, the right also forms part of French law through Article 8 of the European Convention on Human Rights, which has been incorporated into the domestic law of France

---

[15] Warren and Brandeis (1890), 214.

[16] Nerson (1971); Hauch (1994).

[17] Law No. 70–643 of 17 July 1970, now Art. 9 of the Civil Code: 'Everyone has a right to respect for his private life'.

[18] Hauch (1994), 1246–8, summarises the categories of cases where private interests have been recognised: in the informational context, cases have concerned matters of health and illness, family life, sexual activity and orientation, leisure activities; in the personal context, the sanctity of the human body has been found to be at the core of privacy protection; in the territorial context, a person's location or address may attract privacy protection. See also Tissot (1995), 222–3.

[19] Ravanas (1989), 8.

[20] *Supra*, sect. 2.3.1; *infra*, sect. 10.2.

[21] See ALI (1972b), 376–403; Prosser (1960).

and is therefore available to challenge state action. French citizens may individually petition the European Court in Strasbourg, and have done so regularly and successfully.[22] Moreover, French courts may rely upon the rights and principles of the Convention in applying domestic laws. As I will demonstrate below, this has some relevance to the application of human rights in the employment context.

The French law of workplace privacy can be divided into three aspects. First, the French Labour Code stipulates that employers must respect the human rights of workers, thus affording general protection to all rights, including privacy. Secondly, an array of specific provisions of the Civil and Labour Codes, plus the general law governing information privacy, provide more detailed regulation, thus building upon the general protection. Thirdly, French law requires that works councils be informed and consulted on matters affecting employee privacy. This, along with other important institutional and procedural features of French labour law, contributes to resolving disputes over potential privacy invasions. I will consider each of these matters below.

5.3 THE GENERAL RIGHT OF PRIVACY IN FRENCH LABOUR LAW

In 1992, Article L.120–2 was added to the Labour Code: '[n]o one may limit the rights of the individual, or individual and collective freedoms, unless the limitations are justified by the task to be performed and are in proportion to the goal towards which they are aimed'. This wording is identical to an already-existing provision on shop rules, Article L.122–35.[23] In essence, Article L.120–2 permits any employer practice or policy to be challenged as a violation of human rights, and places the onus of justifying the rights infringement on the employer. The rights and freedoms referred to in Article L.120–2 include the right of privacy which, as noted above, is protected under French law through the Civil Code, and is also guaranteed by the European Convention on Human Rights. The criteria for justification are two-fold: the practice or policy must be relevant to the tasks performed by the employees in question, and must be proportional to the objective underlying the practice or policy. Both aspects of this test leave considerable room for judicial interpretation. As I will show below, however, French courts have been more probing and protective in their workplace privacy analyses than their American counterparts.

---

[22] In recent years, France has been challenged before the Court more than any other country (Dickson (1994), 95).

[23] Art. L.122–35 was added to the Labour Code in 1982, and applies to rules of employment concerning safety, health and discipline (ILO (1993a, 2), 47).

5.3.1 The Right of Privacy under French Law (Civil Code and Article L.120–2)

Although many workplace privacy issues are regulated by specific statutory provisions in France, the generous and comprehensive protection afforded to privacy under Article 9 of the Civil Code ensures that a similarly broad conception of privacy has been incorporated into labour law.[24] Today, Article L.120–2 imports human rights into employment. Even prior to the enactment of this article, however, the courts recognised the importance of the right of privacy in the workplace.[25] This is illustrated by the decision of the Conseil d'Etat in a case predating the enactment of Article L.120–2, *Ministre du Travail* v. *Société Peintures Corona*.[26] There, the defendant employer had instituted a work rule requiring employees to submit to blood testing where the employer suspected alcohol intoxication on the job. A refusal to submit was considered an admission of intoxication, and (like a positive test result) could result in discipline. French law requires such work rules to be submitted to a state-appointed labour inspector for approval (an important procedural aspect of French labour law discussed in section 5.5 below). The inspector is empowered to order the modification or withdrawal of rules which, in his opinion, would be contrary to laws and regulations in force.[27] In this case the inspector concluded that the policy was an improper exercise of managerial prerogative because of its unreasonable impact on the human rights of workers.[28] The Minister of Labour agreed, and the matter was eventually appealed to the Conseil d'Etat. The case was argued on the basis of the general proposition, now enshrined in Article L.120–2, that, while an employer may establish work rules for the health and safety of employees and the public, such rules may not limit the rights of employees unreasonably. The position of the minister, which was ultimately endorsed by the court, was that forcing an individual to submit to blood alcohol testing constitutes a serious violation of bodily integrity, and that testing generally is an affront to human dignity since it forces the subject to serve as a witness against himself. For this reason, an employer may institute such a policy only if there is some necessity for it based on health and safety concerns, and must limit the policy to those employees who perform tasks posing a danger to the health and safety of others.[29] In this case, the employer adopted a rule which permitted it to test all employees regardless of the jobs they performed. The rule was, therefore, over-

---

[24] Buy (1993), para. 31.
[25] In fact, the wording of arts. L.120–2 and L.122–35 was inspired by the decision of the Conseil d'Etat in *Ministre du Travail* v. *Société Peintures Corona* (1980) 6 Dr. Soc. 317 (Savatier (1990a), 55).
[26] *Ibid.*
[27] See Labour Code, Arts. L.122–36 and L.122–37.
[28] The 'right of privacy' is not actually mentioned in *Société Peintures Corona*. The minister argued that 'the rights of the person' were affected, and relied upon principles of bodily integrity and human dignity. This view appears to have been endorsed by the court.
[29] Bacquet (1980), 310.

broad. The court agreed, concluding that only those employees who performed certain tasks implicating health and safety or who operated certain dangerous machinery could be tested.[30]

The decision in *Société Peintures Corona* is notable because it gives effect to a more protective approach than similar American case law concerning employment testing. First, the adoption of a test based on 'necessity' led the court to conclude that only the employer's interest in promoting health and safety would be sufficient to justify an invasive testing policy. An employer's economic interests are not sufficiently substantial to overcome employees' rights. Thus, even where the employer suspects that an employee is intoxicated, he cannot require the employee to submit to testing without a safety or health rationale. Of course, the employer could form a reasonable belief of intoxication through observation and supervision, and then take disciplinary measures. Secondly, a testing policy must be individualised. Before requiring an employee to submit to a test, the employer must have some suspicion that the employee is intoxicated, and must be satisfied that health and safety could be jeopardized. French law therefore prevents widespread privacy invasions through random or universal testing practices.

On the basis of *Société Peintures Corona*, commentators have concluded that employment drug testing would infringe Article L.120–2 unless it were restricted to situations where the employer has reason to doubt the sobriety of a particular employee whose job performance could threaten the health and/or safety of others.[31] This view is reinforced by a 1990 Ministry of Labour circular which advised that drug testing would be illegal save in relation to safety-sensitive jobs, and recommended against all pre-employment drug screening.[32] The fact that such a strict approach applies to all French workplaces stands in stark contrast to the deferential American law on the issue of workplace drug testing.

A similar conclusion could be drawn from the French approach to workplace monitoring. In France, the Cour de Cassation concluded in the *Noecel* case that Article 9 of the Civil Code prohibited surreptitious surveillance of employees through hidden cameras, microphones, etc.[33] As a result, the plaintiff-employee could not be disciplined or dismissed on the basis of evidence obtained through such surveillance. Although the court's reasons were very brief in the case, the Advocate General went into some detail on the implications of secret workplace monitoring. In his view, such monitoring offended the dignity of employees and created a climate of distrust which was contrary to the duties of loyalty and good faith implied into the employment contract.[34] Moreover, even where such monitoring has been implemented for legitimate security purposes, its pervasive

---

[30] *Supra*, n. 25.
[31] Ray and Rojot (1996), 65–6.
[32] Ministry of Labour (France) (1990a). See also *Comptoir Lyon Allemand Louyot SA*, Conseil d'Etat, 8 July 1988, JS 89–512 (1989) 42; *Régie nationale des Usines Renault*, Conseil d'Etat, 9 Oct. 1987, JS 89–498 (1988), 623.
[33] Cass. Soc., 20 Nov. 1991 (RDS 1992(2), 77).
[34] *Ibid.*, 75–7.

nature results in every action or word of employees being monitored regardless of its relevance to matters of security. According to the Advocate General, good intentions could not justify the sweeping intrusions resulting from such surveillance.[35] Such a conclusion once again demonstrates the importance placed on individualisation in French workplace privacy law.

Whereas American law has often proved impotent and uncertain in regulating employer policies and practices which systematically limit the privacy of workers,[36] largely due to its focus on consent, French law has been quite effective in providing clear rules and standards related to testing and monitoring which eliminate the possibility that workers could consent to something less. The relative clarity in French law no doubt contributes to the paucity of disputes and legal decisions concerning testing and monitoring.[37] One area of French law has been controversial, namely employer control of employees' off-duty activities. The basic proposition adopted by the French courts is that 'off-duty' behaviour may constitute grounds for discipline or dismissal if, in light of the employee's job functions and the proper management of the enterprise, the behaviour creates identifiable and serious harm or disorder for the enterprise.[38] For example, a security guard may be dismissed for committing a theft against a client of the employer, as the commission of such a crime is incompatible with continuing employment as a security guard.[39] However, an employee's ownership of a brand of car contrary to the employer's wishes is insufficient.[40] Essentially, the test asserted by the French courts involves 'line-drawing'; an employer cannot discipline or dismiss merely for disapproving of off-duty behaviour, but may do so if that behaviour prevents the employee from performing his job tasks or causes some other serious and identifiable harm to the enterprise. This legal position has been criticised as imprecise, since it involves contextual and fact-specific determinations.[41]

A further complication arises because the French recognise certain 'ideological' enterprises (*'entreprises de tendance'*) which may in limited circumstances assert control over employees' off-duty behaviour which is inconsistent with fundamental beliefs. The case of *Painsecq* v. *Association Fraternité Saint Pie X*[42] demonstrates the difficulties of the line-drawing process where ideological beliefs are concerned, but also affirms that French courts will favour the employee's interest in being free from employer control away from the workplace.[43] The case concerned an employee of the Roman Catholic Church who

---

[35] Cass. Soc., 20 Nov. 1991 (RDS 1992(2), 77), 77.

[36] Finkin (1996b).

[37] Institutional and procedural mechanisms unique to France, discussed *infra*, sect. 5.5, also tend to reduce litigation on workplace privacy issues.

[38] *Painsecq* v. *Association Fraternité Saint Pie X*, Cass. Soc., 17 Apr. 1991 (JCP 1991, G, II, 21724).

[39] *Léger*, Cass. Soc., 20 Nov. 1991 (RDS 1992(2), 25 (Info. Rapides)).

[40] *Rossard* [1992] Dr. Soc. 334 (Cass. Soc.).

[41] Tissot (1995), 229.

[42] *Supra*, n. 38.

[43] Ray and Rojot (1996), 66; Savatier (1991b), 485.

performed certain official functions during Church services. He was dismissed when the employer learned of his homosexuality, which contravened the teachings of the Church. The lower courts split on the legitimacy of the dismissal, with the Cour d'Appel de Paris concluding that ideological enterprises may require that their employees share their beliefs. Hence, the Roman Catholic Church could refuse to employ homosexuals, whose beliefs presumably conflict to some extent with those of the Church. The Cour de Cassation disagreed, holding that an employee's beliefs are private and cannot be the subject of discrimination. An employer may only discipline or dismiss an employee for actions undermining the belief system of the enterprise. The fact that an employee's sexual orientation makes it impossible for him to share his employer's beliefs is insufficient, where there is no evidence that the employee *actively* violated those beliefs or encouraged others in the enterprise to violate them.[44] One might conclude from this that if the employer had introduced evidence that Painsecq was a practising homosexual, then the argument in favour of dismissing him would have been stronger. This issue has not been decided.

An examination of the general foundations of French workplace privacy law, as reflected by testing, monitoring and off-duty conduct cases, indicates that a 'floor of rights' approach is at work. In terms of privacy, French labour law is certainly not deferential in a manner indicative of abstentionist thinking, nor is it driven by market concerns. Instead, the French have sought to establish employment standards of comprehensive application which secure the protection of human rights within employment, and render largely irrelevant the question whether or not employees have consented to invasive management policies (a preoccupation of the corresponding American law). Furthermore, the rigorous scrutiny directed at employer interests advanced to justify privacy-invasive policies, and the emphasis placed on individualisation, both indicate that the right of privacy is taken seriously in French labour law.

5.3.2 The Right of Privacy under the European Convention on Human Rights

An analysis of French workplace privacy law provides an opportunity to consider the state of the law under the European Convention on Human Rights, which guarantees the right to private life in Article 8. The Convention is significant because it has been incorporated into French law, and is therefore a source of the rights and freedoms mentioned in Article L.120–2 of the Labour Code.[45] Because the Convention binds only public authorities, its direct role in French labour law is limited to the public sector (although, as will be discussed in section 7.2.1.1 below, Article 8 may place state signatories under certain limited, positive obligations relevant to private sector relationships). Nevertheless, Convention jurisprudence could be of some assistance in interpreting the right

---

[44] *Supra*, n. 38. See also Bossu (1994), 753–4.
[45] See *Noecel*, *supra*, n. 33.

of privacy under Article L.120–2, since the private interests protected by Article 8 and by the French law of privacy are similar. The Article 8 conception of privacy has been interpreted broadly to include matters falling within personal, territorial and informational zones,[46] as has Article 9 of the French *Civil Code*.

One would expect the European Court of Human Rights' approach to public employment cases under Article 8 to be more deferential than that required by Article L.120–2. Although both Convention rights and the rights guaranteed by Article L.120–2 are subject to limitations assessed under a proportionality balancing test, intrusions upon private life are permissible under the Convention if they are necessary to achieve goals related to national security, public safety, the economic well-being of the country, the prevention of disorder or crime, the protection of health or morals or the protection of the rights and freedoms of others. Article L.120–2, in contrast, explicitly requires rights limitations to be justified in relation to *job-performance* concerns. This limits the scope of action of employers, and precludes them from usurping the role of the state in relation to matters such as law enforcement and public morals.[47] Such a limitation is not clearly placed on public employers in Article 8(2). Furthermore, as noted above, the French courts have been sceptical of economic justifications advanced by employers under Article L.120–2, whereas Article 8(2) explicitly mentions 'economic well-being' as a legitimate basis for state limitations of the right of privacy.

The enforcement of Convention rights is also subject to a 'margin of appreciation'—a deferential principle adopted by the European Court of Human Rights which upholds national standards on social and moral issues where no pan-European consensus has emerged.[48] Because the Convention must apply to 38 states[49] with divergent historical and political experiences, the European Court will tolerate state intrusions upon human rights which fall within a particular range of reasonableness. In contrast, domestic courts are concerned with the impact of their rulings on one state, and may therefore be more comfortable with the application of stricter human rights standards where their own national tradition calls for it. For this reason, it may well be that Article 8 imposes a lower privacy standard than has already been adopted in French law, in which case the Convention is largely superfluous.

There has been only one workplace privacy decision of the European Court of Human Rights, *Halford* v. *United Kingdom*.[50] The case concerned a female police officer who had filed a sex discrimination case against her employer, a UK police authority. She had obtained permission from the employer to use the private telephone line in her office to consult with her lawyer; however, she later learned that the employer had intercepted and recorded her telephone conver-

---

[46]   Feldman (1997), 266–8.
[47]   *Infra*, sect. 7.2.2.1.
[48]   Feldman (1997), 274.
[49]   *Interrights Bulletin* (1997), 3.
[50]   See n. 4, Chap. 1.

sations in order to obtain information for use in defending against the sex discrimination claim. Halford's domestic legal efforts failed because the right of privacy does not exist in UK law, and domestic anti-wiretapping legislation[51] does not apply to employer interception of communications in the workplace. However, she took her case to the European Court of Human Rights, and succeeded under Article 8. The Court awarded her £10,000, reasoning that the intercepted telephone calls were private in nature, and that the employer—a public authority—had invaded Halford's privacy by intercepting the calls.

The decision might seem encouraging for workplace privacy law in Europe, since the Court decided that public employees may assert the right of privacy over telephone conversations, even if the telephone calls are made from the employer's premises, on the employer's time, and using the internal telecommunications system and equipment supplied by the employer. The Court also recognised the legitimacy in the employment context of private interests in information (i.e. the contents of telephone conversations) and territory (i.e. the employee's office and the telephone therein). However, the decision itself is based on a very specific set of facts. Not only was Halford given no warning that her telephone calls might be intercepted, but she had a telephone which was designated for personal use, and had received an assurance from her employer that she could use this telephone for legal consultations related to her sex discrimination case. On this basis, the Court emphasised that Article 8 had been infringed because the Police Authority had failed to warn Halford that her telephone conversations were subject to monitoring. Given this, it seems reasonable to conclude that an employer may act consistently with Article 8 by forbidding its employees from making private calls on company telephones, and/or by warning them that any calls bear a risk of interception. Presumably, the rationale for this is that an employer may dictate the terms where an employee is on and/or using company property, and that employees who continue in employment under such terms have given their implied consent to the employer's monitoring policy.[52]

If this is indeed the thinking behind the Court's decision, then it resembles the American approach based on expectations of privacy. The Court effectively decided that Halford had suffered an infringement of privacy because her employer allowed her to expect privacy, and then surreptitiously invaded it. While this reasoning might be a simple way of dispensing with the case, it nevertheless implies that an employee's expectation of privacy is dependent on how much privacy the employer is willing to tolerate in the workplace. Under this interpretation, Article 8 is available for egregious workplace invasions of privacy, but offers little to address systematic invasions flowing from established employer policies and practices.[53] Although this is a legal breakthrough in the United Kingdom, where the right of privacy did not exist in domestic law when

---

[51] Interception of Communications Act 1985 (UK), ch. 56.
[52] Craig and Oliver (1998), 55–6.
[53] *Ibid.*

the *Halford* case arose, it contributes little to extant French employment law. As noted above, the 'floor of rights' emphasis of French workplace privacy law has encouraged the development of generally applicable privacy *standards* based on human rights principles, as opposed to contextual and fact-specific privacy *expectations* arising from the conduct of the parties and their employment contract.

5.4 SPECIFIC PROVISIONS OF FRENCH LABOUR LAW PROTECTING THE RIGHT OF PRIVACY

In addition to the general human rights protection offered by Article L.120–2 of the Labour Code, a wide range of statutory provisions offer specific protection for the right of privacy in employment. The French anti-discrimination provision, found in Article L.122–45, touches on privacy issues through its prohibition of discrimination based on a person's beliefs, political opinions, union activities and religious convictions.[54] Article L.121–8 requires that 'no personal information concerning an employee may be collected by a method which has not been brought to the knowledge of the employee', thus rendering illegal *Halford*-type secret monitoring activities.[55] Genetic testing is limited by Article 16–10 of the Civil Code to medical and scientific research, and then only with the consent of the subject.[56] As a result, employers may not adopt genetic screening at the hiring stage, nor may they impose genetic monitoring[57] as a condition of employment.

Recent amendments to the French Labour Code have now enhanced the privacy protection available to job applicants. Prior to 1992, job applicants could have recourse to Article 9 of the Civil Code, discussed above, or to the general law of information privacy (discussed in section 5.4.1 below). Moreover, the anti-discrimination guarantee found in Article L.122–45 of the Labour Code protects certain private matters, and is available to candidates and employees equally. However, the rights of job candidates were generally viewed as being no different from the rights of citizens, whereas actual employees enjoyed employment-specific rights.[58] A Report by Lyon-Caen to the French Minister of Labour, entitled *Les libertés publiques et l'emploi*,[59] argued that the process of recruitment was a public concern, and that the rights and freedoms of job can-

---

[54] Art. L.122–45 prohibits an employer from refusing to hire, disciplining or dismissing an employee by reason of his origin, sex, beliefs, ethnicity, nationality, race, political opinions, union activities, religious convictions or (except if declared unfit by a workplace doctor) his health or handicap. The use of anti-discrimination law to protect privacy is discussed *infra*, sect. 6.5.2.2.

[55] See, e.g., the case of 22 May 1995 (Cour de Cassation), where the employer infringed this Art. by hiring a private detective to gather information secretly about the employee (CNIL (1995k), 118).

[56] Law No. 94–653 of 29 July 1994; Terré and Fenouillet (1996), 68.

[57] Genetic screening and monitoring are defined and distinguished *infra*, sect. 9.3.1.

[58] Lyon-Caen (1992b), 56.

[59] *Ibid.*

didates should be incorporated into the Labour Code. This provided the impetus for the Law of 31 December 1992 ('Act concerning recruitment and individual freedoms'), which added several new provisions to the Labour Code offering improved privacy protection for both employees and candidates. These include: (1) Article L.121–6, which stipulates that information demanded from candidates/employees must be relevant to the individual's abilities or professional qualifications, and must be directly and necessarily linked with the job in question or with the evaluation of the individual's qualifications; and (2) Article L.121–7, which stipulates that candidates/employees must be expressly notified in advance of the methods and techniques of evaluation to which they will be subject, the methods and techniques themselves must be relevant to the purpose of the evaluation and the results must remain confidential.[60]

The new provisions of the Labour Code on information gathering and evaluation techniques clearly forbid *surreptitious* practices, guarantee procedural protections like prior notification and consultation and ensure confidentiality. As will be seen below in section 5.4.1.1, on these matters the provisions largely repeat the requirements of the general law governing information privacy, and therefore add little to French workplace privacy law.[61] The employment-specific relevance test is, however, a potentially important development, although the generality of the new articles provides little clear guidance on the substantive meaning of 'relevance'. A Ministry of Labour circular was issued in 1993 which elaborated upon the application of the new provisions.[62] According to the Ministry, information falling within certain subject-headings will generally be irrelevant to legitimate employer concerns: state of health, sex life, housing, occupations of parents and spouse, and leisure activities. The circular also recommends against the use of testing and evaluation practices which lack scientific validity, since they provide little or no relevant information. Astrological charts and certain types of honesty testing were specifically mentioned,[63] although psychological testing is not necessarily outlawed.[64] The full impact of the new Articles will likely be appreciated only after the French courts have had the opportunity to develop a body of jurisprudence.

One aspect of French workplace privacy law merits detailed consideration, namely the general law of information privacy, and its application to employment matters.

---

[60] Although Art. L.121–7 does not explicitly require disclosure of evaluation results to the subject, it is assumed that a right of access is implied into the provision as an exception to the confidentiality requirement (Grinsnir (1993), 238).

[61] Lyon-Caen (1992b), 100, proposed that the jurisprudence surrounding recruitment, as developed within the rubric of the general law of information privacy, should be incorporated into the Labour Code.

[62] Ministry of Labour (France) (1993b).

[63] Tissot (1995), 223–4.

[64] Lyon-Caen (1992b), 95, was dubious of the reliability of psychological tests, and this could be persuasive given that the Law of 31 December 1992 was inspired by his Report.

5.4.1 Information Privacy Law (the Law of 6 January 1978)

5.4.1.1 *The Substantive, Procedural and Institutional Features of the Law*

The objective of the Law of 6 January 1978 is to regulate the collection and automatic processing of personal information in both the public and private sectors.[65] The Law is explicitly a privacy initiative, declaring in Article 1 that information processing *'ne doit porter atteinte ni à l'identité humaine, ni aux droits de l'homme, ni à la vie privée, ni aux libertés individuelles ou publiques'*. To this end, the Law imposes substantive limitations on information-gathering, whether or not it is automated, and on automated processing itself:[66] personal information about a subject may not be collected through illegal, fraudulent or dishonest means (Article 25); a subject has the right to object to the collection of personal information for any 'legitimate reason' (Article 26); information concerning a subject's race, political opinions, philosophical or religious beliefs, or union membership may only be collected or recorded with the express consent of the subject (Article 31)[67]; and decisions taken concerning a subject may not be based solely on a personality profile or assessment prepared by automatic means (Article 2). The 1995 decision of *MM v. SNCF*[68] illustrates the operation of these principles in the workplace context. There, the complainant was a railway ticket vendor who was disciplined for being absent from his post. The unauthorised absence came to the attention of the employer because the computer reservation system had recorded the times when the employee was on and off line. The Cour d'Appel de Paris concluded that the reservation system was subject to the Law of 6 January 1978, and that its use to monitor and control employees' movements constituted an abuse, and contravened the employer's contractual duty of good faith. The fact that employees were not aware that their movements could be recorded by the system, coupled with the fact that the employer based its discipline decision in the case solely on the information obtained from the system, led the court to rule in favour of the employee.

In addition to the substantive protection offered by the Law, several procedural safeguards were also introduced. First, prior notification of information gathering activities is required by the Law (and, as noted above, by Article L.121–8 of the Labour Code), and subjects must be informed of the obligatory or voluntary nature of their participation, the consequences of refusing to participate, the persons who will have access to the information and their own rights of access and rectification (Article 27). Secondly, the Law guarantees to all data subjects the right to access files containing their own personal informa-

---

[65] Law No. 78–17 of 6 Jan. 1978 (Act concerning *'l'Informatique, Fichiers et Libertés'*).

[66] The law applies to the collection, recording, elaboration, modification or destruction of information by automatic means (Art. 5).

[67] There is an exception permitting religious, political and philosophical groups, and unions, to compile membership lists.

[68] Cour d'Appel de Paris, 31 May 1995 (reported in CNIL (1995k), 470).

tion and to rectify errors (Articles 34–40). Thirdly, confidentiality is guaranteed, and information holders are under a duty to implement security measures and other safeguards to ensure that information is not disclosed contrary to the Law (Article 29).

The most important aspect of the Law, and what primarily distinguishes it from the American Privacy Act,[69] is its institutional aspect. The Law established the Commission Nationale de l'Informatique et des Libertés ('CNIL'), which has the power to make recommendations and offer legally-binding opinions on particular information privacy issues.[70] The CNIL has therefore been charged with the task of elaborating upon the general terms and principles of the Law, such as the concept of 'legitimacy' in Article 26, and of explaining the operation of those terms and principles in specific contexts. To this end, the CNIL may issue reports on particular issues of concern, and may adopt regulations ('*normes simplifiées*') to assist in compliance. The CNIL has two other important functions. First, pursuant to Chapter III of the Law, public authorities contemplating *automated* information processing (including automated information collection) must obtain the approval of the CNIL prior to undertaking the processing (Article 15). The Law places a reduced obligation on private bodies, who are merely required to make a declaration concerning the proposed automated processing (Article 16). Failure to make a declaration may result in the award of damages to the affected individuals.[71] In both public and private cases, the party proposing the information processing must disclose to the CNIL matters including: the reasons for the information processing, the manner in which the processing will occur, the persons and entities who will have access to the information, the length of time the information will be stored and the safeguards and other security measures which will be taken to ensure confidentiality (Article 19). This information will be used by the CNIL to determine whether a public body may proceed with its proposal, but even in the case of a private body, the CNIL may pass judgement and reject any proposal. This permits the CNIL to take a proactive role in ensuring adherence to the Law.

Secondly, the CNIL may receive and investigate complaints concerning violations of the Law and determine whether or not the Law has been breached (Article 21). Although individuals may pursue challenges under the Law in the French courts (as occurred in *MM* v. *SNCF*[72]), complaints to the CNIL appear to be more common.[73]

---

[69] *Supra*, sect. 4.3.3.4.

[70] Art. 14. For a description of the broad powers of the CNIL, see: CNIL (1988b); CNIL (1994i).

[71] In the employment context, see *Syndicat CGT, HP, JMS* v. *Société Turbomeca*, Cour de Cassation (7 June 1995).

[72] *Supra*, n. 68. Employees may argue that by breaching the Law, employers have also breached the implied covenant of good faith.

[73] The Annual Reports (*Rapports d'activités*) of the CNIL detail the complaints received each year, the decisions of the CNIL, and any action taken to ensure compliance with the Law.

5.4.1.2   *The Operation of the Law and the Activities of the CNIL in the Workplace Context*

How does this regime operate in the employment context? In fact, workplace privacy was of such importance in the work of the CNIL that a permanent sub-commission was established dealing with '*informatiques et libertés du travail*'.[74] Moreover, each Annual Report of the CNIL contains a section dedicated to '*travail et emploi*', and there have been periodic reports and recommendations on specific workplace privacy issues. Although these do not have legal force, they are considered influential and persuasive.[75] In 1985, for example, the CNIL adopted a recommendation concerning information obtained through employment recruiting,[76] which stated the following basic principles: (1) information collected during recruiting should be strictly related to the requirements of the job (i.e. relevance); (2) questions and responses should be put into writing (i.e. formality); (3) the candidate should be notified of the obligatory or voluntary nature of the information requested, the ways in which the information will be used, and the rights of access and rectification (i.e. prior notification); (4) candidates must be given access to information obtained from any analyses or tests performed, and must have the right to rectify erroneous information (i.e. access and rectification); and (5) information obtained should not be kept on file once the recruiting process has concluded (i.e. finality). The significance of the 1985 recommendation is evinced by the fact that it was one of the bases for the Law of 31 December 1992 concerning recruitment.

In 1988, the Commission had the opportunity to apply these principles to automated psychological testing, in which subjects are required to answer questions posed by a computer, and a personality profile is generated from the responses. It concluded that this form of testing could not be used as the sole basis for excluding individuals from a pool of applicants. However, employers may adopt psychological testing as part of the hiring process if the results are merely one of many factors taken into account in hiring, and applicants are informed of how results are reached (i.e. methods of interpretation) and of their right of access to the results. Moreover, a candidate who has been subjected to an automatic evaluation method must be informed of the employer's reason(s) for rejecting his candidacy.[77] The Commission did not consider in detail the inherent inaccuracies of psychological testing, which would clearly implicate the principle of relevance asserted in the 1985 recommendation, nor did the Commission consider specific questions and whether or not they might constitute illegitimate inquiries into private life. As such, the Commission was primarily concerned with procedural matters, in particular prior notification.

---

[74] Mole (1990), 60.
[75] Lenoir and Wallon (1988), 216.
[76] CNIL (1985a), 133 (Déliberation No. 85–44).
[77] CNIL (1988c), 179–80.

It is useful to compare the CNIL's consideration of psychological testing to the analysis undertaken by the California Court of Appeal in *Soroka v. Dayton Hudson Corp.*, where the defendant employer was required to advance a 'compelling interest' to justify specific questions included in its psychological testing of job candidates.[78] Unlike a court deciding a particular case, the CNIL's approach in its reports has been to raise awareness of privacy-invasive practices and provide guidelines to assist employers in complying with the Law. This may in part explain the emphasis on procedure over substance, as the content of tests may vary considerably from employer to employer, whereas the principles of notification, access, rectification, etc. can apply universally. Of course, an individual or group may file a complaint with the CNIL concerning specific questions asked during the hiring process, and in those cases the analysis has focused as much on the nature of the questions as on procedure. In 1988, for example, the CNIL reported its findings on two complaints concerning recruitment questionnaires. In both cases, the Commission concluded that certain questions contravened the substantive privacy guarantees in the Law, in particular Articles 25, 26 and 31,[79] and therefore could not be asked.

In 1995, the CNIL reported on electronic surveillance in employment,[80] and raised two concerns about the proliferation of computerised monitoring systems in French workplaces: first, that the use of monitoring systems threatened to dehumanise the workplace and, secondly, that employers did not appreciate their legal obligations *vis-à-vis* surveillance technology. To this end, the CNIL has publicised with employers the potential negative impact of electronic monitoring on employee morale and productivity, while emphasising that the principles of transparency and proportionality should guide the development and installation of monitoring systems.[81] Furthermore, the CNIL has sought to make employers aware of their legal duties to register surveillance systems, to comply with the substantive and procedural terms of the Law of 6 January 1978, to provide prior notification of monitoring to employees pursuant to Article L.121–8 of the Labour Code, and to inform and consult with enterprise committees and works councils prior to the introduction of monitoring systems (Article L.432–2 of the Labour Code, discussed in greater detail in section 5.5 below).[82]

In addition to its periodic reports and its investigations of complaints, the CNIL has pronounced on specific workplace privacy issues in two other contexts: first, in its legally binding opinions under Article 15 of the Law and secondly, through the development of '*normes simplifiées*'—principles reflecting

---

[78] Discussed *supra*, see n. 137, Chap. 4, and accompanying text.

[79] CNIL (1988e), 180–6. The CNIL objected to questions concerning memberships of organisations, activities of third parties and personal finances.

[80] CNIL (1995k), 113–19 ('*La surveillance dans les entreprises*'); see also CNIL (1994h), 72–5 ('*Les contrôles sur les lieux de travail*').

[81] *Ibid.*, 118–19.

[82] *Ibid.*, 115.

the CNIL's interpretation of the Law in particular contexts.[83] In the former case, it is important to reiterate that only automated information systems are subject to the disclosure requirements of Articles 15 and 16, although the Commission has the mandate to oversee all forms of information collection. A variety of specific information systems have been considered by the CNIL, and have been the subject of legally binding opinions. Recent examples include: electronic recruiting systems containing information which employers can access to search for a suitable employee,[84] electronic voting systems for electing representatives to works councils[85] and automated systems for issuing pay cheques.[86] In each case, the CNIL pronounced upon the legality of the system by considering its purpose, the nature of the personal information required by the system, the procedural protections offered to subjects and security and other measures implemented to ensure confidentiality.

The CNIL's treatment of access control systems illustrates its generally rigorous approach to workplace privacy. In 1986, the CNIL issued an opinion concerning a proposal from Electricité de France to install an automatic access system using magnetic cards in its nuclear power facilities.[87] The system permitted the employer to limit employees' access to certain areas, and to monitor and record the movements of individual employees. The CNIL ultimately endorsed the proposal, emphasising certain limiting factors which ensured compliance with the Law. First, the access control system at issue distinguished between highly sensitive sites (such as a nuclear reactor) and administrative areas, and applied different levels of monitoring. In sensitive areas, security and safety concerns justified an exceptional system to monitor and record each individual employee's movements. In other areas, where individual monitoring could not be justified by safety concerns but the employer still had a security interest in preventing theft, the system merely limited access to employees with appropriate access cards, but did not record individual movements. This effectively limited the privacy-invasive potential of the proposal—only employees working in high-risk areas were subject to pervasive monitoring. Secondly, the principle of finality was respected, as information would be retained for only one month. Thirdly, the procedural requirements of the Law were respected, with employees being notified of the details of the new system, and of their rights to access and rectify information recorded by the system.[88] In essence, the CNIL endorsed the plan because it was premised on a substantial employer

---

[83] *'Normes simplifiées'* are typically asserted following an opinion (or several opinions) on a particular issue, and state the basic principles applied by the Commission. They are more specific than the Commission's reports. Note that they are 'restrictive', but not 'prescriptive'; their purpose is to limit certain information processing practices, but not to indicate which practices should be undertaken (CNIL (1993g), 326, citing Conseil d'Etat, 12 Mar. 1982: *'le contenu d'une norme devait être limitatif et non pas indicatif'*).

[84] CNIL (1996l), 353–5 (Déliberation Nos. 96–107, 96–108).

[85] *Ibid.*, 347 (Déliberation No. 96–016).

[86] CNIL (1994h), 378 (Déliberation No. 94–098).

[87] CNIL (1986c), 307 (Déliberation No. 86–054).

[88] The CNIL's conclusions are discussed in detail in Lenoir and Wallon (1988), 225–7.

objective, was individualised to minimise limitations on worker privacy, and incorporated effective procedural protections.

The '*normes simplifiées*' developed by the CNIL have also assisted employers in conforming to the requirements of the Law. Before 1994, the primary workplace issue giving rise to '*normes simplifiées*' was automated systems for the payment of wages.[89] However, in 1994, the CNIL issued its most significant workplace privacy '*norme*', as it declared the principles which should govern workplace telephone accounting (i.e. call detail) systems.[90] Unlike the OMB's call detail guidelines,[91] the CNIL's *norme simplifiée* No. 40 addresses a full range of privacy issues in detail, providing clear guidance to employers to ensure that their telephone accounting systems comply with the Law. Hence:

(1) Legitimate objective: a telephone accounting system will be permissible under the Law only if its purpose is administrative, relating to matters such as billing or reimbursing employees for calls, or compiling general statistics (Article 2);

(2) Limitations on information collected: only the following information may be collected: the identity of a particular caller, the caller's position with the firm, and the basic details of the call (the number called, its nature (i.e. local, long distance, etc.), its time and duration, and its cost) (Article 3);

(3) Finality: the information may be kept on file for no longer than two billing periods of France Telecom (Article 4);

(4) Confidentiality: (i) when a list of telephone calls is circulated, the last four digits of each number should be removed, and only employees in accounts and personnel departments (and certain other specified managers) should have access to all the information recorded by the system (Article 5); and (ii) employers must implement security and other safeguards to ensure confidentiality (Article 7); and

(5) Prior notification: employers must consult with employees and fully apprise them of the operation of a system prior to its installation (Article 8).

Interestingly, the CNIL also requires that all employers make available a telephone line unconnected to the accounting system, so that employees may exercise their rights and freedoms (particularly, their rights related to collective representation) (Article 6).

---

[89] CNIL (1985a) (Déliberation No. 85–38 (1985), *Norme simplifiée* No. 28 (concerning information about pay for private sector employees)); CNIL (1993g) (Déliberation No. 93–020 (1993), *Norme simplifiée* No. 36 (concerning systems for the payment of wages to state and other public employees)). *Norme simplifiée* No. 36 abrogated several earlier normes on the issue of pay: *Norme simplifiée* No. 1 (1980); *Norme simplifiée* No. 3 (1980); *Norme simplifiée* No. 5 (1980).

[90] CNIL (1994h), 75–81 (Déliberations Nos. 94–112 & 94–113 (1994); *Normes simplifiées* Nos. 39 and 40).

[91] *Supra*, sect. 4.3.3.4.

5.4.1.3 Conclusion

I have demonstrated through the above analysis that the Law of 6 January 1978 provides the CNIL with jurisdiction over all information-gathering practices of public and private sector employers. Through its reports, opinions, determinations of complaints, and '*normes simplifiées*', the CNIL has elaborated upon the Law, and developed a comprehensive body of workplace privacy jurisprudence. The fact that the Law applies in both the public and private sectors, and protects job candidates and employees, gives it comprehensive application. One caveat to this conclusion is the fact that only public sector actors are required to seek the approval of the CNIL prior to implementing automated information processing systems. Even in legal systems emphasising human rights values, like that of France, it would seem that the public/private distinction endures. Nevertheless, in applying the Law, the CNIL has not adopted deferential principles for private sector matters, for situations concerning job candidates or for the employment context generally (all of which have emerged in American law). In fact, the CNIL has been remarkably consistent in its approach to information gathering and automated information processing. Not surprisingly, the principles which have characterised the general law of workplace privacy have emerged in the CNIL's own jurisprudence. Therefore, a rigorous analysis of the objectives underlying information-gathering has been applied, and individualisation has been a paramount consideration. The CNIL has also focused on procedural protection, to the point where procedural issues have sometimes overshadowed substantive concerns.

5.5 Institutional and Procedural Features Unique to French Law

As will be evident to this point, French workplace privacy law differs markedly from its American equivalent, as it provides a relatively coherent and comprehensive 'floor' of privacy for candidates/employees in both the public and private sectors. Many of the substantive and procedural protections available to French candidates/employees are simply not present in American labour law. At the institutional level as well, French labour law is distinct.

In the United States, as in France, collective representation through unions has some potential to protect privacy in the workplace, since it is possible for unions to negotiate terms in collective agreements protecting privacy. In the USA, in fact, matters affecting work conditions, such as drug-testing practices, are compulsory subjects for collective bargaining.[92] In practice, because of the decline and weakness of the union movement in the United States, a much smaller percentage of employees have recourse to collective mechanisms for

---

[92] *Johnson-Bateman Co.* v. *International Association of Machinists, Local 1047*, 295 NLRB 26 (1989).

resolving privacy-related concerns than in France.[93] Moreover, unlike in France, American law fails to provide a coherent 'floor' of principles to buttress collective bargaining on privacy issues. Hence, an American employer may adopt an initial bargaining position which would be highly destructive of employee privacy (yet perfectly legal if implemented), and then hold firm, or bargain to some middle ground offering mediocre protection. The range of legal results in collective bargaining over privacy matters is clearly much narrower in France than in the United States and, in some cases, there is simply no room to bargain because French law is so prescriptive. French unions are therefore rarely presented with the dilemma of sacrificing privacy protection in exchange for economic concessions, since they may always rely on the legislated 'floor of rights' for workers. In fact, if they wish, they may focus their efforts on securing protection beyond that guaranteed by law.[94]

A further crucial feature of French labour law is the role played by elected workers' representatives and works councils in protecting worker privacy. Neither of these institutions has an equivalent in American or Canadian labour law. They exist independent of unions, ensuring that workers in firms with 11 or more employees have a collective voice in a whole range of matters affecting working conditions and the rights of workers.[95] In the case of firms with 11–50 employees, Article L.422–1–1 provides that a workers' representative may bring forward complaints to the employer related to matters affecting individual rights and freedoms. The employer is required to investigate the matter along with the representative, and propose a solution. The representative is empowered to take court action if dissatisfied with the employer's proposed course of action.

Where a works council is in place (generally because the firm has 50 or more employees), then Article L.432–1 stipulates that the employer must inform and consult the works council on questions concerning the organisation, administration and operation of the enterprise and, in particular, on questions concerning the conditions of employment, of work and of professional development. Where the employer wishes to introduce a new work rule, Article L.122–36 stipulates that the employer must first submit it to the works council for an opinion.[96] Under amendments to the Labour Code introduced in 1992,[97] works councils became a pivotal aspect of French workplace privacy law. New provisions were added that require employers to inform and consult with works councils prior to the introduction of new technologies in the workplace (Article

---

[93] See n. 54, Chap. 3.

[94] Lyon Caen (1993c), 6–7.

[95] Art. L.431–4 states that the purpose of a works council is to ensure collective expression by employees, permitting their interests to be taken into account in decisions relating to the economic and financial administration of the enterprise.

[96] Art. L.122–36 adds that if there is no works council (because the entity has fewer than 50 employees), then the proposed rule must be submitted to the workers' representatives for an opinion.

[97] Law No. 92–1446 of 31 Dec. 1992 ('Act concerning recruitment and individual freedoms').

L.432–2) or of any methods or techniques permitting the employer to control the activities of employees (Article L.432–2–1), and to inform works councils of all methods and techniques of recruitment prior to their utilisation, or of any automated information processing system prior to its installation (Article L.432–2–1). Prior to these amendments, the Law of 6 January 1978 was often ignored by small and medium-sized enterprises, but the direct involvement of works councils has heightened private sector compliance.[98]

I must emphasise that French law does not grant a right of co-determination to works councils. The rights are to be informed of employer proposals, and in some cases to be consulted or to provide an opinion. In the case of consultation, the works council must be permitted to respond to the proposal and have some input, although the employer does not have to accommodate any concerns which have been raised. Nevertheless, the rights to be informed and consulted constitute an important procedural step in the implementation of a privacy-invasive policy. Not only does the employer have the benefit of its employees' perspective(s), but the input of the works council could assist in avoiding later legal disputes by reminding the employer of its legal obligations related to the right of privacy or by suggesting privacy-sensitive alternatives. The fact that French law requires employers to involve employees prior to the adoption of privacy-invasive policies, practices and technologies explains in part the relative rarity of workplace privacy litigation (at least in comparison to the United States).

The French emphasis on procedural safeguards to ensure that substantive rights are respected is further exemplified by two matters I have already touched upon in the discussion above. First, French labour law requires employers to obtain the approval of a state-appointed labour inspector for all work rules. The inspector may then assess those rules according to the laws and regulations in force, and if necessary, order their modification or withdrawal.[99] As the case of *Société Peintures Corona*[100] illustrates, an employer who disputes the inspector's interpretation of the law may be challenged in court by the French Ministry of Labour. Secondly, as I noted above, the Law of 6 January 1978 requires employers to register automated information processing systems with the CNIL, and public sector employers must have the approval of the CNIL before adopting the proposed system (Articles 15 and 16). This registration process assists the CNIL in enforcing the Law.

Under French law, an employer contemplating the installation of a system of workplace electronic monitoring to enforce a work rule could be required to negotiate with its union over the system, inform and consult its works council about the system, seek approval for the work rule and the associated system from the labour inspector, and register the system with the CNIL. A public employer must also have the approval of the CNIL prior to proceeding. At each

---

[98] Ray and Rojot (1996), 71.
[99] Arts. L.122–36 and L.122–37.
[100] *Supra*, n. 25; sect. 5.3.1.

of these steps, the opportunity exists for the interests of employees to be taken into account, particularly with regard to their substantive legal rights. This procedural regime contrasts starkly with the American situation, where a non-unionised employer may unilaterally adopt a privacy-invasive policy or practice, and is under no obligation to consider the interests of employees in advance of the adoption.

5.6   CONCLUSIONS

My discussion herein of French workplace privacy law has revealed an elaborate structure of employment rights flowing from the Civil Code, the Labour Code and the general law of information privacy. In substantive, procedural and institutional respects, French workplace privacy law is more coherent, comprehensive and protective than its American counterpart. This is a product of the interventionist tendencies of French political and legal culture, which stand in contrast to the abstentionist and market-oriented foundations of the American labour law system. Of course, not all American jurisdictions pale in comparison to France on the subject of workplace privacy. California's constitutional right of privacy, available to both public and private sector employees and job candidates, flows from a more interventionist conception of the state's role in regulating the employment relationship, and is therefore analogous to the view animating French labour law. Nevertheless, whereas France has erected a 'floor' of privacy protection for all candidates/employees, the state of American law is best described as a complicated, internally inconsistent 'checquerboard'.

The predominant features of French workplace privacy law may be summarised as follows: private interests in the personal, territorial and informational zones are all protected; the law is comprehensive, as it treats the public and private sectors similarly, and in recent times has been amended to ensure that the privacy of job candidates is respected; employers are required to have legitimate and substantial objectives before engaging in invasive practices; invasive practices must be individualised to ensure that they apply only where the stated objective makes it necessary to limit privacy; and there has been an emphasis on procedural rights such as prior notification, access, rectification and finality.

French privacy law has been criticised in the past for its 'preoccupation with grandiose principles and rhetoric to the neglect of effective implementation'.[101] Indeed, some commentators have expressed the concern that while French human rights law aspires to lofty goals, it is undermined by compliance problems and insufficient enforcement.[102] These are serious matters which extend beyond the discussion herein of the substantive content of French workplace

---

[101] Flaherty (1985), 165.
[102] See Besner (1995), 402; Tissot (1995), 226.

privacy law. Nevertheless, it is important to differentiate between the law 'in principle', and the practical impact of the law. One suspects that American workers may not necessarily enjoy the full extent of legal protection provided by law, particularly since enforcement in the United States will often depend on individual workers asserting privacy claims in court—a costly, time-consuming proposition with potential adverse effects on future employability. Of course, organised workers will have other outlets to pursue their grievances, but they amount to only a small minority of the American workforce. If the true impact of French workplace privacy law is to be judged by its enforceability, then the institutional mechanisms discussed above are clearly important. Workers' representatives, works councils, labour inspectors and the CNIL all exist separate and apart from the judicial system and unions. Each of these institutions serves as a potential vehicle for considering and resolving employee concerns related to privacy, and each ensures that French privacy law is implemented and enforced in the workplace. The true advantage of French workers may flow from the institutions empowered to protect their rights. After all, one could envisage American labour law evolving to provide similar substantive and procedural protections for the right of privacy (in certain respects, it already does), but it is difficult to imagine an American labour law system with works councils, labour inspectors and a state-appointed commissioner mandated to safeguard information privacy in employment. The same could be said of the Canadian labour law system, which is the subject of my next chapter, Chapter 6.

6

Privacy in the Workplace in Canada

6.1 INTRODUCTION

The structure of Canadian labour and employment law is similar to that of the United States, although the unique nature of Canadian federalism complicates matters. While the American federal government has a broad and paramount jurisdiction to regulate the employment relationship, thus making possible a *National* Labour Relations Act[1] and national human rights legislation (including the potential for a national workplace privacy law), the Canadian Constitution provides that the federal and provincial governments may exclusively regulate employment relationships existing within their own borders or jurisdictions.[2] It is not essential for my purposes to address the complex issues emerging from this constitutional situation; it is sufficient merely to observe that there are 11 labour relations statutes (ten provincial and one federal) in Canada, and a similar number of human rights codes, employment standards laws, etc. It is therefore not possible to envisage the emergence of a single Canadian regime governing workplace privacy issues, as has occurred in France, or as would be constitutionally permissible in the United States. In fact, the discussion below will reveal that there are important differences in the approaches to privacy in the workplace in the Canadian jurisdictions. At the same time, I will demonstrate that Canadian law (with the exception of the law in Quebec) is considerably less developed on the issue of workplace privacy than its American equivalent, despite the fact that the labour law systems of the two countries are essentially the same. Both the American and Canadian regimes pale in comparison to that of France, however.

In considering the values underlying Canadian labour law, one must first have regard to the political, social, and economic similarities between Canada and the United States, and the predominant influence of the American labour system in the development of Canadian law.[3] An emphasis on freedom of contract, and a general view of employment as a private matter have given rise in the two nations to an abstentionist approach to regulating the employment relationship. Moreover, the judicial attitude to the interests of workers has historically been sceptical, and even antagonistic, in both countries.[4] Given the links between Canada and the United States, it is hardly surprising that similar legal solutions

---

[1] See n. 49, Chap. 3.
[2] Arthurs *et al.* (1993), 11–12.
[3] *Ibid.*, 30.
[4] Weiler (1990b), 120, 161–2.

would be adopted to address matters of industrial justice and industrial stability. Hence, the regimes governing collective labour law (certification of bargaining units, collective bargaining, strikes, etc.) are practically identical. It is noteworthy, however, that a full decade passed between the enactment of the first American labour relations statute in 1933[5] and the first Canadian equivalent, that of Ontario, in 1943.[6] A common theme in Canadian labour and employment law has been that developments tend to lag behind, yet ultimately mirror, those in the United States. This can be seen in the evolution of employment law over the past two decades. Whereas the United States has experienced a notable expansion in state and federal initiatives regulating the individual employment relationship, this same trend is only now becoming apparent in Canada. Historically, Canadian legislators and scholars have focused on collective labour law,[7] with the result that Canadian labour law reflects collective *laissez-faire* thinking, and remains more reliant on collective action than legislation to protect workers' interests. The fact that workplace privacy law is poorly developed in Canada, yet is a growth area in the United States, typifies the general trend in legal reform in the two countries—the United States has been the leader, and Canada the follower.

One factor which may account for much of the difference in approach between the United States and Canada to individual employment law lies in the differing human rights traditions of the two countries. As I noted in section 4.3.1 of Chapter 4, the United States has historically been a rights-conscious society in which the individual values underlying the Bill of Rights, such as dignity and autonomy, have had a significant impact on legal reform. Canada, on the other hand, acquired its constitutional Charter of Rights and Freedoms only in 1982. The rights guaranteed by the Charter, and the values underlying them, can be expected to influence legal developments in the future. However, the essential character of Canadian legal culture was neither rights-conscious nor individualistic prior to 1982. Judicial and legislative initiatives to protect individual workers, and particularly their human rights interests, were unlikely to arise in the absence of a constitutional human rights foundation and an established tradition of respect for individual rights.

Now that the essential human rights tradition is emerging in Canada, there is reason to believe that the potential for protective employment law initiatives is actually greater than in the United States. The influence of market-based thinking has been an important brake on American legal reform in the employment field. However, 'pure market libertarianism', or market individualism, has never been seriously embraced by Canadian legislators, judges and legal scholars.[8] As a result, the influence of *laissez-faire*/freedom-of-contract thinking on employment law is more a matter of legal history than ideology in Canada

---

[5] This legislation is commonly referred to as the Wagner Act.
[6] Arthurs *et al.* (1993), 42.
[7] *Ibid.*, 30.
[8] Weiler (1990b), 132–3.

today. In his examination of Canadian labour law in the post-Charter era, Weiler concluded that a 'pragmatic' approach was emerging, in which neither judges nor legislators were inherently hostile to the interests of workers.[9] Given this, the Canadian political and legal systems may be increasingly open to worker protection initiatives, and particularly ones which are consistent with the value system underlying the Charter.

A further difference between the Canadian and American labour law systems flows from Quebec's unique status as a predominantly French-speaking, civil law jurisdiction within Canada. Although I will say more about Quebec below in section 6.5.3, it is important to note that Quebec's human rights and employment laws are generally more protective than those of other North American jurisdictions. This reflects the emphasis on individual rights and obligations underlying civil law, and also the influence within Quebec of French law (which, as I discussed above in Chapter 5, is substantially more protective than American law). Because of Quebec's importance as a legal jurisdiction within Canada, its innovative approaches to privacy matters may influence the development of the law elsewhere in the country.

In short, the general inadequacy of extant Canadian workplace privacy law, along with the emerging pragmatic approach to Canadian labour law in the post-Charter era, make a comparative analysis with the better-developed American and French regimes highly relevant to future Canadian legal reform. Legislators and judges can be expected to look to historically influential foreign jurisdictions, like the United States and France, in fashioning future legal reforms.

6.2 BACKGROUND—CANADIAN EMPLOYMENT LAW

Like American employment law, Canadian law adheres to the employment-at-will doctrine, with one important modification—the law implies into every employment contract a term requiring an employer to give 'reasonable notice' to an employee prior to dismissal without cause. In practice, an employer is able to dismiss an employee immediately, by paying the employee a lump sum equivalent to the salary for the notice period. An employer may also dismiss an employee for cause immediately without notice. Where an employee alleges wrongful dismissal, the essence of the complaint is not that the employer acted unreasonably or unfairly, but rather that he failed to provide the employee with adequate notice. In fact, Canadian common and civil law impose no duty of fairness or reasonableness on employers at all, although employees owe their employers a duty of trust, confidence and good faith.[10] This anomalous situation, surely a product of an historical systemic bias against worker interests, has been the subject of considerable criticism since it permits employers 'to

---

[9] *Ibid.*, 158–9.

[10] Ball (1994), 570; *Wallace* v. *United Grain Growers Ltd.* [1997] 3 SCR 701, at 735.

terminate at will with caprice and malice, as long as they provide reasonable notice'.[11] The determination of what constitutes reasonable notice is based on matters such as the nature of the job and the employee's length of service; the employer's reasons for dismissing are irrelevant to the analysis, and punitive damages against the employer for arbitrary or unfair dismissal are virtually never awarded.[12] Because Canadian law emphasises reasonable *notice*, as opposed to reasonable *dismissal*, the contract law doctrine of implied good faith and the tort doctrine of dismissal in contravention of public policy have not emerged in the law. As noted in section 4.3.4.1 of Chapter 4, these are two of the most significant doctrinal aspects of workplace privacy law in the United States.

It is important to note, however, that Canadian employers subject to collective agreements are invariably under a duty to act reasonably and in good faith, and arbitral decisions interpreting this duty are a prime source of workplace privacy jurisprudence in Canada. Moreover, three jurisdictions—the federal government, Quebec and Nova Scotia[13]—have statutorily imposed a 'just cause' requirement for dismissal. This modification of the prevailing 'reasonable notice' regime is significant because it tends to transpose the principles developed in the arbitration context into general employment adjudication.[14]

6.3 THE RIGHT OF PRIVACY IN CANADA

As noted in earlier chapters, the right of privacy emerged in American law in the *Pavesich*[15] decision of 1905, and was recognised by French law in the mid-nineteenth century.[16] The right did not appear in Canadian law until 1957, when invasion of privacy was recognised as a general delict under the Quebec Civil Code.[17] Since that time, the right of privacy has been codified in both Quebec's Charter of Human Rights and Freedoms[18] and the Province's Civil Code.[19]

---

[11] Ball (1994), 570; *Wallace* v. *United Grain Growers Ltd.* [1997] 3 SCR 572; Christie *et al.* (1993), 4.

[12] Ball (1994), 574–5. Courts may take into account an employer's conduct in dismissing an employee, and thereby extend the 'reasonable' notice period in a quasi-punitive manner (*Wallace*, *supra*, n. 10, at 737–48).

[13] Canada Labour Code, see n. 48, Chap. 3, ss. 240–6 (just cause dismissal after one year of service); Labour Standards Act (Quebec), RSQ 1977. N–1.1, s. 124, as am. SQ 1990, c. 73, s. 59 (just cause dismissal after two years of service); Labour Standards Code (Nova Scotia), RSNS 1989, c. 246, s. 71 (just cause dismissal after 10 years of service).

[14] England (1982a), 21. See discussion, n. 84, Chap. 6.

[15] See n. 33, Chap. 4.

[16] *Supra*, sect. 5.2.

[17] *Robbins* v. *CBC*, see n. 53, Chap. 2, decided under Art. 1053 of the Civil Code of Lower Canada. The history of privacy law in Quebec is canvassed by Justice Biron in *Aubry* v. *Duclos* (1996), 141 DLR (4th) 683 (Que. CA), 688–91. For a general discussion of privacy in Canada, see Craig and Nolte (1998), 166–9.

[18] See n. 53, Chap. 2. Art. 5 guarantees to everyone 'the right to respect for his private life'.

[19] See n. 53, Chap. 2. Art. 3 states that 'Every person is the holder of personality rights, such as the right to life, the right to the inviolability of his person, and the right to respect of his name, reputation and privacy. These rights are inalienable.'

Quebec's lead in protecting personal privacy has been followed by British Columbia, Manitoba, Newfoundland and Saskatchewan, all of which have enacted privacy statutes declaring invasion of privacy to be a tort.[20] However, invasion of privacy has neither been generally accepted nor rejected as a tort in the Canadian common law.[21] This means that in the five provinces without privacy legislation, including Ontario and Alberta (accounting for approximately half of Canada's population), the status of the right of privacy remains uncertain.

The enactment of the Charter of Rights and Freedoms in 1982 fundamentally changed the Canadian legal landscape in relation to privacy law. Although the right of privacy is not explicitly guaranteed by the Charter, the Supreme Court of Canada construed the right against unreasonable search and seizure guaranteed by section 8 as a broad privacy right, which protected citizens' personal, territorial, and informational private interests from state intrusion. The Court further declared, in light of section 8, that 'privacy is at the heart of liberty in a modern state', 'is essential for the well-being of the individual', and 'has profound significance for the social order'.[22] Privacy thus emerged as a fundamental right and value of Canadian society—a highly significant development since the Supreme Court has declared that the Canadian common law should be developed in a manner consistent with Charter rights and values.[23] To this end, courts in Ontario have indicated that the right of privacy may be an aspect of the common law in the Province,[24] perhaps foreshadowing the eventual judicial recognition of a privacy tort.[25]

The Charter's impact on privacy law in the Canadian public sector has also been significant. Since the enactment of the Charter and the judicial recognition of the right of privacy as an aspect of section 8, the federal government and all but one of the Provinces have enacted privacy legislation governing the collection and processing of personal information by public actors and guaranteeing to citizens a right to access that information.[26] The Province of Quebec has gone

---

[20] See n. 56, Chap. 2.

[21] Craig (1997a), 362–9.

[22] *R.* v. *Dyment*, see n. 66, Chap. 2, 427–8.

[23] *RWDSU* v. *Dolphin Delivery* [1986] 2 SCR 573, 603; *R.* v. *Salituro* [1991] 3 SCR 654, 666–8; *Hill* v. *Church of Scientology* [1995] 2 SCR 1130, 1169.

[24] See *Roth* v. *Roth* (1991), 9 CCLT 141 (Ont. CJ (Gen. Div.)); *Mackay* v. *Buelow* (unreported, 24 Mar. 1995, Ont. CJ (Gen. Div.)); *Gray* v. *Filliter* (unreported, 28 July 1995, Ont. CJ (Gen. Div.)).

[25] Craig (1997a), 370–5.

[26] PCC (1994–5e), 22–3. Only Prince Edward Island, the smallest Province, has yet to legislate. See: Privacy Act, RSC 1985, c. P–21 (federal); Freedom of Information and Protection of Privacy Act, SA 1994, c. F–18.5 (Alberta); Freedom of Information and Protection of Privacy Act (British Columbia), SBC 1992, c. 61, as am.; Freedom of Information Act, SM 1985–6, c. 6 (c. F175) (Manitoba); Right to Information Act, RSNB 1978, c. R–10.3, as am. (New Brunswick); Freedom of Information and Protection of Privacy Act, SNS 1993, c. 5 (Nova Scotia); Freedom of Information and Protection of Individual Privacy Act, RSO 1990, c. F–31 (Ontario); Freedom of Information and Protection of Privacy Act, RSS 1992, c. F–22.01 (Saskatchewan).

further, legislating with respect to both the public and private sectors.[27] This legislation has relevance to the employment context, and I will discuss it in section 6.5.3.2 below.

The relatively recent emergence of the right of privacy in Canadian public and private law has meant that a full and comprehensive theory concerning its application generally, and in particular contexts like employment, has not yet developed. Canadian workplace privacy law is still at an embryonic stage, as evinced by the fact that the seminal textbook on Canadian employment law does not consider the right of privacy as a distinct issue.[28]

6.4 WORKPLACE PRIVACY PROTECTION IN THE PUBLIC SECTOR WORKPLACE

Public sector employees and job candidates in Canada, like their counterparts in the United States, have a significant advantage in the area of workplace privacy because they may assert the constitutional right of privacy directly against an employer. Moreover, government employees are more likely to be unionised, and thereby to benefit from limitations on employer actions flowing from collective agreements. A further advantage accrues to federal public sector candidates/employees, and the great majority of their provincial counterparts, since they may assert a statutory right of privacy in relation to personal information collected, held and processed by governmental bodies in their capacity as employers. The Canadian federal legislation has been particularly important, and I will discuss it in section 6.4.2 below.

6.4.1 Workplace Privacy under Section 8 of the Charter

There has been only one reported workplace privacy decision in which section 8 of the Charter was argued directly. In *Canadian Union of Postal Workers, Calgary Local 710* v. *Canada Post Corp.*,[29] the employer (a Crown corporation subject to the Charter) imposed upon employees a rule permitting searches of items brought into or out of postal sorting plants, lockers inside plants and automobiles owned by the employer (but not employees' own vehicles). Employees who refused to submit to searches were subject to discipline up to and including dismissal. The employer justified the plan by pointing to what it considered a chronic problem of theft and tampering—in the year preceding the implementation of the plan, 21,369 pieces of mail were either stolen, intentionally damaged or opened, resulting in compensation paid to customers of approximately

---

[27] Act Respecting Access to Public Records and the Protection of Personal Information, SQ 1982, c. A–2, as am.; Act Respecting the Protection of Personal Information in the Private Sector, SQ 1993, c. 17.

[28] Christie *et al.* (1993).

[29] (1987), 84 AR 315 (QB).

Cdn$2 million. In considering the constitutionality of the plan, Justice Dixon observed that it was irrelevant whether or not the plan was permitted under the parties' collective agreement; it would still be illegal if it were unreasonable within the meaning of section 8 of the Charter.[30] Justice Dixon then considered the plan's reasonableness. To this end, he remarked that the determination should be made 'in the context of the business relationship or setting that exists between (the employer) and its individual employees'.[31] His analysis then focused on the 'reasonable expectations' of postal employees. In essence, he concluded that employees could not reasonably expect to assert privacy against the employer's search policy because the problems of theft and tampering were significant, and both the employer's interest in limiting losses and the public's interest in the integrity of the mail justified a response.[32] This analysis is reminiscent of the one adopted by the United States Supreme Court in *Von Raab*, where the majority similarly downgraded the employees' expectations of privacy because of a substantial employer interest, while avoiding a rigorous analysis of the private interests at stake.[33] The most deficient aspect of Justice Dixon's approach, however, is his failure to consider alternatives which could have individualised the plan, and thereby limited its impact on worker privacy. The union favoured a reasonable suspicion requirement in advance of a search, but this was not seriously considered by Justice Dixon. Moreover, it is unclear why the employer would have a legitimate interest in searching employees' possessions upon entry *into* the plant—this matter was also not addressed in the judgment.

The decision in *Calgary Local 710* is consistent with the prevailing American approach, itself underlined by deference to employer interests and a general failure to consider less intrusive alternatives. It is somewhat ironic that unionised Canadian employees have fared better in asserting the constitutional right of privacy *indirectly* in the arbitration context. I will consider this aspect of Canadian workplace privacy law in section 6.5.1 below with regard to the private sector.

6.4.2 Information Privacy Law

As I noted above, all but one of the Canadian jurisdictions have enacted information privacy legislation providing access to public records, and placing controls on the collection and processing of personal information by the state. This legislation is important in the workplace privacy context, since public sector candidates/employees may assert the right of privacy in response to information-gathering activities of public employers, and may demand access to

---

[30] *Ibid.*, 319.
[31] *Ibid.*
[32] *Ibid.*
[33] *Supra*, sect. 4.3.3.2, text accompanying nn. 59–74, Chap. 4.

existing personnel records for the purposes of verification and correction. It is not possible to examine each provincial law in detail herein. However, the federal Privacy Act[34] is representative of the other laws, and will be my focus here.

The Privacy Act, introduced in 1983, regulates the collection, processing, retention, disclosure and disposal of 'personal information', defined to include any information capable of identifying an individual, such as information relating to race, national or ethnic origin, colour, religion, age, marital status, education, health, employment history, finances, address, fingerprints and blood type (section 3). The Act is therefore broader than some of its European equivalents, which are concerned primarily with 'automated' (i.e. computerised) collection and processing of data.[35]

The Act places governmental institutions under a series of duties which may be summarised as follows:

(1) A duty to collect personal information only if it relates directly to an operating programme or activity of the institution (section 4);
(2) A duty to collect personal information, where possible, from the individual concerned (section 5);
(3) A duty to retain personal information for a period of time sufficient to ensure that subjects may exercise their right of access (section 6);
(4) A duty to ensure that personal information is as accurate, up-to-date, and complete as possible (section 6);
(5) A duty to use personal information in only three circumstances: (i) with the consent of the individual concerned; (ii) for a purpose for which the information was obtained or compiled by the institution; or (iii) for a purpose permitted by regulation (section 7);
(6) A duty not to disclose personal information to third parties except with the consent of the individual concerned, or in limited circumstances such as where the head of the institution is of the opinion that the public interest in disclosure outweighs any invasion of privacy which could result from the disclosure (section 8).

The Act also confers upon all individuals (including candidates/employees in the federal public service) the rights of access and rectification in relation to personal information concerning them (section 12).

Like France's Law of 6 January 1978, but unlike the equivalent American legislation, the Act establishes an agency with a broad mandate to enforce the leg-

---

[34] *Supra*, n. 26.
[35] Flaherty (1989), 257; see, e.g., the United Kingdom's Data Protection Act, 1984, see n. 5, Chap. 1, discussed *infra*, sect. 10.4. The French Law of 6 Jan. 1978, discussed *supra*, sect. 5.4.1, is also concerned with all information gathering and processing activities, but has a special registration regime for automated processing. Note that as a result of the European Directive on Data Protection, see n. 1, Chap. 1, all Member States of the European Union were required to adopt a regime akin to the French model by 24 Oct. 1998.

islative scheme and promote public awareness of privacy.[36] The Privacy Commissioner of Canada (PCC) is empowered to receive, investigate and resolve any complaints concerning refusals of access to personal information, or the collection, retention, use, disclosure, or disposal of personal information by a governmental body (section 29). The PCC may even institute a complaint himself in an appropriate case (section 29(3)). Moreover, the PCC may, at his own discretion, carry out investigations with respect to personal information held by a government institution to ensure that the Act is being followed (section 37), and may engage in research and prepare reports on privacy issues (section 39). Unlike the French CNIL, the Canadian Commissioner has no formal role in relation to automated processing of information—there is no requirement that automated systems be registered, nor that the PCC approve of them in advance of their use. The PCC also lacks the formal authority to adjudicate claims, or to issue legally binding opinions on privacy issues. His role is primarily advisory and conciliatory. Essentially, the PCC is mandated to receive and investigate complaints, and to resolve each complaint by providing an opinion to the relevant government body. The PCC has no power to enforce his opinion, however. Only in the case where an individual has been denied access to personal information may an action be taken before the courts, and then only after the PCC has been given the opportunity to investigate and resolve the matter (section 41). It should be noted that the Commissioner has been remarkably successful in persuading government bodies to comply with his opinions,[37] perhaps because the risks of non-compliance are substantial: in the case of access, judicial review may occur, and in all cases the PCC may publicise the refusal to comply in his *Annual Report* and with the media.[38]

In the area of workplace privacy, the PCC has received, investigated and resolved numerous complaints in the past 15 years. In fact, it is likely that the lack of workplace privacy claims based on section 8 of the Charter relates in part to the availability of a remedy through the office of the PCC (or through the offices of the PCC's provincial counterparts). The main advantage of the Privacy Act over the Charter is that there is no cost to the individual candidate/employee of having a complaint considered and resolved by the PCC. Whether or not these complaints would have otherwise given rise to constitutional challenges is impossible to know for certain, but the prohibitive costs of asserting a claim in court would probably have discouraged many of the complainants from pursuing a constitutional remedy. While it is beneficial for

---

[36] Many of the provinces have created similar privacy institutions: Information and Privacy Commissioner (Alberta); Information and Privacy Commissioner (British Columbia); Information and Privacy Commissioner (Ontario); Commission d'accès à l'information (Quebec); Information and Privacy Commissioner (Saskatchewan). Manitoba relies on the Office of the Provincial Ombudsman to receive complaints, while Nova Scotia relies on *ad hoc* tribunals appointed by the provincial cabinet.

[37] Prior to 1996, the PCC had applied for judicial review of a refusal to grant access only twice. The first case was settled prior to the hearing. See PCC (1994–5e), 27.

[38] Flaherty (1989), 278–9.

individuals to have an inexpensive means of asserting their right of privacy against public employers, the fact that virtually all federal public sector privacy cases have been dealt with under the Privacy Act makes it difficult to identify the legal principles which have been applied. This is because the PCC's role in dispute resolution is essentially conciliatory, as opposed to adjudicative.[39] His activities have therefore tended to be informal.[40] In cases where the Commissioner has found a claim to be well-founded, he has generally reported only the facts of the case and the resolution which was reached. No formal judgments or reasons are issued.

A review of the PCC's *Annual Reports* for the years 1991 to 1995 indicates that in this five-year period, almost 40 per cent of the cases reported concerned matters of workplace privacy.[41] Because the Commissioner's mandate concerns informational private interests, issues of access to, and collection and disclosure of, personal information have been the focus. A discussion of three cases will illustrate the issues considered by the PCC, and the resolutions which were achieved.

6.4.2.1 *Revenue Canada (1991–2)*

An employee complained to the PCC in 1991 after his office was searched by investigators acting on behalf of his employer, Revenue Canada.[42] The employer suspected that the employee had written anonymous letters that were relevant to a sexual harassment claim filed by another employee. Thus, the office search was ordered, and personal documents were seized (including the employee's personal telephone directory) for the purpose of a handwriting analysis. The PCC's investigation revealed that the seized documents included the employee's benefit statements and a personal record listing his education, previous employment, personal references and family members. These documents were used during the harassment investigation, and were disclosed outside the department without the employee's consent. The Commissioner concluded that the complaint was well-founded in reliance on section 7(a) of the Act, which permits personal information to be used by a government body 'only for the purpose for which the information was obtained or compiled . . . or for a use consistent with that purpose'. In his opinion, the use of personal documentation during an internal investigation 'could hardly be consistent with the

---

[39] Flaherty (1989), 279.

[40] *Ibid.*, 265.

[41] PCC (1990–1f), 35–42; PCC (1991–2g), 52–64; PCC (1992–3h), 57–69; PCC (1993–4i), 58–67; PCC (1994–5j), 31–49. The actual figure is 24 out of 63 cases reported. Note that the PCC receives hundreds of complaints each year, and those included in a particular annual report are ones that were controversial. There are no statistics available on the actual number of employment privacy cases investigated each year by the PCC, nor on the percentage of total cases which concern employment.

[42] PCC (1991–2g), 56–7.

original collection purpose'.[43] Revenue Canada responded by issuing a formal apology to the employee and changing its investigation policy so that an employee's personal information can no longer be used without her consent.

One should note that the office search itself did not contravene the Privacy Act. The Act is concerned with informational private interests only, and not with territorial (or personal) interests. Thus, the territorial privacy analysis adopted in the American office search case of *O'Connor* v. *Ortega*[44] could not be applied by the PCC. The case thus turned on the issue of how Revenue Canada used the personal information it obtained from the search. The PCC offered no thoughts on whether or not the seizure of the information from the employee's office constituted a legal 'collection' within the meaning of section 4 of the Act: '[n]o personal information shall be collected by a government institution unless it relates directly to an operating program or activity of the institution'. Assuming that the investigation of a sexual harassment claim is an 'activity' of Revenue Canada, section 4 would appear to permit the 'collection' of personal information as part of an investigation so long as the information is directly relevant to the investigation. There is no requirement in section 4 that the activity itself must be *legitimate,* nor is there a requirement that the collection of personal information without the consent of the individual concerned should be *necessary* for engaging in the activity. As such, the Act's limitations on personal information collection appear, at least on their face, to be rather weak. Section 5 of the Act does require a government body to collect personal information directly from the individual concerned, where this is possible. This limitation on information collection could have been significant, since Revenue Canada could have asked the employee for a handwriting sample and other personal information, as an alternative to searching his office and seizing the materials without his knowledge. The PCC did not mention this issue, however.

6.4.2.2 *St. Lawrence Seaway Authority (1992–3)*[45]

In his *Annual Report* of 1992–3, the PCC reported on a complaint filed by an employee of the St. Lawrence Seaway Authority, who was denied pay for two days' sick leave when he refused to disclose the nature of his illness to a supervisor. The PCC agreed with the employer's assertion that it had a right to satisfy itself that a returning employee is fit for work, as part of its duty to ensure health and safety in the workplace. However, the complaint was well-founded because the Privacy Act precluded the employer from insisting on disclosure of health information to a supervisor who lacked formal medical training. Hence, the PCC concluded that 'the right to collect medical details to assess an employee's fitness should be reserved only for a qualified medical practitioner',

---

[43] *Ibid.,* 57.
[44] See n. 76, Chap. 2.
[45] PCC (1992–3h), 64–5.

who should then make a determination and inform the employer.[46] As a result, the Authority agreed to change its procedure so that employees returning from sick leave are no longer required to disclose their actual medical details to the employer.

The legal basis of the PCC's conclusion is not readily apparent from the Privacy Act. As noted above, the only substantive limitations placed on the collection of information by governmental bodies (whether or not in their capacity as employer) are that the information must relate directly to an activity of the body (section 4), and that, where possible, the information should be collected from the individual concerned (section 5). The limitation in section 4 is very permissive, and seems to permit a body like the Seaway Authority to collect medical information about employees in order to carry out managerial activities related to promoting health and safety in the workplace. Nothing in the Act regulates the manner in which information is collected, or explicitly supports the limitation recommended by the PCC that medical information should only be disclosed to qualified medical practitioners. Although one cannot know for certain, it appears that the Commissioner must have implied into section 4 a condition of 'legitimacy' *vis-à-vis* activities permitting the collection of personal information. Hence, the assessment of the medical fitness of employees is only a 'legitimate' activity of a government body where it is performed by medically qualified practitioners, and only such a legitimate activity could warrant the collection of personal information concerning employees' health. In any case, the fact that the PCC was able to achieve a resolution which goes beyond the actual dictates of the Privacy Act speaks to the merits of the non-adjudicative, persuasive approach, while highlighting the deficiencies of the Act in relation to information collection.

6.4.2.3 Canada Post Corporation (1994–5)[47]

The most egregious example of a violation of the right of privacy in the federal civil service was reported in the PCC's *Annual Report 1994–5*, and concerned Canada Post Corporation. A letter carrier had fallen and injured her back while delivering mail, and had filed a claim under the workers' compensation scheme. Despite the fact that her own and the employer's doctors agreed about the cause and extent of her injury, Canada Post managers doubted her claim. The employee first complained to the PCC after Canada Post refused her request for access to her employment and medical files. During the Commissioner's investigation of the access complaint, it came to light that the managers had hired a private detective to conduct surveillance of the employee and photograph her. The photographs were destroyed, but photocopies appeared in the employee's compensation file. Furthermore, one particular manager had a file of over 750

---

[46] PCC (1992–3h), 65.
[47] PCC (1994–5j), 35–6.

pages concerning the employee, which he initially refused to turn over to the PCC because he considered the file to be his own personal property. It was also revealed that Canada Post had collected medical information from the employee's doctor without her knowledge or consent (presumably in contravention of section 5 of the Act). In total, the PCC identified 13 violations of the Privacy Act. Canada Post responded by disciplining or dismissing the managers involved, apologizing in writing to the employee, and granting her access to all the personal information in her personnel files.

Although the result in the case appears sound, the legal basis for the PCC's conclusion concerning the surveillance is again unclear. The investigation of an employee's workers' compensation claim is surely an 'activity' of a government body within the meaning of section 4 of the Act, and collecting information about the employee's health is directly related to that activity. On its face, section 4 precludes neither surveillance of employees by private detectives nor the taking of photographs of employees away from the workplace, so long as the information gathered is directly relevant to an 'activity'. In finding that the surveillance and photographing of the employee contravened the Act in this case, the Commissioner again must have implied into section 4 a condition that information may only be collected for a *legitimate* activity. Since Canada Post's own doctor was satisfied that the employee was sufficiently injured to justify the workers' compensation claim, it was illegitimate for Canada Post to investigate the claim by collecting personal information. The PCC may have also been concerned about the employer's covert methods in conducting the investigation. Section 5 discourages surreptitious information-gathering by requiring that personal information be collected, *where possible*, from the individual concerned. The question is whether it would be possible for the employer to conduct effectively an investigation of a worker's compensation claim with the knowledge and consent of the employee concerned. As discussed below, one Canadian arbitration decision has recognised that surreptitious, privacy-invasive investigations of worker injuries may only be justified where there is a reasonable basis for suspecting fraud and no alternative, less-intrusive investigation methods are available.[48] Section 5 of the Act could be interpreted in a similar manner: claims should generally be investigated with the participation of the individual concerned, except in suspicious circumstances where an effective investigation would not be possible without covert information gathering. The PCC has not explicitly adopted this possible interpretation of section 5, however.

6.4.2.4 *Conclusion*

An analysis of the workplace privacy cases resolved by the PCC demonstrates his effectiveness in ensuring that federal government institutions respect the privacy rights of their employees. However, two important limitations of the Act

---

[48] *Re Alberta Wheat Pool and Grain Workers' Union, Local 333* (1995), 48 LAC (4th) 332 (Williams, British Columbia). Discussed *infra*, text accompanying n. 76.

and the PCC's mandate are also revealed. First, with regard to the collection of personal information, the provisions of the Act are quite weak. Section 4 appears to permit the collection of any personal information which is related directly to an 'activity' of an institution, while section 5 requires personal information to be collected from the individual concerned 'where possible'. There is no requirement that the activity itself must be a legitimate pursuit of the institution, nor that the collection of personal information must be 'necessary' to the activity. This may be compared to the more restrictive requirements of the French Law of 6 January 1978, which include a provision that illegitimate information-gathering may be the subject of a complaint to the CNIL.[49] It is notable that despite the generally lax standard imposed by the Act, the PCC appears to be taking a hard line with the federal government in its role as employer. In fact, some of the Commissioner's opinions suggest that he has implied a legitimacy requirement into section 4, and is prepared to pass judgement on whether or not a government activity actually justifies the collection of personal information.

Secondly, the Act is an information privacy statute, and is primarily concerned with informational private interests. For this reason, government actions infringing upon the territorial and personal interests of candidates/employees are only regulated by the Act to the extent that they give rise to personal information about the individual concerned.[50] Hence, in the Revenue Canada case, the Act was infringed not by the search of the employee's office, but by the inappropriate collection, use and disclosure of information acquired during the search. Had no such information been obtained, there would have been no breach of the Act. Similarly, in employment testing cases (drug and genetic testing, for example), the PCC has authority only over the information obtained from testing, and not over the testing itself (which infringes upon personal private interests). Therefore, so long as personal information concerning an individual's drug use or genetic make-up is directly related to some 'activity' of a government body, there is nothing in the Act to prevent the imposition of testing to obtain the information. Fortunately, the PCC has a broad mandate to study, report and issue recommendations on all privacy issues. In fact, his special reports on drug testing and genetic testing[51] have included discussions of their use in both private and public sector employment, and have been highly influential. Moreover, the PCC has been a vocal critic of drug testing in the Canadian military, and took an active role in opposing the military's testing policy. In February 1995, random testing was suspended, largely as a result of the Commissioner's interventions on behalf of military personnel.[52] This again

[49] *Supra*, sect. 5.4.1.1.

[50] The same criticism could be levelled at France's Law of 6 Jan. 1978. However, alternative legal remedies in France protect territorial and personal private interests—this is not necessarily the case in Canada.

[51] *Supra*, nn. 12–20, Chap. 2. The IPCO has also been influential in the area of workplace privacy (see (1993)).

[52] PCC (1994–5j), 16–17. The PCC wrote a letter to the Chief of Defence staff opposing random testing, and publicly criticized the policy.

demonstrates that the PCC has been influential in workplace privacy matters, even where the Act itself is of limited application.

The privacy protection available to private sector employees in Canada depends on whether or not they are among the 37 per cent[53] who are unionised and subject to a collective agreement. The right of privacy has been generally recognised in collective agreement arbitral jurisprudence, and a body of rules and principles have emerged. In contrast, job candidates and non-organised employees have only minimal protection. In five provinces, a statutory right of privacy exists which may be asserted in the employment field. However, this has proven inadequate for reasons similar to those discussed in relation to American law. The result of this inadequacy is that candidates/employees have looked to other legal mechanisms for redress. Thus, anti-discrimination law, which is well developed in Canada, has been asserted against employer drug-testing policies, but with disappointing results. Only the Province of Quebec has enacted information privacy legislation applicable to the private sector.

6.5.1 Privacy in Arbitral Jurisprudence

The single most important Canadian source of principles for the protection of workplace privacy is jurisprudence from collective agreement grievance arbitrations. Such arbitrations generally arise after the unilateral imposition by management of a potentially privacy-invasive policy, and the filing by the union of a grievance. By law, Canadian collective agreements must include a provision requiring disputes over working terms and conditions to be arbitrated during the term of a collective agreement—a result of the fact that strikes and lock-outs are illegal while a collective agreement is in force.[54] In cases where a collective agreement is silent on an issue, the arbitrator will be called upon to determine what is reasonable in the circumstances.[55] Arbitrators have held that employer policies may be unreasonable if they conflict with the privacy rights of employees. One should note that arbitrators have no jurisdiction to consider privacy complaints from job candidates, who are not protected by collective agreements.

The first workplace privacy cases in Canada were arbitrated in the 1960s, when it was recognised that on-site searches of employees and their belongings invaded a 'fundamental right' related to 'personal freedom'.[56] However, it was

---

[53] ILO (1997–8d), 248, Table 3.2.

[54] Brown and Beatty (1984), 3.

[55] *Re Lornex Mining Corp. and United Steelworkers, Local 7619* (1983), 14 LAC (3rd) 169 (Chertkow, British Columbia), 175.

[56] *Re United Automobile Workers, Local 444 and Chrysler Canada* (1961), 11 LAC 152 (Bennett, Ontario), 162.

not until 1974 that the 'right of privacy' was actually mentioned in an arbitration decision. In *Re Amalgamated Electric Corp. Ltd. (Markham)*,[57] the arbitrator considered a grievance arising after the employer searched employees' purses and bags at the end of the working day. The search was part of an audit; there was no evidence that the employer was concerned about deterring or controlling theft. The employer had no search policy, and employees were given no advance warning that searches could occur. The arbitrator noted that the collective agreement was silent on the issue, neither permitting nor prohibiting spot checks of employees' personal effects. Thus, he was required to consider the permissibility of this type of search pursuant to general legal principles. To this end, he concluded that the right of privacy had been infringed by the searches, and this right 'ought to be jealously preserved'.[58] In his view, a spot check would be permissible in three situations: (1) where the collective agreement explicitly provides for it; (2) where the employer has a real and substantial suspicion that an employee has committed a theft; or (3) where the employees voluntarily submit to it. The first two scenarios did not apply in the case, while the arbitrator concluded that the third should be approached with caution. He observed that, although the employees all acquiesced to the search in this case, this was insufficient to make their participation voluntary: 'the voluntary nature of the employees' action might be of concern. Even though employees may voice no objection . . . the fact they are requested by their superiors to do so tends to be a form of compulsion'.[59] Hence, he refused to find that the employees consented to the search through their participation. Furthermore, the arbitrator thought that the employer had alternative, non- or less intrusive methods by which to ensure security (assuming that this was its goal). The employer could place storage lockers outside the plant, and prohibit employees from bringing bags into the workplace.[60] The employer could also establish and publicise a security plan. The arbitrator thought that it would be permissible for such a plan to include searches, so long as employees knew about them in advance, and all employees were searched. In his view, occasional or random spot checks were 'too embarrassing' for employees.[61]

Prior to the enactment of the Charter of Rights and Freedoms in 1982, and for several years thereafter, workplace privacy arbitrations focused on the search issue. The principles which emerged can be summarised as follows: (1) employee searches are insulated from arbitral review where the collective agreement provides for them, or alternatively where employees have submitted to the searches over a period of time, thus establishing a pattern of voluntary participation which would give the employer an implied right to conduct searches[62];

---

[57] (1974), 6 LAC (2nd) 28 (O'Shea, Ontario).

[58] *Ibid.*, 32.

[59] *Ibid.*

[60] *Ibid.*

[61] *Ibid.*

[62] Arbitrators appear to have taken the view that employees are estopped from asserting the right of privacy if they have submitted to a privacy-invasive search policy over a period of time. On this

(2) deterrence of theft is a legitimate and proper concern of the employer, and may justify privacy-invasive search policies; (3) searches of employees' belongings are easier to justify than body searches; the former may be carried out according to a publicised and systematic policy to which all employees are subject, while the latter may only be carried out in extraordinary circumstances (for example, where the employer has clear evidence that a theft has occurred, and the employer's economic interest in preventing theft is substantial)[63]; (4) searches must be carried out in a manner avoiding embarrassment for any individual workers; generally, this requires that individual employees should not be singled out or randomly searched (since a random search can be arbitrary, and may be viewed as singling out)[64]; and (5) where feasible, employers should provide storage facilities for personal belongings outside the workplace, so that employees have the opportunity to avoid being searched.[65] One can conclude that it is reasonable for an employer unilaterally to adopt a policy of searching employees' belongings (purses, bags, etc.) under an abuse deterrence justification, so long as all employees are equally subject to being searched. Apparently, the employer's interest in reducing theft outweighs the employees' private interests related to their belongings. However, employees' personal private interests are viewed as more substantial. Hence, the employer's interest is insufficient to justify body searches.

Although the limitations imposed by arbitrators on workplace searches seem reasonably protective of private interests, particularly in relation to the personal zone of privacy, it is important to note that the right of privacy has been viewed in the private sector[66] as a default term, guiding the regulation of privacy-invasive policies only in the absence of explicit or implicit contractual provisions. Hence, it certainly cannot be said that a 'floor' of privacy exists in the unionised private sector workplace, since arbitrators have recognised that the employer and the union may contract out of the right of privacy. Therefore, according to the jurisprudence, a collective agreement could legally provide for random body searches of employees. Furthermore, arbitrators have taken the view that employers may acquire an implicit right to search employees in any number of ways, if searches had occurred in the past and the union had not filed a grievance. Hence, the right of privacy could be lost by workers through their own (or their union's) failure to assert it.

Since the Charter era began in 1982, arbitrators have faced an increasing number and variety of workplace privacy issues. This trend roughly parallels

---

point, see *Re Glenbow-Alberta Institute and CUPE, Local* 1645 (1988), 3 LAC (4th) 127 (Beattie, Alberta), 149.

[63] See *Re United Automobile Workers, supra,* n. 56, 162; *Re Inco Metals Company and United Steelworkers* (1978), 18 LAC (2nd) 420 (Weatherill, Ontario), 422.

[64] *Ibid.,* 423; *Re University Hospital and London & District Services Workers Union, Local 220* (1981), 28 LAC (2nd) 294 (Picher, Ontario), 301; *Re Lornex Mining Corp., supra,* n. 44, 183.

[65] *Re Glenbow, supra,* n. 62, 150.

[66] As discussed in relation to *Calgary Local 710, supra,* n. 29, public sector employers and employees cannot contract out of s. 8 of the Charter.

the rise of the right of privacy as an aspect of Canada's constitutional and private law, and an increasing popular awareness of privacy issues. Hence, arbitrators have considered grievances concerning workplace fingerprinting,[67] employer efforts to control off-duty activities,[68] off-site surveillance,[69] drug testing[70] and dress and grooming codes.[71] As with the search cases, these decisions generally evince a protective approach to worker private interests, particularly in situations where an impugned policy regulates employees' lives away from the workplace. Moreover, the cases post-1982 demonstrate an increasing awareness of the *constitutional* status of the right of privacy. Although arbitrators have correctly concluded that the principles underlying section 8 of the Charter cannot be asserted directly in a private sector arbitration, they have nevertheless relied on Charter values in determining whether or not an employer's policy meets the test of reasonableness. The key case is *Re Doman Forest Products Ltd.*,[72] where the basic principle was asserted that collective agreements must be interpreted in the context of the fundamental values underlying the Charter. The case concerned the admissibility of videotape evidence obtained by a private investigator who was hired by the employer to look into an employee's absence due to illness. Because of privacy's status as a fundamental value of Canadian society, the arbitrator found that the right was an implied term of the collective agreement in question. He then adopted the three-part 'reasonableness' test developed by the Supreme Court of Canada with regard to surveillance by the state under section 8 of the Charter: (1) was it reasonable in the circumstances for the body in question (i.e. the employer) to request surveillance?; (2) was the surveillance conducted in a reasonable manner?; and (3) were other alternatives open to the employer to obtain the evidence it sought?[73]

The principle that a denial of human rights is unreasonable if an alternative exists which would better respect the right in question is an important feature of Canadian constitutional law,[74] and was effectively imported into the

---

[67] *Re Canada Post and Canadian Union of Postal Workers (Fingerprinting Grievance)* (1988), 34 L.A.C. (3rd) 392 (Bird, Canada).

[68] *Re Bell Canada and Communications Workers of Canada* (1984), 16 LAC (3rd) 397 (Picher, Canada).

[69] *Re Doman Forest Products Ltd. and I.W.A. Local I–357* (1990), 13 LAC (4th) 275 (Vickers, British Columbia); *Re Labatt Ontario Breweries and Brewery, General & Professional Workers Union, Local 304* (1994), 42 LAC 151 (4th) (Brandt, Ontario).

[70] *Re Canadian Pacific Ltd. and UTA* (1987), 31 LAC (3rd) 179 (Picher, Canada); *Re Provincial-American Truck Transporters and Teamsters Union, Local 880* (1991), 18 LAC (4th) (Brent, Ontario); *Re Esso Petroleum and Communications, Energy and Paperworkers' Union, Local 614* (1994), 56 LAC 440 (4th) (McAlpine, British Columbia).

[71] *Re Wardair Canada Inc. and Canadian Air Line Flight Attendants' Association* (1987), 28 LAC (3rd) 142 (Beatty, Canada); *Re Co-op Centre and Retail, Wholesale & Department Store Union, Local 1065* (1990), 17 LAC (4th) 186 (Collier, New Brunswick).

[72] *Supra*, n. 69.

[73] *Ibid.*, 282. The arbitrator ultimately did not apply this test, but chose to convene a new hearing to consider all the evidence.

[74] S. 1 of the Canadian Charter of Rights and Freedoms permits rights to be limited where reasonable, and this has been interpreted by the Sup. Ct. of Canada to include a requirement that the

unionised workplace by the arbitrator in *Re Doman Forest Products Ltd.* Prior to this, arbitration decisions had often ignored or downplayed alternatives as a relevant consideration.[75] However, a focus on alternatives is now typical. This approach was adopted in *Re Alberta Wheat Pool and Grain Workers' Union, Local 333*,[76] where the employee was on long-term disability leave as a result of arthritis. The employer became aware of a rumour that the employee was building a house, and hired a private detective to investigate. In determining the admissibility of certain video tapes, the arbitrator agreed that the employer was justified in investigating the reasons for the employee's absence from work. However, the surveillance and videotaping of the employee were held to be unreasonable breaches of privacy because alternative, less intrusive investigative methods were available to the employer, including confronting the employee or asking the employee to submit to a medical examination.[77]

Recent drug-testing arbitration decisions demonstrate that arbitrators have combined the pre-Charter emphasis on protecting personal private interests from intrusive searches with a focus on limiting employer control of off-duty activities, and requiring employers to adopt less invasive alternatives. The end-result has been to provide stronger protection to Canadian employees than their American counterparts generally enjoy. In *Re Provincial-American Truck Transporters*,[78] the company required all its drivers to submit to urinalysis drug testing in a manner consistent with United States Department of Transportation regulations on the issue.[79] This was despite the fact that the Canadian government had won an exemption from the regulations for Canadian drivers. The union filed a grievance about the drug testing policy, arguing that it was contrary to the implied right of privacy in the collective agreement, and was contrary to Canadian public policy. The arbitrator characterised the policy as a serious infringement of worker privacy because it compromised bodily integrity in a manner analogous to a personal search, and sought to regulate off-duty behaviour.[80] Although the employer had a clear interest in promoting safety, the arbitrator relied on the principles developed in the case of body searches to conclude that a driver could be required to submit to a drug test only if the employer had a reasonable suspicion of on-duty drug impairment. Mandatory universal testing could only be justified, absent a specific term in the collective agreement allowing it, if the employer could bring forward evidence of an actual drug problem in the workplace which could not be combatted by some less intrusive

limitation be a minimal impairment of the right in question. The question whether an impairment is minimal will often turn on whether or not a non- or less impairing alternative exists. See generally *R. v. Oakes* [1986] 1 SCR 103, 139.

[75] See *Re Inco Metals, supra,* n. 63, where the dissent considered the existence of alternatives, but the majority did not.

[76] *Supra,* n. 48.

[77] *Ibid.,* 345. See also *Re Labatt Ontario Breweries, supra,* n. 69, 163.

[78] *Supra,* n. 70.

[79] See n. 152, Chap. 2.

[80] *Supra,* n. 70, 422.

alternative.[81] Because the employer could not bring forward such evidence, the grievance was upheld.

Similarly, in the case of *Re Esso Petroleum and Communications*,[82] the employer's plan to implement a new drug policy, including random urinalysis drug testing for employees in safety-sensitive positions, was challenged. The arbitration panel explicitly adopted Charter values related to privacy in assessing the proposed plan. As a result, the panel applied a two-step test: (1) is there evidence that substance abuse is a problem in the workplace, thereby justifying the employer's proposal?; and (2) is the proposed plan a reasonable means of addressing the problem, or are less-invasive alternatives available? After applying this test, the panel concluded that the employer's interest in promoting safety could be satisfied by testing on the basis of a reasonable and probable suspicion requirement, and held that random testing was generally unreasonable. Testing on a random basis would be justified only where an employee was undergoing rehabilitation for a past substance abuse problem.[83]

The prevailing view in Canadian private sector arbitration jurisprudence is that, absent a term in a collective agreement, drug testing must be individualised, in the sense that it may be imposed only where the employer has a reasonable suspicion that an employee is impaired. Moreover, the employer must be able to point to some safety justification to support the testing. Random and universal drug testing without cause are both generally impermissible. Hence, the Canadian arbitration position is similar to the legal position adopted in France, and certainly offers more protection to workers than American cases applying the constitutional or public policy right of privacy. It is important to emphasise, however, that while the French position on employee testing constitutes a legal standard available to all workers, the Canadian arbitration position only applies to unionised workers[84] whose collective agreements are silent on the issue of drug testing. It remains possible for a private sector employer and its union to agree to a random or universal drug testing policy, even in the absence of a safety rationale. In other words, Canadian arbitrators have recognised that a collective agreement may unreasonably limit the right of privacy. This is only the case in the private sector, however. In the public sector, the workplace privacy principles flowing from arbitration decisions form a 'floor of rights' for public employees by operation of section 8 of the Charter.

---

[81] *Ibid.*, 425.
[82] *Supra*, n. 70.
[83] *Ibid.*, 447–8.
[84] Non-organised workers in Quebec and Nova Scotia, and those subject to Federal regulation, may also enjoy protection from invasions of privacy which have resulted in their dismissal. These three jurisdictions have all statutorily imposed a 'just cause' requirement within dismissal law. Employers are therefore under a duty to act reasonably when contemplating dismissal, which is analogous to the reasonableness duty implied into collective agreements. *supra*, n. 14, Chap. 6. See *Ouellet* v. *Cuisirama* [1995] CT 203, where the right of privacy was considered in the context of a hearing under the Quebec legislation.

6.5.2 Statutory Protection of Privacy

Apart from the two provincial statutes prohibiting the use of the lie detector in the workplace,[85] there are no specific workplace privacy statutes in Canada. Thus, general statutes guaranteeing the right of privacy and prohibiting discrimination in employment have been the focus of workplace privacy litigation.

6.5.2.1 *The Statutory Right of Privacy*

As noted above, five provinces have recognised a right of privacy through legislation: British Columbia, Saskatchewan, Manitoba, Quebec and Newfoundland.[86] Quebec's legislative regime will be considered separately below in section 6.5.3.1. As for the other four provinces, they have effectively created the tort of invasion of privacy by statute, and this tort is certainly available in private sector employment disputes implicating the right of privacy. In arbitration cases, for example, the existence of the statutory tort has been referred to in support of a general public policy favouring the protection of worker privacy.[87] The statutory privacy torts are directly relevant to private sector employment disputes outside the arbitration context, and are also available to job candidates.

To date, the few cases which have interpreted the statutory right of privacy in the employment context have been highly deferential to employer interests, thus mirroring the prevailing approach to the privacy tort in the United States.[88] In fact, each of the privacy statutes recognises two general defences which may be relied upon by employers: (1) consent (express or implied), and (2) defence of property.[89] The availability of a defence of implied consent invites the adoption of the American view that job candidates who accept employment knowing of privacy-invasive policies, or employees who continue to work despite those policies, have implicitly consented to them and cannot assert the right of privacy. This approach appeared in the arbitration decision in *Re Shell Canada Products Ltd.*,[90] which applied the British Columbia privacy statute. There, the employee was injured in an accident at home, and saw his own doctor, who recommended a cessation of work for a period of time. The employer then demanded that the employee submit to a medical examination by a company doctor. The employee complied out of fear of dismissal, but then filed a grievance. The arbitrator held that the essence of privacy is 'choice'—the employee

---

[85] Employment Standards Act (New Brunswick), SNB 1984, c. 42, s. 25; Employment Standards Act (Ontario), RSO 1990, c. E–14, s. 46.

[86] See nn. 53, 56, Chap. 2.

[87] *Re Doman Forest Products Ltd.*, *supra*, n. 69, 281.

[88] *Supra*, sect. 4.3.4.2.

[89] See n. 56, Chap. 2. See British Columbia, s. 2(1)(a) & (b); Saskatchewan, s. 4(1)(a) & (b); Manitoba, s. 5(a) & (c); Newfoundland, s. 5(1)(a) & (b).

[90] (1990), 14 LAC (4th) 75 (Larson, British Columbia).

had the right to consent or not to consent.[91] Thus, by submitting to the medical examination, the employee had consented to it. The arbitrator then observed that the employee would not have been permitted to return to work if he had refused to submit to the medical examination, but that was his 'choice'.[92] Given this, one presumes that the employee would have had no action for breach of privacy if he had refused the employer's demand.

With regard to the defence of property, it appears that the privacy statutes will be interpreted to place fewer limitations on employer monitoring and surveillance than the arbitration right of privacy. In *UFCW, Local 1400* v. *Saskatchewan Co-operative Association Ltd.*,[93] the employer adopted a loss prevention programme which included hidden video cameras in the workplace, the placement of individuals with binoculars outside the workplace to monitor activities within and a series of interrogations of employees concerning alleged thefts. The details of the plan were not brought to the attention of the employees in advance. Their union sued under Saskatchewan's privacy statute as a representative of the employees. The Court concluded that the union could not bring a class action because the statutory right of privacy is personal to each employee,[94] and suggested that the union file a grievance and take the matter to arbitration.[95] The Court nevertheless pronounced on the privacy claim, on the assumption that it could have erred with regard to the class action issue. It refused to find a breach of the privacy tort because '[p]art of an employer's function is to investigate and bring to an end any activities which are causing its business losses'.[96] This function was recognised in Saskatchewan's Privacy Act, which permitted limitations of privacy 'in defence of property'.[97] Remarkably, the Court did not consider the methods adopted by the employer to defend its property and, in particular, whether alternatives could have been adopted which would have reduced or even eliminated the impact on the employees' privacy rights. This seems to have been an obvious issue in the case, since the employer's tactics were so secretive and severe. Although it is not clear whether the matter was ultimately taken to arbitration, it is apparent that the union would have fared better under the privacy principles developed by arbitrators.

6.5.2.2 Anti-discrimination Law

From the discussion above, it should be apparent that the right of privacy is not yet available to non-unionised private sector employees, and private sector job candidates, in five provinces: Alberta, Ontario, New Brunswick, Nova Scotia and Prince Edward Island. Moreover, the statutory protection that is available

[91] (1990), 14 LAC (4th) 75 (Larson, British Columbia), 83.
[92] *Ibid.*, 84.
[93] (1992), 101 Sask. R 1 (QB).
[94] *Ibid.*, 8.
[95] *Ibid.*, 9.
[96] *Ibid.*, 10.
[97] *Ibid.* See *supra*, no. 89.

to their counterparts in four other provinces is relatively weak (leaving aside for the moment Quebec, discussed in section 6.5.3 below). There is certainly no comprehensive floor of privacy rights available to candidates/employees in Canada—like the law of the United States, Canadian law is a muddle. As a result, employees have begun to look to alternative legal remedies to protect their privacy, and anti-discrimination law has become a focus.

All Canadian provinces, and the federal government, have enacted comprehensive human rights legislation guaranteeing the right of equality.[98] Discrimination may be challenged where it is based on a personal characteristic such as sex, race, national or ethnic origin, religion, age, sexual orientation, marital status and disability.[99] Public and private sector employers are prohibited from discriminating in hiring, work assignments, employment terms, benefits and conditions, and dismissal. Hence, the laws have comprehensive application, guaranteeing the right of equality to all candidates/employees. Moreover, the federal and provincial governments have each established commissions mandated to enforce these human rights laws. These commissions are empowered to receive and investigate complaints, to mediate and conciliate disputes and to bring a complaint before a human rights tribunal for adjudication.[100]

Human rights legislation is relevant to workplace privacy since many of the prohibited grounds of discrimination concern personal characteristics generally irrelevant to an individual's ability to perform a job (and therefore not of legitimate employer concern), and which at the same time concern private interests. An individual's religious beliefs, sexual preference or marital status are often considered purely private matters. Where an employer refuses to employ an individual after learning of her homosexuality, one could argue that the employer has discriminated against her (because a heterosexual in her position would have been hired), or one could argue that the employer has invaded her privacy (by taking into account a private interest in hiring, and thereby failing to respect the individual's right to private life). Although anti-discrimination and invasion of privacy actions would both be available in such a case, it is important to note that the two actions are fundamentally different.[101] Anti-discrimination law is activated where an individual is denied an employment opportunity because of a protected personal characteristic. As such, the law is directed at employer practices, policies, decisions, etc. that exclude on particular protected grounds. The right of privacy operates in a much broader sense, prohibiting employer actions infringing upon private interests that are shared by

---

[98] See, e.g., Canadian Human Rights Act, RSC 1985, c. H–6, as am., and Ontario Human Rights Code, RSO 1990, c. H–19, as am.

[99] One result of the Sup. Ct. of Canada decision in *Vriend* v. *Alberta* (1998), 224 NR 1 is that all human rights laws in Canada must protect these grounds. The *Vriend* case held that Alberta's failure to include sexual orientation in its legislation was unconstitutional.

[100] See, e.g., Canadian Human Rights Act, *supra*, n. 98, ss. 40–9.

[101] ILO (1993a, 3), 34, 69.

everyone. An employer policy does not have to exclude an individual in order to constitute an invasion of privacy.

The example of genetic testing will illustrate the differences between the rights of equality and privacy. An employer may demand that all job applicants submit to genetic testing. This in itself does not threaten the right of equality since all applicants are treated similarly, and the employer is not excluding anyone through the testing itself. However, such a demand would implicate the right of privacy of each and every applicant, since such testing would require each applicant to surrender bodily fluids (thus infringing upon a personal private interest), and the information sought from the testing relates to personal health, an informational private interest.[102] Hence, the applicants could assert the right of privacy against the testing *per se*. The right of equality would only be threatened if the employer used the information obtained from the testing to exclude individuals with certain health problems (or risks). Those excluded could conceivably assert discrimination on the basis of physical disability. In effect, the right of privacy could logically be asserted prior to the right of equality, since an invasion of a private interest would be necessary for the employer to obtain the information required to discriminate. The link between invasion of privacy and discrimination is recognised in the Americans with Disabilities Act (ADA),[103] which includes both privacy protection for disabled persons and anti-discrimination protection. The ADA prohibits employers from demanding medical information from, or imposing examinations and tests on, job applicants prior to the making of a job offer,[104] and then outlines an anti-discrimination regime governing the denial of job opportunities to those with physical and mental disabilities. The ADA therefore protects the informational and personal private interests of all job applicants in order to prevent employers from obtaining information about applicants' health that could then be used as the basis for discriminatory hiring. For similar reasons, several Canadian provincial human rights laws prohibit employers from demanding information on employment applications concerning protected personal characteristics.[105]

In the recent case of *Canadian Human Rights Commission* v. *Toronto-Dominion Bank*,[106] an employment drug testing plan was challenged under the

---

[102] See *infra*, sect. 9.5.

[103] See n. 14, Chap. 4.

[104] *Ibid.*, s. 102(d). Note that the Act permits employers to demand a medical examination following the making of a conditional job offer, but requires that the employer must demand such an examination from each person to whom it has made a conditional offer. See Rothstein(b) (1992), 38, 56.

[105] Individual Rights Protection Act (Alberta), RSA 1980, c. I–2, s. 8(1)(b); Human Rights Code (British Columbia), RSBC 1979, c. 186, s. 7(1)(b); Human Rights Act (Manitoba), RSM 1987, c. H175, s. 6(4); Human Rights Act (Nova Scotia), RSNS, c. 214, s. 8(3); Charter of Human Rights and Freedoms (Quebec), *supra*, see n. 53, Chap. 2.

[106] (1996), 96 CLLC 230–021/145,222 (Fed. Ct., TD). Two other recent decisions have assessed employment drug-testing policies under anti-discrimination law: *Entrop* v. *Imperial Oil Ltd.* (1997), 27 CHRR D/210, appeal dismissed (1998), 98 CLLC 145,072 (Div. Ct.); *Re: Sarnia Cranes Limited*, unreported, Ontario Labour Relations Board (4 May 1999).

Canadian Human Rights Act. The decisions of the two appellate courts which considered the case demonstrate that Canadian human rights legislation has not yet sufficiently linked anti-discrimination protection with privacy protection, and is therefore inadequate in protecting candidates'/employees' private interests from employer-imposed testing policies.

In 1990, Toronto-Dominion Bank instituted a comprehensive drug-testing programme for applicants to whom job offers have been made. Pursuant to the policy, an applicant must provide a urine sample for drug testing as a condition of employment. Those who test positive are required to participate in mandatory drug abuse rehabilitation (including counselling) if they wish to secure employment. The job offer will be withdrawn if the individual refuses to participate in the rehabilitation or fails to complete it successfully. Moreover, individuals who complete the treatment programme are subject to future testing, and another positive drug test could lead to dismissal. In short, the policy imposes burdens on, and/or denies employment opportunities to, individuals who test positive regardless of whether or not they are in fact drug dependent, and whether or not their drug use has an impact on their job performance.[107] Furthermore, the Bank offered no evidence that it had experienced human resource problems related to drug use in the past. Its justification for the policy was speculative—it assumed that a drug-free workforce would be more productive, and that there would be a reduced risk of employee theft. The Bank did not, and could not, advance a safety justification for the policy.

The Canadian Civil Liberties Association, on behalf of the Bank's employees, filed a complaint with the Canadian Human Rights Commission[108] alleging that the testing programme constituted discrimination against those with a disability, drug dependence (an existing or previous dependence on drugs is included in the Act's definition of disability[109]). A Human Rights Tribunal was then convened. The Tribunal rejected the argument that the policy *directly* discriminates against drug addicts because both non-dependent casual users, who are not disabled and therefore not protected under the Act, and the protected group of dependent users, could lose employment opportunities under the policy. The Tribunal then considered the possibility that the policy *adversely affects* drug dependents, but avoided deciding the question by reasoning that the policy adequately accommodates such persons through the provision of drug rehabilitation and counselling.

An appeal was then brought to the Federal Court, Trial Division, by the Human Rights Commission and the Civil Liberties Association. In her decision, Justice Simpson agreed with the Tribunal that the Bank's testing policy was not direct discrimination. She found insead that the policy constituted indirect or adverse effect discrimination against job candidates who were drug addicts

---

[107] *Toronto-Dominion Bank, supra*, n. 106, 145/224.

[108] Because banks are federally regulated in Canada, the appropriate legislation and commission was that of the federal government.

[109] *Supra*, n. 97, s. 25.

because it was more difficult, if not impossible, for them to abide by a policy requiring employees to refrain from drug use. This finding was significant because, under the legislative scheme, an employment policy that directly discriminates must be justified as a *bona fide* occupational *requirement*.[110] In this case, it would have been difficult for the Bank to prove that working in a financial institution *requires* employees to abstain from off-duty drug use. However, because the policy was characterised as adverse effect discrimination against drug addicts, it would be valid if the Bank could show a rational connection between the policy and job performance issues (a lower test than the one applied in the case of direct discrimination) and that the policy reasonably accommodates drug addicts. Justice Simpson expressed the view (shared by the Tribunal) that the policy satisfied the test for accommodation, but found that the Tribunal erred in not considering the rational connection element.

Justice Simpson's decision is important because it illustrates the difficulties inherent in arguing a privacy matter under anti-discrimination law. Because the Bank offered no evidence that drug use had affected its productivity or security, it is reasonable to characterise the impugned policy as an attempt to obtain information about, and control, candidates' off-duty activities and private lives through invasive testing. As such, the policy infringes upon the informational and corporeal private interests of all job candidates. In contrast, the policy is discriminatory only to the extent that it denies opportunities or imposes burdens upon a sub-group of candidates, namely drug addicts. Although Justice Simpson remarked upon the privacy ramifications of the policy, she flatly rejected the submission that the Human Rights Tribunal should be required to consider privacy matters as part of its discrimination analysis:

> In my view, these privacy issues are outside the jurisdiction of the Tribunal. It is charged with considering the complaint. It is made under s. 10 of the CHRA and makes no reference to privacy issues or to the validity of the Bank's contracts of employment. If the Tribunal had jurisdiction to consider these issues, then it might have been appropriate to use Charter principles in such a consideration. However, without fundamental jurisdiction to consider the issues, the question of importing Charter values does not arise.[111]

On this view, privacy concerns have no place in anti-discrimination analysis. However, the application of anti-discrimination law leads to the paradoxical result that drug addicts, but not mere drug users, are legally protected from discrimination by the Bank, and must be accommodated. Casual drug users have no such protection, and can be dismissed by the employer after a positive test. Thus, the individuals who pose the least threat to the employer's interests are the ones who enjoy no protection under anti-discrimination law. If the matter were analysed within privacy law, and in particular in relation to the principles developed by arbitrators (as discussed above in section 6.5.1), then Toronto-

---

[110] *Ibid.*, s. 15(a).
[111] *Toronto-Dominion Bank, supra,* n. 106, 145/226.

Dominion Bank would be prohibited from testing anyone without individualised reasonable suspicion of impairment, and could be wholly precluded from applying the policy, given the absence of a legitimate health and safety rationale.

The inadequacies of assessing employment drug-testing within anti-discrimination law were further highlighted when the *Toronto-Dominion Bank* case was appealed to the Federal Court of Appeal.[112] In that court, each of the three judges on the panel delivered a separate decision. Justice McDonald found that the Bank's drug-testing plan constituted indirect discrimination against workers disabled by reason of drug addiction, and further held that the Bank had failed to accommodate those drug-addicted workers in a manner sufficient to meet the requirements of the Canadian Human Rights Act. Justice Robertson took the view that the plan was actually direct discrimination against drug-dependent employees, and that the Bank had failed to lead convincing evidence that the plan was a *bona fide* occupational requirement. Chief Justice Isaac, in dissent, agreed that the plan constituted indirect discrimination, but held that the Bank had accommodated drug addicts by offering rehabilitation programmes for those who tested positive for drug use. Ultimately, the imposition of discipline and dismissal on employees who test positive for drug use was held to be illegal, indirect discrimination, but only in the case of those disabled due to drug addiction.

If, as appears to be the case from the *Toronto-Dominion Bank* decision, the only way to attack employment drug testing under anti-discrimination law is to characterise the testing as indirect discrimination against drug addicts, then there is nothing within that law to prevent testing *per se*, or to prevent the disciplining or dismissal of drug users who cannot be characterised as 'disabled' (i.e. 'casual' drug users). Anti-discrimination law merely contributes one limiting element to employment drug testing: employees who test positive for drug use and self-identify as addicts/disabled must be accommodated by the employer through the provision of treatment and rehabilitation. Both Justices McDonald and Robertson adverted to the fact that an analysis of drug testing within a privacy framework could lead to broader limitations.[113] Justice McDonald stated:

> The [Banks's] policy applies to prohibit any continued use of illegal drugs regardless of the reason for that use. Casual drug users who continue to use drugs after testing positive risk dismissal whether or not they are dependent on drugs. The policy is designed to catch all drug users not merely dependent drug users. It is only because it is designed to catch all drug users that drug dependent employees are caught. While the rule negatively impacts on drug dependent users, it does not directly discriminate against them. *I would note that if the CHRA protected the right of privacy, casual users would be protected from invasive drug testing procedures. As my colleague states, however, this case is not argued on privacy grounds.* Drug dependent users are

---

[112] [1998] 4 FC 205 (CA). The case was subsequently abandoned by the Bank, and there will be no appeal to the Sup. Ct. of Canada.
[113] *Ibid.*, at 250 (*per* Justice Robertson); at 281 (*per* Justice McDonald).

therefore the only individuals protected from this policy under the Act.[114] [emphasis added].

Because the Canadian Human Rights Act and its provincial equivalents do not regulate employment drug testing *per se*, but at the most prohibit discrimination against drug addicts based on the information obtained from testing, it would seem that there is little hope of successfully challenging private sector drug testing policies in the five provinces which have not yet created a statutory right of privacy. In contrast, candidates/employees in the public sector may challenge drug testing under section 8 of the Charter, and unionised workers may rely upon the right of privacy developed in the arbitration context.

6.5.3 Workplace Privacy in the Province of Quebec

Privacy law in the Province of Quebec has two unique features relevant to employment: first, the Province's human rights legislation protects both the rights of equality and privacy, and, secondly, the Province has enacted an information privacy law applicable to the private sector. Although workplace privacy has not, to date, been a significant source of litigation in Quebec, the remedies available to public and private sector candidates/employees are broader and more coherent than elsewhere in Canada.

6.5.3.1 Quebec's Charter of Human Rights and Freedoms

Not only was Quebec the first Canadian jurisdiction to recognise the right of privacy in its private law, but it was also the first (and remains the only) jurisdiction to include the right of privacy in its human rights legislation. Section 5 of Quebec's Charter of Human Rights and Freedoms guarantees to everyone 'the right to respect for his private life'. Quebec's Charter is quasi-constitutional, as it takes precedence over all provincial laws (meaning that it may be employed to challenge laws in the courts) (section 52). However, it also applies to private dealings such as employment. For this reason, the privacy right in Quebec's Charter is analogous to the one contained in California's Constitution, as both may be asserted against public and private bodies. This means that all Quebec employers are legally obliged to respect the privacy of candidates/employees—the right of privacy thus forms part of the legal 'floor' regulating the employment relationship.

Furthermore, the right of privacy falls within the mandate of Quebec's quasi-judicial Human Rights Commission, which is given the responsibility of ensuring 'by all appropriate measures' the promotion and respect of the rights contained in Quebec's Charter (section 71). Although the Commission's powers of investigation and adjudication are limited to matters concerning anti-dis-

---

[114] [1998] 4 FC 205 (CA), at 281.

crimination law (sections 71, 74), it may play an advisory role in relation to other rights such as privacy. To this end, the Commission has issued various reports on privacy-related issues, although none has yet focused on privacy in the workplace.[115] Nevertheless, rights like privacy may be enforced by the judiciary even where the Human Rights Commission lacks jurisdiction (section 49). This means that employees and job candidates may rely upon section 5 to challenge privacy-invasive management policies in court, while organised employees and unions may assert the right in the arbitration context.

There is a fundamental difference between privacy-based arbitrations in Quebec and in the other provinces, since it is not possible for private sector employers and unions to contract out of section 5 of Quebec's Charter by agreeing to limit workers' privacy rights. Employers would also not be able to take advantage of implied contractual terms permitting privacy invasions which might arise through employee acquiescence to, or acceptance of, unilaterally imposed invasive policies. One must be cautious, however, in declaring Quebec employment law to be highly protective of private interests. Very few workplace privacy cases have been litigated in the Province, and at least one arbitration decision reflects a deferential approach to privacy in the employment context. In *Re Bridgestone/Firestone Canada Inc.*,[116] the arbitrator had to decide whether videotapes taken of an employee by a private investigator during off-duty hours were admissible as evidence. Although the arbitrator noted that the right of privacy is a fundamental human right under Quebec's Charter,[117] he observed that all such rights are subject to limitations and must be applied in context. In his view, employment is a special context in which the employee places himself under the direction and control of the employer, and owes the employer a duty of loyalty. These factors constitute a 'renunciation' on the part of the employee of aspects of his private life, which thereby reduces the force of the right of privacy.[118] The arbitrator concluded that the videotapes were admissible because the employer had a legitimate interest in investigating the employee (who had filed a claim for injury compensation), and the employee's expectation of privacy was reduced both as a result of the employment context, and because he was in public view when the videotapes were taken.

It is notable that the arbitrator's view that expectations of privacy are reduced in the employment context is similar to the approach taken by the court in *Calgary Local 710*,[119] although this constitutional decision was not mentioned in the *Bridgestone/Firestone Canada Inc.* reasons.

If future tribunals adopt the view taken in *Bridgestone/Firestone Canada Inc.* that the right of privacy has reduced force in the employment context (and that

---

[115] Lamarche (1996), 68–70. See Quebec Commission on Human Rights (1991), 9, concerning the impact of new technologies on the right of privacy.

[116] [1995] TA 505 (Quebec).

[117] *Ibid.*, 518.

[118] *Ibid.*, 519.

[119] *Supra*, n. 29.

employees therefore have a lower expectation of privacy), then this could convert Quebec's law of workplace privacy into a mere reflection of the prevailing
law governing non-organised private sector candidates/employees in the United
States and elsewhere in Canada. At the same time, the comprehensive application of the right of privacy in employment means that there is at least a legal
floor of privacy protection in Quebec, as in France and California. Given the significance of Quebec as a jurisdiction within Canada, it is possible that other
provinces will eventually follow Quebec's lead by adopting a similar comprehensive approach to privacy.[120]

6.5.3.2 *Quebec's Law of Information Privacy*

Quebec is the only jurisdiction in North America which has enacted information privacy legislation applicable to the private sector.[121] As a result of the Act
Respecting the Protection of Personal Information in the Private Sector,[122]
private sector candidates/employees in the Province now enjoy rights similar to
those of their public sector counterparts, including the right to access human
resource files, and demand that errors be corrected (sections 27–29).
Furthermore, the legislation requires that whenever a private sector actor
(including an employer) opens a file containing personal information about an
individual, the actor must have a 'serious and legitimate reason' for establishing
the file, must collect the personal information by 'lawful means' and must generally obtain the information from the subject (sections 4–7). The actor is also
under a duty to inform the subject of the purpose of the file, the use which will
be made of it, the persons who will have access to it, the place where the file will
be kept and the rights of access and rectification (section 8). Other legal duties
include a duty to ensure that the file is accurate (section 11), and a duty to disclose information to third parties only with the consent of the subject (section
13). Section 18 of the Act provides a very strict definition of 'consent': consent
to the communication or use of personal information must be manifest, free and
enlightened, and must be given for specific purposes.

The Act also confers a mandate upon the Access to Information Commission
(Quebec's equivalent of the federal PCC) to investigate and adjudicate[123] complaints concerning access to information and rectification (sections 42–69). In
relation to other matters concerning the protection of personal information
(including information collection, communication and use), the Commission

---

[120] Quebec was the first province to enact a public sector information privacy regime, and this is
credited with influencing the other provinces to adopt similar laws. See Comeau and Ouimet (1995),
652–3.

[121] *Ibid.*, 651. The federal government is presently considering a proposal to extend its information privacy legislation into the private sector. See Bill C–54, Personal Information Protection and
Electronic Documents Act (1998).

[122] *Supra*, n. 27.

[123] Quebec's Commission has a formal adjudicative role, unlike the federal PCC, whose role is
advisory and conciliatory.

may receive complaints, initiate its own complaints and investigate (section 81). In such cases, however, the Commission's function is not adjudicative. Instead, it may make recommendations (section 83), and if these are not followed to its satisfaction, then it may publish an opinion and direct public attention to the matter (section 84). Although the Commission is analogous to the French CNIL, both of which oversee information privacy laws applicable in the public and private sectors, its power is more limited. While the Commission has developed for itself an advisory role, issuing general guidelines and recommendations on the implementation of, and compliance with, the Act,[124] its opinions on issues of information collection, use, etc. do not have the force of law. Moreover, there is no registration regime which would permit the Commission to assert control over automated processing.[125] Quebec's information privacy regime is, therefore, less interventionist than the French version.

The Quebec Act is nevertheless more protective than other Canadian laws, and this is not simply because it applies to the private sector. As I observed above, the collection of personal information must not only be linked to a 'serious and legitimate reason', but must also be 'lawful'. The first condition is not present in the analogous federal legislation, although the federal PCC appears to have read a legitimacy requirement into the Privacy Act. The second condition is even more significant, as Quebec law recognises the right of privacy in the Civil Code, and in Quebec's Charter. As a result, information collection is lawful only if it complies with Quebec's privacy law (as discussed in section 6.5.3.1 above). This means that in a case of workplace drug testing, for example, employees could complain about the practice to the Access to Information Commission, which would then investigate and issue an opinion on whether or not such testing constitutes a 'lawful' means of collecting information. Unlike the federal legislation, which is primarily concerned with privacy over personal information after its collection, Quebec's law reflects a more comprehensive approach to privacy, effectively prohibiting information collection which infringes upon all the private interests protected by the right of privacy.

6.6 CONCLUSIONS

The extent to which a Canadian candidate/employee is legally protected from privacy-invasive employer policies depends on the government (federal or provincial) which has regulatory control over the particular employer, and whether the employer is a public or private body. Moreover, unionised employees will generally enjoy greater protection than their non-unionised counterparts. The range of protection in the country is quite astounding: in the Province

---

[124] Comeau and Ouimet (1995), 666–7.

[125] *Ibid.*, 667. Quebec's lawmakers apparently believed that a French-style registration system would be opposed by business interests. Comeau and Ouiment describe the Quebec law as 'pragmatic'.

of Ontario, candidates and non-unionised employees in the private sector appear to have no remedy for invasion of privacy while, in the Province of Quebec, all candidates and employees may assert the right of privacy in Quebec's Charter. Canadian workplace privacy law is far from comprehensive, thus making it analogous to the law in the United States. Both countries' regimes are less coherent, comprehensive and protective than the French system.

As I noted in section 6.1 of this Chapter, the evolution of workplace privacy law towards a more comprehensive and protective model is ultimately more likely in Canada than in the United States. In the past 15 years, as a result of section 8 of the Charter of Rights and Freedoms, the legal trend in Canada reveals growing protection for privacy. This trend is evinced by the enactment in the 1980s and early 1990s of information privacy laws by the federal and provincial governments, and by the adoption of Charter privacy principles in private sector arbitration cases. Furthermore, Quebec's rejection of the public/private distinction in the application of its privacy laws indicates that Canada may be moving towards the French model, which itself treats all actors (such as employers) in a qualitatively similar manner. Although there is a trend in both the United States and Canada toward heightened privacy protection in both the public and private sectors, the efficiency arguments and general influence of market individualists in the United States may discourage a rapid expansion of law in the American employment context. However, there is no evidence of a similar market individualist tradition in Canada. Canadian labour law has remained tied to the collective *laissez-faire* model which, as I noted in section 3.3.1 of Chapter 3, will accommodate legal initiatives to promote industrial justice and stability. The pragmatic nature of present-day Canadian labour law, combined with a general societal enthusiasm for measures protecting human rights, should make possible 'floor-of-rights' initiatives in the field of workplace privacy.

7

Seven Legal Principles

7.1 INTRODUCTION—CONVERGENCE, DIVERGENCE, AND HARMONISATION

In Chapters 4, 5 and 6, I considered the law of workplace privacy in the United States, France and Canada respectively. The analyses revealed a basic similarity in the laws of the three countries, as each recognises a right of privacy within its constitutional human rights (i.e. public law) and private law regimes that protects personal, territorial and informational private interests. Moreover, in each, the right has played a regulatory role in the employment context—a role that appears to be expanding over time. Beyond these points, however, fundamental differences remain. French law is clearly more comprehensive and protective than American and Canadian law. The federal systems in the two North American countries complicate matters further, as some subsidiary jurisdictions, like California and Quebec, have taken a more protective approach than others.

Nevertheless, it is clear that a process of convergence is taking place in the three countries. Bennett has defined 'convergence' as a 'dynamic process' through which domestic laws in different jurisdictions tend to evolve toward common solutions to shared problems.[1] In each of the countries examined to this point, workplace privacy has been identified as a legal problem, and the laws in the three are evolving to address the problem, albeit at different paces. This process is exemplified by the flurry of statutes which have been enacted in the United States[2] and France,[3] and by the growth of Canadian workplace privacy law since the entrenchment of the Charter of Rights and Freedoms in 1982.[4] Of course, absolute convergence is neither likely nor desirable. Differing legal and political cultures can be expected to impact upon domestic legal reforms, and give rise to 'divergence' (a point which will be of crucial importance when I consider United Kingdom law in section 10.2 of Chapter 10 below). In the case of workplace privacy, the institutional mechanisms for enforcing the right are likely to remain the most notable point of divergence, even if the essential legal principles converge. As Kahn-Freund observed, a nation's institutions are a reflection of its unique social, political and economic power structure.[5] The French system of works councils, labour inspectors, etc. is a product of a

---

[1] Bennett (1992), 111.
[2] *Supra*, sect. 4.3.4.4.
[3] *Supra*, sect. 4.4.
[4] *Supra*, sects. 6.5.1, 6.6.
[5] Kahn-Freund (1974d), 18–20; *supra*, sect. 4.2.1.

power structure which accepts and relies upon state intervention to ensure compliance with laws. American political and legal culture, and to a lesser but important extent that of Canada, rejects state intervention in preference to self-help through the assertion of legal rights before courts and administrative tribunals.[6] In short, the legal principles governing the right of privacy in the workplace may be expected to converge over time, but the institutions that enforce the right are likely to remain divergent.[7]

It may well be that legal convergence is a natural phenomenon in jurisdictions at a similar stage of economic development. In the case of workplace privacy, however, this process may be rather slow since domestic laws are presently quite diverse. A concerted effort to harmonise laws would obviously expedite convergence, and would be desirable for two reasons. First, from the perspective of inter-jurisdictional trade and business activity, there are advantages to common employment standards, which would permit the implementation of firm-wide human resource policies.[8] Given the differences in the protection of privacy in the domestic laws of the United States, France and Canada, multi-jurisdictional employers may not only be prevented from developing firm-wide policies on matters affecting worker privacy, but may also face some uncertainty in determining the relevant legal standards to guide their policies. This point has already been made in the case of inter-American business,[9] but it could equally be made in relation to firms operating in more than one Canadian province and subject to provincial jurisdiction. In the case of drug testing, for example, a national employer could be prevented from developing a single policy because of divergent and ambiguous provincial employment laws. Similarly, businesses operating in two or all three of the national jurisdictions will be required to cope with diverse, and even conflicting, laws. This point is well illustrated by the dilemma faced by Canadian trucking companies which operated in both Canada and the United States prior to 1992. American law required periodic drug testing of drivers, whereas Canadian law imposed no such requirement, and arbitration jurisprudence indicated that suspicionless testing would be an unreasonable exercise of management prerogative in the absence of a collective agreement permitting it.[10] This conflict became a serious concern in Canada, as many employers chose to adopt the American requirement.[11] A similar conflict can be seen in the case of Esso, an American oil company that has courted controversy by implementing in its French operations an employment drug-testing policy developed in the United States. Because French laws on the subject are considerably more protective of candidates'/employees' private interests, it is likely that Esso's policy is illegal in France.[12]

---

[6] Bennett (1992), 218.
[7] *Ibid.*, ch. 7.
[8] PCC (1990b), 8.
[9] See n. 147, Chap. 4.
[10] *Supra*, sect. 6.5.1.
[11] PCC (1990b), 7; see *Re Provincial-American Truck Transporters*, n. 70, Chap. 6.
[12] ILO (1993a, 3), 227.

Secondly, divergent employment standards are problematic for more protective jurisdictions, and for the workers who benefit from the higher standards. I discussed the phenomenon of worker protection erosion, or 'social dumping', in section 3.3.3 of Chapter 3. Although of general concern with regard to employment standards, worker protection erosion is particularly troublesome in the case of matters related to domestic human rights law, since the worker interests protected are often conceived as being of a higher order, or as fundamental in nature. Social dumping could place downward pressure on domestic human rights protection—a phenomenon that could be avoided if all relevant jurisdictions committed to common levels of protection. This reasoning is, in fact, the basis of the social rights movement within the European Union as discussed in Chapter 3, which seeks to implement a set of fundamental social rights as the foundation of European-level labour law.[13] In the case of workplace privacy, protective jurisdictions like France, Quebec and California would naturally be concerned about lower standards in other jurisdictions if business perceived compliance with more protective standards as a competitive disadvantage and chose to locate elsewhere. Such jurisdictions can therefore be expected to push for the *upward* harmonisation of employment standards related to privacy as a means of preventing other jurisdictions from securing or maintaining a competitive advantage in attracting foreign trade and investment through reduced standards. The European Directive on Data Protection,[14] which harmonises information privacy law throughout the European Union by imposing on all Member States a system of information privacy similar to that of France, is an example of upward harmonisation[15] securing a common standard of protection among trading partners. Since each Member State will be required to maintain the same essential standards of protection, no state will be able to set itself up as an information haven, and thereby gain a competitive advantage. This demonstrates the use of privacy law to prevent social dumping. The fact that the Directive applies in the employment context, in the same manner as the French Law of 6 January 1978, means that it secures common standards of workplace information privacy protection throughout the European Union.

The harmonisation of employment standards among trading partners is desirable from the perspective of economic certainty, and *upward* harmonisation discourages the pursuit of economic advantage through social dumping, thereby preventing the reduction of employment law to the lowest common denominator. In this chapter, I will advance seven legal principles that, in my view, should form the basis of a common approach to the upward harmonisation of workplace privacy law in the United States, Canada and France. Furthermore, I will suggest in Chapter 10 below that these principles may also form the basis for the emerging law of workplace privacy in the United Kingdom. These principles constitute a 'best practice' model, and represent a

[13] *Supra*, sect. 3.3.3, and text accompanying nn. 83–85, Chap. 3.
[14] *Supra*, n. 1, Chap. 1.
[15] The Directive is certainly upward harmonisation in relation to the UK (*infra*, sect. 10.4).

protective approach to the right of privacy in the workplace. I outlined the basic premises underlying this approach in Chapters 2 and 3: (1) privacy is recognised as a human right in each of the jurisdictions; (2) the right of privacy protects important interests in autonomy, dignity, trust and pluralism; (3) the right, and the interests which it protects, are threatened by invasive management practices; and (4) the industrial justice objectives of labour law will permit legal regulation of management practices in order to protect worker privacy. Because of privacy's status as a human right safeguarding important individual interests, it is appropriate for the labour laws of the jurisdictions considered herein to converge toward a highly protective stance.

Before proceeding to outline the seven legal principles, it is important to emphasise that these principles relate to substantive law. As I discussed above, and as I detailed in Chapters 4, 5 and 6, there are significant differences at the institutional level in the workplace privacy laws of the United States, France and Canada, and remedial approaches differ as well. I intend the principles discussed herein to serve as guides to the legal reform of workplace privacy law in terms of both the development of new legislation and the application by tribunals/decision-makers of general privacy rights in the workplace context. The institutions that should be entrusted with the interpretation and enforcement of workplace privacy law, and the remedies that should be available for breach of these laws, are matters beyond the scope of my present discussion.

7.2 LEGAL PRINCIPLES FOR THE PROTECTION OF THE RIGHT OF PRIVACY IN THE WORKPLACE

I will proceed here by suggesting seven legal principles for the protection of the right of privacy in the workplace. The principles can be divided into three categories: two concern matters of application; four concern the reconciliation of competing interests; and the final principle relates to procedural and other safeguards for protecting informational private interests. I will justify each principle in relation to the laws of the United States, France and Canada, and in terms of more theoretical considerations.

7.2.1 Principles Concerning the Scope of Application of the Right of Privacy

7.2.1.1 Principle 1: Comprehensive Application Regardless of Status

---

Principle 1: Comprehensive Application Regardless of Status

(a) The right of privacy should apply to both public and private sector employment;
(b) The right of privacy should provide qualitatively similar protection to both employees and job candidates.

My analyses of American, French and Canadian law revealed tremendous diversity in the application of workplace privacy law. The protection available to an individual may depend on his status in three respects: (1) whether he is a public or private sector employee; (2) whether or not his employment is governed by a collective agreement; and (3) whether he is an employee or a job candidate. I take the view that the right of privacy should have comprehensive application in employment law, meaning that all individuals should enjoy qualitatively similar protection. Because my basic premise is that employment *law* (as opposed to employment *contracts*) should determine the standards governing matters related to workplace privacy (see Principle 2 below), I will not consider the role of collective agreements in protecting privacy here. This does not mean that I reject collective agreements as a mode of workplace privacy regulation. On the contrary, employment contracts, whether individual or collective, could provide enhanced protection beyond the protective legal floor that I believe is necessary. My primary concern here, however, is to describe the principles and features of the 'floor'.

(a) Comprehensive Application vis-à-vis *Public and Private Sector Employment*

Public sector employees in all three national jurisdictions enjoy privacy protection flowing from constitutional or statute law. The same cannot be said of private sector workers. Although French law has generally adopted a single approach to the right of privacy in the public and private sector workplaces, the two North American jurisdictions exhibit at least three different approaches to privacy protection in the private sector. First, private sector workers in some jurisdictions such as New York and Ontario[16] have no identifiable right of privacy that exists independently of their employment contracts or collective agreements. Secondly, the majority of jurisdictions offer a cause of action for invasion of privacy to all employees, although courts have adopted a deferential and reduced standard of protection in private sector cases.[17] Thirdly, two jurisdictions—California and Quebec[18]—have taken a comprehensive approach that does not differentiate between the public and private sectors. In resolving these conflicting approaches, it is necessary to confront the general issue of the appropriate role of human rights law in regulating relationships traditionally viewed as 'private'.[19] This is because human rights laws, including laws giving effect to the right of privacy, have often distinguished between the citizen–state relationship, and private sector relationships such as employment. Thus, in many jurisdictions, state action is subject to human rights restrictions to a much greater extent than that which is generally considered to be 'private' action. In Canada

---

[16] *Supra*, nn. 97, 107, Chap. 4 (New York); sect. 6.6 and text accompanying nn. 21, 22, Chap. 6 (Ontario).
[17] *Supra*, text accompanying nn. 105, 122–3, Chap. 4 (United States); 89–96, Chap. 6 (Canada).
[18] *Supra*, sects. 4.3.4.3 (California); 6.5.3.1 (Quebec)
[19] Ewing (1995), 111.

and the United States, for example, constitutional guarantees of free speech and privacy constrain public employers directly, whereas employers in the private sector are subject only to those limits found in statute law, common/civil law or the employment contract.

While the distinction sometimes drawn by human rights law between public and private employment has been characterised by some as an 'historical accident',[20] it rests in part on the assumption that state power is potentially so much more coercive than private power that the state, even as an employer, should be subject to stricter limitations.[21] It also reflects the attitude of *laissez-faire* thinkers that while the state may limit its own actions, state-imposed legal constraints on the labour market create inefficiencies, and should therefore be avoided. The private quality of employment is reinforced by its contractual nature. It was this fact which, 26 years ago, led the United Kingdom's Younger Committee to conclude 'that most of the privacy complaints in employment are a matter of the relationship between the employer and the employee or prospective employee', and that legal intervention to protect worker privacy was unnecessary.[22] Still today, an enduring argument against protecting human rights in the private sector is simply that legal intervention would interfere unnecessarily with private action, including freedom of contract.[23]

The importation of individual human rights into the employment context has also been criticised as potentially antithetical to the collective nature of labour law. Hence, collective representatives may be sympathetic to the assertion of human rights law against employers, yet ultimately oppose the extension of such rights into the workplace if this would permit individual workers to rely on human rights to frustrate collective action.[24] While this argument is not exclusive to private sector employment, it is clearly relevant to the question whether rights already existing in public law should be *extended* into the private sector.

The denial of human rights protection to individual workers in order to protect unions from these same rights rests on the assumption that it is somehow problematic to hold collective representatives answerable for actions which, if committed by employers, would raise human rights concerns. In a liberal-democratic society, one could forcefully advance the opposite proposition, that collective actors should be particularly accountable in the realm of human rights because of the potential threat of collective power to individual autonomy. To illustrate, it would be most peculiar to immunise racial or sexual discrimination committed by unions from human rights review, when such discrimination would be intolerable if committed by the state or an employer. Similarly, one

---

[20] Samar (1991), 186.

[21] Fredman and Morris (1989), 7–8, argue that the state is distinct from private employers because the government has the unique power to initiate legislation and make executive decisions affecting employment, and because the state can justify limiting its employees' human rights in reliance on the 'public interest'. However, Chap. 2 (sect. 2.3.4.5) discussed the ways in which private sector employers have justified drug testing policies by reference to the 'public interest'.

[22] Committee on Privacy (1972), 97.

[23] Epstein (1992b); *supra*, sects. 4.3.1, 4.3.2.

[24] Clapham (1996b), 23–4; Holloway (1993), 136.

might well conclude that privacy-invasive policies of unions should be subject to no less demanding human rights scrutiny than employer policies threatening workers' private interests.

In fact, concerns about the application of human rights to collective worker representatives largely centre on fears that individuals may invoke freedom of expression or freedom of association to destroy closed shops and undermine worker solidarity.[25] These issues are obviously controversial, and a full consideration of the competing perspectives lies beyond the scope of this book. It should suffice to observe that it is difficult (if not impossible) to imagine how the assertion of the right of privacy could threaten collective organisation to the same extent as freedom of association or freedom of expression. There is nothing in the *collective* nature of organised labour that makes it problematic for unions to respect fully the personal, territorial and informational private interests of their members.

Furthermore, in an era of declining union influence, where the employment relationship is becoming increasingly individualistic in character (i.e. is based on the individual contract of employment as opposed to collective agreements), the application of individual rights like privacy to employment is particularly valuable as a means of protecting and empowering individual workers, and assisting both workers and employers in determining the scope and limits of the management prerogative. Hence, a focus on individual rights within increasingly individualised labour law systems creates an appropriate symmetry.

Another argument against the importation of human rights into the employment relationship rests on the historical lessons of the American *Lochner* era (1900–37).[26] It was during this period that the United States Supreme Court declared unconstitutional several pieces of worker protection legislation, including key elements of President Roosevelt's 'New Deal',[27] on the theory that such legislation interfered with the freedom of contract of workers and their employers. In a manner echoing the premises of collective *laissez-faire*, one might well point to the *Lochner* experience as evidence that industrial relations is a matter best kept out of judicial hands. This indeed is Holloway's point when he argues against the 'constitutionalisation' of labour law because such an approach would call on judges to pronounce upon employment standards according to their own personal views of the appropriate scope of state regulation in private sector industrial relations.[28]

In response to the school of thought which raises the spectre of an anti-worker judiciary to oppose the importation of human rights into private sector employment law, I would observe that there is a basic fallacy in equating the protection

---

[25] Clapham (1996), 23–4, 28.

[26] *Lochner* v. *New York*, 198 US 45 (1905). See Gunther (1992), 110–28.

[27] *Lochner, ibid.*, itself concerned the constitutionality of legislation limiting the working hours of bakers. The Court, per Justice Peckham, 49, stated: '[t]he question whether this act is valid as a labor law, pure and simple, may be dismissed in a few words. There is no reasonable ground for interfering with the liberty of person, or the right of free contract, by determining the hours of labor, in the occupation of a baker.'

[28] Holloway (1993), 123.

of worker interests through the application of human rights principles with judicial activism voiding worker protection legislation (as occurred in the *Lochner*-era United States). In both situations, it is true that 'rights' are being called upon to support state intervention—freedom of speech, anti-discrimination or the right of privacy in the former case; freedom of contract or property rights in the latter case. However, the enduring labour law lesson of *Lochner* is not that the judiciary should vacate the field of worker protection, but rather that the judiciary should avoid frustrating worker protection initiatives in the private sector through a simplistic reliance on freedom of contract. As I argued in section 3.3.2 of Chapter 3, the employment relationship is not one of contractual equals, and state (including judicial) intervention to support the interests of workers falls squarely within the industrial justice objectives of labour law.

Ultimately, the application of human rights like privacy to the private sector workplace is supported by the nature of the contractual relationship between non-governmental employers and employees, which cuts across the traditional public/private divide. In fact, over the course of the twentieth century, the employment relationship has become increasingly *public* in nature, making the notion of the workplace as a private sphere seem outdated. Thus, even if we continue to hold to the public/private distinction in human rights law,[29] the workplace may well fit more comfortably on the public side of the dichotomy. There are at least four reasons for this.

First, despite the influence of collective *laissez-faire*, the private employment contract has been extensively regulated by the state, through labour relations codes, occupational health and safety legislation, employment standards statutes, etc. The state's pursuit of industrial justice and stability policies demonstrates that employment is a matter of general public concern, and renders *freedom* of contract in the employment context rather illusory.

Secondly, not only is a sizeable portion of the workforce employed by the state itself, but as many, if not more workers are employed in private industries subject to considerable state regulation. Also, the past decade has been marked by governmental downsizing, privatisation, and contracting out, all of which have contributed to a significant transfer of jobs from the public to the private sector.[30] Thus, many 'private' jobs have a decidedly 'public' flavour to them. Yet, if the traditional public/private distinction were controlling, and if the non-governmental workplace were automatically considered private and therefore beyond the scope of human rights law, then fewer workers would enjoy the protection available against state action.[31]

---

[29] Many commentators, most notably those from the critical legal studies school, have attacked the public/private distinction. See, e.g., Harlow (1980), 265; Kennedy (1982); Pateman (1983); Clapham (1993a), 94, 128–32. It is beyond the scope of this book to explore the general criticisms of the public/private distinction. Only the application of the distinction in the employment context will be considered. On this issue, see in particular Klare (1982). Clapham himself includes trade unions and corporations in his list of 'new fragmented centres of power' whose actions *vis-à-vis* individuals should be subject to human rights review (137).

[30] Clapham (1996b), 21–2.

[31] Summers (1986), 691.

Thirdly, the employment contract often permits the employer to exert considerable economic power and control over workers, and this control can sometimes extend beyond the confines of the workplace (a matter which itself implicates the right of privacy).[32] The power of an employer to regulate the lives of its employees is not dissimilar to the regulatory power exercised by the state, but without constitutional safeguards. One commentator, writing in the context of drug testing, has observed that the ultimate sanction available to an employer to punish *suspected* drug use by an employee, namely termination of employment, may be more severe than the criminal sanction imposed upon that same drug user after a successful state prosecution.[33] Given the expanding demands placed on workers in the 1990s, the regulatory power of the employer is surely as significant to the daily lives of workers as that of the state, and perhaps of greater significance in many cases.

Fourthly, private employers and unions are often used as tools by the state for achieving larger public policy goals. Consider, for example, the imposition on the private sector of wage controls to fight inflation, or employment equity/affirmative action policies. In the privacy context, as I discussed in section 2.3.4.5 of Chapter 2, the United States Government has actively encouraged employers to initiate drug-testing programmes as part of its 'war on drugs'. Tripartism, through which public policy is implemented by state, employer and union co-operation, may well increase in the future.[34] As a result, the private sector employer will slide further toward the public side of the public/private dichotomy.

By taking these four considerations into account, we can see that state and public interests are so bound up in the employment relationship that the traditional public/private distinction underlying human rights law becomes difficult to apply. This surely speaks to the merits of reconsidering the relevance of the distinction to human rights law, and in particular to the notion that the categories of 'private' and 'public' employment are watertight compartments. In fact, it may be helpful to view private employment as falling closer to the public side of a public/private *continuum*. Alternatively, one might well label private sector employment as 'quasi-public' in nature, thus recognising a new middle-ground category. There is ample precedent in American, French and Canadian law for a conception which extends the bounds of employment beyond the 'private' sphere. French labour law on the issue of human rights is most obviously helpful in this regard, as it draws very few distinctions between public and private sector employment. In North America, both California and Quebec have moved beyond a strict application of the public/private distinction in employment law. Moreover, decisions of courts and labour arbitrators also reflect a trend toward viewing employment as a matter of 'public' concern. This

---

[32] Grodin (1991); Summers (1986). See Kelly (1994).

[33] Feldthusen (1988), 94.

[34] See France, *supra*, sect. 5.1; Sciarra (1996), 6, argues that management and labour together constitute a 'political public sphere' whose 'strongest power resides in their capacity to interact with governments as necessary partners of national political economy'.

is revealed by the adoption in Canadian arbitration jurisprudence of constitutional human rights principles to guide the resolution of workplace privacy disputes,[35] and by the public policy doctrine in the United States, which similarly applies constitutional human rights principles to the private sector workplace.[36]

The breakdown of the public/private distinction in human rights law can also be seen in the approach of the European Court of Human Rights to the right of privacy guaranteed by Article 8 of the European Convention. The Court has stated:

> although the essential object of Article 8 is to protect the individual against arbitrary interference by the public authorities, there may in addition be positive obligations inherent in an effective respect for private life, albeit subject to the State's margin of appreciation . . . These obligations may involve the adoption of measures designed to secure respect for private life even in the sphere of the relations of individuals between themselves.[37]

The Court has thus taken tentative steps towards recognising that Article 8 not only controls state action, but may also require state intervention in relationships traditionally considered private. The failure of a state party to the Convention to provide a remedy for an invasion of privacy committed by a private actor may thus constitute a violation of Article 8.[38] This is, of course, different from applying Article 8 directly to private relationships, but nevertheless evinces the recognition that private actors may threaten human rights, and should be under legal constraints emanating from public law.

By viewing private sector employment as quasi-public in nature, and thereby appropriately subject to human rights law, it becomes clear that any distinction between the rights of workers on the basis of their status as governmental or non-governmental employees is artificial. The human rights interests of all workers (including their *private* interests) are the same, regardless of their employment status.[39] Moreover, the 'public' nature of all employment demonstrates why any management policy which impacts upon the human rights of employees should be approached as a matter of general legal concern, as opposed to a private matter to be determined by the employment contract, or regulated according to a watered-down, deferential legal approach. I therefore conclude that workplace privacy law should apply to all employment relationships.

---

[35] *Re Doman Forest Products*, see n. 69, Chap. 6; *supra*, sect. 6.5.1.

[36] *Luedtke*, see n. 94, Chap. 4; *supra*, sect. 4.3.4.1.

[37] *X & Y* v. *Netherlands* (26 Mar. 1985), Series A, No. 91 (ECHR), 11; see also *Airey* (9 Oct. 1979), Series A, No. 32 (ECHR), 17; de Meyer (1973), 272–3; Van Dijk and Van Hoof (1990), 596–7; Naismith (1996), 156–8.

[38] This is analogous to an action before the European Court of Justice (ECJ), where a citizen alleges that the government of a Member State of the European Union has failed to transpose a European directive into national law, and has thereby denied the citizen the benefits of the directive. See Case 41/74 *Van Duyn* v. *Home Office* [1974] ECR 1337, 1347–9 (ECJ).

[39] This was the view adopted by the ILO (1995e), 13.

(b) Comprehensive Application vis-à-vis *Employees and Job Candidates*

Workplace privacy law in the United States, France and Canada also evinces divergent approaches to the protection of applicants. French law was recently amended to provide heightened protection for job candidates, in a manner consistent with the analysis of Lyon-Caen.[40] In a similar vein, courts in California have adopted the same level of scrutiny for constitutional privacy claims by candidates and employees.[41] However, in most other North American jurisdictions candidates either have no cause of action[42] or enjoy a reduced level of protection.[43] Private sector applicants may be doubly disadvantaged in advancing a privacy claim, since the right of privacy may have reduced force in the private sector *and* in the hiring process. The issue therefore arises whether the status of a job candidate is sufficiently different from that of an actual employee to justify a more deferential legal approach to privacy-invasive hiring policies.

Generally, one would expect the most rigorous examination of an individual's background and character to occur prior to, as opposed to during, employment. The hiring process is designed specifically to identify the individual who is best suited (or qualified) for the relevant position. Hence, an employer conducts interviews, contacts referees and attempts to gather any information that will provide guidance in making the hiring decision. For this reason, there is great potential for invasions of privacy at the time of hiring. In fact, candidates are more likely than employees to be subjected to employer-imposed testing practices such as drug and psychological testing, hand-writing analysis or genetic screening. It might well be argued, however, that at the hiring stage an employer should be at liberty to use all means at its disposal to determine whether a candidate is a drug user, health risk, etc., including testing. If a candidate does not wish to be subject to such testing, then she may withdraw her application (and avoid a potential invasion of privacy) without suffering any significant loss, since she merely gave up the opportunity to obtain a job, as opposed to the job itself. Similarly, if a candidate agrees to submit to a test, then this should be taken as voluntary consent to any invasion of privacy that may result, on the theory that no coercion to act affirmatively can exist where the subject is free to choose between consenting or refusing. As I discussed in Chapters 4 and 6, this reasoning has appeared in both American and Canadian workplace privacy law to support reduced privacy protection at the time of hiring.[44]

Superior legal protection for actual employees has also been supported by the fact that in the employment context there exists a contractual relationship which creates legal obligations flowing from the employer to the employee. In

[40] Lyon-Caen (1992b); text accompanying nn. 59–65, Chap. 5.

[41] *Soroka*, see n. 137, Chap. 4 (and accompanying text).

[42] Consider job applicants in the 5 Canadian provinces lacking a statutory privacy right, *supra*, sect. 6.5.2.2.

[43] See text accompanying n. 121, Chap. 4.

[44] *Soroka*, see n. 137, Chap. 4; text accompanying nn. 109–17, Chap. 4 (United States); *Re Shell Canada Products Ltd.*, *supra*, n. 90, Chap. 6 (and accompanying text).

some jurisdictions, employers may be under an implied contractual duty of good faith.[45] In the unionised workplace, an employer will be under constraints related to good faith and reasonableness flowing from the collective agreement. No such contractual duties exist in the pre-employment situation. Hence, it could be argued that the legal regulation of the hiring process should reflect the more tenuous link between employer and applicant, and thereby provide both parties with greater room to manœuvre.

While the existence of a contractual relationship, with associated obligations and rights, may support a rigorous application of the law in regulating the employment relationship, it does not follow that job applicants should for that reason be denied equivalent legal protection. Any argument whose basic premise is that candidates are free to choose whether or not to submit to privacy-invasive policies is a manifestation of the false analogy between workers and consumers that I outlined in section 3.3.2 of Chapter 3. As I noted there, market individualists have argued that workers are free to withdraw their labour in protest over employment policies they dislike, in exactly the same manner in which consumers may withdraw their business from retailers. This analogy is flawed, however, because it fails to appreciate the fundamental importance of employment to the lives of individuals, and the fact that individuals face many obstacles in shifting their labour (or the potential supply of their labour) from one employer to another. Hence, it is unrealistic to claim that job candidates are always free to choose whether or not to submit to privacy-invasive policies in the hiring process.[46] Since refusing to submit almost inevitably will mean giving up the opportunity for employment, the loss to the individual from the refusal will be considerable. On the other hand, if the individual does submit, then the impact on her right of privacy is no different than if she were an actual employee. Hence, in relation to any privacy-invasive employer policy, it can be said that: (1) the private interests affected are the same regardless of the status of the subject; (2) the potential harm to the values underlying privacy (i.e. autonomy, dignity, trust and pluralism) is similarly equivalent; and (3) the penalty to the subject of avoiding the harm, whether it be loss of a job or loss of the opportunity for a job, is a significant hardship.

In addition, a reliance on the existence of a contractual relationship to determine the level of protection available for the right of privacy is inconsistent with the legal approach to the right of equality in the three national jurisdictions considered herein. American, French and Canadian anti-discrimination laws are equally available to job applicants and actual employees.[47] This supports the

---

[45] See, e.g., *Luedtke*, see n. 94, Chap. 4 (Alaska); text accompanying n. 132, Chap. 4 (California).

[46] Slane (1995), 89; Mole (1990), 66. Even Britain's Committee on Privacy (1972), which did not take the issue of workplace privacy very seriously (*infra*, sect. 10.2), conceded that 'although theoretically an (existing or prospective) employee is quite free to choose who he shall work for, in practice social and economic pressures limit that freedom in greater or less measure' (at 95).

[47] Civil Rights Act of 1964, see n. 13, Chap. 4; Americans with Disabilities Act, see n. 14, Chap. 4 (United States); Labour Code, Art. L.122–45, see n. 54, Chap. 5 (France); Canadian Human Rights Act, see n. 98, Chap. 6 (Canada).

view that human rights law should be unconcerned with the precise nature of the relevant relationship, and instead should intervene in any situation where the exercise of power by an employer results in an infringement of a human right. Hence, the existence of a contractual relationship, or the lack thereof, is of no importance; what matters is that any relationship between an employer and an actual or prospective employee can be characterised as one of unequal power. It is certainly the case that the employment contract permits an employer to exert considerable control over its employees (a point I discussed in section 2.3.3.1 of Chapter 2). However, it is also the case that the relationship created through the application process implies unequal power. The employer is offering to the public a 'good'—a job—of considerable importance, and applicants may well feel pressure to acquiesce to employer demands which infringe upon private interests because of their desire (and even their need) for employment.

A further, practical consideration justifies rigorously protecting individuals from privacy-invasive hiring practices. Because candidates do not have a contractual relationship with the employer, they are more vulnerable to privacy-invasive policies. The case of drug testing illustrates this point. As I will discuss below in Chapter 8 (section 8.4) one of the concerns surrounding drug-testing technology is inaccuracy, and particularly the possibility of false-positive test results. Employees who are disciplined or fired on the basis of a drug test will know the reason for the employer's actions, and will generally have recourse to grievance procedures, legal appeals, second-test confirmation or some other means of challenging the results of the test.[48] They may even be able to keep their jobs by entering and successfully completing a rehabilitation programme. While the drug testing of employees is likely to be transparent, the same cannot be said of candidate testing. Applicants who test positive will most likely be removed from consideration without ever knowing the reason why.[49] They are unlikely to be asked to take a second, confirmation test, nor are they likely to be given the opportunity to challenge positive test results.[50] This demonstrates that the absence of a formal, contractual relationship between employers and job candidates can be an argument in favour of human rights protection for job applicants.[51]

For these reasons, workplace privacy law should provide qualitatively similar protection to job candidates and actual employees. This conclusion and the conclusion above that public and private sector employees should enjoy legal protection are the bases for the principle of 'Comprehensive Application Regardless of Status'.

---

[48] An employee who is dismissed following a positive drug test may be able to launch an action in wrongful dismissal, and will be able to bring forward evidence of negative test results to demonstrate the wrongfulness of the employer's actions. Organised employees will have the additional support of the union, and the grievance procedures contained in the collective agreement.

[49] Axel (1991), 151.

[50] Feldthusen (1988), 86.

[51] This point influenced the OLRC (1992a), 111, to recommend legislative protection for job applicants from drug testing; Normand *et al.* (1994), 9.

7.2.1.2 Principle 2: Floor of Rights Application

Principle 2: Floor of Rights Application

The right of privacy should establish a single set of legal standards, or a 'floor of rights', in the employment context. It should not be possible for employers and employees to contract out of the right, nor should candidates or employees be taken to consent implicitly or expressly to privacy invasions which would otherwise be unwarranted.

The second principle, that the right of privacy should establish a floor of protection for workers, is linked to the principle of 'Comprehensive Application Regardless of Status'. It should be clear from Chapters 4, 5 and 6 that the privacy protection available to employees in a particular case could depend on two factors: (1) the legal source of the right of privacy, and (2) certain circumstances which operate to reduce 'expectations' of privacy. With regard to the legal source of privacy protection, some rights of privacy, for example constitutional privacy or the privacy guaranteed by the French Labour Code,[52] exist independently of the employment contract and may be asserted by workers against policies which are contractually permissible. Other rights, such as the right developed by Canadian labour arbitrators, can be limited, or even eliminated, by contractual agreement or past conduct.[53] Still other rights, for example the right existing in American tort law, are subject to broad exceptions premised on implied consent.[54]

Moreover, as I observed in relation to American law, and then repeated in my Canadian law discussion,[55] a reliance on the concept of 'expectations' of privacy has made the protection offered by the right highly circumstantial. This aspect of the law (which has also appeared in the only workplace privacy case decided under the European Convention on Human Rights[56]) has significantly reduced the impact of the right of privacy as a mechanism for standard-setting within employment law, since the protection available in a particular case will depend on circumstances such as prior notice, acquiescence, and implied consent—circumstances which bear little or no relation to the competing interests at stake. This means that two identical employment policies, affecting the same private interests and supported by the same competing interests, could be treated differently under the right of privacy if, in one case, the employer gave prior notice to employees of the policy (or if employees continued to work under the policy

---

[52] *Supra*, sect. 5.3.1.

[53] *Supra*, sect. 6.5.1.

[54] *Supra*, sect. 4.3.4.2. Compare this to the approach to consent under public policy privacy, *supra*, text accompanying nn. 113–14, Chap. 4.

[55] *Supra*, text accompanying n. 109, Chap. 4 (United States); *supra*, text accompanying nn. 29–33 and 117, Chap. 6 (Canada).

[56] *Halford* v. *United Kingdom*, *supra*, n. 4, Chap. 1, discussed *supra*, sect. 5.3.2.

for a period of time), but in the other case, the employer gave no notice (or the employees complained about it at the first opportunity).

Although the principle of comprehensive application discussed above does not necessarily require that the *same* source of privacy should govern all employment situations, the principle would effectively be undermined if the various sources of privacy offered qualitatively different protection depending on the status of the candidate/employee. Therefore, it is necessary to adopt a second principle, namely that the right of privacy establishes a single, unified standard applicable to all employment relationships. This means that employers and employees cannot contract out of the right, and that candidates/employees cannot consent either expressly or implicitly to privacy invasions which would otherwise be unwarranted. In essence, an approach premised on the 'floor of rights' school of labour law, as I outlined in section 3.3.3 of Chapter 3, should be adopted for regulating workplace privacy.

7.2.2 Principles Concerning Competing Candidate/Employee, Employer, and Public Interests

7.2.2.1 Principle 3: Legitimate and Substantial Limitations

The purpose of all law is to mediate between competing individuals, groups, organisations, institutions, etc., and to reconcile their often-conflicting interests. Human rights law, in its common/civil law, statutory and constitutional forms, is an important (although certainly not atypical) example of the mediating role of law. When a human rights claim arises, it is usually true that the alleged violator of a right has acted for some purpose, or in reliance on some interest, distinct from the interest of the party whose right has allegedly been violated.[57] Thus, the newspaper that publishes information about a criminal accused may have acted in reliance on freedom of the press, or on the public's 'right to know', or for the purpose of selling more newspapers and thereby increasing profits. Such a newspaper may be able to advance a range of rights and interests which can compete with the right of the accused to a fair trial—a right which could be jeopardized because of the publicity resulting from the newspaper's actions. In the workplace privacy context, consider the conflict that could arise where a hospital adopts a policy of blood-testing its employees for a particular disease. The employees could surely object that the testing policy invades certain private interests. On the other hand, the hospital's interest in protecting patients and staff from disease transmission, and the interest of the hospital's patients and staff in being secure against disease, are important countervailing interests.

The fact that the essence of human rights law is the management of conflict-

---

[57] Leaving aside the possibility that a human rights violation might be perpetrated simply for the purpose of denying human rights, and for no other reason, as might occur in some cases of discrimination.

ing interests is exemplified by the presence in constitutional and conventional human rights documents of provisions allowing for 'reasonable limits' on guaranteed human rights. For example, section 1 of Canada's Charter of Human Rights and Freedoms states that guaranteed rights and freedoms are subject to 'reasonable limits demonstrably justifiable in a free and democratic society'.[58] Human rights are rarely framed in absolute terms, in recognition of the fact that competing interests may justify rights-limitations. Hence, the right of privacy does not appear in common/civil law, statutory law or constitutional law as an absolute right. In fact, my legal analyses in the three preceding chapters demonstrated that limitations are permitted in various circumstances, and according to various tests (the most common of which is 'reasonableness').[59]

In section 2.3.1 of Chapter 2, I outlined a functional approach to the right of privacy, through which it is possible to determine whether a private interest of an individual is infringed by the actions of another. I offered a host of examples in the chapter of management policies (e.g. drug testing, electronic surveillance, etc.) which potentially limit private interests. If, indeed, private interests are threatened, why should this not be sufficient to justify the conclusion that the right of privacy itself has been infringed? The short answer is that the identification of private interests is only the first step in the privacy analysis, and that the second (and perhaps most important) step involves an evaluation of the competing interests of management and the public. A more complete response, however, must take into account the distinction between 'coverage' and 'protection' in human rights law.

The concept of human rights 'coverage' refers to the domain or class of acts to which a particular human right extends, whereas 'protection' involves a determination of the relative strength of the right when measured against competing rights and interests.[60] In simpler terms, 'coverage' includes all the *potential* states, conditions, actions, etc. protected by a human right, whereas the *actual* 'protection' afforded by the right in a given circumstance can only be determined by evaluating the competing interests which have been set up against the right, and by deciding whether or not these interests have greater force than the right.[61] Hence, to return to my example above concerning a hospital's policy of blood-testing its employees for a disease (probably with a view

---

[58] The European Convention on Human Rights and the American Convention on Human Rights both contain similar limitation provisions. Reasonable limits have been implied in the interpretation of the United States Bill of Rights. The French Labour Code's guarantee of human rights includes a proportionality test for limitations (Art. L.120–2).

[59] American and Canadian private law both premise privacy protection on the concept of 'reasonable expectations' (*supra*, n. 55). French law (*ibid.*) adopts a proportionality balancing test. Similarly, the relevant constitutional provisions in Canada and the United States refer to 'reasonableness' as the standard by which to judge an invasion of privacy (see Craig (1997a), 256–9; the Fourth Amendment of the United States Bill of Rights, and s. 8 of the Canadian Charter of Rights and Freedoms).

[60] Samar (1991), 77.

[61] Schauer (1982) offers the following analogy to explain the difference between 'coverage' and 'protection' in human rights law: 'If I'm wearing a suit of armour, I am *covered* by the armour. This will *protect* me against rocks, but *not* against artillery fire. I can be wounded by artillery fire despite the fact that I am covered by the armour. But this does not make the armour useless. The armour

to reassigning or dismissing those employees who test positive), it is evident that the employees' right of privacy provides 'coverage' because private interests would be implicated by a policy requiring employees to submit to blood tests. These private interests would fall into the personal zone, in the sense that obligatory blood testing would be invasive of the body, and also into the informational zone, as the information obtained through the testing would relate to personal health. Employees might also be concerned that this information could be disclosed beyond the confines of the hospital administration, leading to embarrassment and humiliation in the community at large. While these private interests are substantial, to say that they are sufficient in themselves to 'protect' staff from the hospital's testing policy is clearly incorrect. In other words, the existence of a threatened private interest is necessary, but not sufficient, to make out a privacy claim. A full analysis must take into account the hospital's purpose in subjecting employees to the testing policy, and its choice of method. Questions one might ask include: how serious is the disease at issue?; what is the risk of its transmission within the hospital?; what alternatives are available to the hospital in protecting patients and staff from the disease?; and what safeguards have been established to ensure the security of the health information obtained through the blood testing? Even if one's bodily integrity and personal health are generally considered to be private interests, the right of privacy may not afford protection in the case where one's health (or lack thereof) poses a threat to others. One might well conclude that information about personal health loses its private nature where the public is at risk. Similarly, although the private interest in bodily integrity will generally shield individuals from invasive medical procedures, a high risk of disease transmission, coupled with a lack of an alternative, less invasive method for detecting the presence of disease in health care workers, might well justify blood testing as a condition of employment. Again, it could be said that bodily integrity loses its private quality in such a situation.

The result above follows from the very nature of privacy itself. When one makes a privacy claim, one is implicitly stating that a certain interest is 'private', and should for this reason be protected from public intrusion. The assessment of a privacy claim must therefore focus on whether, in the circumstances, the interest at issue has a private character sufficient to justify privacy protection. The counter-argument to any privacy claim is that the interest, even if generally accepted to be of a private nature (i.e. to be 'covered' by the right of privacy), is not 'protected' in the circumstances because the competing interests of other parties creates a public dimension inconsistent with a claim of privacy.[62]

The justifications I offered in Chapter 2 for protecting privacy as a human

does not protect against everything; but it serves a purpose because with it only a greater force will injure me' (quoted in Samar (1991), 77).

[62] One can rely on the Millian 'harm principle' for this result. As Mill (1859), 32, wrote, the sphere of action protected from societal encroachment is 'that portion of a person's life and conduct which affects only himself, or if it also affects others, only with their free, voluntary, and undeceived consent and participation'.

right also provide insights into why certain competing interests can defeat a privacy claim. Consider first the autonomy-based justification. Privacy advances autonomy, and the related concept of independence, by providing the individual with the means to resist social control over her thoughts, actions, beliefs, relationships, etc. Nevertheless, no person can expect to enjoy perfect autonomy or independence while at the same time reaping the benefits of modern society— autonomy is not equivalent to anarchy.[63] This is because it is entirely possible that in exercising one's autonomy (perhaps through an assertion of privacy), one might frustrate the exercise of autonomy or independence by others. In order for all individuals to have an equal opportunity to pursue their interest in autonomy, compromise between competing autonomy-related claims will be necessary. In the case of the hospital's blood-testing policy, as described above, an assertion by employees of their right of privacy to oppose the policy could well be characterised as promoting their autonomy, since any mandatory policy is, by its very nature, a limitation on autonomy. Yet, what of the patients and staff who might conceivably be exposed to a serious, contagious disease? Their autonomy and independence could be reduced dramatically if they were prevented from protecting themselves against exposure to disease because of the operation of the right of privacy. One author, who has written extensively on the relationship between privacy and autonomy, has suggested that conflict situations should be resolved by determining whether, in any given circumstance, autonomy would be maximised through the assertion of privacy, or through the vindication of competing rights and interests.[64]

The same approach could be taken where privacy is justified on the basis of promoting individual well-being and dignity. To return to the hospital example, the well-being and dignity of those seeking to resist mandatory testing might well be jeopardized under such a policy. However, the very purpose of the policy would be to safeguard and promote the well-being and dignity of those potentially threatened by disease. Again, this illustrates how the assertion of a human right may, at the same time, both advance an important interest of the rights-claimant, yet jeopardize the same interest (or an interest of a qualitatively similar nature) of competing claimants. It is certainly not inevitable that human rights law will permit the assertion of privacy in furtherance of autonomy or dignity (or, for that matter, healthy relationships or pluralism) when that assertion threatens the same interests of others.[65] Similarly, human rights law will not necessarily condemn a policy seeking to maximise autonomy or dignity for some, where a denial of autonomy or dignity for others is an inevitable consequence of the policy. That is not to say that such a policy would necessarily be endorsed, of course. This leads me to the difficult question of how competing

---

[63] The classic illustration of this point involves the rules of the road. Individuals cannot be allowed to set their own personal rules (e.g., which side of the road to drive on) because this would result in chaos on the streets, and would put at risk the safety of other drivers and pedestrians.

[64] Samar (1991), 103.

[65] Clapham (1993a), 146, goes further, and implies a duty on the part of all individuals and private bodies 'not to subject others to indignities'.

privacy claims should be assessed and balanced, particularly in the employment context. The first legal principle relevant to the balancing of interests can be stated as follows:

Principle 3: Legitimate and Substantial Limitations

The right of privacy is not an absolute right, and may be limited by certain competing employer and public interests. However, in justifying a limitation on an individual's private interests, an employer should be required to advance a substantial interest related to a legitimate management concern. An employer should not be permitted to act beyond the scope of the employment relationship, and therefore should not place itself in the position of the state by limiting private interests without a management-related justification.

The issue of interest balancing must be informed by the fact that a human right, privacy, is at stake. This is not simply a rhetorical observation conveniently bolstering the case for protecting candidate/employee privacy. In asserting the right of privacy, a claimant is at the same time asserting those interests underlying the right, and which give it force. Hence, as I argued in section 2.3.3 of Chapter 2, a privacy claim advances interests in autonomy, well-being and dignity, pluralism and healthy relationships. Although all of these interests will not necessarily be threatened in a particular case, the fact that privacy is in jeopardy means that one or more of the interests must be. For this reason, the right of privacy is by its very nature substantial and a matter of pressing public concern; for competing interests to trump the right, they too should be of a substantial nature. One certain way in which competing employer interests may be regarded as insubstantial would be if they bear no relation to any of the justifications I discussed in section 2.3.4 of Chapter 2 for interfering with privacy: improving economic conditions, protecting health and safety, deterring abuse of the employment relationship, complying with state-imposed regulatory requirements or promoting the public interest. This is so because a failure or refusal to assert a management-related justification clearly indicates that the employer has acted beyond the scope of the employment relationship, which itself is fairly convincing evidence that the right of privacy has been infringed unjustifiably. As I noted in Chapters 4 and 6, some American states and Canadian provinces permit private sector employers to dismiss employees at will, with the result that employers are able to exert control (through the threat of dismissal) over employees' lives to a much greater extent than should be permissible under the right of privacy.[66] This is surely a significant structural problem with the employment laws of the two countries.

An employer must also be prevented from placing itself in the position of the

---

[66] See *Brunner* v. *Al Attar*, *supra*, n. 23, Chap. 4 (United States); *supra*, sect. 6.2 (Canada).

state for the purpose of invading privacy. To illustrate this point, a state policy discouraging the consumption of alcohol and drugs by employees in the transportation sector (perhaps reflected in a law permitting alcohol and drug testing of those employees, or by a ministerial statement encouraging a 'crack-down' on the use of alcohol and drugs by truck drivers, airline pilots, etc., or by an awareness campaign) could be advanced by employers in support of testing truck drivers, train operators, airline pilots, etc. However, this state policy could never justify an employer policy of testing workers whose jobs do not require the operation of a motor vehicle. Indeed, all workers might at some time engage in the operation of a motor vehicle while intoxicated. While this is surely of great public concern, it is only of management concern if it occurs in the context of the employment relationship (i.e. because the worker is operating an employer-owned vehicle while intoxicated, or is engaging in work-related duties while driving in an intoxicated state, etc.). Any other conclusion would permit employers to behave no differently from the state, and would expose the lives of workers to pervasive and endless interference by their employer.

Even where a policy or practice meets the legitimacy standard, it remains necessary to assess rigorously the employer and public interests advanced in opposition to employee private interests, in order for the competing interests to be weighed properly in the balancing exercise. It is evident, however, that this approach has not necessarily been adopted in the national jurisdictions. It is generally the case that employers in France are prohibited from infringing privacy for frivolous reasons unrelated to legitimate employer interests. However, in the United States, privacy-invasive management policies have often survived judicial scrutiny on the basis of flimsy or speculative justifications unsupported by evidence, while candidates'/employees' private interests have been downgraded through a reliance on 'reasonable expectations' and implied 'consent'.[67] The same phenomenon has occurred in the application of the tort of invasion of privacy to employment situations.[68]

The better (i.e. more protective) view is that workplace privacy issues should be regulated according to the interests at stake, and that only a substantial competing interest will justify the infringement of a private interest. This higher test is evident in the constitutional jurisprudence from the state of California,[69] in the French proportionality analysis under Article L.120–2 of the Labour Code,[70] and in the Canadian arbitration approach post-1982.[71] Of course, the adoption of a legal principle that only a 'substantial' or 'compelling' competing interest can overcome private interests provides general guidance. However, this may be further refined through the two related principles that I discuss next.

---

[67] Consider the workplace privacy jurisprudence of the US Supreme Court, *supra*, sect. 4.3.3.2.
[68] *Supra*, sect. 4.3.4.2.
[69] *Luck* v. *Southern Pacific Transportation Co.*, *supra*, no. 129, Chap. 4; *supra*, section 4.3.4.3.
[70] *Supra*, sect. 5.3.1.
[71] *Supra*, sect. 6.5.1.

7.2.2.2 *Principle 4: Sufficiency of Limitations Premised on Third Party Interests*

> **Principle 4: Sufficiency of Limitations Premised on Third Party Interests**
>
> Employer policies (or policies imposed on employers by the state) which limit private interests for the purpose of protecting third party interests in autonomy, dignity and well-being, healthy relationships, and pluralism (i.e. interests similar in nature to those underlying the right of privacy) are most likely to meet the 'legitimate' and 'substantial' tests. For this reason, an employer's interest in protecting the health and safety of employees, consumers and the public is a compelling justification for placing limitations on private interests.

As I observed in section 2.3.4.2 of Chapter 2, some privacy-invasive employer policies have as their primary aim the protection of the health and safety of employees, consumers and the public. Such policies have important economic motivations, as accidents are surely bad for business,[72] yet offer important benefits to third parties. For example, a hospital's blood-testing policy may have some economic advantages for the hospital (and taxpayers if the hospital is publicly funded), but its function in protecting employees and patients from disease transmission is most significant. Where third parties are the direct beneficiaries of a privacy-invasive policy, and the interests advanced by the policy include ones qualitatively similar to those protected by the right of privacy (such as autonomy, dignity, etc.), then we might easily conclude that such a policy meets the requirement of being 'legitimate' and 'substantial'. It is this reasoning that underscores the emphasis placed on safety justifications in some American,[73] French[74] and Canadian[75] decisions concerning employment testing.

7.2.2.3 *Principle 5: Insufficiency of Limitations Premised on Economic Interests*

> **Principle 5: Insufficiency of Limitations Premised on Economic Interests**
>
> An employer's economic interest is generally less likely to support limitations on private interests, since it is problematic to subordinate individual rights like privacy to economic goals.

---

[72] The economic impact of accidents can be severe: increased insurance premiums, negative publicity, clean-up costs, law-suits from a variety of interested individuals and groups, and costs associated with the replacement of affected workers and equipment.

[73] *Luck v. Southern Pacific Transportation Co., supra*, n. 129, Chap. 4.

[74] *Société Peintures Corona, supra*, n. 25, Chap. 5.

[75] *Re Esso Petroleum and Communications, supra*, n. 60, Chap. 6.

Employers can generally point to third-party interests in justifying privacy-invasive policies, merely because consumers and the public benefit whenever an organisation is able to reduce production costs, increase efficiency and offer lower prices. As I argued in Chapter 3, however, the subordination of individual rights to economic interests is cause for concern.[76] Workplace privacy law should therefore be sceptical of economic justifications for invasions of privacy since, otherwise, the entire issue could devolve into the realm of management theory, where the cost-benefit analysis dictates the policies to be applied. One should therefore expect invasions of privacy premised on economic justifications alone to be permissible only in rare cases, perhaps where private interests are threatened minimally, and the economic benefits are manifest and significant.

The three nations exhibit considerable diversity in their legal approaches to economically-motivated invasions of worker privacy. American law is most likely to tolerate such invasions, given the emphasis placed on promoting economic efficiency.[77] In contrast, French law demonstrates great scepticism of economic justifications.[78] Although Canadian law largely mimics the American view, arbitration decisions concerning workplace searches demonstrate a more interest-sensitive approach. Thus, employers who have experienced significant losses due to theft may be entitled to adopt search policies for employees' belongings in order to prevent future economic losses, but arbitrators have generally frowned upon any policies or practices involving body searches. Arbitrators have taken the view that an employer's economic interests may outweigh employees' private interests in material objects such as purses and bags, but not private interests related to bodily integrity since the latter are generally of more substantial weight.[79]

7.2.2.4 *Principle 6: Least Restrictive Means*

> **Principle 6: Least Restrictive Means**
>
> Even where an employer is able to advance a legitimate interest sufficient to limit private interests, the right of privacy should require that the least restrictive means of accomplishing the interest be adopted. An employer should adopt a less invasive alternative, if this could reasonably satisfy its interest. If an invasive policy must be adopted, then it should be *individualised* in the sense of being sensitive to individual circumstances, and should be *particularised* in the sense that the policy should impact only upon private interests to the extent necessary to achieve the employer's objective.

[76] *Supra*, text accompanying nn. 25–6, Chap. 3.
[77] Consider the US Supreme Court's workplace privacy jurisprudence, discussed *supra*, sect. 4.3.3.2. Consider also the Employee Polygraph Protection Act, *supra*, n. 144, Chap. 4, and *supra*, text accompanying n. 154, Chap. 4. which permits employers to use the polygraph to protect their own economic interests.
[78] *Société Peintures Corona, supra*, no. 25, Chap. 5.   [79] *Supra*, sect. 6.5.1.

The sixth principle requires that a privacy-invasive policy must restrict the right of privacy only to the extent necessary to achieve the legitimate and substantial interest supporting the policy. This essentially means that the least intrusive alternative must be adopted, in order to ensure that incidental invasions of privacy, unjustified by the interest, are minimised or even eliminated. This, I would submit, follows from the significance of the right of privacy and the interests it protects, and the corresponding need to preserve as much of the right as possible in a particular circumstance. Therefore, the existence of an employer interest capable of overriding certain private interests of employees does not mean that the right of privacy enjoyed by those employees is destroyed. This point is crucial in two respects, both of which can be illustrated by the hospital example I have used throughout this chapter.

First, it may be that the hospital's objective of protecting patients and staff from disease transmission could be accomplished without intruding upon employee's private interests. The fact that the objective *could* justify limits on privacy does not mean that such limitations are inevitable. It may be, for example, that a programme to educate staff about disease transmission, coupled with improved sanitation (rubber gloves, face masks, etc.) would be a non-invasive alternative to a disease-testing programme. Hence, an analysis of alternatives becomes crucial. The fact that much of the case law on workplace privacy in the United States and Canada has avoided consideration of alternatives should therefore be considered an important weakness.[80] This deficiency in the legal analysis is a reflection of the general deference adopted by courts in assessing employer justifications for privacy-invasive policies. Given that some courts have resisted applying a 'substantial' interest test, it is hardly surprising that they have also been unwilling to require employers to adopt the least restrictive means of achieving the interest.

Secondly, if the hospital's interest in protecting patients from the transmission of a disease necessitates some sort of privacy-invasive testing policy, we might well conclude that because of the manner in which the disease is transmitted, limitations are required in order to prevent employees who are unlikely to pose a risk from being subjected to a serious invasion of a corporeal private interest. If, for example, the disease in question can only be transmitted through contact involving the exchange of bodily fluids, then staff who do not engage in close contact with patients should be excluded from the testing policy. In other words, employees who pose a risk should be included; those who do not should be excluded. This means that privacy-invasive policies should, as a matter of principle, be *individualised* in the sense of being sensitive to individual circumstances. An employer policy which subjects all employees, regardless of individual risk, to privacy-invasive treatment will be suspect if the result is that some workers will be exposed to unjustified invasions of privacy.

---

[80] *Supra*, text acompanying nn. 122–3, Chap. 4 (United States); 96–8, Chap. 6 (Canada).

The failure to individualise privacy-invasive employment policies has been fatal in some French and Canadian cases,[81] but has not been an important consideration in American jurisprudence.[82] A requirement that body searches or drug testing may only be imposed on a reasonable suspicion basis is an important example of individualisation, since random or universal searches will inevitably expose the vast majority of employees to pointless invasions of privacy. While subjecting all individuals to invasive searches in order to catch a few (i.e. a dragnet) arguably has some deterrence value, and may even be administratively efficient, it is almost certainly excessive in light of the important private interests involved.[83] Dragnet searches of the general population by law enforcement authorities would be constitutionally unthinkable in the United States, France and Canada, and should be illegal if conducted by employers in the workplace.[84]

Not only must an employer policy threatening private interests be individualised where possible, but in the case of those individuals subject to the policy, the employer must also ensure that the policy impacts upon only the private interests necessary to achieve the employer's objective. In other words, the policy must be sufficiently *particularised*. As I observed in section 2.3.2 of Chapter 2, private interests fall into three general categories: personal, territorial and informational. Personal and informational interests are the two typically threatened in the employment context. A privacy-invasive employer policy, whether it involves testing or monitoring, will generally threaten personal interests at the first instance. However, such policies have information-gathering as an objective, with the result that informational private interests of employees may also be jeopardized. To return to the hospital example, a testing policy to identify the presence of a disease in employees will compromise the private interest in bodily integrity (a personal interest) and the private interest in information about personal health (an informational interest). A hospital should not be able to use the opportunity presented by such testing to conduct a sweeping analysis of employee health. Privacy is lost only to the extent necessary for the hospital to achieve its objective of preventing the transmission of a disease from employees to patients and other staff.

Particularisation has considerable relevance in the case of employment monitoring, which may be justified in relation to legitimate employer concerns such as ensuring safety and security in the workplace, but may also be pervasive and excessive, thereby permitting the monitoring of activities attracting privacy. In order to limit the impact on privacy of telephone monitoring in American workplaces, the ECPA has been interpreted to permit such monitoring only 'to

---

[81] *Société Peintures Corona*, *supra*, n. 25, Chap. 5, and text accompanying n. 30, Chap. 5 (France); *supra*, text accompanying nn. 78–84, Chap. 6, but see *Calgary Local 710*, *supra*, n. 29, Chap. 6, and text accompanying nn. 29–32, Chap. 6 (Canada).
[82] See the dissenting views in the Supr. Ct. of Canada, *supra*, text accompanying nn. 68–71, Chap. 4; Employee Polygraph Protection Act, *supra*, n. 144, Chap. 4 and accompanying text.
[83] *Von Raab*, *supra*, n. 47, Chap. 4, 33–6, Chap. 7, *per* Justice Scalia (dissenting).
[84] Feldthusen (1988), 97.

the extent necessary to guard against unauthorized use of the telephone or to determine whether a call is personal or not'.[85] Similarly, the proposed PCWA would have prohibited the monitoring of employees' activities unrelated to work, and would in particular have prohibited monitoring in places where employees have territorial private interests (e.g. bathrooms, locker rooms, and dressing rooms).[86] One can also see an emphasis on particularisation in the French CNIL's approach to telephone accounting systems,[87] and in its analysis of automatic security systems. [88] In both cases, the C.N.I.L. imposed limitations on monitoring to ensure that employers would not collect unnecessary information. The CNIL has also sought to limit unnecessary information-gathering during the hiring process, taking the view that personal information should only be demanded by employers where it is strictly related to the requirements of the job in question.[89]

The twin concepts of individualisation and particularisation should serve as guides in assessing privacy-invasive employer policies. In principle, a legitimate policy should impact upon private interests only to the extent necessary to accomplish the objectives underlying the policy. A policy that is insufficiently individualised and particularised will be illegitimate because a less intrusive alternative will exist which could better preserve private interests.

7.2.3 *Principle 7: Procedural and Other Safeguards Related to Informational Private Interests*

Principle 7: Procedural and Other Safeguards

The right of privacy requires that procedural and other safeguards should be incorporated into any privacy-invasive employer policy to protect informational private interests. These safeguards should promote the transparency of the policy, ensure the accuracy of information obtained about candidates/employees and preserve the confidentiality of information to the fullest extent possible.

The principles I outlined above have concerned the application of the right of privacy in employment, and the substantive rules for balancing the competing interests of candidates/employees, employers and the public. However, a separate yet fundamental issue involves the procedural and other safeguards that should be implemented in relation to information acquired through privacy-invasive policies. These safeguards are necessary since the purpose of all such

---

[85] *Watkins, supra*, n. 91, Chap. 2.
[86] *Supra*, n. 15, Chap. 4, ss. 9(a)(1) and 9(b).
[87] *Supra*, text accompanying n. 90, Chap. 5.
[88] *Supra*, text accompanying nn. 87–8, Chap. 5.
[89] *Supra*, text accompanying nn. 75–6, Chap. 5.

policies is to collect information about employees. Hence, all privacy-invasive policies necessarily threaten informational private interests.

One of the greatest causes for concern in the field of employment privacy is that private interests may be threatened surreptitiously, with candidates/ employees being ignorant of an invasion at the time of its occurrence. Electronic surveillance can be conducted without the knowledge or consent of the subjects. Body fluids obtained for limited purposes can be extensively tested,[90] again without the knowledge or consent of the subject. Since surreptitious monitoring and testing can constitute significant invasions of privacy, with profound effects on the individuals concerned, it is necessary that the operation of privacy-invasive policies be transparent. Only in this way will candidates/employees be in a position to protect themselves from unjustified intrusions. Transparency also promotes the accuracy of any information collected through a privacy-invasive monitoring or testing policy. Where employment-related decisions are taken by management on the basis of findings from testing or monitoring, then the individuals concerned should be informed of those findings in advance of management decision-making, and should have the opportunity to challenge those findings for possible inaccuracy.

A further cause for concern is that information collected legitimately by an employer may fall into the hands of third parties and/or may be used for purposes unrelated to the purpose for which it was legitimately collected. Although the initial collection of information may be justified, later uses of that same information could have an undue impact on privacy.

Fortunately, there are plentiful sources in the laws of the United States, France, and Canada for the procedural and other safeguards that are necessary to protect informational private interests. Furthermore, there are international sources on the subject, including ILO[91] and Council of Europe[92] guidelines, and the European Directive on Data Protection.[93] Commentators who have examined information privacy laws have remarked that the fundamental legal principles are remarkably similar from jurisdiction to jurisdiction.[94] At this stage it may be helpful for me to summarise the essential information privacy safeguards which have emerged:

(a) Prior notification—individuals should generally be informed prior to the occurrence of any event that could threaten private interests. In principle, information-gathering activities should not be surreptitious. Notice should include not only the fact that a privacy-invasive event is about to occur, but also details concerning how it will occur and its purpose. Personal information (i.e. information relating to a person and which permits that person to

---

[90] Blood or urine obtained for legitimate purposes can be tested for pregnancy and certain illnesses or conditions. Genetic tests, providing a vast amount of information about personal health, could also conceivably be performed. See *infra*, sects. 8.5.2, 9.5.2.

[91] ILO (1995e).

[92] Council of Europe (1989).

[93] *Supra*, n. 1, Chap. 1.

[94] Flaherty (1989); Bennett (1992).

be identified) should be collected from the subject unless this is not feasible, in order to ensure the subject's prior knowledge.[95]

(b) Access—individuals should have the right to access any personal information held by an employer concerning them, including any information obtained about them as a result of a privacy-invasive policy such as drug testing or electronic monitoring. Access should be provided prior to the taking of any management decisions based on this information.[96]

(c) Verification and rectification—where an individual disputes the accuracy of personal information obtained through a privacy-invasive event, then he must be permitted to demand verification and correction. This should occur prior to the taking of any management decisions based on the disputed information.[97]

(d) Confidentiality and security—an employer may not disclose personal information concerning any subject to third parties without the subject's explicit consent, and must implement adequate security measures to prevent unauthorised or accidental disclosures.[98]

(e) Finality—information should be held by an employer only for a period justified by the purpose for which the information was originally collected. Thereafter, it should be destroyed.[99] However, information should be held by the employer for a period sufficient to ensure that individuals may exercise their rights of access, verification and rectification.[100]

Ultimately, procedural and other safeguards will be an essential aspect of any legal response to workplace privacy issues. Such protections are particularly important where a privacy-invasive management policy is nevertheless justified by a legitimate and substantial interest, and meets the requirements of the principle of least restrictive means. Safeguards such as prior notification, access and rectification protect candidates/employees by promoting the accuracy of information obtained through a privacy-invasive policy, while safeguards such as confidentiality and finality ensure that personal information is not used beyond

[95] *Luedtke, supra*, n. 94, Chap. 4, 1136–7; Privacy Act (United States), *supra*, n. 79, Chap. 4, s. 552(e)(2); French Labour Code, Art. L.121–8; Law of 26 Jan. 1978 (France), Art. 27; Privacy Act (Canada), *supra*, n. 26, Chap. 6, s. 5(2); Act Respecting the Protection of Personal Information in the Private Sector (Quebec), *supra*, n. 27, Chap. 6, s. 8; ILO (1995f), Arts. 6.1, 6.2, 6.14, 11.1; Council of Europe (1989), Arts. 4.1–4.2, European Directive on Data Protection, *supra*, n. 1, Chap. 1, Arts. 10–11.
[96] Privacy Act (United States), *supra*, n. 95, s. 552(d)(1); Law (France), *supra*, n. 95, ss. 34–36; Privacy Act (Canada), *supra*, n. 95, s. 12–13; ILO, *supra*, n. 95, Arts. 11.2, 11.3; Council of Europe, *supra*, n. 95, Arts. 11, 12.1; Directive, *supra*, n. 95, Art. 12.
[97] Privacy Act (United States), *supra*, n. 95, s. 552(d)(2); Law (France), *supra*, n. 95, ss. 34–40; Privacy Act (Canada), *supra*, n. 95, s. 12(2); Act Respecting the Protection of Personal Information in the Private Sector (Quebec), *supra*, n. 27, Chap. 6, s. 11; ILO, *supra*, n. 95, Arts. 11.9, 11.10; Council of Europe, *supra*, n. 95, Arts. 12.1–12.3; Directive, *supra*, n. 95, Art. 12(b).
[98] Privacy Act (United States), *supra*, n. 95, s. 552(e)(10); Law (France), *supra*, n. 95, Art. 29; Privacy Act (Canada), *supra*, n. 95, s. 8(2); Act (Quebec), *supra*, n. 95, s. 13; ILO, *supra*, n. 95, Arts. 7.1, 10; Council of Europe, *supra*, n. 95, Arts. 8, 13; Directive, *supra*, n. 95, Arts. 16–17.
[99] Law (France), *supra*, n. 95 Art. 42; ILO, *supra*, n. 95 Art. 8.5; Council of Europe, *supra*, n. 95 Art. 14; Directive, *supra*, n. 95 Art. 6(e).
[100] Privacy Act (United States), *supra*, n. 79, Chap. 4, s. 552(e)(5); Privacy Act (Canada), *supra*, n. 24, Chap. 6, s. 6(1).

the purposes for which it was originally collected. The existence of such safe-guards minimises the severity of the impact of a privacy-invasive management policy—an objective surely required by the human rights nature of the private interests at stake.

7.3 CONCLUSIONS

In this chapter, I have suggested the adoption of seven legal principles for the protection of the right of privacy in the workplace. These are: (1) the right of privacy should apply to all employees and job candidates regardless of their sta-tus (*comprehensive application regardless of status*); (2) the right of privacy should establish one set of legal standards applicable to all employees and job candidates (*floor of rights application*); (3) the right of privacy should be subject to only those limitations justified by legitimate and substantial competing inter-ests (*legitimate and substantial limitations*); (4) competing third party interests similar in nature to those protected by the right of privacy are more likely to meet the 'substantial' test (*sufficiency of limitations premised on third party interests*); (5) competing economic interests are less likely to meet the 'substan-tial' test (*insufficiency of limitations premised on economic interests*); (6) any limitation of the right of privacy should be the least restrictive means of satisfy-ing competing interests (*least restrictive means*); and (7) procedural and other safeguards should be implemented to protect informational private interests (*procedural and other safeguards*). These seven principles emerged from my analyses of workplace privacy law in the United States, France and Canada, and from more theoretical considerations related to the nature of privacy as a human right. They constitute a 'best practice' model.

In Chapters 8 and 9, I will demonstrate the utility of these principles by apply-ing them to two controversial workplace privacy issues: drug testing and genetic testing. The analyses will demonstrate the operation of the principles in prac-tice, while suggesting how best to resolve the competing interests of candi-dates/employees, employers and the public in relation to each issue. In Chapter 10, I will advance these same principles as a normative model to guide the devel-opment of workplace privacy law in the United Kingdom.

8

Employment Drug Testing

8.1 INTRODUCTION

Employment drug testing is perhaps the most controversial of today's workplace privacy issues. In the past decade, tribunals in each of the three national jurisdictions have confronted the issue, although their approaches have varied considerably. American courts, with some exceptions, have been highly tolerant of drug testing, including suspicionless random and universal testing.[1] Canadian arbitrators, in contrast, have found suspicionless testing to be unreasonable under collective agreements, and have rejected testing without a compelling safety justification.[2] However, many private sector candidates/employees in Canada have no privacy right in law that could be asserted against drug testing.[3] French law largely reflects the Canadian arbitration approach, although all French workers are protected equally.[4]

My primary purpose in this chapter is to analyse employment drug testing with the guidance of the seven legal principles developed in Chapter 7. Through these principles, it will be possible to develop a single legal response to drug testing which could be implemented as a comprehensive floor of protection, as demanded by *Principle 1, Comprehensive Application Regardless of Status*, and *Principle 2, Floor of Rights Application*.

8.2 COMPETING POLICY APPROACHES TO CONTROLLING DRUGS

The use and abuse of narcotics such as heroin and cocaine, and societal efforts to curb their negative impact, obviously have a long history, but it was only in the early 1980s that the technology became available to permit the efficient and inexpensive testing of individuals for the presence of drugs or drug by-products (metabolites[5]) in their systems.[6] Drug testing in the employment context first became popular in the United States, and continues today to be a significant workplace privacy issue there. In Canada and the nations of the European Union, drug testing has occurred, but not to the same extent.[7] The reasons for

---

[1] *Supra*, sect. 4.3.3.2.
[2] *Supra*, sect. 6.5.1.
[3] *Supra*, sect. 6.5.2.2.
[4] *Supra*, sect. 5.3.1.
[5] See Appendix—Glossary of Terms.
[6] Ackerman (1991), 3.
[7] *Supra*, n. 23, Chap. 2, and accompanying text.

this disparity stem from differing policy approaches to drug control. While the United States has historically approached drugs as immoral and a source of serious social and economic harm, the issue has been viewed in other countries as primarily a matter of public health. Hence, while American policy has emphasised the need to stamp out drugs through the criminal law, other countries have preferred to emphasise 'harm reduction' policies[8] such as treatment, needle exchanges and the distribution of methadone.[9]

The American 'war on drugs' has fuelled a more coercive approach to drug control in the United States. The objective of this 'war' has been to eliminate drug use through the identification and punishment of traffickers and users. Given the punitive climate created by the drug war, and the branding of drug users as 'the enemy', or 'throw-away people who should be ignored or locked up',[10] it is hardly surprising that the workplace has been converted into a battlefield through the implementation of drug testing.[11] In effect, drug testing has become a strategy of social control, made possible by technological developments that have made widespread testing feasible.[12] Canada and the European Union have been caught up in the drug war too. This is a function both of American companies exporting the American drug attitude overseas (a particularly acute problem for Canada because of its geographical proximity to the United States, and its trading links through the North American Free Trade Agreement,[13] but also for France[14]), and of the government of the United States pressuring its main trading partners to adopt similar policy approaches to drugs.[15] Of course, the 'public health' approach to drugs is not universally supported in countries where it has prevailed to date; hence, home-grown advocates in both Canada and the United Kingdom have spoken in favour of a more activist and punitive approach like that of the United States.[16]

Because the primary objective of drug testing in employment has been to eliminate drug *users* from the workplace by identifying them through mandatory testing, depriving them of job opportunities or possibly requiring them to enter and successfully complete rehabilitation programmes as a condition of employment, the coercive and punitive nature of anti-drug policy has been felt in the employment setting. This has placed the civil liberties of candidates/employees

---

[8] Reuter *et al.* (1993), 17–18; Bertram *et al.* (1996), 7, 205–8. The Netherlands is perhaps the best example of a non-punitive approach to drugs. See Horstink (1996), 97. Sneiderman (1997), 499, 527, writes that Canada's approach to drugs has resembled the American 'Police Model', although it has not been as extreme.

[9] See Appendix—Glossary of Terms.

[10] Bertram *et al.* (1996), 174.

[11] *Ibid.*, 27.

[12] Jacobs and Weider (1996), 120.

[13] Sneiderman (1997), 522.

[14] *Supra*, n. 12, Chap. 7.

[15] ILO (1993a, 3), 227; Reuter *et al.* (1993), 17–18.

[16] At one time, the Canadian federal government contemplated the passage of legislation providing for random drug testing of federal transportation workers (*supra*, n. 154, Chap. 2). The American approach is also evident in the UK. See, *The Scotsman* (1997a), 1, referring to Dr Ian Oliver, Chief Constable of Grampion and an influential spokesman for tougher narcotics controls; *The Scotsman* (1997b), 5; Institute of Personnel and Development (1997).

in jeopardy.[17] The scenario of a candidate/employee testing positive for drug use, and being denied employment as a result, has played itself out with disturbing regularity in the United States, France and Canada. This is the product of an approach to drugs which emphasises punishment and deprivation of opportunity over personal privacy and rehabilitation. It is an approach which often places no emphasis on the concern which should be foremost in an employer's mind: whether or not a candidate's/employee's drug use actually or potentially impedes job performance.

8.3 FORMS OF DRUG TESTING POLICIES

Drug testing policies are often divided into two main categories for analytical purposes: (1) pre-employment, under which candidates (i.e. job applicants, or candidates for transfer or promotion) are subjected to drug testing; and (2) employment, where existing employees are required to submit to drug testing. The relevance of this distinction to my legal analysis herein is limited because the first principle I outlined in Chapter 7 (*Principle 1, Comprehensive Application Regardless of Status*) dictates that employees and job applicants should receive qualitatively similar privacy protection.

There are other variations in employment drug-testing policies which are relevant to my discussion below. For example, a candidate/employee may be tested *with cause* where the employer has a reasonable basis or some suspicion for believing that the subject is a drug user.[18] Alternatively, testing may be performed *without cause*, in which case all candidates/employees may be tested (i.e. universal testing), or the subjects may be chosen randomly (i.e. random testing). An employer may apply its testing policy to all candidates/employees, or may require tests of only those related to particular categories of employment, such as jobs the employer considers to be safety-sensitive. In the case of existing employees, an employer may adopt a policy requiring drug tests following certain events, for example accidents or the return of an employee from a leave of absence (i.e. post-event testing). Such tests may be random or universal in application, or may be triggered by some 'cause' condition. The timing of employment testing is also important, as such tests can be scheduled and publicised to employees in advance (i.e. scheduled testing), or may be administered without warning (i.e. surprise testing). The following chart illustrates the policy options available to an employer:

---

[17] Bertram *et al.* (1996), 47.
[18] Axel (1991), 148, observes that pre-employment drug testing is generally universal and without cause, although firms may restrict it to serious candidates or finalists for positions.

Drug Testing Policy Options

(1) *Individuals Tested (Who?)*
All Individuals   **OR**   Individuals in Particular Categories of Employment
(2) *Reason for Testing (Why?)*
Testing Without Cause   **OR** Post-Event   **OR** Testing With Cause
(3) *Method of Testing (How?)*
Random Testing   **OR**   Universal Testing
(4) *Notification of Testing (When?)*
Scheduled Testing   **OR**   Surprise Testing

8.4 METHODS AND LIMITATIONS OF DRUG TESTING

Before considering the competing interests involved in drug testing, it is necessary to appreciate the manner in which drug testing is carried out, and the limitations of such testing.

In order to test for the presence of drugs in a subject's system, a body fluid must be procured from the subject—generally, blood or urine. Urinalysis tends to be the testing method of choice in the employment context because a urine sample is easier to obtain from a subject than blood (particularly in a non-medical environment),[19] while other forms of testing are either too expensive for widespread use or are still in developmental stages.[20] The testing of saliva, sweat, hair samples, and even brain-waves may someday be possible, but none of these tests is presently viable.[21]

The most common form of urinalysis test is known as the 'enzyme immunoassay method' (EIM),[22] an inexpensive[23] means of detecting drug

---

[19] Blood testing is rarely employed because, (1) it is considered a more invasive procedure than urinalysis, and (2) extraction of blood samples must be performed by medically trained personnel (OLRC (1992a), 11).

[20] PCC (1990b), 11.

[21] Hobbs and Scrivner (1988), 626; Normand *et al.* (1994), 183. At least two American companies, HairTrac and Psychemedics Corp., are marketing hair analysis products for workplace drug testing. The latter company, based in Culver City, Cal., claims to hold US and foreign patents for detecting the presence of marijuana, cocaine, heroin and PCP in hair. Skin patches, which are worn for a period of time and then analysed for drugs, are now being marketed (*Fresno Bee* (1997), 3).

[22] See Appendix—Glossary of Terms.

[23] In Mar. 1999, a perusal by the author of Internet sites dedicated to workplace drug testing revealed 46 companies in the USA, Canada and the UK marketing workplace drug-testing services. The price range varied considerably depending on the drugs being tested, the services provided and the size of the relevant workforce. Basic EIM tests were being marketed for between US$9.00 and US$18.00 per worker.

metabolites which can be performed without specialised equipment.[24] Hence, it is ideal for large-scale use by employers, since they can administer the test and obtain results on-site.[25] EIM tests have been widely criticised for inaccuracy, although there is controversy about the extent of this problem. Syva, the manufacturer of a brand called 'EMIT', estimates that its test is 95 per cent accurate at identifying marijuana use, with a 1 per cent false positive rate.[26] Hoffmann-La Roche, the producer of a similar 'Abuscreen' kit, claims a 99 per cent 'confidence level'.[27] The Addiction Research Foundation provides a higher figure for false positives—2 per cent to 5 per cent.[28] One medical commentator has suggested that EIM tests are 'virtually worthless' because of a false positive rate higher than 25 per cent.[29] False positives may arise because the test is so sensitive that it can detect the presence of marijuana through passive inhalation, and can be fooled by natural body chemicals or cross-reactions with other substances such as aspirin.[30] False positives can also result from human error in the process of administering the test. This danger was vividly demonstrated in 1984, when the United States Air Force discovered that 46,000 'positive' drug tests were doubtful due to human error and poor quality control.[31]

The inaccuracy rates of EIM drug tests make it inevitable that many subjects who have not consumed the drugs covered by the tests will nevertheless be identified as drug users, and may be refused employment, disciplined or forced into rehabilitation as a result. If the EIM test has a false-positive rate of 5 per cent (which is, apparently, a reasonable estimate), then five out of every 100 subjects will be found erroneously to have used drugs. Given the low numbers of employees who actually consume drugs, the number of false-positive results will almost certainly be a substantial proportion of the total number of positive results, and may even exceed that of true-positives.[32]

Rates of testing inaccuracy drop when an EIM positive result is considered presumptive of drug use, but not conclusive, and second-test confirmation

---

[24] A similar form of test, known as the 'radioimmunassay method', employs radioactive material and requires complex equipment. Hence, it is as rare as a pink elephant in the workplace setting (Committee on Labor and Employment Law (1988), 453).

[25] Many tests are packaged for use outside a laboratory.

[26] This figure is provided in *National Federation of Federal Employees, Local 2058* v. *Weinberger*, 640 F Supp. 642 (DDC, 1986), 647–8.

[27] McGovern (1987), 1458, reports this figure, which can be found in Roche Diagnostic Systems (1984).

[28] Addiction Research Foundation, *Employee-Related Drug Screening* (1987), cited in Feldthusen (1988), 85.

[29] Dr David Greenblatt, Tufts-New England Medical Center, quoted in *New York Times* (1985), 17.

[30] Manfield (1997), 292, notes that EIM tests are over-inclusive because they identify metabolites with properties similar to those of drugs. Hence, over-the-counter cold remedies such as Contact C and Sudafed have registered positive for amphetamines, pain relievers like Advil have led to false-positive results for marijuana, and poppy seeds may result in a positive test for heroin.

[31] Coombs and West (1991), p. xix.

[32] Feldthusen (1988), 87, reaches this conclusion in reliance on estimates showing that 3% of workers use cocaine, and less than 1% of workers use other drugs. He notes, however, that perhaps 10% of workers use marijuana. Hence, if a workforce of 100 is tested using an EIM test with a false positive rate of 5%, one might expect to find 18 positive tests, of which 5 are false and 13 true. There have been many claims against American employers and laboratories resulting from false-positive test results. See Manfield (1997), 292.

occurs. This is particularly so where the second test is of a more rigorous type. Several forms of testing are more accurate than EIM, yet are rarely used at the initial stage because they are expensive, labour intensive, and must be performed in a laboratory. These include thin-layer chromatography, gas chromatography and gas chromatography combined with mass spectrometry.[33] The latter method is considered the most accurate means of testing, as it can identify drugs in concentrations as low as parts per billion. However, a single urine test can cost over US$100, making it unlikely to be a popular option with employers who, it can be assumed, prefer the cheaper methods of drug testing.[34]

While inaccuracy is an important limitation of drug-testing technology, it may be that testing technology will improve in the future, with more accurate tests becoming available at a sufficiently low cost to permit their routine use in the employment context. However, there are certain limitations inherent in testing results which technological improvements are unlikely to solve. A positive drug test (assuming it is accurate) indicates that the subject has consumed a drug during some period prior to the test being carried out. EIM tests can generally detect marijuana use up to three weeks prior to the test,[35] cocaine use within the previous three days and amphetamine use within 24 hours.[36] A positive drug test does not indicate that the subject was impaired at the time of the drug test,[37] nor does it ascertain whether the subject is a casual drug user, a drug abuser or is drug dependent.[38] Moreover, because certain drugs clear the system quickly and cannot be detected by tests a few days after ingestion, a negative drug test may wrongly label a subject as a non-user. Therefore, a drug testing policy may weed out candidates/employees who are casual users of marijuana, while failing to identify those who are dependent on amphetamines.

The inaccuracy of drug tests, coupled with the limited information provided by an accurate positive result, form the background against which to assess the competing candidate/employee, employer, and public interests as part of the interest balancing approach I outlined in Chapter 7 above.

8.5 THE IMPACT OF DRUG TESTING ON PRIVATE INTERESTS

The first step in assessing the competing interests surrounding employment drug testing is to develop a full appreciation of the private interests which are threatened. As will be seen, these are significant. In fact, employment drug testing, regardless of its form, impacts upon two distinct private interests.

---

[33] See Appendix—Glossary of Terms
[34] Manfield (1997), 290, 294.
[35] *Ibid.*, 287, suggests that EIM tests may detect marijuana use up to 3 months after the subject has consumed the drug.
[36] Addiction Research Foundation (1991), 25; Feldthusen (1988), 88; OLRC (1992a), 23.
[37] This is the fundamental difference between breathalyser tests for alcohol, which can measure actual impairment, and urinalysis tests for drugs, which can only measure ingestion prior to the test.
[38] See Appendix—Glossary of Terms.

8.5.1 Personal/Corporeal Private Interests

The administration of a drug test inevitably implicates personal/corporeal private interests because the subject is required to offer up a body fluid such as urine, blood, saliva, etc. Blood testing requires an invasion of the body by a needle, can be painful and carries with it a small risk of infection. Urinalysis testing can be embarrassing and uncomfortable for the subject, since the act of urination may be observed by those performing the test to prevent tampering with the urine sample.[39] Alternatively, subjects may be asked to remove clothing or strip completely, or may be searched in advance, to ensure that they are not carrying substitute urine or adulterating substances.[40] It is difficult to imagine anything more private than the disposal of body wastes. Yet, even if a less intrusive means were found to conduct drug testing (such as hair analysis which, as noted above, is not presently viable), personal private interests would still be affected. The suggestion that hair analysis would 'drastically diminish' or even 'eliminate' the privacy problems of drug testing[41] is incorrect because any test which uses a part of a person's body to obtain information about her is intrusive,[42] and violates the sanctity of the human body.

8.5.2 Informational Private Interests

The private interests implicated by drug testing are not limited to the realm of the body. Significant informational private interests are also at stake, and this is true regardless of the testing method. First, a test subject is often required to disclose any medications he might be taking, as these could affect the test results and lead to false positives or negatives. This in turn may disclose information about the health of the subject.[43] Secondly, the body fluids which are surrendered could conceivably reveal a wealth of information about the subject's health, if other tests were performed. Blood and urine samples could reveal that a candidate/employee is pregnant or carries the HIV virus. In providing a sample to an employer, an individual has no guarantee that the sample will be used only for the limited purpose of drug testing. Hence, the fear arises that an employer could surreptitiously carry out wide-ranging health testing, and discriminate against those who have conditions unrelated to drugs.[44]

---

[39] *Supra*, n. 113, Chap. 2.
[40] Oscapella (1992), 332; PCC (1990b), 2, 18. The US Department of Health and Human Services recommends that drug test subjects should be required to 'remove any unnecessary outer garments' and that 'all personal belongings must remain with the outer garments'. The subject 'shall remain in the presence of the collection site person and not have access to water fountains, faucets, soap dispensers, or cleaning agents' (US Department of Labor Memorandum, 18 Aug. 1986, quoted in Chapnik (1990), 103). Similar recommendations have come from Canada's Ministry of Health and Welfare (1990).
[41] Jacobs and Weider (1996), 129.
[42] *Société Peintures Corona, supra*, n. 25, Chap. 5.
[43] PCC (1990b), 16.
[44] Feldthusen (1988), 94–5.

Thirdly, and most importantly, drug testing provides employers with information about a subject's off-duty conduct which may be unrelated to any legitimate employer interest, and thereby violates *Principle 3, Legitimate and Substantial Limitations*. As I discussed above, an accurate positive drug test reveals that an individual has consumed drugs at some time in the past, but says nothing about whether she was under the influence of drugs at the time the test was administered, or whether her work performance has been impaired by drugs in the past. When an employer requires candidates/employees to refrain from consuming drugs (this being the inherent purpose of a drug-testing policy which punishes those who test positive) then the employer is seeking to regulate their activities away from the workplace. This regulation becomes very significant where it is implemented through mandatory, privacy-invasive testing. After all, most of those subjected to the testing will not be drug users, while only a small proportion have a drug problem serious enough to impair their work. Where an employer insists on testing candidates/employees in the absence of any belief that their performance is suffering from drug use, then the employer is attempting to obtain non-work related information, and is thereby regulating off-duty life.

A testing policy requiring individualised suspicion of drug use as a precondition of the test, such as a post-accident policy where there is suspicion that drugs may have been a contributing cause, is consistent with *Principle 6, Least Restrictive Means*, and would be more respectful of informational private interests. Although some speculation is still involved in the decision to administer the test, there is at least a basis for believing that the individuals subject to the testing have conducted themselves in a manner affecting their job performance. I would thus conclude that any drug testing policy which lacks a 'with cause' element is a serious infringement of private interests. Testing with cause is a lesser infringement of private interests, although its impact on the corpus remains significant.

The objection may be made that no person can rely on an informational private interest where the information pertains to conduct which is illegal. After all, the consumption of narcotics like marijuana and cocaine is a criminal act in many European Union and North American countries. However, recognising that conduct away from the workplace has a public dimension because of its illegality does not mean that the conduct loses its private nature *vis-à-vis* the employer. Drug consumption as a general issue is a matter for public authorities such as the police, and it certainly would not be possible for such authorities to subject a person (whether or not a member of the workforce) to a drug test without individual cause. Where an employer imposes drug testing to discourage drug consumption, to assist the state in the war on drugs, or to boost its public image, then we should be concerned that the employer is really attempting to usurp the power of the police (see *Principle 3*). The ramifications of this are troubling, at the very least because police investigations of criminal activity are constrained by legal and constitutional limitations, while the actions of employers are not to the same extent.[45]

[45] Feldthusen (1988), 94.

8.5.3 The Significance of these Interests

In Chapter 2, I argued that the autonomy justification underlying the protection of privacy dictated the general proposition that there must be a sufficient link between the controls placed on the independence of employees by an employer and job performance. This idea emerged again in *Principle 3, Legitimate and Substantial Limitations*. Management policies lacking the requisite link constitute illegitimate limitations of private interests. Workplace drug testing, and in particular random and universal testing imposed upon candidates/employees, will often lack this link because such testing provides the employer with information about off-duty conduct which is generally unrelated to work performance, and which can be used to control independence.

The use of workplace drug testing as a form of social control, and as an indirect method by which the state can implement drug policy, demonstrates how a privacy invasive practice can undermine pluralist thought and debate in society, as I suggested in Chapter 2. It is surely obvious that there is no societal consensus about the legal or moral standing of narcotics, and particularly of 'soft drugs' like marijuana. This is reflected in the diversity of legal approaches to the issue,[46] and in the fact that many people knowingly, regularly and happily flaunt drug laws. Regardless of one's personal view, there is a strong current of opinion in favour of the de-criminalisation (if not the legalisation) of some of the drugs for which candidates/employees are presently being tested. The right of privacy becomes particularly relevant here, because one of its key functions is to protect alternative opinions, beliefs and lifestyles. When employers declare a policy of a drug-free workplace, refuse to tolerate drug use and institute drug tests to catch and discipline drug users, they may be seeking to impose their particular viewpoint on workers, and to 'have their way' on a matter which attracts the protection of privacy *vis-à-vis* the employer. In the short term, workers might disagree vehemently with an employment drug policy, yet acquiesce to it in order to keep their jobs. In the long term, however, this form of social control threatens to take hold of lifestyles, thoughts, and opinions, and to mould them in the form desired by the employer. Such is the threat to pluralism.

Further to this, the intrusions upon private interests inherent to drug testing threaten to undermine the employment relationship through, as the ILO has put it, 'fear, mistrust, polarization between management and workers, lack of openness, and social control'.[47] Drug testing is also an affront to the dignity of candidates/employees, as discussed in section 2.3.3.2 of Chapter 2. In some respects, drug testing is a throw-back to turn-of-the-century classical management practices, through which employers sought to control and manipulate workers' lives for moral or religious purposes.[48] As I noted in section 2.3.3.3 of Chapter 2,

---

[46] Compare the harm reduction approaches of the Netherlands and Italy (*infra*, n. 98) with the criminal approach taken in the USA.

[47] ILO (1996c).

[48] *Supra*, sect. 3.2.

employment is one of the most important relationships in people's lives. The infusion of distrust, moralistic manipulation and conflict into the relationship through intrusions upon private interests is serious not only due to its effect on worker productivity and labour relations, but also because of its impact on the psychological well-being of the individuals involved.

8.5.4 Conclusion

Workplace drug testing infringes upon two crucial private interests. First, it impacts upon personal privacy by imposing, as a condition of hiring or continuing employment (or as a condition of not being disciplined), that a candidate/employee submit to an invasive, painful and/or embarrassing testing procedure which requires her to offer up a body fluid for analysis. Secondly, testing infringes upon informational privacy, not only because it reveals health information about the subject, but also because it provides information about the subject's behaviour away from the workplace, and constitutes an attempt by the employer to dictate an aspect of this behaviour related to drug consumption. Hence, drug testing resembles more a form of social control than a legitimate tool of management. The assertion of such control by employers is highly problematic due to its negative impact on autonomy, dignity, and pluralism, and its destruction of trust in the employment relationship.

8.6 JUSTIFICATIONS FOR DRUG TESTING

The second step in the interest balancing exercise is to determine whether any of the justifications for employment drug testing are sufficiently legitimate and substantial (*Principle 3*) to overcome the private interests at stake. In Chapter 2, I canvassed the types of employer and public interests which could be advanced to justify privacy-invasive employment practices, and identified five justifications supporting workplace privacy invasions: (1) improving economic conditions, such as productivity and service quality; (2) protecting the health and safety of workers, consumers and the public; (3) deterring abuse of the employment relationship; (4) complying with state-imposed regulatory requirements; and 5) promoting public policy. Each of these is relevant to drug testing.

8.6.1 Economic Conditions

It is often assumed that drug use is correlated with reduced productivity, on the theory that drug users are less productive during on-duty hours, while imposing costs on the employer related to absenteeism and accidents.[49] As I explained

---

[49] Kaestner (1992b), 6.

above, however, it is unreliable to infer a relationship between a positive test result and the capacity of an individual to perform a job—the information provided by a positive test is simply too limited. A positive test merely indicates that an individual has used drugs in the past. It is a considerable leap from this information to the conclusion that an individual's drug use has stunted workplace productivity, or will do so in the future.

Moreover, the results of studies seeking to identify a link between drug use and reduced productivity are inconclusive. Some purport to show that illicit drug use leads to delayed entry into the labour market,[50] or is positively correlated with weeks unemployed and increased resignations.[51] Others, however, were unable to find any correlation between illicit drug use and labour force participation[52] or hours worked.[53] Two studies by Kaestner and the National Bureau of Economic Research in the United States demonstrate the inconclusive findings of drug/productivity studies. The first, which examined the impact of illicit drug use on the labour supply of young adults, reached the conclusion that 'there appears to be no systematic effect of illicit drug use on labor supply'.[54] The author further concluded:

> Taken at face value, these results would have important policy implications. They would suggest that drug use among young adults is a highly idiosyncratic experience that has different effects on different people. There does not appear to be a common experience, and public policies should reflect this fact if they are to be effective and cost efficient. The goal of policy would be to identify those individuals for which illicit drug use does become problematic, and further research is clearly needed in this area.[55]

In other words, one cannot generalise about the impact of drug use on workers and, in fact, drugs may have no effect at all on many individuals' work performance. The need for caution is demonstrated by the results of the second of the two studies, which considered the effect of drug use on wages, and assumed that drug use would correspond to lower wages because of the adverse impact of drugs on the physical and psychological well-being of the individual worker.[56] However, the study actually found that there was a correlation between increased frequency of drug use and higher wages.[57]

The validity of all these studies is limited for a number of reasons. First, they depend on self-reporting, and there is no way to ensure that individuals are

---

[50] Johnson and Herring (1989).
[51] Kandel and Davies (1990); Kandel and Yamaguchi (1987).
[52] White *et al.* (1988).
[53] Kagel *et al.* (1980).
[54] Kaestner (1992b), 25.
[55] *Ibid.*
[56] Kaestner (1990a).
[57] *Ibid.*, 14. It would, of course, be a mistake to assume that drug consumption is causally linked to increased wages. Kaestner himself does not draw this conclusion. One should keep in mind that because of the high cost of narcotics, it may well be that those with higher salaries can afford to purchase more of them, with the result that drug consumption rises along with wage rates.

honest when answering questions about their drug use.[58] Secondly, the studies attempt to gauge productivity by considering labour market participation, total hours worked, wages or costs to the employer of substance abuse, yet these are surely imprecise measures of a complex concept such as productivity.[59] Thirdly, productivity can be measured in relation to the economy as a whole, and in relation to particular firms.[60] Those individuals with the most severe drug problems (i.e. drug dependents) are most likely to be unemployed.[61] Hence, their drug consumption would impact upon a measure of overall productivity, but because they are out of the workforce, this necessarily means that their consumption is irrelevant to the productivity of a fully staffed firm.[62] Fourthly, the majority of workers who consume narcotics are casual users of soft drugs like marijuana.[63] One would not expect the productivity of such workers to be substantially affected by their drug use.[64] Hence, only a minority of a firm's employees who use drugs will potentially contribute to reduced productivity *within the firm*. This would include those whose drug problem is serious enough to result in lateness or absenteeism, and those whose drug consumption affects their ability to carry out tasks.[65] For this reason, one can reasonably conclude that little in a

---

[58] One would anticipate that respondents would under-report their drug use, as opposed to over-report (Kaestner makes this assumption, *ibid.*, 22, as does Zwerling (1993), 169). If this is the case, then illicit drug use may have even less of an impact on productivity than is revealed in the studies. Productivity is measured by objective criteria such as labour force participation, hours worked per week, wage rates and annual salary. At present, the recorded levels of drug consumption cannot be conclusively correlated with productivity as measured by these criteria. If drug consumption were even higher, then the correlation between drug usage and productivity would be even more tenuous.

[59] Normand *et al.* (1994), 7. McVicar *et al.* (1995), 4, in their survey of economic studies of workplace substance abuse, observe that '[t]he issue of how to measure 'the cost of substance abuse' has been a controversial one', and that the measurements chosen in various studies are diverse, and therefore the results of the studies cannot be compared easily. Berry and Boland (1977) defined the cost of substance abuse as the productivity that is lost due to substance abuse, and then determined this by calculating the difference between the wages of abusers and non-abusers. This approach has been widely criticised (McVicar *et al.* (1995), 4).

[60] Studies may seek to determine the 'net social impact' of drug and alcohol abuse (the cost of abuse on all members of society), or may determine the 'net budgetary impact' of abuse on specific organisations (*ibid.*, 5).

[61] Illicit drug use is more common among unemployed than employed persons, with 14% of the unemployed reporting drug use, compared to 7% of the employed (figures provided by Normand *et al.* (1994), 4). Hobbs and Scrivner (1988), 605–6, estimate that as at 1988, the American economy was suffering an annual loss of six billion dollars due to long-term unemployment associated with drug use. This was 6 times the one billion dollar figure which these same authors advanced as the total annual loss to American business of drug use.

[62] Some commentators make the mistake of relying on the overall economic impact of drug use to justify workplace drug testing. See, e.g., LaVan *et al.* (1994), 346.

[63] This fact is borne out by the results of a study conducted by the Canadian Department of National Defence (1992). Approximately 5,500 urine samples were collected from members of the Canadian Forces, and 1.3% (or 75) tested positive for narcotics. Of the 75, 70 had used marijuana, 3 had used cocaine, 1 had used PCP, and 1 had used amphetamines. These results are mirrored by all the workplace studies considered by Normand *et al.* (1994), 82–3.

[64] The fact that there may be 16 million illegal drug users in Canada and the USA, of whom 11 million are workers, and of whom 1 million have used drugs in the past month, tells us nothing about the actual impact of this drug use on firm productivity because such statistics fail to differentiate between different kinds of drugs, and users/abusers/dependents. LaVan *et al.* (1994), 348, imply that such raw figures support workplace drug testing without critically analysing their real value. Hobbs and Scrivner (1988), 605–6 make the same mistake.

[65] Keastner (1992a), 2, states that only 7% of employees surveyed reported consuming drugs while in the workplace. However, see Heller and Robinson (1991), 120.

positive drug-test result indicates whether the subject of the test will be more prone to absence, or less productive, than those who test negative.[66] This reinforces my conclusion above that positive drug tests have limited informational value, while demonstrating that blanket drug testing may itself be an inefficient and wasteful means of promoting firm productivity.

8.6.2 Health and Safety

Health and safety concerns are another popular justification for the adoption of workplace drug testing.[67] Employers generally are under a legal duty to take positive action to reduce health and safety risks in the workplace.[68] One can hardly doubt that an employee performing tasks under the influence of a narcotic could, depending on the nature of the task, pose a threat to the safety of herself and others. Therefore, some employers have instituted drug testing programmes in order to identify drug users who might potentially be involved in a drug-related accident. Post-accident testing has also become a feature of safety-justified drug testing policies, as employers seek to identify the causes of accidents, and prevent their recurrence.

There are very few studies of the link between drug use and workplace safety.[69] In fact, much of the evidence supporting drug testing for safety reasons is anecdotal[70]—reports of employees arriving at work while under the influence of drugs,[71] and well-publicised accidents in which those responsible tested positive for drugs in their systems.[72] One scientific study has reported that prolonged drug use may result in decreased reaction time, co-ordination, logic and vigilance, all of which are relevant to the safety issue.[73] Nevertheless, after studying the available empirical evidence, including two studies which found that drug use is not a significant safety issue,[74] the OLRC reached the following conclusion:

---

[66] Feldthusen (1988), 89.

[67] A 1988 Gallup survey of several hundred large American companies with drug testing programmes found that 54% started their programmes to protect their safe work record or reduce the number of accidents: Gallup (1988), 17–18. See also Linowes (1988), 40, 52–3, who found that 97% of companies surveyed justified their drug testing policies on the basis of safety.

[68] *Supra*, n. 138, Chap. 2.

[69] Zwerling (1993), 181–2.

[70] ILO (1996c).

[71] According to the survey by Linowes (1988), 69% of respondents were influenced to introduce drug testing because of incidents of drug use on the job.

[72] Consider the case of a limousine driver who was involved in an accident seriously injuring 3 members of the Detroit Red Wings Ice Hockey Team. A drug test performed subsequent to the accident identified marijuana in the driver's system (*International Herald-Tribune* (1997), 22).

[73] Heller and Robinson (1991), 33. These authors conceded, however, that 'there is a lack of published evidence which would permit assessment of the effectiveness or benefits of workplace drug testing programmes' (at 43).

[74] These studies were conducted by Health and Welfare Canada and the Niagara Institute (1988), and Transport Canada, Heffring Research Group (1990).

no empirical studies exist which demonstrate that drug abuse in the Canadian work-force is a significant problem. In fact, the research that has been conducted indicates the contrary: drugs have not been found to be a major factor in workplace accidents.[75]

In fact, according to the Addiction Research Foundation, less than 1 per cent of employees in Canada's workforce can be classified as 'heavy drug users'.[76] Even if this figure were several times higher in the United States and France, only a very small percentage of workers would suffer from a drug problem with employment implications. The inevitable conclusion is that the great majority of employees pose no risk whatsoever since they either do not use drugs, or are casual users whose drug consumption has no impact on their work perfor-mance.[77] This contrasts with the problem posed to workplace safety by alcohol consumption,[78] since it is estimated that 10 per cent of employees are excessive alcohol drinkers.[79] Considerably more employees are reporting to work under the influence of alcohol (or suffering from its 'hangover' effect) than of drugs,[80] and alcohol is by far the most common impairing drug implicated in workplace accidents.[81]

The evidence further suggests that the overwhelming majority of individuals subjected to random or universal drug tests will either be non-drug users, or drug users who nevertheless pose no safety risk. Therefore, large-scale drug test-ing premised on safety considerations may well be a colossal waste of resources.

McGovern has defended drug-testing in *high-risk* employment settings on the rationale that,

> the chief benefit of urinalysis, saliva, or blood tests is that they can detect the use of drugs before the visible symptoms of drug abuse show themselves in the workplace. This ability is an advantage no trained supervisor can duplicate. The underlying premise . . . is that this 'edge' should not be sacrificed when the safety of the employee, co-workers, or the general public is at stake.[82]

He argues that employees[83] performing tasks posing a 'substantial risk of seri-ous bodily injury' (e.g. airline pilots, nuclear power plant workers and surgeons) may be subjected to random or universal drug testing because of the risk to other employees and the public of a drug-related accident.[84] This is essentially an argument based on risk assessment. McGovern has concluded that in certain employment fields, the risk of an employee's drug use causing or contributing to

---

[75] OLRC (1992a), 3–4.
[76] Addiction Research Foundation (1991).
[77] OLRC (1992a), 93. From 1970 to 1983, the Province of Alberta tracked workplace fatalities for drug involvement. 42 of the 254 victims showed traces of illicit drugs, while 54 showed evidence of alcohol use. In 11 cases, alcohol was probably a contributing cause. There was no evidence of a causal connection between illicit drug use and the causes of the fatalities (see Weir (1994), 456).
[78] Alcohol is, of course, an addictive drug. The main distinction between alcohol and narcotics is that the former is a legal substance (often sold by the state itself), while the latter is illegal.
[79] Addiction Research Foundation (1991).
[80] Normand *et al.* (1994), 5.
[81] Canadian Medical Association (1992), 2232A.
[82] McGovern (1987), 1498–9.
[83] Presumably, he would include job candidates as well.
[84] McGovern (1987), 1498–9.

an accident, when considered alongside the potential impact of such an accident, will justify drug testing in advance of an accident occurring.

Leaving aside for the moment the relevance of drug testing's impact on private interests, the decision to 'safety test' could conceivably depend on an assessment of the risk associated with performing an employment task while under the influence of a drug. Hence, the risk of an impaired grocery store cashier causing damage to himself, fellow employees and the public is probably very low. On the other hand, the risk associated with an impaired aeroplane pilot may be very great, when one considers the lives that could be lost if a drug-related accident were to occur. In other words, testing 100 employees 100 times (i.e. 10,000 drug tests) in order to identify a few drug users might be viewed as an effective safety policy if the risk associated with impairment on the job is very high.

It is claimed that drug-testing serves another purpose relevant to safety because it deters employees from using drugs, and from becoming safety risks.[85] Others have suggested, however, that if drug abuse has a 'disease' component over which the individual has reduced or no control, then the deterrent effect of drug testing will be reduced.[86] There is, as yet, no conclusive scientific evidence that employment drug testing widely discourages future drug use.[87] Moreover, the deterrence factor of drug testing is dependent on the form of testing adopted by a firm. Pre-employment testing alone will have no long-term deterrence value on employees. Hence, employers who wish to deter employees from future drug use must implement programmes which provide for repeated random or universal testing. Given the few employees who are drug users, and the fewer still whose drug use could pose a potential safety problem, the resources required for a long-term testing plan could probably be put to better use. In certain limited cases, however, risk assessment could lead to a different conclusion.

8.6.3 Abuse Deterrence

Deterring employee abuse of the employment relationship is probably the least significant justification for workplace drug testing. Some reports have suggested that by discouraging drug use, and thereby reducing the number of employees using drugs, testing programmes curtail workplace theft (since drug users may steal from their employers to finance their expensive drug habits).[88] This was the rationale advanced by the defendant bank in the Canadian anti-discrimination

---

[85] The data on this point are limited, although this has not prevented some authors from relying on the deterrent effect of drug-testing to support its use in the employment context: Hobbs and Scrivner (1988), 630; McGovern (1987), 1453.

[86] McGuire and Ruhm (1991), 10.

[87] Normand *et al.* (1994), 236.

[88] PCC (1990b), 6; OLRC (1992a), 5. Drug-testing companies often emphasise crime deterrence as a justification. In fact, Drug Testing Services of Austin, Texas lists 'theft of property' as its first reason to drug test employees.

challenge to drug testing that I discussed in Chapter 6.[89] However, because few employees are drug users, and even fewer are drug-dependent, drug-related workplace theft probably accounts for only a tiny percentage of the overall annual loss to businesses from employee abuse.

8.6.4 Regulatory Compliance

Employer drug testing programmes adopted as a result of state-imposed regulatory requirements are, as I noted in Chapter 2, to be found mostly in the United States. Thus, United States Department of Transportation Regulations require drug testing for the aviation, motor carrier, rail, marine and pipeline industries.[90] Moreover, under the 1988 Drug-Free Workplace Act,[91] all employers wishing to contract with the United States Government for the provision of goods or services in excess of US$25,000, and all recipients of federal grants, must undertake to provide a drug-free workplace as a condition of the contract.[92] There are presently no regulations in Canada and France which either impose or encourage employment drug testing in the private sector.

8.6.5 Public Policy

State efforts to combat drug use run the gamut from employment-related initiatives (public sector drug testing, regulations requiring private sector drug testing and policies encouraging employers to be pro-active in creating drug-free workplaces), to more general public awareness campaigns against drugs (e.g. 'Just Say No!'[93]), to tougher criminal law sanctions. All of this has occurred against the backdrop, and as part, of the war on drugs that I discussed earlier in this chapter. This has undoubtedly created an anti-drug/anti-drug users social climate. How has this affected employers? Surveys indicate that a substantial number of American employers have chosen to adopt drug-testing policies to help curb illegal drug traffic,[94] suggesting a willingness on the part of companies to assist the state in the anti-drug campaign. Moreover, the same surveys suggest that many employers believe that drug testing will improve their organ-

---

[89] *Toronto-Dominion Bank, supra,* n. 106, Chap. 6, and accompanying text.
[90] *Supra,* n. 152, Chap. 2. These regulations apply to 538,000 air carrier employees, 90,000 rail industry workers and 5,500,000 truck drivers.
[91] 41 USC paras. 701–7 (1988).
[92] This is an extension of Executive Order 12564, *supra,* n. 161, Chap. 2, through which President Reagan sought to make all agencies of the US government, 'drug free'. Under the Order, all Federal employees were required to refrain from the use of illegal drugs (s. 1(a)), and Federal agencies were authorised to implement drug-testing programmes (ss. 2(b)(5), 3). The Drug-Free Workplace Act sought to achieve similar results in private sector firms contracting with the US Government.
[93] 'Just Say No!' was the anti-drug slogan popularised by former United States First Lady, Nancy Reagan.
[94] According to Gallup (1988), 10% of employers identified the desire to curb illegal drug traffic as the main reason for adopting a drug testing plan.

isation's public image.[95] Even employers who claim to have legitimate productivity, safety and abuse-deterrence rationales for their drug testing policies are probably influenced by the public policy of discouraging drug use by exposing drug users, and disciplining, punishing or rehabilitating them.[96] How else can one explain the expenditure of resources[97] on comprehensive drug-testing plans which provide so little relevant information about productivity and safety, and which are prone to high rates of inaccuracy? Alcohol consumption is surely a more pressing workplace problem than drug use, yet employers have certainly not been as quick to develop alcohol awareness policies for their employees. This must relate to the differing public policy approaches to drugs and alcohol, and in particular to the fact that the former is illegal (and therefore socially unpopular), while the other is legal (and socially acceptable).

8.6.6 Conclusion

Drug testing appears to contribute very little information to its two main employment-related justifications, improving economic conditions and promoting health and safety. A positive drug test merely identifies the subject as having used a drug at some point in the past. It indicates nothing about whether that person will have a negative effect on firm productivity, nor whether she poses a safety risk. The link between a positive drug test and both productivity and health and safety is the assumption that a person who is a drug user will be more likely than a non-drug user to be an unproductive or unsafe worker. This assumption is tenuous for two reasons. First, the most popular form of drug testing, EIM, has a significant inaccuracy problem. In fact, false-positive results may outnumber true-positive results. Secondly, a positive test brands a subject with the label 'unproductive', or 'unsafe', on the basis of a generalisation about the group to which the individual belongs (i.e. the group, 'drug users'), even though most drug users are neither unsafe nor unproductive.

What all drug users have in common, however, is that they are participating in an illegal activity.[98] Workplace drug testing seems to be most concerned with (and most effective at) identifying these individuals, for the purpose of depriving them of employment opportunities. Whether the point is to punish drug users, discourage drug use generally or boost a firm's public image by weeding out drug-using candidates/employees, it seems clear that the promotion of

---

[95] Linowes (1988), 52–3. twenty-two percent of respondent companies with drug-testing policies felt that these policies improved their public image: Schottenfield (1989), 415.

[96] Feldthusen (1988), 94.

[97] In 1993, it was estimated that US$1.2 billion was spent on workplace drug testing in the United States (*Los Angeles Times* (1993), 2).

[98] Under Dutch law, the possession of drugs for one's own use is not subject to any criminal penalties (Van den Hurk (1997)). Italy's drug laws are also liberal. Drug use was de-criminalised there in 1993. Use remains contrary to the law, but no criminal sanctions attach to it. Instead, administrative measures (i.e. compulsory treatment) may be imposed upon drug users (Bricolo (1997)).

anti-drug public policy is the single most significant justification underlying workplace drug testing.

Through the application of Principles 3 to 7, I am now able to draw conclusions about the objectives supporting drug testing, the means chosen to achieve these objectives and the procedural and other safeguards which must be implemented in relation to drug testing and the information derived therefrom.

8.7.1 Reconciling Competing Interests (Principles 3, 4 and 5)

8.7.1.1 Weighing the Private Interests at Stake

It should be clear that the right of privacy is implicated by any employer-imposed drug-testing policy. It does not matter whether the policy is random or universal, scheduled or surprise, or with cause/without cause/post-event. In all these cases, a personal private interest will be impacted upon by the imposition of a drug test. Informational interests are also threatened. As I noted above, the impact is significant in light of the underlying values protected by privacy: autonomy, well-being and dignity, healthy relationships and pluralism.

8.7.1.2 Weighing the Employer and Public Interests at Stake

Against this backdrop, I turn to assess the justifications advanced in favour of drug testing. When the significance of private interests is manifest, as it is in the case of drug testing, then the right carries with it considerable power. Therefore, competing employer and public interests must themselves be legitimate and substantial to have any hope of overcoming the limitations imposed by the right. For this reason, a workplace drug testing programme solely justified by anti-drug public policy cannot survive scrutiny under *Principle 3, Legitimate and Substantial Limitations* because an employer must advance an interest which bears some relation to an employment matter, such as health and safety, productivity or abuse deterrence. An employer cannot place itself in the position of the state by, for example, usurping the police power. The failure or refusal of an employer to assert a legitimate management justification is conclusive that an unjustified invasion of privacy occurs every time a candidate/employee is required to submit to a drug test. No employer may adopt drug testing to deter drug use in society, punish drug users or improve its public image.

Similarly, workplace drug testing mandated by legislation or other state action must also rely on an employment-related justification, and not simply on anti-drug public policy. The state can combat drug use through a variety of means, including public awareness campaigns and its own police power (with all the associated safeguards), but the state should not be permitted to recruit employers in the war on drugs, and require drug testing in employment solely to identify and punish drug users.

It can be assumed, however, that privacy-invasive workplace policies will rarely be justified only on public policy grounds, although they may be justified *primarily* on public policy grounds, or they may be public policy measures masquerading as something different. Employers can be expected to fall back on the productivity and/or safety rationales. For this reason, careful scrutiny should be applied in assessing the true purposes behind drug testing programmes.

The promotion of productivity is not a compelling justification for workplace drug testing. Concerns about the productivity of those who use drugs are decidedly economic, and *Principle 5, Insufficiency of Limitations Premised on Economic Interests* dictates a sceptical approach to justifications for privacy violations premised on economic considerations. This scepticism is hardly misplaced in the case of drug testing, as studies to date are inconclusive in linking productivity with simple drug use. Although it could be considered a common sense conclusion that drug users will, on aggregate, be less productive than non-drug users, this says nothing about the impact of drug use on the individual. Thus, to expose all candidates/employees to random or universal drug testing without cause, for the purpose of identifying a few drug users, labelling them as less productive, and denying them employment, disciplining them or forcing them into rehabilitation is simply not justifiable. The private interests at stake clearly outweigh any productivity justification advanced to support drug testing for two reasons: first, drug testing provides little useful information about productivity, while impacting significantly on personal and informational private interests; and secondly, even if testing did provide some useful information, an economic interest cannot be relied upon to justify a manifest and serious infringement upon private interests.

Where an employer drug tests 'with cause' for productivity reasons, the private interests at stake are perhaps less compelling (because the impact on private informational interests is not as severe), yet they cannot be said to be merely incidental or insignificant. Given this, the result is the same regardless of whether productivity testing is conducted with or without cause—an employer should be prohibited from doing it. This result is reinforced when one considers the alternatives available to employers (which I discuss below).

Drug testing for safety purposes presents a dilemma, however, because its point is to protect the autonomy, dignity and personal security interests of third parties. Pursuant to *Principle 4, Sufficiency of Limitations Premised on Third Party Interests*, such a policy is more easily justified. However, the real issue in the context of drug testing is not whether a policy has a protective objective (many drug testing policies surely do), but, rather, whether a policy actually contributes to achieving greater workplace safety, and whether this contribution can outweigh the costs in terms of loss of personal privacy for the individuals affected. Commentators fall into three camps on the safety question. Some take the view that drug testing should be impermissible because the tests are too inaccurate to provide meaningful information on any issue, and because the link between drug use and safety risks is weak. These commentators hold to the view that drug testing contributes so little relevant information to the question whether a person poses a safety risk that the benefits are outweighed by the impact on privacy.[99] Others observe that while safety testing cannot generally be justified because of the limitations of drug testing, it may be carried out where the employer has reasonable cause to believe that an employee's drug use is affecting work performance, and that this poses a risk to the safety of others.[100] Finally, there are those who argue in favour of testing where impaired performance of a work task carries with it a high risk of a catastrophic event such as injury or death to third persons.[101]

The latter position, which supports random or universal drug testing for safety-sensitive positions, is based on the view that some jobs are so risky that those who perform them must abstain from drug use altogether. The following assumptions underlie this position:

- Drug abuse can pose a risk to workplace safety because an abuser may perform employment tasks while impaired. Before an individual becomes a drug abuser, the individual logically must be a drug user. The deterrent effect of drug testing contributes to preventing workers from using drugs, thus ensuring that workers never become drug abusers.[102]
- By the time the physical manifestations of drug abuse become apparent to an employer, it may be too late. The strength of drug testing is that it can identify drug use before the visible symptoms of drug abuse show themselves in the workplace. This is an advantage that no trained supervisor can duplicate.[103]
- Off-duty drug use can negatively impact on work performance by reducing reaction times, motor control, and co-ordination.[104] This could conceivably result in, or contribute to, accidents.

These three propositions are not, in themselves, compelling. The first two draw a link between drug use and work performance which, as I noted above, is not strong. The third is supported by minimal and controversial research.[105]

---

[99] OLRC (1992a), 112–13; Canadian Bar Association (1987).

[100] Feldthusen (1988), 109, concedes that some jobs may not permit the employer to ascertain reasonable cause, and in those cases random testing may be justifiable. See judicial decisions on employment testing from Canada and France, *supra*, sects. 5.3.1, 6.5.1.

[101] McGovern (1987); Hobbs and Scrivner (1988).

[102] Hobbs and Scrivner, *ibid.*, in their defence of random safety testing, appear to subscribe to the view that anyone consuming illicit drugs is a drug abuser, while failing to distinguish between drug use, drug abuse and drug dependence (see Appendix—Glossary of Terms). The proposition that the mere use of drugs is 'abuse' is not adopted herein because it fails to recognize that many people consume drugs, in particular marijuana, without their consumption having an impact on their work performance.

[103] McGovern (1987), 1498–9.

[104] *Supra*, n. 73.

[105] Normand *et al.* (1994), 6. The authors report that some drugs, such as cocaine and amphetamines, may actually result in short-term work performance improvements because they are stimulants (at 121).

However, taken together, they surely support the view that the imposition of accurate drug testing must contribute *in some way* to reducing the risk of work-place accidents. Logically, a workplace free of drug users would be safer than a workplace with even one drug user, since in the former case there is no chance of a drug-related accident, whereas in the latter, there is at least some chance (although perhaps small) that one worker will perform a task while impaired by drugs. This may nevertheless be a very weak argument in support of random or universal drug testing, since such tests will catch only a small number of drug-using candidates/employees while exposing a great many more to significant (and ultimately unnecessary) intrusions upon private interests. One might well hold to the view that the employer and public interest in promoting safety cannot overcome the force of the private interests affected.

Where the risk associated with impaired work performance is high, in the sense that an accident would threaten human life or result in some other catastrophic event, then it has been argued that the balance shifts. Advocates of safety testing make this argument by observing that employees in safety-sensitive positions have a reduced expectation of privacy *ab initio*. Typically, at the pre-employment stage, candidates for such jobs are subject to rigorous background checks and medical examinations.[106] After hiring, periodic medical check-ups may be required. Those who accept safety-sensitive employment recognise that their health and off-duty activities will be relevant to their continuing employment. Hence, the nature of their jobs prevents them from asserting personal and informational private interests to the same extent as other workers.

The 'diminished expectation of privacy' argument has appeared in United States Supreme Court decisions, where employees' private interests have been downgraded *because* competing interests were found to be substantial.[107] However, this reasoning could easily be turned on its head, by arguing that employer and public expectations of invading privacy for safety reasons are reduced in value because the private interests at stake are so important. Premising privacy protection on 'shifting' expectations is clearly prone to manipulation. In any event, it would be incorrect to conclude that the risk of accidents renders the personal and informational private interests of, say, airline pilots less substantial than the same interests of airline sales representatives. A blood or urine test carries with it the same intrusion upon the corpus, and seeks to acquire the same information about off-duty conduct. Even if the employer and public interests in preventing catastrophic accidents are great, they could still be outweighed by the private interests which are infringed. One therefore must return to the question whether or not the safety interest underlying certain drug testing meets the 'substantial' standard of *Principle 3*. The short answer is yes, by reason of *Principle 4*, but this would only be the case in certain narrow, high risk cases.

---

[106] Hobbs and Scrivner (1988), 628; McGovern (1987), 1501.
[107] *Supra*, text accompanying nn. 66–7, Chap. 4.

8.7.1.3 Conclusion

The above discussion demonstrates that reconciling candidates'/employees' private interests with the employer and public interest in safety raises complex issues. I would nevertheless draw the conclusion that the promotion of workplace safety is the only one of the various employer and public interest justifications that is sufficient to support drug testing. This follows from the fact that the safety justification promotes third party interests similar in nature to the interests underlying the protection of privacy (*Principle 4, Sufficiency of Limitations Premised on Third Party Interests*). It is also consistent with legal positions adopted in the United States, France and Canada.[108]

However, a safety objective cannot justify random or universal drug testing in all cases, since the link between the fact that a person is a drug user and work performance is weak. Moreover, in many cases, the risk associated with performing tasks while impaired is sufficiently low that it cannot justify subjecting candidates/employees to invasive drug testing. However, there may be a limited category of job positions where the risk of catastrophe resulting from impairment on the job is very high. In such cases, the privacy-based argument against drug testing becomes less convincing.

At this stage, it is apparent that the drug testing issue has been narrowed considerably, since testing based on anti-drug public policy, economic considerations, and abuse deterrence have all been ruled out through the application of Principles 3, 4 and 5. Further refinement is still possible through the application of *Principle 6, Least Restrictive Means*.

8.7.2 Ensuring that the Least Restrictive Means are Adopted (Principle 6)

Even if safety concerns can justify employment policies impacting upon private interests, *Principle 6, Least Restrictive Means* requires that such a policy should limit privacy only to the extent necessary to accomplish the objectives underlying the policy. I explained this Principle in Chapter 7. It dictates that a privacy-invasive policy may be adopted only if: (1) no reasonable alternative exists which could accomplish the objective with a less intrusive impact; and (2) the invasive policy is individualised and particularised to ensure that it minimally impairs private interests.

8.7.2.1 Alternatives to Drug Testing

Having concluded that the employer interest in promoting the safety of employees and the public may be sufficiently substantial to justify limitations on private

---

[108] *Luck, supra*, n. 129, Chap. 4, and text accompanying nn. 129–32, Chap. 4; *Societé Peintures Corona, supra*, n. 25, Chap. 5, and text accompanying non. 26–30, Chap. 5; *supra*, sect. 6.5.1.

interests through drug testing, I now turn to whether or not drug testing is necessary and, if so, how the impact of such testing on private interests can be limited. Are there alternatives available which respect private interests better than drug testing? This is important because drug testing has arguably become a convenient alternative to the traditional employer method of detecting impaired work performance—supervision. One of the peculiar aspects of the drug-testing debate is the assertion by pro-testing advocates that drugs cause chronic absenteeism, significant losses in productivity, diminished work performance, and safety dangers, coupled with a claim that drug testing is the preferred solution.[109] One would think that if employees are chronically late or absent, or perform shoddy work, then employers who are able to supervise would become aware of this without drug testing. Of course, the real point of most drug-testing policies is to screen-out drug users, who it is assumed will become tardy, shoddy workers at some point in the future. Perhaps drug testing is so popular because it relieves managers from having to make employment decisions on the basis of subjective observation. After all, a candidate/employee who is drug-tested is either a 'drug user' or 'clean', and management decisions are facilitated by such simplistic categorisation.

Drug testing should not be used because it is convenient and simple, but because it is necessary. Hence, we can see again why productivity concerns cannot justify drug testing. If an employee is not as productive as the employer would like, then the employer should be able to determine this by adopting objective and non-invasive work performance tests measuring hours worked, efficiency, output, etc. As one commentator has put it, '[t]he way to measure performance is to measure performance. Rather than testing the typist's urine for drug traces, why not test the typing?'[110] Moreover, supervision may be coupled with Drug Evaluation and Classification training (DEC) to assist managers in identifying drug and other performance problems. DEC is a standardised, systematic method of examining a subject's behaviour, appearance, eyes, vital signs and results in performance tests to determine whether the subject is acting under the influence of a mind-altering substance. Although initially developed for police investigations, employment supervisors may be trained in certain DEC methods in order to recognise performance problems related to drugs, alcohol, and even stress and fatigue.[111] DEC is an imperfect means of identifying drug use, since symptoms related to other factors (illness, fatigue, etc.) may be mistaken for drug use.[112] However, an employer's primary concern should be the quality of work performance, as opposed to the causes of inadequate work. Hence, DEC could prove quite valuable.

---

[109] The article by Hobbs and Scrivner (1988) is a prime example.
[110] Wisotsky (1987), 776.
[111] Normand *et al.* (1994), 203–6.
[112] Ironically, DEC has little value in the workplace in identifying drug use specifically, since supervisors would need continual practice in detecting drug use to be effective, and employment drug use is simply too rare to provide sufficient practice opportunities (*ibid.*, 206).

Many companies have responded to the problem of substance abuse by implementing a comprehensive workplace substance abuse programme (WSA). Such a programme incorporates training for supervisors in DEC methods, along with an education and awareness programme to inform all employees of the health and other consequences for them, and the impact on the company, of drug and alcohol abuse.[113] A WSA provides confidential counselling to workers suffering from substance abuse, through which they are directed to appropriate community services, and are provided with follow-up support. Although some WSAs have included drug testing, this is certainly not an essential feature. In fact, the basic premise of WSA is that educating and supporting employees is preferable to coercing and punishing them with measures like drug testing. The strength of this type of programme is its ability to tackle a range of problems, including the abuse of alcohol, tobacco, prescription drugs and narcotics.[114] WSAs may also be useful in helping employees to deal with stress related to work or family problems, both of which may be more serious threats to work performance than the use of drugs.[115]

Even with regard to jobs in which the physical safety of employees or the public is at risk, there are non-intrusive testing alternatives available. Psychomotor or functional testing[116] determines whether an employee's work performance is *actually* impaired by evaluating visual perception, fine motor control and neuromuscular response. A flight simulator, in which the performance of airline pilots is evaluated, is one such test. The FACTOR 1000 test is another example. This test, essentially similar to a video game and inexpensive to administer, requires the subject to keep a randomly moving icon centred between two fixed points on a computer screen. The speed of the icon continually accelerates until the subject can no longer compensate for the movement, at which time the test ends. Upon completion, a computer calculates the subject's current hand-eye co-ordination result, and compares it to previous results.[117] Psychomotor testing involves no infringement of a personal private interest, and because it measures the subject's ability to perform the actual skills required for a job, it entails no incursion upon informational private interests.

Not only does psychomotor testing avoid the serious impact on private interests inherent to drug testing, but it also provides meaningful information about work performance. Because it tests for actual impairment, as opposed to possible causes of impairment, it eliminates the need to speculate which is inherent to drug testing.[118] The combination of psychomotor testing and a WSA programme (including DEC training for supervisors) would be a formidable and

---

[113] United States Department of Labor (1996).

[114] Coshan (1994), 415.

[115] *Ibid.*, 415–16.

[116] See Appendix—Glossary of Terms.

[117] McCourt (1992). Notably, the cost of performing a FACTOR 1000 test per employee is about one dollar, which is appreciably less than the cost per employee of urinalysis drug testing (OLRC (1992a), 118).

[118] The OLRC (1992a) endorsed psychomotor/functional testing, while advocating that workplace drug testing in all its forms should be illegal; Normand *et al.* (1994), 206.

effective means of ensuring safety in the great majority of industries. After all, an employer cannot meet its positive duty to protect its employees and the public from safety hazards by merely adopting a drug testing programme. If the hazards are significant enough to overcome employees' private interests, then surely the employer has a duty to supervise intensely, to provide adequate education and support to workers, and to implement a rigorous testing programme for detecting work-performance problems which may result from a host of causes—ageing, illness, fatigue, alcohol, drugs, etc. No one would seriously argue that an employee is 'safe' merely because she has passed a drug test. There is, however, a great danger that a 'drug free workplace' will wrongly be equated with a 'safe workplace', and other, more pressing dangers will go undetected until disaster strikes.

Advocates of safety testing in employment argue that the benefit of drug testing is its ability to identify an emerging problem before the physical symptoms of drug abuse show themselves in the workplace.[119] The flaw in this argument is the failure to recognise that alternative testing methods may exist which are less intrusive and as (if not more) effective. Such an argument recognises the importance of the employer's (and public's) interest in promoting workplace safety, as incorporated into *Principle 4, Sufficiency of Limitations Premised on Third Party Interests*, but then fails to consider the need for an employer to pursue this interest in the manner least restrictive of privacy (i.e. *Principle 6, Least Restrictive Means*). Therefore, it is very significant that psychomotor testing would probably be more effective than drug testing in identifying an emerging problem (since it provides *meaningful* information concerning work performance).[120] It is equally significant that a comprehensive WSA programme would encourage safe practices by offering education and support to workers. This would be a constructive addition to the employment relationship, unlike drug testing.

8.7.2.2 *Individualisation and Particularisation*

The concepts of individualisation and particularisation provide further guidance in applying *Principle 6, Least Restrictive Means*. Individualisation requires that an employer impose a privacy-invasive policy only on those employees for whom it is reasonably necessary. In effect, this means that an employer may only require employees to submit to safety drug testing if they perform jobs which carry a significant risk of harm to other workers or the public, and if no reasonable alternative method of gauging work performance is available. The onus is on the employer to make out these two conditions. Because few employees perform dangerous jobs, and because drug testing is such an unsatisfactory

---

[119] McGovern (1987), 1499.

[120] McGovern, *ibid.*, states that airline pilots, nuclear plant workers and surgeons should be subject to safety testing. Employees holding these jobs could be tested with psychomotor techniques on regular occasions, and emerging work performance problems—lack of concentration, reduction in hand-eye co-ordination, etc.—could then be identified.

means of predicting work performance compared with supervisory observation or psychomotor testing, it is difficult to imagine cases in which a drug-testing policy will be justified. Nevertheless, assuming that a safety testing policy could be implemented, then it would have to be individualised. Limitations which seek to individualise drug testing policies have been suggested on two fronts.

First, some advocates of safety testing argue that it may be effectively individualised if it occurs only after the employer has formed a reasonable suspicion that a subject's work performance may be impaired by drugs. The reasonable suspicion standard limits the number of individuals subject to testing by excluding those who do not exhibit outward behaviour indicative of safety risk. Moreover, it seems fair to conclude that an employee who exhibits behaviour in the workplace indicative of drug use, thus allowing the employer to form a suspicion of drug use, cannot assert informational privacy with the same force as the general workforce, since there is reason to believe that the employee's off-duty conduct is affecting her work performance. However, effective supervision (assuming it is possible) may well pick up this fact in advance of intrusive testing. An employer would then be able to question the employee concerned, and require the employee to submit to a psychomotor test to confirm the work-performance problem. Thus, it is unclear why a reasonable suspicion would necessarily require drug testing for confirmation, since the employer's concern is not with drug use, but with the work performance of the employee. Tests of actual work performance would more naturally flow from a reasonable suspicion.

Advocates of random or universal safety testing reject the reasonable suspicion standard on the argument that it would prevent pro-active measures on the part of employers to ensure safety in the workplace.[121] An employer would have to observe behaviour consistent with impairment, or come into possession of information pointing to drug use, before demanding a drug test. In certain job settings, it may be very difficult for the employer to supervise the conduct of employees—consider the case of truck drivers, for example. Moreover, a reasonable suspicion standard would not protect against those cases, albeit rare, where an employee is impaired yet does not exhibit observable symptoms of impairment.[122] Even the most vigilant employer might not be able to form a reasonable suspicion although an employee has a drug problem with the potential to impact upon his work performance. On this basis, a second suggestion for individualisation has been made, namely that employees performing ultra-hazardous jobs may be subject to drug testing if continual, effective supervision is not feasible.[123] Again, this assumes that alternative methods of gauging work performance are not available. There is nothing preventing employers from being pro-active by implementing an aggressive programme of education and

---

[121] McGovern (1987), 1495, 1498–9.

[122] *Ibid.*, 1495.

[123] Even Feldthusen (1988), 110–11, who strongly objects to workplace drug testing, thinks that it may be justifiable in such circumstances.

psychomotor tests for work performance. The opportunities to administer such testing will be the same as for drug testing, yet the information provided may be superior because it concerns the subject's actual abilities. It is difficult to imagine circumstances in which the administration of alternative, less intrusive methods would not be feasible, but drug testing would be. Furthermore, these alternative methods could be applied to all employees, thus avoiding the potentially thorny issue of identifying those employees who may and may not be drug tested. Standards for distinguishing between employees and their jobs, such as 'ultra-hazardous', 'high-risk' and 'not conducive to effective supervision', are not particularly precise.

Turning to particularisation, only a brief comment is necessary. An employer must ensure that its drug testing policy impacts upon only the private interests necessary to achieve the employer's objective. In the case of drug testing, informational private interests must be respected through particularisation. If it could be established that drug testing were necessary in certain limited cases for the purpose of promoting safety, and if a sufficiently individualised policy could be implemented, then the employer should only test specimens for drugs with the potential to cause work performance problems. Under no circumstances should other types of analyses (i.e. pregnancy, HIV, etc.) be conducted.[124] Moreover, information acquired through drug testing should remain private except in so far as it assists the employer in promoting safety. Therefore, this information should only be used for legitimate employment purposes, such as making hiring decisions, re-assigning work, disciplining, etc. An employer should not publicise the results within or outside the organisation, nor should an employer release the results to the authorities.

8.7.2.3 Conclusion

Although the employer and public interest in safety may be sufficient to justify limitations on candidates'/employees' private interests (*Principle 4*), an examination of alternatives (*Principle 6*)—supervisory observation, DEC training, comprehensive WSA programmes, and psychomotor testing—suggests that non-intrusive management practices are available which provide more meaningful information concerning work performance than drug testing. Only in rare cases would such alternatives be impractical, thus permitting drug testing. In any event, if a drug testing policy is sufficiently individualised, then only in rare cases will it be justifiable to subject candidates/employees to drug tests of any kind. Moreover, a drug-testing policy which is sufficiently particularised will prevent an employer from using the information acquired through testing for any purpose other than to improve safety.

---

[124] ILO (1996c).

8.7.3 Guaranteeing Procedural and Other Safeguards (Principle 7)

Procedural issues have loomed large in the drug-testing debate, as it has been through procedure that many advocates and opponents have sought to address concerns about testing inaccuracy. Although it will be clear by now that employment drug testing is not generally permissible under the legal principles I advanced in Chapter 7, it is still necessary to consider procedural and other safeguards which must be implemented alongside any drug-testing programme to protect informational private interests (*Principle 7, Procedural and Other Safeguards*). Certainly, all the safeguards I discussed in Chapter 7 should be guaranteed. However, drug testing raises some unique considerations.

The nature of drug testing generally dictates that candidates/employees will be aware in advance of the testing. This is because subjects must donate a body fluid such as blood or urine, thus necessitating their co-operation. However, if new methods of drug testing were to become more viable, such as hair analysis,[125] it might then be possible for an employer to conduct a drug test without the knowledge of the individuals concerned. Employers should therefore be under an obligation to inform subjects prior to any drug test, and this notification should include both the fact that testing will occur, and the relevant details of how it will occur. Employers may be hesitant to provide much advance notice, out of concern that drug users will abstain in order to ensure a negative test. The deterrent effect of drug testing, lauded by many testing advocates,[126] will surely necessitate a general announcement to employees of a drug-testing plan. Therefore, there is no justification in principle for an employer to fail to notify well in advance of a drug-testing plan, and at least one or two days prior to the administration of the actual tests. Providing such notice, and accompanying details about how testing will be carried out, will prevent the degrading scenario whereby a candidate/employee is told to attend at a location with no idea of why, and is then ordered to urinate (and perhaps watched in the process) or to give blood, for the purpose of a drug test.

Procedural protections can go far in ensuring that no employment decisions are taken on the basis of potentially inaccurate drug testing results. As I noted earlier in this chapter, employers may prefer cheaper methods of testing such as EIM even if this means sacrificing accuracy. This is particularly the case in relation to low-skilled employment positions where the competition for jobs is strong. The cost to an employer of rejecting a candidate/employee due to a false positive result is low, since there will likely be many others who have tested negative and are eager to fill the position. However, the cost to the individual who has tested positive is high because of loss of employment opportunity. The stigma of 'drug user' which attaches to a person who tests positive will also be harmful, causing stress and perhaps interfering with future job prospects. For

---

[125] *Supra*, n. 21.
[126] *Supra*, n. 85.

this reason, subjects will prefer more accurate (and more expensive) testing methods. The result is a conflict of preferences between employers and candidates/employees. This conflict should be resolved in favour of candidates/ employees because the information revealed by a drug test attracts privacy. Management decisions should only be taken on the basis of such information if it is accurate.

As a first step, since the information provided by a drug test relates to a subject's private interest, the subject has the right to have the information at the first possible opportunity. Therefore, a subject should be notified of the results of a drug test as soon as possible following the administration of the test, and certainly before management decisions are taken. Moreover, providing the information to the subject permits scrutiny of drug tests which, as noted above, do have a considerable inaccuracy problem. Presumably, the subject will be in the best position to know whether a false positive has occurred.

Furthermore, any employer who adopts drug testing should provide a subject who tests positive with a reasonable opportunity to rebut or explain the result. Rebuttal is best facilitated by permitting the subject to demand verification of a positive result with a more accurate method of testing (I described several of these in section 8.4 of this chapter). Preferably, employers should be required to perform second-test confirmation in all cases where a single test produces a positive result. Follow-up tests should be carried out at the employer's expense, by an independent and licensed laboratory,[127] on the same sample as the first test, and the confirmatory method should be different from the original method. This would largely eliminate the inaccuracy problem inherent in the EIM test.[128] However, as a final step, a subject who has tested positive on both initial and confirmatory tests should be interviewed by a Medical Review Officer (MRO), who will examine the results of the tests and determine if other explanations (i.e. legally prescribed medications, foodstuffs, exposure to second-hand marijuana smoke) could have caused a false-positive.

A procedure which involves the candidate/employee both before and after the drug test is administered, and before any management decisions are taken on the basis of a positive test result, prevents subjects from being disciplined or deprived of employment opportunities on the basis of flawed information. It also renders drug-testing programmes transparent, which will contribute to preventing abuses such as tampering with samples to achieve a positive result, or testing for private health matters unrelated to drugs.

---

[127] The ILO (1996c) has called for the development of international standards for workplace drug testing. Here, the term 'licensed' refers to licensing under domestic law in relation to quality assurance and quality control protocols which ensure accuracy.

[128] Where a positive EIM test is confirmed by a gas chromatography/mass spectrometry test, the error rate can be reduced to less than 1 per cent (OLRC (1992a), 20).

8.8 CONCLUSIONS—A LAW GOVERNING EMPLOYMENT DRUG TESTING

In light of the seven legal principles governing workplace privacy, what would be an appropriate legal response to employment drug testing? In my view, two possibilities emerge from the above discussion.

First, employment drug testing in all its forms could be prohibited entirely. This result could be achieved either by statute or by judicial interpretation of the right of privacy. An approach of outright prohibition would be premised on the view that employers should always be able to achieve the safety, productivity and abuse deterrence objectives related to employment drug testing through non-intrusive methods such as psychomotor testing and/or WSA programmes. This approach would have one over-riding advantage: *certainty*. It would also encourage employers to develop and adopt non-invasive supervisory and performance evaluation methods, while being highly protective of private interests.

The second option would leave minimal room for employment drug testing, but would suffer from some uncertainty. This option would permit employers to subject candidates/employees to drug testing as a condition of employment if the following four conditions were satisfied:

Proposed Legal Conditions for Employment Drug Testing

---

(1) *Safety justification*: only individuals holding or being considered for positions with a significant safety element would be subject to the policy;

AND

(2) *Individualisation*:

   (a) *Impossibility of supervision*: the employer is able to demonstrate that it would not be possible to supervise effectively employees in safety positions, perhaps because they typically work off-site;

   OR

   (b) *Reasonable suspicion*: the employer has a reasonable suspicion that a particular candidate/employee has a diminished capacity to perform tasks by reason of drug use;

AND

(3) *No reasonable alternatives*: the employer is able to demonstrate that there is no alternative, less intrusive method of determining whether or not a candidate/employee is able to perform job functions safely;

AND

(4) *Procedural and other safeguards*: the employer has guaranteed a full range of procedural and other safeguards in relation to drug testing and the information derived therefrom, including: prior notification of

testing, notification of results as soon as possible, verification of positive results through second-test confirmation, access to an MRO prior to any employment decision being taken on the basis of results and confidentiality in relation to the results.

This second option could be implemented by statute, or by judicial interpretation of the right of privacy. It would permit safety testing in those *rare* cases where an employer can prove that alternative methods of performance evaluation would not effectively address genuine safety concerns. In practice, the application of this approach could well result in the end of employment drug testing, since it may be very difficult for employers to meet the burden of proving that drug testing is the appropriate means of achieving safety objectives.

The disadvantage of this second option is the uncertainty of determinations surrounding which jobs have a sufficiently significant safety component, whether or not effective supervision is impossible, and whether or not reasonable alternatives are available. However, the employment testing case law from the United States, France and Canada reveals that courts and tribunals do have experience in dealing with such difficult issues.

9

Employment Genetic Testing

9.1 INTRODUCTION

In Chapter 8, I applied the seven legal principles from Chapter 7 to employment drug testing. Drug testing is already a reality for candidates/employees in North America and the European Union, and has attracted considerable scholarly attention. Another workplace testing issue now looms on the horizon, and threatens to equal drug testing as a source of privacy concern: employment genetic testing. In Chapter 9, I will consider the existing and potential uses of genetic testing in the employment context and, as in Chapter 8, I will seek to identify and reconcile the competing interests of candidates/employees, employers and the public. As will become apparent, the analysis of employment genetic testing is not simply a restatement of the discussion concerning drug testing. Genetic testing raises unique questions, the resolution of which is informed by the legal principles that I have developed herein.

9.2 THE SCIENCE OF GENETICS AND THE HUMAN GENOME PROJECT

Genetic science is a complex field, and volumes of literature are available on the subject. While I will not attempt to provide a comprehensive analysis of genetics here, some scientific background is required in order to appreciate the potential future role of genetic testing in the employment context.[1]

The term 'gene' first appeared at the turn of the twentieth century as part of a theory that minute particles existed within the body of a biological organism which determined its physiological traits. These particles (i.e. genes) were thought to pass from parents to offspring, thus explaining physiological similarities between generations of the same family.[2] It later became clear to scientists that genes have no independent existence *per se*, but are simply discrete areas of deoxyribonucleic acid (DNA) which are responsible for the synthesis of certain proteins linked to certain physical characteristics. Nevertheless, the concept of a gene has become so much a part of popular parlance that one tends to view genes in exactly the manner first envisaged in the early 1900s. Regardless of the term employed ('gene' will be used here for simplicity), it must be recognised that the physiological structure of any biological organism is largely

---

[1] A good primer on genetics is Watson *et al.* (1987).
[2] Hubbard and Wald (1993), 11, 42.

determined by its genetic composition. Hence, in the case of human beings, physical characteristics such as a person's sex, eye and hair colour, blood type and bone structure are all genetically-determined.

To understand the link between the genetic composition of a person and her health, one must first realise that the human body is composed of millions of cells, each of which (with a few exceptions such as red blood cells) contains that person's full DNA. DNA itself is a string of over 3 billion pairs of chemical nucleotides,[3] organised in a linear fashion into a series of genes. Scientists estimate that there are between 50,000 and 100,000 genes in human DNA Each gene is a specific sequence of nucleotides which carries the information required for constructing proteins. Some of these proteins are the 'raw materials' which make up the structures of cells and tissues, while others form enzymes essential to biochemical reactions within the body. A further wrinkle is added by the fact that the body's DNA, and there-fore its genes, are organised into 23 distinct chromosomes. At conception, each parent contributes a set of chromosomes, which combine to form a new and unique human being. Therefore, each human being is composed of cells, which contain DNA, which is divided into thousands of genes, which are organised into 23 chromosomes.[4] The complete set of an individual's genetic information is known as the human genome, and every person's genome is distinct.

Because genes regulate the creation of proteins, they embody the instructions through which chemical components are organised, modified or transformed into a living biological form.[5] Human genes might be analogised to a 'recipe'.[6] Any error in the recipe could manifest itself in the ultimate outcome. This is the link between genes and health—a genetic abnormality may result in physical disorders and disease. It has long been recognised that certain medical condi-tions may have genetic causes, particularly those of a hereditary nature which pass from one generation to the next, or which are shared by individuals linked by familial, racial or ethnic background. Given this, it is not surprising that sci-entists have increasingly looked to the human genome for answers in research-ing the causes of, and treatments/cures for, disease. However, understanding human genetics in any meaningful sense requires information about complex matters such as the locations of genes within DNA, their functions and how they interrelate. Obtaining this preliminary information is the first stage in the Human Genome Project (HGP), an internationally co-ordinated effort to com-pile information on the genetic and physical features of the human genome. The objective of the HGP is to map the 23 human chromosomes through the identi-fication and ordering of the three billion base pairs of nucleotides in human DNA.[7] Commenced in 1990, it is estimated that the mapping phase of the HGP will be complete by 2005.[8]

---

[3] See Appendix—Glossary of Terms.
[4] PCC (1992c), 7.
[5] Casey (1997).
[6] Hubbard and Wald (1993), 11–12.
[7] US Department of Energy (1998).
[8] Iles (1996), 29–30.

The HGP is an effort to understand and explain the relationship between genes and genetic disease. The sequencing of DNA is the first step in this process, as it will provide the basis for identifying those genes which are responsible for particular biological characteristics. This will then tell scientists where to look for genetic flaws responsible for disease.[9] The location of these genetic flaws will permit predictive testing for genetic conditions and, it is hoped, will make possible the development of treatments and even cures. The potential health benefits flowing from the successful completion of the HGP are considerable when one realises that there are presently over 4,000 medical conditions known or believed to be genetic in nature, and that, according to estimates, each human being carries 20 harmful genes.[10] Among the disorders linked to genetic causes are coronary artery disease, cystic fibrosis, diabetes, Down's Syndrome, Huntington's Disease, sickle-cell anaemia and certain forms of cancer.

Although the potential health benefits of the HGP are undoubtedly impressive, it is important to put these into perspective. Even if human DNA is sequenced, and all human genes are identified, the utility of this information is limited by the fact that only a small minority of genetic disorders are linked *solely* to inherited genes. Such conditions are termed 'monogenic'[11] where they flow from a single defective gene, or 'multigenic' where they involve the interplay of two or more defective genes. However, the great majority of genetic illnesses have an environmental component, and therefore cannot easily be predicted solely from the human DNA map.[12] Some, termed 'multifactorial' disorders, result when an inherited genetic weakness is triggered or exacerbated by environmental conditions. In such cases, the identification of the genetic weakness in a particular person's DNA would only raise some possibility that the person could develop the disorder. Hence, even where all family members share the genetic weakness, there is no certainty that any of them will become ill.

Furthermore, environmental agents such as chemicals and radiation may interfere with the normal chemical processes within DNA, thereby causing genetic abnormalities and disease. Such disorders are not inherited, and occur during a person's lifetime in response to non-genetic factors. Even monogenic and multigenic disorders may be exacerbated by environmental factors, since the severity of symptoms can vary considerably from one person to the next.[13] Researchers now believe that the environment is an overarching factor across

---

[9] Genetic maps have already been used to find the exact chromosomal locations of several important disease genes, including those responsible for cystic fibrosis, sickle-cell anaemia, Tay-Sach's disease and monotonic dystrophy (Casey (1997), 2).

[10] Estimates also suggest that 1 in 12 individuals suffer from some sort of genetic disorder. See Milunsky (1993), 1308; Malinowski and Blatt (1997), 1217.

[11] See Appendix—Glossary of Terms.

[12] NIH–DOE Working Group (1993), 8; Holmes (1997), 516.

[13] Gostin (1991), 114; Hubbard and Wald (1993), 31, 64. In the cases of monogenic disorders like Huntington's Disease and cystic fibrosis, the age of onset is variable as between those affected, as are the severity of symptoms and the progress of the disease. Note that a positive test for Huntington's Disease is thought to be 95% accurate in predicting that the subject will develop the disease, and the disease is incurable and fatal (Rothstein (1989a), 72–3).

the spectrum of genetic disease. For this reason, critics of the HGP have suggested that its value in combatting disease is too limited, and that it should be re-focused on the relationship between the environment and genetics.[14]

9.3 TESTING FOR GENETIC CONDITIONS

The medical community has long recognised that family health history is a relevant diagnostic tool, since physiological traits and conditions can be inherited from parents. Hence, genetic considerations are hardly a new concern of doctors. However, only recently has it become possible to test for genetic defects and disorders. The development of genetic tests requires both an understanding of the gene(s) responsible for a particular disorder and a means of isolating the gene(s) in a particular person for analytical purposes. In the case of some diseases, such as sickle-cell anaemia, reasonably accurate testing methods predated the HGP.[15] However, the vast amount of genetic information provided by the HGP, and the advances in genetic technology associated with it, will make it possible to develop a whole new range of genetic tests.[16] Furthermore, the HGP has generated considerable public interest in the issue of genetic health, which may heighten public demand for genetic tests.[17] The combination of technological capability and public demand creates the potential for an expansion of genetic testing in the future.

Because the information acquired through genetic testing can be used to predict the future onset of disease, it has attracted the interest not only of the medical community, but also of two private sector actors: insurers and employers. Companies in the life and health insurance fields have primarily been interested in testing for genetic disorders as a means of determining the health risks embodied by a particular individual, and thereby setting premiums accordingly (or in some cases excluding those at risk of genetic disease from coverage).[18] Employers' interest in genetic testing is more complex, and will be explored below in section 9.6. However, for purposes of preliminary discussion, employers have identified genetic testing as a means of reducing the costs associated with genetic disease (i.e. costs related to reduced productivity, absenteeism, associated health care costs), and of protecting worker health by ensuring that genetically vulnerable employees are shielded from exposure to hazardous substances. Before exploring these employer justifications for workplace genetic testing, I will consider three issues in more detail: (i) the purposes served by

[14] Hubbard and Wald (1993), chs. 4, 5; Beckwith (1991), 6–7.

[15] The OTA (1990), 95, reports that as at 1989, tests were available for genetic conditions such as adult polycystic kidney disease, Duchenne muscular dystrophy, Huntington's Disease, haemophilia, and retinoblastoma.

[16] The OTA, *ibid.*, predicted that genetic tests would soon be available for conditions such as hypertension, dyslexia, cancer, schizophrenia, manic-depressive illness, and multiple sclerosis.

[17] Gostin (1991), 116–17.

[18] See Meyer (1993); Berry (1996); Holmes (1997).

genetic testing; (ii) methods of genetic testing; and (iii) the value of the information obtained from genetic testing.

9.3.1 The Purposes Served by Genetic Testing

Genetic testing can be defined generally as any procedure whereby the genome (or an aspect thereof[19]) of a particular individual is analysed for abnormalities known to be associated with an increased risk of development of a disease or disorder.[20] Within this broad notion of genetic testing lie two distinct forms, with two distinct purposes. The first of these forms is *genetic screening*. Screening is a single test, the purpose of which is to identify pre-existing genetic abnormalities, disorders or conditions in the genome of a particular subject. Parents may choose to submit their infants to genetic screening for certain disorders, particularly if there is a history of those disorders in the family. Individuals may also be interested in discovering whether or not they carry a defective gene associated with a condition. As a precondition to insurance coverage or employment, insurers or employers may require applicants to submit to genetic screening for a list of conditions. The basic point of genetic screening, then, is that a single analysis[21] of an individual's DNA may be used to identify any genetic abnormalities, and certain decisions may then be made on the basis of the information obtained from the analysis.

Secondly, *genetic monitoring* involves periodic examinations of an individual's genome to identify changes over time. Such changes may involve chromosomal damage or genetic mutations, and may result from ageing, personal habits such as cigarette smoking or exposure to radiation or chemicals. The differences between genetic screening and monitoring are substantial. Beyond the fact that the former involves a single test, whereas the latter requires periodic testing, there is a significant difference in their purposes. Genetic screening emphasises the diagnosis of genetic disorders by providing information about the pre-existing genetic make-up of the subject. Although the information obtained through screening may benefit the subject by facilitating treatment, some forms of genetic screening—particularly those implemented in the insurance industry—have a purely exclusionary purpose, using genetic information to the subject's detriment. In contrast, genetic monitoring not only facilitates the diagnosis of genetic disorders, but also provides information about their causes. Tracking the genetic health of individuals exposed to substances with the

---

[19] Aspects of the genome include chromosomes, genes, DNA, RNA, or proteins encoded by genes.

[20] This is similar to the definition of 'genetic testing' offered by proposed Vermont legislation (H.89): 'analysis of a chromosome, a gene, DNA, RNA, or protein encoded by a gene' (*Human Genome News* (1997), 3–4). See also Meyer (1993), 1277.

[21] Screening could occur on different occasions for different traits, and technological improvements could make it possible to screen more thoroughly for a trait which has already been screened (OTA (1990), 5).

potential to cause genetic harm has a protective dimension as well, since the early detection of genetic disease is made more likely by a monitoring programme that detects genetic alterations before they manifest themselves in physical harm.[22] The differences between exclusionary genetic screening and protective genetic monitoring demonstrate why it is important to distinguish between the two modes of genetic testing.

9.3.2 Methods of Genetic Testing

In order to appreciate the privacy implications of genetic testing, it is necessary to note what may be obvious, namely that a genetic test must be performed on some aspect of the subject's corpus—blood, hair, skin, etc.[23] The particular method of testing will depend on what is being tested for,[24] and there are differences in the testing methods employed for screening and monitoring. These methods are constantly changing due to the advances made in the development of genetic technology as a result of the HGP.[25]

Since only around 10 per cent of monogenic and multigenic disorders have been conclusively linked to particular genes, tests which screen for actual genetic disorders remain relatively rare. More common at present are indirect screening tests, falling into two categories. First are tests that identify abnormal gene products (i.e. the consequences of abnormal gene function). In the case of sickle-cell anaemia, for example, the trait can be identified indirectly through a process known as 'haemoglobin electrophoresis'.[26] Secondly, there are an increasing number of 'linkage analysis' tests[27] which look for abnormalities in the general area of DNA where the relevant gene is believed to be located. Thousands of such linkages were known prior to the commencement of the HGP, and the identification of new linkages has accelerated quickly as a result of intensive research over the past five years. The identification of genetic markers is, not surprisingly, the first step in identifying an actual gene.[28] Thus, it is estimated that the successful mapping of the human genome through the HGP will make it possible to identify up to 50,000 genetic markers, and presumably the corresponding genes.[29] Given that the identification of a marker or gene

---

[22] Seifert (1984), 353.

[23] DNA can be extracted from any tissue containing nucleated cells, including blood.

[24] To illustrate, linkage analysis (see Appendix—Glossary of Terms) requires the application of a restriction enzyme to a DNA sample. The particular enzyme used will depend on the condition being tested. See, generally, OTA (1990), 78.

[25] One example of such a technological advance involves the use of fluorescent light, as opposed to radiation, in linkage analysis. The new method is more accurate, and has health benefits for those carrying out the tests (OTA (1990), 79).

[26] Rothstein (1989a), 73; OTA (1990), 77. It is also possible to test for sickle-cell anaemia directly, as the relevant gene has now been identified.

[27] See Appendix—Glossary of Terms.

[28] Malinowski and Blatt (1997), 1222–4.

[29] Boyle (1995), 2. Rothstein (1989a), 74, suggests that eventually direct gene probes will be able to analyze specific genes.

linked to a genetic disorder permits the testing for the presence of that marker or gene in individuals, it is clear that the potential number of genetic tests which could be developed is enormous. Malinowksi has estimated that the world market for DNA testing will amount to over US$700 million in 1998.[30]

In the case of genetic monitoring, testing methods look for actual mutational activity in the genome, as opposed to pre-existing genetic abnormalities which may or may not result in future illness. Prior to the HGP, monitoring programmes focused on testing for the presence of mutagens (i.e. substances such as radiation and chemicals capable of producing changes in the genetic materials of cells) in individuals, in order to determine whether significant exposures had occurred which could threaten genetic health.[31] New tests are now being developed which go beyond simply identifying exposure to mutagenic substances, and analyse actual genetic mutations.[32] Advances resulting from the HGP could make it possible to monitor the entire genome of an individual subject, and determine on a gene-by-gene basis whether any mutations have occurred over time.

9.3.3 The Value of the Information Obtained from Genetic Testing

A wide range of new genetic tests are clearly on the horizon. At present, most remain experimental, yield information of dubious accuracy or are prohibitively expensive to administer.[33] One can only speculate about the accuracy of testing technologies which could be developed in the future. However, several points can be made which will remain true regardless of evolving science.

First, genetic testing will be primarily predictive in nature. Once a genetic abnormality manifests itself in observable physical harm in an individual, the point of testing will be merely to assist in, or confirm, a diagnosis. However, genetic testing will serve to alert individuals who are seemingly healthy of genetic flaws which could result in future health problems for themselves or, if they are carriers of a genetic disorder, for their offspring. This information can be invaluable where there is a treatment (or even a cure) available for the genetic condition, since detection prior to the onset of physical symptoms might assist individuals in avoiding health problems entirely.[34] Moreover, in the case of

---

[30] Malinowski and Blatt (1997), 1221; Malinowski (1996), 123–33.

[31] Over 25,000 substances are believed to be genetically-threatening (OTA (1990), 59).

[32] The OTA (1990), 62, 66–9, discusses in a comprehensive manner the tests for actual mutations (as opposed to exposures to mutagenic substances) which have been developed for use in monitoring programmes. It is possible, e.g., to analyse sperm from male subjects to identify mutations, particularly on the Y chromosome.

[33] Holmes (1997), 562. The following are the costs in US$ of some common genetic tests: Charcot-Marie-Tooth Disease—$385; Cystic Fibrosis—$125 to $245; Huntington's Disease—$205; Sickle Cell Anaemia—$210–$500 (sources: Ohio Task Force on Genetic Testing (1995), App. 5); Malinowski and Blatt (1997), 1213–14.

[34] E.g., newborn infants identified as suffering from sickle-cell anaemia can be treated with antibiotics, in order to reduce infection and the risk of death. See Gaston *et al.* (1986).

multifactorial genetic conditions, it may be possible to identify the environmental factors which trigger genetic disease, so that a vulnerable individual will be able to take pro-active steps to avoid these factors.[35] Finally, information about genetic abnormalities may be valuable to individuals in making decisions about reproduction, particularly if they face the risk of passing on debilitating genetic diseases to their offspring. In essence, the information derived from genetic testing can enhance autonomous decision-making by providing individuals with useful health information on which to base important decisions about lifestyle, while promoting intervention and treatment.[36]

Despite the potential benefits flowing from genetic testing, many commentators have expressed serious reservations. In the hands of the individual concerned, information from genetic testing may promote autonomous decision-making. However, that same information can be used by others to deprive individuals of opportunities. In this context, the value of information obtained through genetic testing must be re-examined. As I noted above, the fact that an individual may test positive for a genetic disorder (or the linkage associated with an abnormality) is often a poor predictor that the individual will develop a disease. This is because most genetic diseases are multifactorial, with environmental causes playing a contributory role. Even monogenic diseases differ in timing of onset and severity from individual to individual. Hence, while a genetic test may be perfectly accurate in identifying the presence in an individual of a genetic abnormality associated with a disease, its predictive power in relation to disease development may be weak. The individual may never develop the disease, or may develop only mild symptoms which are not life-impairing. Predictive power will only increase with a better understanding of the environmental factors influencing genetic disease, but this may be highly variable as between individuals. In fact, for the majority of genetic conditions (and certainly those which are multifactorial), it is highly unlikely that a test can be developed which has significant predictive power. Hence, one could conclude that most genetic tests will lack accuracy in predicting the development and severity of disease.

There is, then, a basic similarity between the information derived from both drug and genetic testing. As I observed in section 8.4 of Chapter 8, a positive drug test indicates merely that metabolites are present in the subject's body, and that she has therefore consumed a drug at some point in the recent past. The test does not provide meaningful information about the amount of drug consumed, whether the individual was under the influence of drugs at the time of the test, or whether the individual will use drugs in the future. In fact, any conclusions to be drawn from a positive drug test about the subject's future use are premised

---

[35] Individuals who are Glucose-6-Phosphate Dehydrogenase deficient ('G-6-PD deficient') are at enhanced risk for haemolysis (destruction of red blood cells) if they are exposed to certain aromatic amino and nitro compounds. Hence, they can protect themselves by avoiding exposure to such compounds (OTA (1990), 85).

[36] Gostin (1991), 111.

on speculation that one who has consumed drugs in the past is more likely than a non-drug user to consume drugs in the future. Similarly, a positive genetic test merely indicates the presence in the subject's body of a genetic abnormality. A positive test does not provide information about the subject's state of health at the time of the test, since most people have genetic abnormalities yet are perfectly healthy by societal standards. Moreover, in most cases it is impossible to predict with accuracy that a genetic abnormality will manifest itself in disease. All that can be said is that one who tests positive is more likely to develop a genetic disease than one who tests negative. Even where it is probable that the subject will develop a genetic disease, the timing of onset and the severity of the illness cannot be predicted with accuracy. Hence, both drug and genetic tests are, by their nature, poor indicators of both present and future conditions.

Although the value of genetic testing in assessing present and future health is low, there is a danger that information from such testing will be interpreted and used without a full appreciation of its predictive limitations.[37] Hubbard and Wald argue that there is confusion in society on the complex subject of genetic health, fuelled by 'grandiose scientific announcements' about discoveries of genes 'for' particular conditions such as alcoholism, schizophrenia, cancer and homosexuality.[38] In their view, the public reporting of such discoveries creates the impression that genes cause certain conditions, while failing to explain adequately the more complex inter-relationship between genes and the environment. The result is an incomplete understanding which places too much faith in the predictive power of the gene,[39] and raises the spectre of discrimination against individuals because, in superficial genetic terms, they are labelled 'sick' or 'abnormal'.[40] This leads to the concern that individuals will reject genetic testing which could have important health benefits in order to avoid the stigma of illness and the potential deprivation of opportunities.[41] The autonomy gains promised by genetic testing could therefore be illusory.

9.4 GENETIC TESTING IN THE WORKPLACE

The extent to which genetic testing is presently used by employers to screen and monitor candidates/employees is difficult to gauge. Two comprehensive surveys conducted by the United States Office of Technology Assessment (OTA) in 1982 and 1989 provide some insights into the attitudes of American employers

---

[37] The experience of carriers of sickle-cell trait in the USA bears this out. In the early 1970s, 20 States implemented programmes to screen for sickle-cell anaemia. However, many individuals who were carriers of the trait, but did not suffer from the disease itself, nevertheless experienced deprivation of opportunities in employment and insurance. See Levine (1982).

[38] Hubbard and Wald (1993), 68–71, 94–8.

[39] *Ibid.*, 68. See also Holmes (1997), 529.

[40] Billings (1992), 481; Guyer and Collins (1995), 10847; AMA (1991), 1827.

[41] Weisner (1997), 22.

towards genetic testing.[42] Both surveys were directed at Fortune 500 companies and large unions. In the case of the 1982 survey, 18 companies reported the current or past use of a form of genetic testing, while the 1989 survey identified 20 companies.[43] The number of current users of genetic testing doubled from six companies in 1982 to 12 in 1989. In terms of future use, the 1982 survey found that four companies anticipated using genetic testing at some point in the next five years, while 55 thought that the adoption of genetic testing was 'possible'. In 1989, six companies expected to adopt genetic testing within five years, while 102 companies were 'not sure'.[44] The predominant reasons offered for genetic monitoring were, (1) it was part of a voluntary research programme, and (2) it was necessary for follow-up medical diagnosis. This second reason was also advanced for genetic screening, as was the fact that the screening was requested by the employees concerned. Only a few companies reported taking a personnel decision on the basis of the results of a genetic test: two companies had rejected job applicants, while three had transferred employees to different jobs.[45]

Although the 1989 OTA survey concluded that there was 'little evidence that companies anticipate the use of any kind of genetic monitoring or screening in the foreseeable future',[46] it was conducted before the commencement in 1989 of the HGP. The HGP has fundamentally changed the genetic testing landscape, and has increased significantly the potential applications of genetic science in the workplace. As new forms of genetic tests are marketed, and as the costs of testing decrease, one can expect employers to take a greater interest in using the tests for human resource purposes. In the past, employers have embraced testing methods such as drug testing and various forms of psychological screening (e.g. handwriting analysis, honesty tests and polygraph tests).[47] It seems probable that genetic testing will be added to this list.

As with genetic testing generally, employment genetic testing may fall into the two categories of genetic screening and genetic monitoring. Screening may be used by employers to identify potential health problems in prospective or actual employees, for the purpose of denying them employment opportunities or of

---

[42] Stone (1991b) conducted a survey of 54 Fortune 500 companies. None of the companies reported using genetic testing. The PCC (1992c), 16–17, noted that no empirical evidence existed in Canada as at 1992 concerning the use by employers of genetic testing. He relied on the results of the OTA surveys.

[43] O.T.A. (1990), 173–8. The 1989 survey found that 12 companies were currently conducting biochemical genetic screening, while one large petroleum company was currently performing genetic monitoring. 8 companies reported past use of genetic screening, while 5 reported past use of genetic monitoring. Some of the companies responded affirmatively to questions about both present and past use, with the result that 20 companies in total reported use at some time of genetic testing. The 1989 survey also asked respondents about the use of genetic testing in voluntary contexts: as part of a 'wellness' programme, or at the request of employees. 13 companies responded affirmatively, with the result that genetic testing took place in the workplaces of 33 of the companies surveyed.

[44] *Ibid.*, 178–9.

[45] *Ibid.*, 182–3.

[46] *Ibid.*, 183.

[47] Rothstein (1989a), 79.

assigning them to positions and tasks which will minimise health risks. In some cases, the results of an initial screen will form the baseline reference for a programme of genetic monitoring, through which the genome of workers is continually tested to determine whether any mutations are occurring as a result of exposure to hazardous substances. The point of such monitoring is to identify genetic changes at the earliest possible opportunity, in order to remove the worker from the genetically-compromising situation before irreparable harm occurs.

Unlike drug testing, there is no legitimate role for 'random' or 'surprise' genetic testing, since individuals have no control over the make-up of their genome, and there is therefore no deterrence element to either genetic screening or monitoring. Genetic testing differs in another important respect from drug testing—genetic testing may be of benefit to the individuals tested. Testing could provide individuals with important information about their genetic susceptibilities, thus allowing them to avoid an unsafe work environment.[48] For this reason, workers may participate in employer-sponsored testing programmes voluntarily, and may even request that their employer establish such programmes.[49] This separates genetic testing from other workplace privacy issues such as drug testing, handwriting analysis, polygraph testing, etc. which have an underlying exclusionary and/or punitive nature. This is not to say that workplace genetic testing lacks an exclusionary and/or punitive potential. However, it also has a protective aspect, and it is certainly foreseeable that individuals would voluntarily submit to genetic testing because of the health benefits.

9.5 THE IMPACT OF GENETIC TESTING ON PRIVATE INTERESTS

Although genetic testing may impact profoundly upon candidates'/employees' private interests, it is important to recognise at the outset that this is not necessarily the case. One would be hard pressed to conclude that a programme of voluntary participation, in which workers' genetic health is monitored, and those experiencing mutational activity are reassigned without negative employment consequences (such as loss of salary, seniority, benefits, etc.), is privacy-invasive.[50] Nevertheless, genetic testing programmes that are mandatory, or that carry with them negative employment consequences, impact upon both personal/corporeal and informational private interests.

---

[48] Guay *et al.* (1992), 251.
[49] Both the 1982 and 1989 employer surveys reported by the OTA (1990), 180, indicated that some employers had provided genetic testing services because they were requested by workers.
[50] *Ibid.*, 31–2.

9.5.1 Personal/Corporeal Private Interests

Genetic testing implicates personal private interests in precisely the same manner as drug testing. In order for a genetic test to be carried out, the subject must provide a sample of body fluid or tissue from which DNA can be extracted. As I argued in section 8.5.1 of Chapter 8, any test which uses a part of a person's body to obtain information about her is intrusive, and violates the sanctity of the human body. In some cases, genetic testing can even impact upon the personal private interests of members of the subject's family. This is because linkage analysis, presently used in testing for genetic illnesses such as polycystic kidney disease and Alzheimer's disease, requires the participation of relatives of the subject.[51]

9.5.2 Informational Private Interests

It is difficult to imagine a more profound informational interest than that concerning the human genome.[52] A single cell acquired for genetic testing may reveal the subject's complete genome. From this information, it is possible to identify a host of health matters concerning the subject *and* the subject's family. Hence, the circle of individuals affected by workplace genetic testing expands to include any relatives who could share in the hereditary traits and disease predispositions identified by the testing.[53] Mandatory genetic testing deprives subjects of informational privacy in two distinct ways. First, such testing limits the subject's right to control access by third parties to personal genetic health information. Secondly, by requiring a subject to submit to a genetic test, the employer may be forcing that person to learn about the traits and disorders present in her genome. In essence, genetic testing denies to the subject the right *not* to know about matters of personal health.

As genetic research continues, the personal and health information which could be acquired through a genetic test will increase, as will the significance of the impact on informational private interests. Already, there has been speculation about the existence of genes for 'inherited tendencies'—sexual orientation, depression, alcoholism and honesty[54]—and research resources have been dedicated to their discovery. The potential development of genetic tests, and the potential impact of those tests on informational private interests, seem virtually limitless.

---

[51] OTA (1990), 79.
[52] PCC (1992c), 2; Feldbaum (1996), 704.
[53] Merkett (1996), 208–9.
[54] Hubbard and Wald (1993), 93–107.

9.5.3 The Significance of These Interests

In the employment context, genetic information concerning mutational activity on the subject, his predisposition to disease, and his 'tendencies' attracts privacy not only because of the way the information is obtained (i.e. invasive testing), but also because it relates to a matter, personal health, which has traditionally been recognised as a private interest at the core of the right of privacy. In principle, the private interests at stake are significant, yet this is clearly exacerbated by the limitations on autonomy and well-being inherent to workplace genetic testing, and the impact of such testing on relationships and pluralism.

First, the decision to undergo genetic testing is by no means an easy one, given the ramifications to the individual of discovering that the genome contains a flaw which could manifest itself at some future time in disease. At present, it is possible to diagnose many genetic disorders for which there are no cures or treatments. Therefore, a positive result can have devastating effects for the subject.[55] Sharpe has observed that the reactions of subjects to the results of genetic tests can range from relief and happiness in the case of a negative test, to depression, anxiety, shock, shame and guilt in the case of a positive result.[56] Individuals testing positive may then be faced with difficult decisions, such as whether or not to disclose the results to family members who might also be affected, and whether or not to have offspring. Given the lack of treatment for many genetic disorders, the low probability that any particular individual has the disorder, and the similarly low probability in many cases that the disorder will result in illness, it is reasonable to assume that some individuals would prefer to avoid predictive genetic testing.[57] Such testing in the workplace, where a candidate/employee is required to undergo and pass a test as a precondition to opportunities or benefits, effectively limits the ability of the individual to make an independent, autonomous choice. In most cases, individuals can be expected to submit to mandatory screening programmes, as opposed to giving up opportunities or benefits by refusing participation, yet this will surely result in some learning that they could develop genetic disorders—information they might have preferred to avoid discovering. In other cases, individuals who already suspect (perhaps on the basis of family history) that they might suffer from a genetic disorder could actively avoid employment opportunities conditioned on genetic tests, out of fear that a positive result could be disclosed to third parties such as insurance companies.[58]

Secondly, genetic information can be highly speculative, since it merely indicates a likelihood that the subject will develop some disorder at some point in the future. Denying employment opportunities or benefits to an individual who

---

[55] Berry (1996), 234; Knoppers (1991a), 62–3.
[56] Sharpe (1996), 126. See also Holmes (1997), 573; Laurie (1996), 74.
[57] Knoppers (1995b), 13.
[58] Holmes (1997), 573.

may develop a genetic illness which *could* affect that person's work performance and/or impose future costs on the employer constitutes a substantial limitation on individual autonomy. After all, the individual's employment options may be narrowed by reason of a genetic predisposition which could fail to manifest itself in an actual illness.

Thirdly, the acquisition of genetic information about an individual through workplace genetic testing is the first step in the process leading to genetic stigmatisation and discrimination, both of which are serious affronts to dignity. Holmes has observed that despite the poor predictive value of much genetic information, the fact that it could lead to the denial of employment opportunities and benefits threatens to create a 'biological underclass of people branded as poor risks for employment, marriage, child-bearing'.[59] Such individuals may be stigmatised as 'sick' or 'disabled' despite the fact that they suffer from no observable illness. They may be viewed merely as embodiments of genetic failure, as opposed to productive employees and members of society. Denial of opportunities to the 'genetically deficient' is analogous to racial and sexual discrimination, in the sense that a person has no control over all aspects of his genetic endowment, including his race or sex.[60] In fact, genetic discrimination could be used to mask other forms of invidious discrimination, since some genetic disorders are linked to a person's race or sex.[61] Sickle-cell anaemia, for example, is a disorder primarily affecting individuals of African descent, while BRCA1, a gene associated with breast cancer, is often found among women of Ashkenazi Jewish origin.[62]

I find it notable that much of the academic literature on genetic testing has expressed concerns about discriminatory decision-making resulting from the acquisition of genetic information, while seemingly ignoring the relevance of the right of privacy to the question whether genetic information can be obtained in the first place.[63] If, however, the acquisition of genetic information by an employer is considered an unreasonable invasion of a private interest, then it would follow that any decision taken by the employer on the basis of that information would be impermissible regardless of its discriminatory impact. As discussed in section 6.5.2.2 of Chapter 6, privacy considerations may logically come before anti-discrimination issues. Since the existence of a genetic predisposition in an individual can only be ascertained through invasive testing or some other form of pro-active informational inquiry, the right of privacy has a pivotal regulatory role.

I would offer further comments on the relationship between genetic testing and the two other justifications for the right of privacy I advanced in Chapter 2, healthy relationships and pluralism. The imposition of genetic testing by an

---

[59] Holmes (1997), 505.
[60] Berry (1996), 240.
[61] Brokaw (1990), 323–5.
[62] Weisner (1997); Tay Sach's disease is also associated primarily with Ashkenazi Jews.
[63] Rothstein (1992b), 56.

employer is clearly not conducive to the promotion of trust within the employment relationship because, as with drug testing, the exercise of control in this manner by employers seems certain to lead to conflict.[64] In terms of pluralism, the issue arises whether genetic diversity in the workplace should be viewed as a goal of (or necessary to) a pluralistic society. If the right of privacy were to block workplace genetic screening, then it is safe to assume that this would promote genetic diversity in employment, since it would prevent the marginalisation and exclusion of individuals because of the perception that they are genetically 'flawed'. To the extent that the right of privacy operates to prevent the exclusion of individuals from institutions (including business organisations), then it promotes their participation, and the possibility that their perspectives, experiences and beliefs will contribute to the development of ideas, attitudes, opinions, lifestyles, etc. While this is a valid argument in support of the right of privacy, it says nothing about whether genetic diversity *per se* is necessary to pluralist debate—it merely tells us that debate is invigorated by maximising participation. Given the mysteries of genetics, it remains to be seen whether an individual's genome has any influence over the development of perspectives relevant to pluralist debate. However, the possibility should not be discounted, since scientists have already explored the link between genes and 'tendencies' like sexual orientation.[65] Moreover, the life challenges faced by those who experience genetic disorders may contribute to the formation of ideas which have intrinsic value for society. For this reason, the pluralism justification underlying the right of privacy may well have force in the case of workplace genetic testing.

9.5.4 Conclusion

Workplace genetic testing impacts upon personal private interests because it is carried out on body fluid or tissue obtained from the subject. Moreover, because testing reveals matters concerning the health of the subject and his family, it threatens informational private interests of the highest order. Genetic testing also implicates the four primary justifications underlying the right of privacy— autonomy, well-being and dignity, healthy relationships and pluralism. Therefore, it is clear that the use of genetic testing to exclude individuals from employment benefits and opportunities constitutes a substantial affront to privacy.

---

[64] Collective labour representatives are virtually unanimous in their opposition to workplace genetic testing. See Peirce (1985), 772–3, 779.

[65] *Supra*, n. 54.

9.6 JUSTIFICATIONS FOR WORKPLACE GENETIC TESTING

In Chapter 2, I identified five distinct interests supporting privacy-invasive employment practices. In the case of genetic testing, only two of these need to be considered in detail in relation to *Principle 3, Legitimate and Substantial Limitations*: protecting health and safety and improving economic conditions. Genetic testing appears to have no role in abuse deterrence,[66] and to date there are no state-imposed regulatory requirements in the area. Although public policy has not yet developed sufficiently *vis-à-vis* genetic testing, I will offer brief comments on this issue.

9.6.1 Health and Safety

The idea of 'sorting out workers according to their susceptibility to occupational hazards' has been with us for over half a century.[67] This reflects the fact that occupational illness resulting from workplace exposure to chemicals or radiation has been common in all industrial societies, imposing great costs on individual workers, their families, employers and society generally.[68] With advances in genetic science, researchers have concluded that some individuals may be particularly susceptible (or 'hypersusceptible') to occupational illness because of abnormalities in their genes. As early as 1963, Stokinger published an article advocating genetic testing to identify hypersusceptible individuals.[69] He published a follow-up article in 1973 in which he criticised industry for failing to embrace genetic testing.[70] Twenty-five years later, as a result of the HGP, there has been increased interest in the development of predictive screening tests for genetic abnormalities, in order to identify the hypersusceptible prior to any health-threatening exposure.

The OTA reports that 50 human genetic diseases are believed to enhance an individual's susceptibility to toxic or carcinogenic substances.[71] These include: glucose-6-phosphate dehydrogenase deficiency,[72] sickle cell anaemia,[73] thalassemias,[74] acetylation phenotype,[75] ataxia telangiectasia[76] and genetic

[66] This could change if researchers were to identify a gene which made it more likely for a person to behave dishonestly (i.e. a 'criminal' gene), or if an 'addiction' gene were found, and employers thought that a worker with a genetic predisposition to alcohol or drug addiction would be more likely to engage in theft or fraud in the workplace.

[67] Haldanae (1938), 179.

[68] In the USA alone, estimates from the mid-1980s indicated that occupational illness resulted in an annual loss of close to a million working days (Williams (1987), 182).

[69] Stokinger and Mountain (1963).

[70] Stokinger and Scheel (1973).

[71] OTA (1990), 83.

[72] *Supra*, n. 35.

[73] See Appendix—Glossary of Terms.

[74] See Appendix—Glossary of Terms.

[75] See Appendix—Glossary of Terms.

[76] See Appendix—Glossary of Terms.

predispositions to certain forms of cancer.[77] Assuming that accurate genetic tests become available for these conditions, employers may well conclude that their duty to take pro-active steps to provide a safe workplace[78] supports the adoption of genetic screening to identify hypersusceptible individuals, and protect them from exposure to dangerous substances. Employees and their collective representatives may also support employer efforts to use genetic screening for health purposes.

Employees who do not have a genetic susceptibility to certain substances in the workplace may nevertheless suffer from genetic mutations (in particular cancer) due to exposure to radiation and toxic agents.[79] In order to protect employees who work in areas where they may come into contact with mutagenic substances, employers may wish to introduce monitoring programmes whereby each employee is initially tested in order to secure a baseline genetic reference. Subsequent tests would then be performed on a periodic basis to determine whether any signs of mutational activity are present. As I noted above, developments in genetic science resulting from the HGP are expected to make possible the detection of mutations throughout the genome.

As at 1997, very few employers had instituted either genetic screening or monitoring programmes to protect workers from exposure to chemicals or radiation. The reasons for this include prohibitive costs, insufficiently developed technology and ignorance of genetic testing as an employment practice. Some have suggested a more sinister explanation, namely that employers may not wish to admit that workplace chemicals are a source of harm, since this could expose them to employees' lawsuits.[80] In any case, little documentation exists on how such programmes might be instituted. A programme established in 1992 by a Danish cotton mill could serve as a prototype, however. There, the employer decided to screen its employees for alpha-1-antitrypsin (A1AT) deficiency, which is linked to the early onset of emphysema. It is believed that people exposed to airborne particles such as cotton fibres are at an increased risk for emphysema. The employer was able to use this genetic information to provide protective masks, install better ventilation and reassign vulnerable employees.[81]

Genetic screening and monitoring policies directed at employee health concerns have come under some criticism. The point of such policies is to identify those who are 'hypersusceptible' because of their genetic makeup, or those who are experiencing genetic mutations, and to remove them from work situations where they will be exposed to toxic agents. While this may indeed protect

---

[77] OTA (1990), 88.

[78] *Supra*, n. 138, Chap. 2; Guay *et al.* (1992), 257–9.

[79] There is substantial scientific evidence supporting the view that radiation exposure induces chromosomal aberrations. Other substances linked to genetic mutation include: arsenic, benzene, chromium, coal tars, cadmium, lead, zinc, diesel fumes, styrene and vinyl chloride (OTA (1990), 56–65).

[80] Hubbard and Wald (1993), 131; Andrews and Jaeger (1991), 101; Seifert (1984), 365.

[81] This example is discussed by Reilly (1993), 1348.

employee health, it risks approaching the problem of occupational hazards from the wrong perspective. Instead of concentrating on identifying and excluding those who are vulnerable, employers could focus their efforts on reducing the number and amount of dangerous substances to which all workers are exposed, and on finding ways of protecting all workers from genetic disease.[82] It would be unfortunate if genetic testing were used to perpetuate the use of toxic agents, by making it possible for employers to select the most tolerant (or 'hypertolerant') workforce.[83]

This problem is exacerbated when one considers the inaccuracy problems related to genetic screening. The American Medical Association (AMA) has argued that regardless of developments in genetic testing technology, tests used in screening will always have poor predictive value. Hence, it is possible that individuals identified as hypersusceptible 'will never express the gene, will express the gene mildly, or will not express it for a long time', while those considered to be genetically tolerant to radiation and chemicals may nevertheless develop genetic mutations and cancer.[84] Furthermore, since all individuals may be susceptible to genetic mutations resulting from certain exposures, but to different degrees, it becomes problematic to label some as hypersusceptible and some as tolerant.[85] Engaging in such labelling is more an exercise in arbitrary line-drawing than systematic classification.

Genetic monitoring programmes have a similar inaccuracy problem. Monitoring may be capable of detecting immediate genetic mutations occurring in employees, but there may also be long-term effects of exposure to toxic substances which cannot be identified by genetic testing at the time of employment. Hence, workers who consistently test negative in genetic monitoring programmes may continue to be exposed to mutagens which will lead in the long-term to a genetic disease such as cancer.[86] This is not an argument against adopting genetic monitoring. It is merely a reminder that genetic monitoring is not the solution to occupational disease, and that undue emphasis on testing may divert attention away from efforts to combat genetic disease in the long term. Initiatives to reduce toxic agents in the workplace, to replace them with safer substances and to develop technologies to protect workers from exposure are clearly necessary.

It has been suggested that genetic testing could also be used to promote public safety, by permitting employers to screen out candidates/employees who perform safety-sensitive tasks, yet suffer from genetic predispositions to certain diseases which could impede their performance. To illustrate, individuals who suffer from sickle-cell anaemia might be excluded from jobs involving the oper-

---

[82] In fact, it is for this reason that the US Occupational Health and Safety Administration has officially opposed the use of genetic testing in the workplace. See Note(a) (1981), 1209. See also Gostin (1991); Hubbard and Wald (1993), 132–3.

[83] AMA (1991), 1829.

[84] *Ibid.*

[85] Hubbard and Wald (1993), 132.

[86] *Ibid.*

ation of aircraft, since low oxygen levels at high altitudes can result in painful 'sickling' episodes which impede performance.[87] Candidates/employees in safety-sensitive jobs who test positive for genes linked to degenerative diseases such as Huntington's[88] or Alzheimer's[89] could similarly be excluded. As with genetic screening and monitoring for worker health reasons, genetic screening for public safety is problematic because of the poor predictive value of genetic tests.

9.6.2 Economic Conditions

If genetic testing becomes a widespread employment practice, it will probably be due to the cost advantages of selecting a genetically healthy workforce.[90] The development of genetic testing technology makes it possible for employers to screen candidates/employees for a wide range of genetically-related health problems, the list of which grows annually. As I observed above, some of these disorders could be triggered, or exacerbated, by exposure to toxic substances in the workplace. Not only may employers wish to protect the health of their employees, but they may also be concerned about the costs associated with industrial illness, such as lost work hours and increased workers compensation premiums. Of course, genetic testing can identify many more abnormalities which, at some point in the future, could develop into diseases regardless of workplace exposures.[91] Employers could refuse to hire candidates who might be considered poor employment investments because of their predisposition to genetic disease. The cost savings from avoiding such employees arise on various fronts: reducing lost work hours due to employee illness; improving worker efficiency by having the healthiest workforce possible; and focusing recruitment and training/development resources on individuals who are more likely to remain healthy in the long term, thereby avoiding costs associated with replacing sick employees.[92] Furthermore, employers can reduce the costs of the insurance benefits offered to employees and their families, such as health, dental, drug and life insurance, by screening out those candidates/employees whose own or family's genetic makeup threatens to impose special burdens on the benefit schemes,[93] or

---

[87] OTA (1990), 84.
[88] Underwood and Cadle (1985), 689, offer the hypothetical of a candidate for a position in a police department being required to submit to a test for the gene linked to Huntington's Disease. This is a chronic, degenerative disorder resulting in the gradual loss of mental faculties. Guay *et al.* (1992), 261, speculate that an employer could exclude an individual testing positive for Huntington's Disease from becoming an aeroplane pilot.
[89] OTA (1990), 152.
[90] Brokaw (1990), 319.
[91] Rothstein (1989a), 79. The OTA (1990), 88–94, lists various 'non-occupationally related diseases' which could be the subject of workplace testing: various cancers (colon, lung, bladder), mental disorders, addictive disorders (such as alcoholism), atherosclerosis and diabetes.
[92] Miller and Huvos (1994), 370–1.
[93] Berry (1996), 236.

alternatively by requiring them as a condition of employment to accept limited or no insurance benefits.

In countries such as Canada and France, state-run health insurance systems ensure that all citizens have access to medical care regardless of their ability to pay for that care. Employers may offer benefit packages to employees which extend beyond the care guaranteed by the state (i.e. 'extended health insurance plans'), which could include coverage for dental care, prescribed drugs, eyewear and medical procedures excluded from state coverage. Such benefit packages are clearly an attractive element of the remuneration offered to employees. If the cost to the employer of extended health care benefits is 'experience rated', meaning that it is based on the value of previous claims from its own employees, then the employer has an incentive to keep the value of claims down. Genetic tests could be employed to screen out those candidates/employees who are predisposed to illness, and may make repeated and expensive claims.

Although it is doubtful that the goal of reducing claims to extended health care programmes would justify expenditures on workplace genetic testing, it is important to realise that the unique health care situation in the United States could fuel demand for, and the development of, workplace genetic testing technology. Before explaining how this might affect workplaces outside the United States, it is necessary to consider the state of American health care. Because there is no state-organised health insurance system in the United States, individuals and families are generally required to make their own provisions for such insurance. Not surprisingly, health insurance has become a significant employment benefit. Although 40 million Americans remain without health insurance,[94] the great majority of those who do have insurance are covered by programmes provided by their employers. Statistics demonstrate that there is an important, yet costly, link between employment and health care. According to one study, 97 per cent of medium and large employers in the United States offer health insurance as an employment benefit,[95] with the cost of the benefit accounting for over 20 per cent of total payroll costs.[96] The largest employers spent US$2,500 per employee on health insurance in 1990.[97]

There is a substantial body of literature available on the use of genetic testing by insurance companies in setting premiums.[98] Sixty per cent[99] of American employers who provide health care benefits choose to self-insure, setting themselves up as quasi-insurance companies by establishing and administering their own programmes for their employees. The rest purchase insurance from third-party providers. The provider may set premiums through experience rating, in which case the employer has an incentive to reduce the value of claims in order to benefit in future years. Alternatively, the provider may base premiums on a

---

[94] Reilly (1993), 1345.
[95] US Chamber of Commerce (1988).
[96] Hubbard and Wald (1993), 131.
[97] Rothstein (1989a), 6.
[98] See Gostin (1991); Guay *et al.* (1992); Meyer (1993); Berry (1996); Holmes (1997).
[99] Reilly (1993), 1346.

periodic risk assessment of the actual workforce.[100] In this case, and in the case of self-insurance, the employer will be affected by actuarial premium-setting, which is the standard method employed in the insurance industry to determine rates. Actuarial science involves the use of complex mathematical formulae to assess the probability (or risk) of an event occurring. In general, where there is a greater actuarial probability of an individual becoming ill, then that person's insurance premium will be higher. This is why individuals must typically answer questions about their lifestyle, health and family history as a precondition to receiving insurance coverage. Those individuals who engage in activities known to constitute health risks, such as cigarette smoking, are charged more for their insurance.[101]

The information derived from genetic testing is particularly well suited to insurance use because, like actuarial science itself, a genetic test indicates a likelihood of illness occurring at some point in the future. Those who test positive for a genetic abnormality are more likely to develop the associated disease than those who test negative, and are therefore more likely to impose substantial costs on the insurer. For this reason, it has been argued that insurance companies are justified in linking premiums, or the types and extent of coverage, to genetic test results. If insurance companies are entitled to rely upon genetic probabilities in setting premiums, then employers may argue that they should be permitted to use the same genetic tests to make hiring and work assignment decisions which will reduce the costs of providing health care benefits. Epstein takes the view, for example, that it is rational for employers to screen out candidates with genetic disorders, since it is more costly to employ them.[102]

How could this largely American phenomenon spread to other countries? If the market for genetic testing technology in the United States were to expand as more companies seek to reduce health care expenses, then the cost of the technology is likely to drop. This would then make the technology affordable for companies in other countries where the pressures of health care costs are not as severe, but where cost containment in relation to health-related benefits is still a concern. Moreover, as genetic testing emerges within American corporate culture, it may be exported by American firms to foreign offices and affiliates, as has occurred in the case of drug testing.[103] The use of employment genetic testing to reduce expenses related to health care could therefore become an international phenomenon.

[100] Andrews and Jaeger (1991), 104, observe that an insurance company might impose genetic testing on an employer as part of its rate-setting procedure. In particular, an insurance company might do this where an employer has a high workforce turnover.
[101] Meyer (1993), 1276–7.
[102] Epstein (1994c), 18.
[103] *Supra*, text accompanying nn. 10–13, Chap. 7; 13–15, Chap. 8.

9.6.3 Public Policy

At this early stage in the development of genetic technology, it is difficult to discern any clear public policy in support of workplace genetic testing. This has not stopped some commentators from speculating about possible state initiatives to encourage genetic screening and monitoring as a means of promoting worker health and safety,[104] or of limiting health-care costs.[105] Unlike the case of drug testing, where employer initiatives (at least in the United States) were actively encouraged by anti-drug public policy, workplace genetic testing has received virtually no formal state support to date. In fact, jurisdictions have been more likely to take a restrictive regulatory approach to employment genetic testing than virtually any other workplace privacy issue.[106] Furthermore, the HGP has been accompanied by a vigorous and controversial debate about the ethical, legal and social implications of genetic testing in all contexts.[107] Concerns about the private interests of those undergoing genetic testing have been central to this debate. This is certainly different from the drug-testing case, where privacy has been, at best, an afterthought.

9.6.4 Conclusion

Although genetic testing technology is still in its infancy, its workplace applications have already been identified by academic commentators, governmental reports and some employers. Genetic monitoring may have a role to play in the promotion of health and safety. Genetic screening has wider implications, since it may be used not only to identify genetically susceptible individuals and protect them from harmful exposures, but may also be used to screen out candidates/employees who are predisposed to costly genetic illnesses unrelated to employment. In fact, cost containment in relation to employee health benefits is the factor most likely to result in the widespread adoption of workplace genetic testing.[108] However, genetic testing in all its forms has one overarching drawback. A genetic test can only predict the *likelihood* of an individual becoming ill, but can never predict with certainty the timing of its onset and/or its severity. It is therefore highly problematic to impose negative employment consequences upon an individual on the basis of a genetic test, since that individual may become ill much later in life, may not develop a life-impairing condition, or may never become ill.

---

[104] Seifert (1984).

[105] Mykitiuk and Penney (1995).

[106] *Supra*, nn. 141, Chap. 4 (United States), 56, Chap. 5 (France) (and accompanying text).

[107] From its inception, the HGP has included funding for the study of the ethical, legal and social implications of genetic technology (US Department of Energy (1988)).

[108] PCC (1992c), 18.

Having concluded that substantial private interests are threatened by workplace genetic testing, I will now consider whether any of the justifications offered for such testing can meet the standard of *Principle 3, Legitimate and Substantial Limitations*, and the complimentary standards of *Principle 4, Sufficiency of Limitations Premised on Third Party Interests* and *Principle 5, Insufficiency of Limitations Premised on Economic Interests*.

9.7.1 Reconciling Competing Enterests (Principles 3, 4 and 5)

9.7.1.1 Employment Genetic Screening

Employment genetic screening, whether involving testing for disorders related to occupational exposures or for non-occupational disorders, threatens vital private interests. For this reason, the right of privacy has considerable force. Any justification advanced by employers in support of workplace genetic screening must itself be substantial if it is to overcome the right (*Principle 3, Legitimate and Substantial Limitations*). At this stage, my analysis is assisted by the findings in Chapter 8 regarding workplace drug testing. In reliance on *Principle 5, Insufficiency of Limitations Premised on Economic Interests* I concluded that an employment test which provides little useful information about productivity, while impacting significantly upon personal and informational private interests, cannot be justified on a rationale linked to an employer's economic interests. I would draw the same conclusion in the case of genetic screening. Genetic tests have limited predictive power because a positive test merely indicates a likelihood that a subject will become ill at some point in the future. The tests do not account for variations in individuals resulting from environmental, lifestyle and other factors, nor can they predict with accuracy the timing of onset or the severity of the illness.[109] Any conclusions drawn about the future costliness of an individual who tests positive for a genetic disorder are highly speculative. Hence, while an employer may have a legitimate interest in reducing costs associated with labour (e.g. health-care-related costs), such an interest is not sufficiently substantial to justify subjecting candidates/employees to privacy-invasive genetic screening, and then excluding a few from opportunities and benefits on the basis of speculative positive test results.

In the future, genetic research may produce more sophisticated screening technology, offering improved predictive power. Yet even if employers were able to obtain reliable and useful information about the future costs likely to be imposed by a candidate/employee, it is unlikely that an employer's economic interests would be adequate to overcome the private interests at stake. *Principle*

---

[109] It is for this reason that the AMA (1991), 1827 has strongly opposed genetic screening.

5 dictates that economic considerations cannot be relied upon to justify a manifest and serious infringement of privacy, since only in rare cases should economic goals be permitted to trump individual rights.[110]

Genetic testing for health reasons raises different considerations, since it would appear to be more easily justified within the terms of *Principle 4, Sufficiency of Limitations Premised on Third Party Interests*. As I observed earlier in this chapter, both genetic screening and monitoring may be employed in an effort to protect vulnerable persons from exposures to toxic agents which could trigger or exacerbate genetic illness. Screening may be used to exclude 'hypersusceptible' individuals from dangerous work environments, while monitoring may be employed to detect the development of genetic mutations as a result of exposure to mutagenic substances. Where such testing is made a condition of hiring or continued employment, in the sense that refusal to submit carries with it negative employment consequences, then it may be argued that a conflict arises between the objective of the testing—the promotion of the health and well-being of the subject—and the well-being justification underlying the right of privacy. The question thus arises whether or not an individual may assert the right of privacy to avoid testing which he feels is an affront to his autonomy and dignity, even if the privacy-invasive practice is a well-meaning attempt to protect his health? In other words, will *Principle 3, Legitimate and Substantial Limitations* permit an employer to invade the privacy of candidates/employees 'for their own good'? These questions differ from the ones considered in the case of drug testing, where the primary issue was whether the right of privacy could be asserted to avoid an invasive practice intended to protect the interests of *third parties*.[111] In that case, *Principle 4* led me to the conclusion that the interests underlying the policy were legitimate and substantial, and that limitations on privacy would be more easily justified.

In the case of genetic screening for health purposes, concerns about inaccuracy and unreliability make it doubtful that there is an actual conflict between a salubrious invasive practice, and the right of privacy. In 1991, the AMA stated that 'there is insufficient evidence to justify the use of any existing test for genetic susceptibility as a basis for employment decisions', and that even with advances in genetic technology, a positive test should never be used to deny employment due to the 'poor predictive power' inherent to genetic tests.[112] A further concern arising from the use of genetic screening for health reasons is that employers may relax their efforts to make the workplace safe by excluding vulnerable workers,[113] as opposed to reducing the toxic substances to which employees are

---

[110] *Supra*, text accompanying nn. 27–8, Chap. 3, and sect. 7.2.2.3.

[111] Peirce (1985), 790, distinguishes between a justification for invasive testing premised on third-party safety, and a justification concerning protecting individuals from self-harm. The latter may be subject to a stricter test.

[112] *Ibid.*, 1829.

[113] The US Occupational Health and Safety Administration has officially opposed workplace genetic testing for this very reason (Williams (1987), 189). See also Field (1983), 126; Peirce (1985), 823–4.

exposed. In this way, the employee health rationale merges with the economic rationale discussed above—it may be more cost-effective to hire genetically-tolerant workers, as opposed to incurring costs associated with cleaning up the workplace or replacing ill workers. This approach is problematic not only because it once again threatens to subordinate private interests to the employer's economic goals, but also because it may result in exposing so-called 'tolerant' individuals to dangerous substances. Given the limits and inaccuracies of testing technology, there is no guarantee that subjects who test negative for genetic susceptibility will actually be tolerant. Some affected individuals may not be detected, while others may only exhibit symptoms of genetic disease in the long term. In both cases, worker health may be put at risk because of undue reliance on genetic testing. For all of these reasons, the health justification offered in support of 'susceptibility' screening is not compelling, and would not meet the 'substantial' requirement of *Principle 3*.[114]

The AMA thought that there could be a role for mandatory genetic screening in the highly unusual situation where a pre-existing genetic illness would be triggered by exposure to a toxic substance, and the resulting disease would develop so rapidly that significant and irreversible injury would occur before genetic monitoring could be effective in preventing the harm.[115] The AMA added, however, that exclusion of persons suffering from such a genetic disorder (and none are known to exist) would only be justified if the genetic tests involved were performed with the informed consent of the subject and were highly accurate in predicting the subject's susceptibility, and if the employer demonstrated that it would require undue cost to protect susceptible employees by lowering the level of the substance in the workplace.[116] The highly improbable scenario contemplated by the AMA is one which eliminates the uncertainty of genetic screening. Should an employer test for a genetic susceptibility which will *inevitably* result in disease, and then exclude any candidates/employees who test positive? In fact, this situation raises the very same issues as workplace genetic monitoring since, in both cases, the genetic testing would be directed at existing vulnerabilities (in the AMA's example, a pre-existing genetic abnormality and, in the case of genetic monitoring, a genetic mutation) for which there is a strong probability of exacerbation if the subject remains in the workplace. For this reason, it is helpful to turn to the issue of genetic monitoring.

9.7.1.2 Employment Genetic Monitoring

Genetic monitoring, which identifies actual mutational activity in a subject, could avoid the inaccuracy and unreliability criticisms levelled against genetic screening. Where the monitoring detects a mutation in the genome of the subject, then there is a much greater probability that continued exposure to

---

[114] Williams (1987), 204.
[115] AMA (1991), 1829–30.
[116] *Ibid.*

mutagenic substances will lead to increased mutational activity. In theory, the subject's health interests would best be served by removing her from any work environment where she might experience further exposures. The question then becomes whether the health benefits of genetic monitoring are sufficiently substantial (*Principle 3*) to overcome the employees' right of privacy, thereby allowing the employer to impose genetic testing.

It is important to note, however, that while employee health is a concern of employers, both because legislation generally requires employers to provide a safe workplace, and because of the costs to the employer of employee illness, the private interest in health remains that of the *employees*. The removal of health decisions from employees, even where well-intentioned, constitutes a denial of autonomy. A Canadian study has surveyed the social and legal norms which have emerged to date in the field of genetics, and has emphasised an autonomy-based approach[117] premised on the view that a fully informed individual is in the best position to make his own health decisions, and that paternalistic control of health (whether by employers, the state or any other individual or entity) should be avoided.[118] In the employment context, respect for autonomy demands the conclusion that the informed individual is in the best position to weigh the benefits of employment against the risk of possible future illness in deciding whether to submit to genetic testing.[119]

Where participation in a genetic monitoring programme (or in a screening programme such as that envisaged by the AMA) is made a condition of hiring or continuing employment, then control over genetic health is effectively denied to employees, and autonomy is limited. This in itself is reason to doubt that an employee health justification would be sufficiently substantial to support the imposition of genetic testing on workers. Furthermore, the use of genetic monitoring to remove 'affected' employees from the work environment, regardless of their personal preference, poses the same danger to overall occupational health discussed in relation to screening out 'genetically susceptible' workers. Employers may use genetic monitoring as a cost-effective means of avoiding occupational illness, while failing to take steps to make the work environment safer for everyone. Again, one can see how a justification premised on employee health can easily serve as a disguise for an economic motivation.[120]

In my view, the only justification for mandatory workplace genetic testing which would be sufficient to overcome the private interests at stake follows from *Principle 4, Sufficiency of Limitations Premised on Third-party Interests*. No genetic illness is contagious, so there is no argument that testing is needed to protect the health of others. However, arguments have been advanced that certain genetic disorders could impact upon a worker's physical and mental facul-

---

[117] Knoppers (1995b); Note (1995e), 325. See also AMA (1991).
[118] Laurie (1996), 80 and 90; Williams (1987), 205.
[119] *Ibid.*
[120] The AMA (1991), 1830, pointed to this in justifying its policy response generally opposing genetic screening.

ties, thereby creating a safety risk for others.[121] The nature of third-party safety as a substantial justification capable of limiting the right of privacy is thoroughly reviewed in Chapters 7 and 8, and there is no need to repeat that discussion here.[122] Suffice it to say that if genetic testing were capable of promoting the safety, security, bodily integrity and autonomy of other employees, consumers, or the public, then such testing could constitute a legitimate and substantial limitation on worker privacy. For any form of genetic testing to be a meaningful safety tool, however, it would have to achieve a high degree of accuracy in predicting the effects of a genetic disorder. This is unlikely.[123]

Even assuming the accuracy of genetic testing, testing for safety purposes would only be permitted if no other reasonable alternatives existed (*Principle 6, Least Restrictive Means*). I consider the issue of alternatives next.

9.7.2 Ensuring that the Least Restrictive Means are Adopted (Principle 6)

My analysis of workplace genetic testing has, to this point, been quite negative. That is not to say that such testing has no role to play in promoting occupational health and safety. Genetic screening and monitoring, where made available to individuals on a truly voluntary basis, may someday save lives. However, *Principle 3* will not permit the imposition of an invasive testing practice unless the employer can advance a substantial justification. The employer's economic interests are simply not sufficient to overcome the private interests at stake with regard to genetic testing (*Principle 5*). A justification premised on worker health is also insufficient because it denies individual autonomy over health matters, assists employers in avoiding measures directed at reducing occupational hazards for the benefit of all workers, and is too easily advanced to mask employers' economic interests.

Furthermore, all the justifications which could support genetic screening or monitoring are hobbled by the generally poor predictive value of genetic testing. On this point, several commentators have called for the creation of an independent body to oversee the licensing of genetic tests, and to ensure that only tests which meet a certain standard of accuracy and reliability are permitted.[124] There is clearly merit in a formal certification process for genetic tests. In the context of workplace genetic monitoring, where the results of a test could indicate *actual* mutational activity in a subject, it is essential that the use of a test should only be permitted where the potential for false negatives and false positives is very low. However, it is doubtful that *predictive* genetic screening tests

---

[121] *Supra*, nn. 87–9.

[122] *Supra*, sects. 7.2.2.2, 8.6.2.

[123] The AMA (1991), 1829, thoroughly rejects the use of genetic testing for safety purposes because of its inaccuracy.

[124] Peirce (1985), 826 ('A Commission on Genetic Testing'); Malinowski and Blatt (1997), 1289–97 (arguing for a 'Genetics Advisory Panel' under the American Food and Drug Administration); Williams (1987), 201–3.

will ever be sufficiently reliable to justify using the results to make negative employment decisions.[125]

Even if one were to conclude that health and safety considerations could justify reasonably accurate genetic testing as a condition of employment, such testing could only be imposed in a manner consistent with *Principle 6, Least Restrictive Means*. This stipulates that a privacy-invasive policy may be adopted only if: (1) no reasonable alternative exists which could accomplish the objective with a less intrusive impact; and (2) the invasive policy is individualised and particularised to ensure that it minimally impairs private interests.

9.7.2.1 *Alternatives to Mandatory Genetic Testing*

The adoption of genetic testing to screen out individuals who could constitute safety risks suffers from the same flaw I discussed in Chapter 8 in relation to drug testing: privacy-sensitive alternatives exist which could equally (and perhaps better) achieve safety objectives. Reliance on predictive testing results, whether drug, genetic or another variety, may simplify management decision-making, since a candidate/employee either tests positive and is excluded, or tests negative and is included. However, such simplicity does not necessarily promote safety. All testing methods are susceptible to false-negative results, in which case some workers acquire the aura of 'safety', yet still constitute a risk.[126] Moreover, predictive testing cannot determine actual risk, since it does not take into account the subject's actual mental and physical capacities. Criteria such as 'past drug use' or 'genetic abnormality' are poor predictors of how an individual will actually perform on the job. The most reliable form of employee safety testing is one which assesses the actual mental and physical skills required to perform a task safely. For this reason, the AMA has rejected the use of genetic testing for public safety reasons because it is 'unnecessary'. Instead, the AMA suggests the use of 'functional testing', which it claims would be more precise than genetic testing.[127] Hence, my comments in section 8.7.2.1 of Chapter 8 regarding psychomotor testing could equally be made here. It is clearly preferable for employers to test the actual skills required of employees in safety-sensitive positions, as opposed to employing privacy-invasive testing methods with limited predictive value.

Earlier in this chapter, I argued that the issue of workplace genetic testing differs from many other privacy-invasive management practices because genetic testing has the potential to promote occupational health and thereby benefit workers. Given this, individuals who face workplace exposure to mutagenic substances might be expected to participate voluntarily in certain genetic screening and monitoring programmes. If such a programme provided candidates/ employees with full disclosure concerning both genetic risks and the limitations

[125] AMA (1991), 1828.
[126] *Ibid.*
[127] *Ibid.*

of genetic testing, minimised the employment consequences of a positive test (perhaps by permitting removal of employees from dangerous work environments only with their consent, while guaranteeing alternative, safe positions within the organisation to candidates/employees where feasible), permitted the candidates/employees to decide for themselves whether or not to submit to genetic testing (with a refusal carrying with it no negative employment consequences), and included necessary procedural and other safeguards (as I discussed in section 9.7.3 below) then one can assume that most candidates/employees would voluntarily participate.[128] This alternative would significantly reduce the impact on private interests, since it would be highly respectful of autonomy, would clearly promote health and well-being, would preserve trust within the employment relationship and would avoid exclusions threatening pluralism. At the same time, this alternative programme would prevent employers from relying unduly on genetic testing to prevent occupational illness. So long as candidates/employees maintain control over their genomes, employers will have to continue efforts to reduce the dangerous workplace substances to which individuals may be exposed.

At least one commentator has suggested that it is possible to require the informed consent of employees to workplace screening, while permitting the employer to exclude any employees who refuse to participate, or test positive. In her draft legislation on the subject, Peirce states that to ensure that all testing is 'voluntary', 'the informed consent of the employee' must be obtained.[129] However, she proposes that an employer may decline to hire an individual who refuses consent, or who tests positive. She justifies what she terms 'mandatory tests' because this would allow employers to 'monitor employee health and curtail [their] liability for workers' compensation and disability claims'.[130] The flaw in Peirce's reasoning is evident in her own analysis: how can 'voluntary' genetic screening be 'mandatory'? The concepts are mutually exclusive. Where negative employment consequences are attached to a candidate's/employee's refusal to participate in genetic testing, then it is not possible to view any consent obtained from the candidate/employee as truly voluntary. In any event, Peirce's proposal undermines individual autonomy, while giving preference to employer economic interests. Her conclusion is at odds with *Principle 5, Insufficiency of Limitations Premised on Economic Interests*, and fits more comfortably within the labour law conceptions of a market individualist.

9.7.2.2 Individualisation and Particularisation

It will be clear from the foregoing analysis that *mandatory* workplace genetic testing is virtually impossible to justify under Principles 3 to 6. Given this, I will add only brief comments on the issues of individualisation and particularisation.

---

[128] Williams (1987), 203–6.
[129] Peirce (1985), 842.
[130] *Ibid.*

Any genetic testing programme, whether mandatory or voluntary, should be individualised in the sense that it should only be directed at those individuals for whom it is reasonably necessary. Obviously, in the case of genetic testing for health reasons, only those who are exposed to dangerous workplace substances should be tested. Similarly, safety testing should be limited to those employment positions involving safety-sensitive tasks. Within these categories, however, it will be difficult to limit the extent of testing because there is no way to know in advance of testing whether or not a particular candidate/employee could suffer from a relevant genetic abnormality.[131] In fact, in the case of genetic monitoring, it would be necessary for all vulnerable individuals to be tested.

In some cases, a genetic disorder may be associated with a particular racial or ethnic group, or may primarily affect one of the sexes. Sickle-cell anaemia, for example, predominantly affects those of African origin. However, to individualise in this manner would be unwise for two reasons. First, the fact that a genetic disorder may affect a disproportionate number of individuals from a particular group does not exclude the possibility that it may manifest itself in others. Hence, to be thorough, nobody should be excluded. Secondly, to base testing inclusions and exclusions on group membership creates the possibility that the testing will be viewed as discriminatory.

On the issue of particularisation, my comments below in section 8.7.2.2 of Chapter 8 concerning drug testing and informational private interests apply equally in the case of genetic testing. Thus, employers should only conduct tests to identify genetic conditions or abnormalities with the potential to affect employee health or safety. In no case should a wide-ranging analysis of the genome be undertaken, since this could reveal a host of health matters entirely unrelated to any legitimate employer interest.

9.7.2.3 Conclusions

Even if employer interests in safety and employee health could justify limiting privacy through genetic testing, reasonable alternatives exist which make limitations on privacy unjustifiable. Hence, genetic testing in all its forms conflicts with *Principle 6, Least Restrictive Means*. As in the case of drug testing, an employer's interest in protecting the safety of employees, consumers and the public is best served by psychomotor or functional testing, as opposed to predictive genetic testing. Moreover, a truly voluntary scheme of genetic testing for health reasons would be likely to attract considerable participation of candidates/employees, thus avoiding the severe impact on private interests of mandatory testing. It is particularly significant that a voluntary scheme would respect autonomy over health matters. At the same time, it would prevent the use of

---

[131] Preliminary consideration of matters such as a candidate's/employee's family history may demonstrate a greater probability that the individual will be susceptible to genetic mutations, but this is hardly a conclusive indicator of whether or not it will be necessary to monitor an individual.

genetic testing by employers as a means of avoiding pro-active measures to make the workplace safe for everyone.

9.7.3 Guaranteeing Procedural and Other Safeguards (Principle 7)

The implementation of procedural and other safeguards protective of informational private interests, as required by *Principle 7*, is crucial in the case of genetic testing, since there is a need to ensure that testing is only performed for legitimate purposes, that the information acquired through testing is accurate and that this information is not disclosed outside the employment context. Several commentators have suggested that the following fundamental principles should guide the development of genetic testing policies: communication, control, consent and confidentiality.[132] Each of these promotes the transparency of the testing process, while ensuring that the autonomy of subjects is respected to the fullest extent possible.

It is significant that a genetic test may be carried out without the subject's knowledge or consent. This is because a single cell, obtained from a discarded hair or eyelash, contains an individual's full genome, and could be tested. In order to ensure that individuals maintain control over their genomes, it is necessary to place employers under an obligation to inform candidates/employees prior to any genetic test. Hence, pursuant to *Principle 7*, individuals should not only be informed that testing will occur, but should be provided with full details on the manner of testing, the genetic conditions which are the focus of the testing, and the accuracy and limitations of the testing. Only through the communication of all relevant information in advance of testing can it be said that candidates/employees are capable of exercising autonomy, or control, in the area of genetic health, and of giving truly informed consent.

Following testing, a number of issues arise. First, test results should be communicated to the subject at the first possible opportunity.[133] Secondly, in the interests of testing accuracy, any positive genetic test result should be confirmed by a second test. Genetic testing, like drug testing, is subject to errors which can result in false positive results. No employment decisions should be taken on the basis of a positive test result until it has been confirmed.

Thirdly, post-testing counselling should be provided. A positive test result could be very disturbing to a candidate/employee.[134] Consider the reaction of an employee upon discovering that a genetic monitoring programme has detected mutational activity in her genome. The employee would naturally feel considerable distress, and would likely have many questions and concerns she would wish to discuss. For example, it is virtually certain that such an employee would want to explore her medical options (i.e. treatment, likelihood of recovery, etc.).

---

[132] Note (1995e).
[133] Andrews and Jaeger (1991), 88–90.
[134] See Malinowski and Blatt (1997), 1264–72.

If the employee has the choice of remaining in a position where she will be exposed to toxic agents, then she may wish to consult with experts to gain a full appreciation of the risks.[135] An employee who has tested positive may also suffer from psychological harm, such as feelings of inadequacy. For these reasons, post-test counselling should be provided by an expert in the field of genetics counselling, who can assist the employee in relation to medical, employment and other issues.[136]

Fourthly, health information acquired through genetic testing should remain confidential, and should not be disclosed either within or outside the organisation if the information is in a form which would permit it to be linked to a particular individual.[137] The need for strict confidentiality in the case of workplace genetic testing arises from the stigma which may attach to genetic illness, and from the fact that genetic information could be used by third parties such as insurance companies and other employers to the detriment of the individual. Williams would carve out an exception to the confidentiality requirement in order to permit disclosure by employers to unions because '[u]nions have an interest in knowing the number of hypersusceptible employees they represent' since they must negotiate on matters related to workplace health and safety.[138] However, he does not address three obvious alternatives: first, that the employer could advise the union of the existence of hypersusceptible employees without naming them[139]; secondly, that the employer should be required to obtain the employees' consent prior to disclosure to the union; or thirdly, that disclosure could be made voluntarily to the union by the employees without the involvement of the employer. Since an employee's informational private interest is so strong in relation to her genetic health, she should always maintain control over disclosure to third parties, including unions.

Genetic testing is not a routine medical procedure, given that it assesses the very essence of the subject through an analysis of the genome. Because of its magnitude, it is essential that the procedural and other safeguards discussed in relation to Principle 7 be fully implemented. Only in this way will employment genetic testing be carried out in an open manner, with those subject to testing being fully informed both before and after testing. A transparent process promotes autonomy, and ensures that any consent offered by subjects in advance of testing, and any decisions made subsequently, are fully informed.

---

[135] Williams (1987), 204.

[136] Peirce (1985), 841; Knoppers (1995b), 11–12.

[137] Disclosure of aggregate testing results which do not permit identification of any individual worker would not be in breach of confidentiality (Andrews and Jaeger (1991), 96).

[138] Williams (1987), 206.

[139] Andrews and Jaeger (1991), 96–7.

9.8 CONCLUSIONS—A LAW GOVERNING EMPLOYMENT GENETIC TESTING

In this chapter, I applied the legal principles from Chapter 7 to the issue of employment genetic testing. It should be obvious from my analysis that no employer interest is sufficient to support the imposition on individuals of mandatory genetic testing (i.e. genetic testing linked to negative employment consequences). Therefore, by statute or judicial interpretation of the right of privacy, such testing should be prohibited. This is, in fact, the extant legal position in France.[140]

The health benefits of some types of genetic tests may nevertheless be attractive to both employers and candidates/employees, with the result that candidates/employees may participate voluntarily in a testing programme, or may even encourage employers to provide such testing. If accurate tests become available for genetic disorders or mutations which could be exacerbated by future exposure to hazardous substances in the workplace, then the state could even require employers to make such tests available. Genetic testing would be consistent with the legal principles I developed in Chapter 7 if each of the following conditions were met:

Proposed Legal Conditions for Employment Genetic Testing

(1) *Health justification*: genetic testing should only be permitted as a means of protecting employee health from mutagenic substances (i.e. chemicals and radiation) which will exacerbate a pre-existing genetic disorder or result in a genetic mutation;

(2) *Accuracy*: genetic tests should be used only if they are reasonably accurate, and second-test confirmation should always be performed before any decisions are taken based on test results;

(3) *Voluntary Participation*: no individual should be obliged to participate in a genetic testing programme as a condition of employment;

(4) *Accommodation*: if a subject tests positive, then the employer should be required to accommodate the subject, either by removing the mutagenic substance(s) from the workplace, or by assigning the subject to a position which would eliminate exposure;

(5) *Control*: if accommodation of a subject is impossible, then the decision whether or not to work in a hazardous environment should be exclusively that of the subject;

(6) *Procedural and other safeguards*: subjects should be fully informed both prior to and after participating in genetic testing. Post-test counselling for those who test positive is crucial. Safeguards related to the information obtained from genetic testing should also be guaranteed.

[140] *Supra*, n. 56, Chap. 5.

These would include: access to test results at the first possible opportunity, a guarantee of confidentiality, and security measures to ensure confidentiality.

In the future, accurate genetic testing could become a valuable tool for preserving employee health. However, testing should never be imposed on candidates/employees. The right of privacy and the underlying values of dignity, autonomy, trust in relationships and pluralism dictate that only a voluntary programme of genetic testing would be permissible. Nevertheless, such a programme would still result in the collection of information concerning personal health, thus necessitating the implementation of a full range of procedural and other safeguards through the operation of Principle 7.

10

The Emerging Law of Workplace Privacy in the United Kingdom

10.1 INTRODUCTION

In the preceding chapters, I developed seven legal principles for the protection of the right of privacy in the workplace through an examination of the extant laws of the United States, France and Canada, and advanced these principles as a 'best practice' model to guide the regulation of workplace privacy issues like drug testing and genetic testing. This approach has an obvious limitation, since the principles which emerged were those already existing in one, two, or all three of the national jurisdictions. As it turned out, a protective model was developed, but this was heavily influenced by French legal principles. If my analysis had been limited to the United States and Canada, then some of the protective principles I advanced in Chapter 7 would not have emerged since they are not presently recognised in the laws of those two countries.[1] My choice of jurisdictions was therefore a crucial element in the outcome of my legal analysis.

I could have taken a different approach, however. If the right of privacy is, indeed, a 'fundamental' human right,[2] then I could have developed a set of protective principles independent of extant domestic law, and then advanced these principles as a normative model to assess critically the laws of jurisdictions like the United States, France and Canada, and to guide the development of workplace privacy laws there and elsewhere in the future. An analysis incorporating a normative model is an accepted mode of reasoning within comparative law.[3] Proceeding in this manner could be justified in the case of workplace privacy because of the significance (or fundamental importance) of workers' private interests, as I demonstrated in section 2.3.3 of Chapter 2. This mode of analysis would reflect the nature of privacy as a fundamental human right, as opposed to the treatment of privacy under extant legal regimes. As such, it would avoid the potentially impoverishing impact of premising legal reform on what already exists somewhere else, and would permit law to aspire to something beyond the *status quo* (albeit broadly defined). A theoretical and normative analysis of workplace privacy as a fundamental human right could also give rise to

---

[1] In particular, Principle 1, Comprehensive Application Regardless of Status, and Principle 2, Floor of Rights Application, could not have been advanced with much force absent the French example.

[2] ILO (1988g), 48–9.

[3] The comparative method using 'models' is discussed by Blanpain (1993), 13.

protective principles of universal application, since the private interests of candidates/employees and the competing interests of employers and the public will be similar regardless of the jurisdiction.

Although I have not (at least to this point) explicitly adopted a comparative analysis premised on a normative model, I have nevertheless advanced a highly protective view of workplace privacy. In fact, I applied the principles that I identified in Chapter 7 to the issues of drug testing and genetic testing in a decidedly normative fashion, for the purpose of determining the appropriate legal responses to those issues. A logical progression from the application of the principles to specific issues would be to apply the principles as a normative model for the development of workplace privacy law in other jurisdictions. Legal reform in other countries could therefore proceed by reference to the protective model which was developed from American, French and Canadian law.

On this basis, it is now possible to come full circle by returning to the issue I outlined in Chapter 1: the emerging law of workplace privacy in the United Kingdom. The United Kingdom is an appropriate jurisdiction for applying the legal principles developed herein as a normative model to guide legal reform. While the UK is at the same stage of economic development as the United States, France and Canada, it has no independent right of privacy, and therefore no identifiable body of workplace privacy jurisprudence. Recent legal developments outlined in Chapter 1, namely the incorporation of the European Convention on Human Rights and the implementation of the European Directive on Data Protection,[4] will result in the right of privacy emerging in UK domestic law by the year 2000. In this chapter, I will consider the emerging law of privacy in relation to employment, with a view to demonstrating that UK law can be developed in light of the experiences of the three national jurisdictions I have considered herein. First, however, I will explore the features of UK legal and political culture which have precluded the emergence of this body of law to date. It may be that these features will continue to make the United Kingdom a 'divergent', as opposed to 'convergent', jurisdiction.[5]

10.2 PRIVACY AND LABOUR LAW IN THE UNITED KINGDOM

Essentially, the privacy vacuum in pre-1999 UK labour law was a result of the nation's abstentionist approach to the regulation of the employment relationship, coupled with its lack of a human rights tradition which could form the basis of judicial or legislative intervention to vindicate privacy interests.

As I discussed in section 3.3.1 of Chapter 3, UK labour law has adhered historically to the 'collective *laissez-faire*' model, and the related approach of 'legal abstentionism'. In fact, the UK may be considered the quintessential abstentionist jurisdiction, since regulation of the employment relationship remains

---

[4] *Supra*, n. 1, Chap. 1.
[5] *Supra*, sect. 7.1.

constrained relative to other jurisdictions at a similar stage of economic development. Adherence to the abstentionist approach does not necessarily preclude legislative and judicial intervention in employment. Even Kahn-Freund's abstentionist vision allows room for state regulation in furtherance of industrial justice and stability objectives, where collective *laissez-faire* is unlikely to achieve justice or preserve stability. In an era of declining unionisation,[6] one would expect a commensurate rise in the state's 'gap-filling' role, in response not only to the failure of collective bargaining to address particular issues adequately, but also to the fact that many workers do not have access to collective bargaining at all. In the case of the United Kingdom, however, the expansion of the state's role in employment regulation has been restrained relative to its Western counterparts. In fact, during the recent era of Conservative government in the United Kingdom (1979–97), the state pursued a policy of labour market deregulation as a means of reducing the costs of labour, and thereby promoting job creation and economic development. Supporters of this approach rejected state intervention in the employment relationship by arguing that it would be inefficient and ultimately unnecessary.[7]

The United Kingdom's restraint in employment regulation has been particularly noteworthy in the context of human rights, since this has been a growth area in the United States, France and Canada, all of which have been influenced to some extent by collective *laissez-faire* thinking.[8] Human rights issues like equality, freedom of expression and privacy are ones affecting all workers, regardless of their status, and the state could reasonably implement standards, or a 'floor of rights', applicable to all workplaces in order to guarantee a particular result. Moreover, absent a guaranteed 'floor', human rights issues are not appropriate subjects for collective bargaining or for individual employee–employer contract negotiations since the range of potential results in an unregulated bargaining environment will extend far beyond the range of acceptable results from a normative perspective. Although UK law has made some important advances towards a floor of rights in areas such as anti-discrimination law, it pales in comparison to the comprehensive and protective law of France. As I noted in Chapter 5, a basic proposition of French employment law is that the rights and freedoms of candidates/employees must be respected by employers,[9] and specific provisions of the Labour Code protect the rights of equality and privacy.[10] The law of human rights in employment has been less progressive in the North American systems than in France, but there has been considerably more enthusiasm, debate and action than in the United Kingdom.[11] The results

---

[6] Deakin and Morris (1995), 42–5.

[7] See Hayek (1980); *supra*, sect. 3.3.2.

[8] *Supra*, sect. 3.3.

[9] *Supra*, sect. 5.3.

[10] *Supra*, sect. 5.4; Labour Code, Arts. L.120–2, L.122–45, L.121–6, L.121–7, L.121–8.

[11] For Canada, see Glasbeek (1993b); Weiler (1990b). For the United States, see Fried (1984a); Summers (1986).

include: Canadian innovations in the fields of pay equity[12] and anti-discrimination law[13] which extend beyond similar UK efforts; a national anti-discrimination regime for the disabled in the United States which is considerably broader and more interventionist than the United Kingdom's new legislation on the subject[14]; and numerous employment law initiatives at the state-level in the United States which are relevant to human rights like privacy.[15]

Why has the United Kingdom lagged behind in the protection of human rights in the workplace?[16] Clearly, legal abstentionism does not provide a complete explanation since other labour law systems influenced by collective *laissez-faire* and abstentionist thinking have been more active in legislating human rights guarantees for workers. In fact, the inaction of the United Kingdom government is best explained by the lack of a human rights tradition which could overcome *laissez-faire* thinking on matters implicating the fundamental human rights of workers. Countries such as the United States, France and Canada all share a commitment to constitutional human rights, with the result that constitutional rights and values like equality, dignity, autonomy, etc. have influenced the development and interpretation of both public and private laws, including labour and employment law.[17] This commitment has simply not been evident in the United Kingdom, a jurisdiction which lacks constitutionally-entrenched human rights. On the contrary, some British commentators have expressed concerns about the importation of human rights 'rhetoric' into employment law,[18] while others have predicted that human rights protection could be appropriated by management to undermine workers' interests.[19]

Nowhere has resistance to judicial innovation or legislative action in support of human rights been more evident than in the case of the right of privacy. In

[12] See Ontario's Pay Equity Act, RSO 1990, c. P–7, as am.

[13] All Canadian provinces, and the federal government, have enacted comprehensive human rights legislation prohibiting discrimination on grounds such as sex, race, national origin, marital status, sexual orientation, age and physical and mental disability. See *supra*, sect. 6.5.2.2. The UK presently has distinct statutes prohibiting sex, race, and disability discrimination, and religious discrimination in Northern Ireland (Race Relations Act 1976, ch. 74; Sex Discrimination Act 1975, ch. 65; Disability Discrimination Act 1995, ch. 50; Fair Employment (Northern Ireland) Act 1989, ch. 32).

[14] ADA, *supra*, note 267. The United Kingdom's legislation, the Disability Discrimination Act 1995, protects an individual in the case of 'a physical or mental impairment which has a substantial and long-term adverse effect on his ability to carry out normal day-to-day activities' (s. 1(1)). The concept of a 'perceived disability' is nowhere to be found. Hence, it remains legal to discriminate against individuals suffering from a condition which does not meet the restrictive statutory test, even where the discriminator has an irrational belief that the condition is sufficient to deny employment. Individuals who are HIV-positive, or those who have some genetic abnormality which may manifest itself in disease in the future, are examples of two groups who remain unprotected by British anti-discrimination law.

[15] *Supra*, sect. 4.3.4.4. See Finkin (1995a), 165–6.

[16] In all fairness, however, some UK commentators have called for state action to implement a floor of rights for workers: Ewing (1995); Deakin and Wilkinson (1991a); Muckenberger and Deakin (1989); Collins (1987).

[17] *Supra*, secs. 4.3.3.1, 4.3.3.2, 4.3.4.1 (USA); sects. 5.1, 5.2 (France); sects. 6.3, 6.4.1, 6.5.1 (Canada).

[18] Fredman (1992), 35, 41.

[19] *Supra*, sect. 7.2.1.1(a); Clapham (1996b), 23–4, 28; Holloway (1993).

1972, the Younger Committee examined the issue of workplace privacy, and considered specific problems such as intrusive questionnaires, polygraphs, and personality tests. The Committee did not view these as pressing matters, and concluded (in a typically abstentionist manner) that workplace privacy issues should be dealt with in the context of 'good relations between employer and employee'.[20] On the more general issue of introducing the tort of invasion of privacy into United Kingdom law, the Committee posited that the concept of 'privacy' could not be defined sufficiently.[21] Since that time, the British privacy debate can best be characterised as a seemingly endless argument about whether or not it is possible to 'define' privacy in a legally meaningful manner.[22] In 1993, the Lord Chancellor recommended the adoption of a civil remedy for invasion of privacy,[23] although six years later there is still no indication that the government is prepared to move forward on the matter.

The recent decision of the European Court of Human Rights in *Halford* v. *The United Kingdom*[24] illustrates the present gulf which exists between UK privacy law, and the approach required under Article 8 of the European Convention on Human Rights. There, the plaintiff-employee had no cause of action under UK law against her employer's telephone tapping activities, but successfully obtained a remedy from the European Court pursuant to Article 8 of the Convention. What explains the intransigence of British judges, who have rejected developing a common law tort of invasion of privacy, and of parliamentarians, who have so far failed to legislate to fill the privacy gap? Some have suggested that the British media have succeeded in blocking reform by arguing that the right of privacy will create uncertain limitations on freedom of the press.[25] While this is certainly part of the problem, it is a symptom of two features underlying British legal culture which have a conservatising effect on legal reform. First, legal certainty and predictability are highly valued in the United Kingdom. British common law, for example, has evolved into a rather inflexible set of legal categories and rules, and reasoning from first principles is generally avoided. As evidence of this, one merely has to examine the privacy debate itself. It could well be argued that the right of privacy is premised on, and is therefore a natural extension of, the basic principles of individual autonomy and security of the person which underlie the entire range of personal, intentional torts (i.e. assault, battery, false imprisonment, and infliction of mental distress).[26] This argument has never been entertained seriously by the UK judiciary because the

---

[20] Committee on Privacy (1972), 95; *supra*, Chap. 7, text accompanying n. 22.

[21] *Ibid.*, 5.

[22] The seeds of this debate are evident in Brittan (1963), 267. See Wacks (1980a); Committee on Privacy and Related Matters (1990), 49; Lord Chancellor's Department/Scottish Office (1993).

[23] Lord Chancellor's Department/Scottish Office, *ibid.*, 11: 'The right to privacy should be seen as sufficiently important to justify its recognition *per se*, rather than having it be dealt with piecemeal.'

[24] *Supra*, n. 4, Chap. 1, discussed in detail *supra*, sect. 5.3.2, and in Craig and Oliver (1998).

[25] Markesinis (1990d), 806.

[26] Craig (1997a), 203–7.

full range of interests protected by the right of privacy has not been defined to the satisfaction of judges and many commentators. Even in an egregious case where the invasion of privacy is obvious for all to see, the courts have refused to provide a remedy because future cases might not be so clear-cut.[27] Concerns have been raised, for example, that the right of privacy might chill freedom of expression and freedom of the press—this 'uncertainty' then provides a justification for refusing to recognize the right.

Secondly, the British adhere to the conception of judges as interpreters of law, but not as law-makers. While this view defies the very nature of the common (i.e. 'judge-made') law, judicial activism in the United Kingdom is rare. When faced with a novel claim, judges are inclined to comment that the provision of a remedy is for Parliament, and not for the courts. This has certainly been true in the case of privacy, as illustrated by the *Halford* case. In fact, commentators and policy-makers have often been heard to doubt the ability of the judiciary to decide privacy cases on a casuistic basis pursuant to general principles, since this would encroach upon the legislative function.[28]

The defining features of United Kingdom legal and political culture relevant to workplace privacy law—judicial conservatism, a lack of a human rights tradition, and an abstentionist approach to labour law—all must be considered in assessing the potential impact of the Human Rights Act and the new Data Protection Act 1998.

10.3 INCORPORATION OF THE EUROPEAN CONVENTION ON HUMAN RIGHTS

The enactment of the Human Rights Act (i.e. incorporation) may mark the genesis of a human rights tradition within United Kingdom law which poses challenges, and creates opportunities, for both legislators and judges. Incorporation will place human rights considerations on the legislative agenda, and should lead to a comprehensive review of all existing laws to ensure their conformity with Convention principles. Moreover, incorporation will expand the role of the British judiciary beyond that of merely interpreting and applying law. Instead, Parliament itself will have given the judiciary a mandate to scrutinise laws according to a governing set of human rights principles.[29] In short, tradi-

[27] Kaye, *supra*, n. 2, Chap. 1, is an example of an egregious invasion of privacy. The plaintiff was an actor who had been hospitalised with serious head injuries. The defendant newspaper's reporters entered Kaye's private room, ignoring a notice on the door not to disturb the actor. They then photographed him, and these photographs were later published. The Court was sympathetic to Kaye's privacy claim, but ultimately rejected it because no tort of invasion of privacy exists in UK law.

[28] Markesinis (1990d), 807–8; Craig (1998b).

[29] The Human Rights Act empowers UK courts to 'strike down' secondary legislation (i.e. regulations) inconsistent with Convention rights (s. 4(3)). In the case of primary legislation, the High Court, the Court of Appeal, and the House of Lords may make a 'declaration of incompatibility' with the Convention that triggers an accelerated process for amending the legislation by ministerial remedial order (s. 4(1)(2)). Other courts may express their views, but cannot make a 'declaration of incompatibility'.

tional conservative legal values such as certainty and restraint may be challenged by dynamic and fact-sensitive values like fairness and justice. As in many other countries with a human rights tradition, the *quality* of results will become the focus of British legal debate. Labour and employment law will not be immune to this process. In fact, the emerging human rights tradition could, in time, overcome judicial conservatism and abstentionism and lead to greater judicial and legislative activity in the employment field.

10.3.1 The Immediate Impact of Convention Incorporation

Incorporation of Article 8 of the Convention will have an immediate impact on UK employment law in both the public and private sectors. With regard to the public sector, candidates/employees will be able to assert the right of privacy directly against public employers in domestic courts. For example, an employee in the position of Halford will be able to challenge her employer's telephone tapping under the incorporated version of Article 8, and will no longer be required to exhaust other remedies first. Incorporation would place United Kingdom courts in a position analogous to those in the United States and Canada which are able to apply constitutional human rights provisions in public sector employment disputes.

Private-sector employment will also be affected by incorporation, through the operation of UK employment dismissal law. At present, a person with one year of seniority whose employment is terminated may launch a claim for unfair dismissal under the Employment Rights Act (ERA).[30] In addition, the legislation has been interpreted to permit an employee with the requisite seniority to resign and allege constructive unfair dismissal (i.e. the employer's actions were tantamount to dismissal, and therefore made it reasonable for the employee to resign). 'Unfair' dismissal will arise where the employer has acted in a manner which could be characterised as a repudiation of the employment contract. It is therefore critical to ascertain the parties' contractual rights and obligations. On this point, tribunals have implied into every employment contract, 'terms obliging the employer to maintain the relationship of trust between employer and employee, or not to treat the employees arbitrarily, capriciously, or inequitably, or not to behave intolerably and not [*sic*] in accordance with good industrial practice'.[31] In short, the employer is under a contractual duty of good faith, requiring him to preserve a relationship of trust with employees, and to treat them with fairness and respect. Tribunals will generally apply a test combining considerations of fairness and reasonableness in assessing whether or not an employer's actions were consistent with this implied contractual duty (i.e. were

---

[30] *Supra*, n. 68, Chap. 3, ss. 94–104 and s. 108(1). Employees with less than one year of seniority may have recourse to the common law of wrongful dismissal, which is essentially identical to the Canadian law of wrongful dismissal outlined *supra*, sect. 6.2.

[31] Upex (1994), 116.

the employer's actions unreasonable and unfair in the circumstances?). Moreover, under the ERA, an employer may avoid liability for unfair dismissal by proving that the dismissal was motivated by (1) the employee's lack of capability or qualifications; (2) the employee's conduct; (3) redundancy; or (4) statutory requirements (section 98(2)). There is also a residual category covering other 'substantial' reasons (section 98(1)(b)). Even if one of these conditions is satisfied, however, tribunals will hold a dismissal to be unfair if the employer acted unreasonably in the circumstances of the case.

To date, United Kingdom tribunals have failed to recognise that a dismissal premised on a violation of privacy constitutes a breach of the statutory duty of good faith. One commentator who has analysed 'lifestyle dismissal' cases (i.e. cases where an employer disapproves of an employees' lifestyle and thereby effects a dismissal) has concluded that unfair dismissal law permits employers to dismiss for irrational reasons so long as the employer does so to preserve its relations with consumers, the public, and other employees.[32] In one case, for example, an employer survived an unfair dismissal challenge after it terminated the employment of a cook at a children's camp who was homosexual. The employer successfully justified the termination by relying on its belief, unsupported by any empirical evidence, that gay men were a risk to the safety of children.[33] Such a result reflects the fact that British tribunals have traditionally placed no weight at all on the protection of an employee's private life when assessing the reasonableness of a dismissal.

The Human Rights Act 1998 will promote enlightenment within the law of unfair dismissal, as it requires courts and other tribunals to interpret domestic laws, such as the ERA, in a manner compatible with Convention rights.[34] Clearly, concepts such as 'trust', 'respect', 'fairness', 'equitable', 'reasonable' and 'substantial' are open to interpretation, and reference to human rights principles, such as those underlying Article 8, will be of assistance in determining whether the actions of an employer are consistent with the implied good faith duty. Consider, for example, a private-sector employee in Halford's position. It could well be argued that the implied duty requires a private employer to respect the values and principles underlying Article 8 of the Convention as incorporated into domestic law through the Human Rights Act. Therefore, an employer who has surreptitiously intercepted an employee's telephone conversations has acted in an unfair and inequitable manner, and has therefore breached the implied contractual duty.[35] The employee could then seek an injunction against future breaches, sue for damages or resign and make a claim for constructive dismissal.

---

[32] Ford (1998), 23.

[33] *Saunders* v. *Scottish National Camps Association Ltd.* [1980] IRLR 174.

[34] S. 3(1).

[35] One commentator has speculated that Halford may have been able to recover under UK domestic law for a breach of the implied duty of trust, even without incorporation of the Convention. See IDS (1997), 1.

In fact, this has been the result in some American states with a similar implied duty of good faith linked to the law of wrongful dismissal.[36]

An important case, which foreshadows the potential future role of the Human Rights Act in UK employment law, is *Ahmad* v. *ILEA*.[37] Ahmad was a full-time schoolteacher, and a devout Muslim. He desired to attend religious services on Friday afternoons, but this conflicted with his teaching timetable. The defendant education authority refused to allow him to absent himself from the classroom unless he agreed to become a part-time teacher (with a resulting loss of pay and benefits). Ahmad rejected this arrangement, resigned, and then challenged the employers' action as an unfair constructive dismissal. The Employment Appeal Tribunal concluded that the employer had acted reasonably, and this was upheld by the Court of Appeal in a split decision (two to one, Scarman LJ dissenting). Scarman LJ's dissent is notable for his reliance on the human rights principles of the Convention in interpreting the employer's obligations to Ahmad in the circumstances. He concluded that the employer was under a duty to accommodate Ahmad's religious beliefs, and also thought that a provision of the Education Act barring religious discrimination against teachers should be interpreted expansively to contain a positive right to religious accommodation.[38] The majority (Lord Denning and Orr LJ) took a narrower view, concluding that the employer was under no obligation to alter timetables or teaching loads to permit a teacher to attend religious services during the school day. Of course, following incorporation of the Convention, a plaintiff in the position of Ahmad will be able to assert freedom of religion (guaranteed in Article 9) directly against a public education authority. However, a private-sector employee could rely on the human rights value of freedom of religion embodied in the Convention to argue, as Scarman LJ did, that the employer's implied duty of trust requires greater efforts at religious accommodation.

Incorporation of the Convention should result in the reinterpretation of an employer's implied contractual duty of trust and good faith to include a duty to respect the human rights of employees. If this occurs, then a workplace privacy right will effectively arise in the private sector. Although this would be a welcome development, the law would remain unsatisfactory for the reasons I outlined in relation to American wrongful dismissal law in section 4.3.4.1 of Chapter 4: (1) employees would generally only be in a position to assert privacy as part of an unfair dismissal claim, and loss of employment as a precondition to asserting a workplace privacy right is a high price which most workers cannot afford to pay; (2) unfair dismissal law offers no protection for job candidates; and (3) the law of workplace privacy would develop in an incremental and reactive manner, although a proactive and comprehensive regulatory framework may be required to deal with complex matters such as employment drug and genetic testing.

[36] See in particular California, *supra*, sect. 4.3.4.3, and *Luck*, *supra*, n. 127, Chap. 4.
[37] [1978] QB 36 (CA).
[38] *Ibid.*, at 48–50.

10.3.2 Convention Incorporation in the Long Term

The fact that the right of privacy will be available to public sector candidates/ employees and private sector employees in the United Kingdom following the enactment of the Human Rights Act says nothing about how the right will be applied in practice by the judiciary. Two distinct paths present themselves. First, United Kingdom workplace privacy law could evolve in a manner similar to the existing American and Canadian regimes, with diverse causes of action and levels of protection depending on an individual's status. The fact that the Human Rights Act is itself directed only at the public sector may influence the judiciary to take a less rigorous approach to private sector workplace privacy disputes. Given the abstentionist tradition underlying United Kingdom labour law, it would not be out of character for the judiciary to limit the employment applications of the right of privacy as much as possible, perhaps by reducing the protection available to job candidates and private sector employees, and/or by adopting a deferential approach to the economic interests of employers. If this course is chosen, the judiciary will be able to draw upon American and Canadian precedents for support.

There is, of course, a second and much different approach which could animate the development of United Kingdom workplace privacy law. The Human Rights Act will not merely be one law among many; instead, it will become a supreme law, in the sense that all existing and future laws will be required to conform with the provisions and principles of the Act. The Act may well lay the groundwork for a human rights tradition within United Kingdom law, which could then inform, guide and even generate future legal reform. One need merely look at Canada's experience over the past 15 years with its Charter of Rights and Freedoms to appreciate how quickly a human rights tradition can emerge.[39] Such a tradition may justify greater judicial and legislative action in defence of human rights. Thus, the influence of the incorporated version of Article 8 of the Convention could lead to the judicial development of a common law tort of invasion of privacy in the United Kingdom,[40] which would then be available to all candidates/employees who wish to challenge privacy-invasive hiring practices. Comprehensive employment privacy legislation might someday become a reality, as Parliament awakens to the need for greater activism in defence of the human rights interests of both employees and job candidates, and for more precise guidelines for the benefit of employers. In short, Convention incorporation could lead to the diminution of abstentionism in UK employment law, and the adoption of a more interventionist approach by both the judiciary and the legislature.

[39] *Supra*, sects. 6.3, 6.5.1.

[40] Laws (1993), 65, has already argued that a privacy tort could be developed by reference to Art. 8 even without incorporation. A common law tort of invasion of privacy may be emerging in Canadian law, as a result of the Charter (*supra*, sect. 6.3).

Potential sources of workplace privacy law such as the Human Rights Act, the ERA (i.e. unfair dismissal law), and a judicially-created privacy tort could be interpreted and applied by the judiciary in a manner consistent with the seven legal principles I outlined in Chapter 7. Moreover, privacy legislation applicable to employment could be framed (and interpreted) with those same principles as a normative guide. A comprehensive, coherent, and protective employment privacy regime could then be developed in the United Kingdom.

10.4 IMPLEMENTATION OF THE EUROPEAN DIRECTIVE ON DATA PROTECTION

The rise of UK workplace privacy law will also be fuelled by the implementation of the European Directive on Data Protection through the Data Protection Act 1998 (the '1998 Act'). This new legislation will impose substantive limitations on the processing of personal data by public and private sector actors such as employers, while providing essential procedural protections for data subjects such as job candidates and employees.[41] Both the Directive and the 1998 Act define the concept of 'processing' personal data to include the acts of collecting and using information,[42] meaning that any effort by an employer to obtain information about any identifiable candidate/employee will fall within the regulatory ambit of the Directive/1998 Act, as will any subsequent use of that information for employment decision-making. As with the information privacy laws of France and Canada,[43] the 1998 Act has the potential to improve dramatically the protection available for the private interests of job candidates and employees. However, enthusiasm must be tempered by the fact that past United Kingdom governments have resisted the expansion of information privacy legislation, and have only legislated to meet international trade obligations. Human rights (in particular, privacy) considerations have been absent from previous UK efforts in the field. This is no doubt a function of the lack of a human rights tradition in United Kingdom political and legal culture that I described in section 10.2 above.

---

[41] The 1998 Act contains expanded procedural protections going beyond those of the DPA. Hence, a data subject will enjoy the following rights: (1) the right to be notified of data processing relating to the subject (s. 7(1)(a)); (2) the right to access data and to a full explanation of the purpose(s) underlying the data processing (s. 7(1)(b) and (c)); and 3) the right to rectify, erase, and destroy inaccurate information (s. 14).

[42] Art. 2(a) of the Directive defines 'personal data' as 'any information relating to an identified or identifiable natural person ("data subject"); an identifiable person is one who can be identified, directly or indirectly, in particular by reference to an identification number or to one or more factors specific to his physical, physiological, mental, economic, cultural or social identity'. Art. 2(b) defines 'processing of personal data' as 'any operation or set of operations which is performed upon personal data, whether or not by automatic means, such as collection, recording, organization, storage, adaptation or alteration, retrieval, consultation, use, disclosure by transmission, dissemination or otherwise making available, alignment or combination, blocking, erasure or destruction'. See also the 1998 Act, s.1, which mirrors the Directive by defining 'processing' to include 'obtaining' and 'using' data.

[43] *Supra*, sects. 4.4.1, 5.4.2.

10.4.1 The 1984 Data Protection Act and the Directive

To appreciate the potential impact of the Directive and the new 1998 Act, one must first consider the United Kingdom's now-repealed DPA,[44] which was considerably narrower in scope. While the DPA regulated the 'processing' of 'personal data', this was limited to actions performed upon information recorded by automatic equipment such as computers (section 1(2), (3) and (7)). The DPA required data users to register with a 'Registrar' in advance of any data-processing activities (sections 4 and 5), and to provide particulars such as a description of the personal data to be held by the user, the purposes for holding the data, the source(s) from which the user intended to obtain the data, and the person(s) to whom the user could disclose the data (section 4(3)). Registration could be denied if the Registrar were satisfied that the data user was likely to contravene 'any of the data protection principles' (section 7(2)(b)). These principles were found in Schedule 1 of the DPA, and included the following: (1) the information contained in personal data should be obtained, and personal data should be processed, fairly and lawfully; (2) personal data should be held only for specified and lawful purposes; (3) personal data held for any purpose should not be used or disclosed in any manner incompatible with that purpose; (4) personal data held for any purpose should be adequate, relevant, and not excessive in relation to that purpose; (5) personal data should be accurate and up-to-date; (6) personal data held for any purpose should not be kept for longer than is necessary for that purpose; (7) an individual should be entitled to be informed by any data user if the user holds personal data of which the individual is subject, to have access to any such data, and to have erroneous data corrected or erased; and (8) in the case of computer bureaux, appropriate security measures should be taken against unauthorised access to, or alteration, disclosure, or destruction of, personal data, and against accidental loss or destruction of personal data.

Following registration, data users were not permitted to process data in a manner inconsistent with the particulars disclosed during the registration process, and were required to continue to abide by the data protection principles (section 5(2)). Moreover, the DPA conferred the following rights upon data subjects: the right of access to personal data (section 21), the right to rectification and erasure of inaccurate personal data (section 24), and the right to sue in court for damages suffered as a result of inaccuracy (section 22) or unauthorised disclosure (s. 23).

The limitations of the DPA were considerable, but three should be mentioned here. First, it was not enacted as a civil liberties measure, and was never intended to protect the human rights interests of data subjects such as candidates/employees. In fact, the DPA was introduced primarily as a means of facilitating trade relations between the United Kingdom and other European Union nations, many of which had enacted data-protection laws that prohibited transfers of

---

[44] *Supra*, n. 5. The DPA was repealed by the 1998 Act.

personal information into countries lacking equivalent regimes.[45] The D.P.A. was therefore an economic/trade initiative, in contrast to information privacy regimes in countries such as France and Canada, which have as a central goal the protection of the right of privacy. One would not expect data-protection laws enacted under an economic/trade rationale to be as interventionist as civil liberties measures, and this is certainly true in the case of the D.P.A.

Secondly, the DPA applied only to data recorded in a manner permitting *automatic* processing. In short, the DPA was directed at the manipulation of information held in computer databases; its terms applied solely to information which existed in an electronic format. If an actor did not intend to convert personal information into personal data through computerisation, then there was no duty to register under the DPA in relation to that information. Employers were therefore able to avoid the DPA by collecting information from candidates/employees through non-automatic means, and by maintaining human resource files and employee medical records in manual format.

Thirdly, even where a data user was subject to the legislation, the DPA offered little substantive regulation of information-gathering activities. Although the first data-protection principle stipulated that the information contained in personal data should be obtained fairly and lawfully,[46] data users were not required to disclose to the Registrar the methods they proposed to use in acquiring personal information.[47] The purpose of the disclosure requirements of the DPA was to facilitate the regulation of data users' activities after personal information had been acquired and entered onto a computer. In any event, the concept of 'fairness' merely pointed to the manner in which information was obtained,[48] while the requirement of 'lawfulness' had little meaning since UK law placed few limitations on information-gathering activities.[49] As such, the DPA did not effectively regulate the kinds of information which could be obtained by a data user. The result in the employment context was that employers were generally free[50] to demand information of a private nature from candidates/employees, to penalise those who refused, and to make adverse employment decisions based on the information obtained.

[45] Bennett (1992), 91.

[46] The 'Interpretation' section of Sched. 1 of the DPA stated that 'in determining whether information was obtained fairly, regard shall be had to the method by which it was obtained, including in particular whether any person from whom it was obtained was deceived or misled as to the purpose or purposes for which it is to be held, used or disclosed'.

[47] Napier (1992), 12, observed a related problem with the DPA, namely that the Data Protection Registrar was not aggressive in enforcing the regime, and preferred persuasion and education over the exercise of legal powers. However, Napier added that in recent times, the Registrar had adopted a stricter line in enforcing the principle that personal data should be processed fairly.

[48] Generally, information was considered to have been obtained unfairly where the data subject was not aware of the data user's information-gathering activities.

[49] Prior to 1999, the only limitations within UK law were found in the criminal law. Information would be obtained unlawfully if its acquisition resulted from an illegal interception/wiretap (Interception of Communications Act, *supra*, n. 51, Chap. 5) or through theft.

[50] It is conceivable that an employer's information-gathering activities could be in breach of the implied duty of trust, as described *supra*, n. 35, but there is no jurisprudence on this matter.

In contrast to the DPA, the Directive has an unmistakable civil liberties emphasis which complements its economic/trade harmonization goal.[51] Furthermore, the Directive applies to all information whether manually or automatically processed. In terms of the substantive regulation of information collection practices, the most significant reform of the Directive *vis-à-vis* UK law is found in Article 7, which stipulates that all information processing must be 'legitimate'. This constitutes a substantive limitation on the acquisition of information by an actor, and applies regardless of whether or not the information is collected automatically or is destined for a computer database.[52] In the case of employers, the test of legitimacy may be satisfied where a subject has 'unambiguously given his consent' to data processing (Article 7(a)), or where the employer is able to advance a legitimate interest furthered by the data processing which is capable of overriding the privacy interests of those employees subject to the processing (Article 7(f)). The former provision clearly discourages covert surveillance, while the latter provision performs two functions which are new to United Kingdom law. First, it outlaws arbitrary or capricious information-gathering by employers, such as the interceptions which occurred in *Halford*. Generally, an employer must be able to advance a purpose for acquiring information from applicants and employees which is relevant to some legitimate management interest. Secondly, it recognises that the right of privacy is implicated by all information-gathering activities of an employer, and that the existence of a legitimate employer interest does not necessarily override the privacy expectations of candidates/employees. Instead, the Directive imposes a balancing test which weighs the employer's interest and the privacy interests of affected persons.

Article 7 is complimented by Article 8, which applies a more restrictive test for information processing relating to racial or ethnic origin, political opinions, religious or philosophical beliefs, trade union membership, health and sex life. Employers may only compile such information about candidates/employees if this is necessary for carrying out rights and obligations 'in the field of employment law', and if adequate safeguards are in place to ensure confidentiality (art. 8(2)(b)). Alternatively, the 'explicit consent' of the data subject will suffice to permit the processing of the information enumerated in Article 8 (Article 8(2)(a)).

---

[51] *Supra*, n. 10 Chap. 1, and accompanying text. See also Preamble (2): 'Whereas data-processing systems are designed to serve man; whereas they must, whatever the nationality or residence of natural persons, respect their fundamental rights and freedoms, notably the right of privacy, and contribute to economic and social progress, trade expansion and the well-being of individuals'.

[52] Art. 3 states that '[t]he Directive shall apply to the processing of personal data wholly or partly by automatic means, and to the processing otherwise than by automatic means of personal data which form part of a filing system or are intended to form part of a filing system'. The collection of information about individuals in the hiring or employment context will fall within the ambit of the Directive, where that information becomes part of a filing system. 'Filing system' is defined in art. 2(c) as 'any structured set of personal data which are accessible according to specific criteria, whether centralized, decentralized or dispersed on a functional or geographical basis'.

Another substantive limitation which is relevant to employment is found in Article 15 of the Directive, which grants to all persons the right not to be subject to adverse decisions 'based solely on automated processing of data intended to evaluate certain personal aspects relating to him, such as his performance at work'. This is intended to prevent an employer from basing hiring or other employment decisions exclusively on data obtained through electronic performance evaluation. Article 15(2) provides, however, that electronic performance monitoring may be used as the exclusive basis for employment decision-making so long as measures are included to safeguard the subject's 'legitimate interests, such as arrangements allowing him to put his point of view'. Safeguards of this nature must also be incorporated into any law which authorizes the use of electronic performance evaluation (Article 15(2)(b)).

Although the Directive creates the potential for a protective regime governing information privacy to emerge in United Kingdom employment law, much depends on how the Directive is implemented through legislation. I therefore turn to this issue.

10.4.2 Implementation of the Directive through the 1998 Act

Implementation of the Directive will occur in the United Kingdom through the 1998 Act. The structure of this new legislation is identical to that of the repealed DPA, in the sense that both laws regulate data processing by public and private bodies by requiring those bodies to register with a governmental institution[53] and to abide by a list of data protection 'principles'. Moreover, like the DPA (but unlike the Directive), the 1998 Act makes no mention whatsoever of the right of privacy or of human rights generally—it would perhaps be expecting too much at this early stage to see the word 'privacy' used in a UK statute. Nevertheless, the 1998 Act represents a significant expansion in the regulation of personal information, particularly in the employment context, as it gives effect to the two key features of the Directive described above: (1) the regulation of both automatic and manual information processing[54]; and (2) the substantive regulation of information collection practices. This second feature will be my focus below. However, there are three specific reforms in the 1998 Act which have a direct impact on the employment context, and should be mentioned.

---

[53] In the case of the DPA, the institution was the Data Protection Registrar. The 1998 Act transforms the Registrar into a Data Protection Commissioner (s. 6).

[54] It should be noted that the application of the 1998 Act to certain types of manual information will occur over time according to a remarkably complicated schedule to the Act (s. 39 and Sched. 8). Also, registration under the Act is restricted to the automatic processing of data; manual processing is excluded (s. 17(2)).

10.4.2.1 Reforms in the 1998 Act with a Direct Impact Upon Employment

First, as required by the Directive, the 1998 Act regulates employment decisions based on automatic evaluations. The Act stipulates that workers whose job performance is evaluated automatically have the right, upon making a formal request and paying a prescribed fee, to be notified by the employer of the 'logic involved in that decision-taking' if the employer intends to base a 'significant' employment decision solely on the results of the automatic evaluation (section 7(1)). Furthermore, an employee's 'performance at work' should not be evaluated solely on the basis of information obtained through automatic means (section 12(1)).[55] This provision is quite limited, since it does not actually prohibit automatic evaluation methods; any such method is only regulated by the Act to the extent that it is the *sole* basis for decisions taken by the employer. Moreover, the Act provides that decisions based on automatically processed information are exempt from regulation so long as the subject has requested automatic evaluation, or (as permitted by the Directive) the subject's legitimate interests are safeguarded by being allowed to 'make representations' (section 12(7)). Exempt decisions include those related to the entering into or performance of a *contract* (section 12(6)). It would therefore appear that if an employer wishes to evaluate job candidates in order to decide whether to enter into an *employment contract* with them, or to assess the performance of employees under the existing employment contract, then it may do so through automatic means so long as the subjects of the evaluations are permitted to make 'representations' (upon which the employer is under no statutory obligation to act). If this interpretation is correct, then the exceptions to section 12 of the 1998 Act effectively gut one of the basic principles underlying the provision, which is that candidates/employees should be protected from pervasive and dehumanising surveillance methods. This result would appear to run counter to the intentions of the framers of the Directive upon which the Act is based. I will return to the interpretation of section 12 of the 1998 Act in section 10.4.2.3 below.

Secondly, section 56 of the 1998 Act provides new protection in the employment sphere by prohibiting employers from requiring candidates/employees to make access to information requests for the purpose of obtaining information to which the employer would not otherwise be entitled. It is a general principle of information privacy legislation that access to personal information should be limited to those who collected it (assuming they acted for a legitimate purpose) and to the subjects of the information. Third parties, such as employers, are generally prohibited from access. In the past, employers have avoided this prohibition by requiring as a condition of employment that candidates/employees make access requests and then hand over the requested information. Access to criminal records has been particularly problematic in the United Kingdom, as many

---

[55] S. 12(1) grants to individuals the right to take steps up to and including a court action to prevent decision-making based solely on the processing by automatic means of personal data of which the individual is subject.

employers have demanded that candidates/employees request and disclose their criminal records in situations where the employers themselves have no access to the information. Section 56 effectively ends this practice.

Thirdly, the Data Protection Registrar under the DPA has now been replaced in the 1998 Act by a Data Protection Commissioner with expanded powers. The Commissioner has the duty to promote good practice, and may develop and disseminate codes of practice on particular issues of data protection (section 51(1) and (2)). Implied in these sections is the power of the Commissioner to engage in research and to prepare studies, which would then form the basis for codes of practice. The 1998 Act also encourages the Commissioner to consult with trade associations and representative of data subjects such as unions in the process of developing codes of practice (section 51(3)), and permits those same groups to develop their own codes of practice with the assistance of the Commissioner (section 51(4)). Furthermore, individuals may apply to the Commissioner for an opinion on whether processing affecting them is consistent with the Act (section 42), and the Commissioner may provide assistance to individuals who are parties in court proceedings under the 1998 Act where the case involves a 'matter of substantial public importance' (section 53). The Act does not stipulate the nature of the assistance which the Commissioner may provide, although aid would probably come in the form of legal advice and monetary support. Nothing in the 1998 Act permits the Commissioner to initiate proceedings itself, however.

The strengthening of the powers of the Data Protection Commissioner has specific relevance to employment law because, as should be clear from my discussions of information privacy legislation in the United States, France and Canada,[56] experience dictates that the impact of such legislation in the employment context will largely depend on the existence of strong institutions which are empowered to promote and enforce the legislation. In the United Kingdom's case, the impotence of the DPA in relation to employment matters was, in part, related to the weaknesses of the Data Protection Registrar.[57] The new Data Protection Commissioner is clearly empowered to take a more proactive role in promoting information privacy in employment. In fact, the Commissioner is already focusing on employment issues, establishing a research unit in the area, and announcing that it will develop and promulgate guidelines on electronic surveillance in the workplace by the year 2000. Already, the research unit has recommended the strict regulation of genetic testing in employment, and is proposing limits on the use of surveillance technologies such as video cameras and e-mail monitoring systems.[58]

---

[56] *Supra*, sects. 4.3.3.4, 5.4.1, 6.4.2.
[57] *Supra*, n. 47.
[58] *The Times*, 4 May 1999.

10.4.2.2 *The Substantive Regulation of Information Collection in Employment*

As I noted above in section 10.4.1, the Directive requires the United Kingdom to implement substantive limitations on the collection of personal information, including heightened protection for 'sensitive' data (i.e. information pertaining to a subject's race, religion, political opinions, sexual life, etc.). The 1998 Act gives effect to this aspect of the Directive in section 4(4) by requiring all 'data controllers' (such as employers engaging in information collection) to comply with a set of Data Protection Principles governing the processing of all personal data including 'sensitive' data.[59] Section 10 then grants to individuals the right to block information collection or other processing which is contrary to these Principles, if the collection or processing is likely to cause 'substantial damage or substantial distress' to the individual concerned. The Data Protection Principles are found in Schedule 1 of the 1998 Act, and are in fact remarkably similar to the principles from the DPA that I described above. The first Principle has particular relevance to information collection practices:

> Personal data shall be processed fairly and lawfully and, in particular, shall not be processed unless—(a) at least one of the conditions in Schedule 2 is met, and (b) in the case of sensitive personal data, at least one of the conditions in Schedule 3 is also met.

This principle requires that information collection be conducted in a fair and lawful manner. This was also the case under the DPA, as I noted above. The 1998 Act goes much further than the DPA, however, by stipulating that data processing can only be fair and lawful if it complies with a further set of conditions found in Schedule 2 of the Act. Three of these have relevance in the employment context, yet each raises concerns that the 1998 Act will be impotent in protecting the privacy of candidates/employees.

(a) Consent

The first of the conditions in Schedule 2 is that '[t]he data subject has given his consent to the processing'. In other words, information collection by an employer will be considered fair and lawful if the candidates/employees concerned have consented. One should immediately note that the 1998 Act fails to incorporate the concept of 'unambiguous consent' from the Directive; it merely refers to 'consent'. In my view, the standard of 'unambiguous consent' is sufficiently high that it would preclude *acquiescence* to employer information requests from rendering the collection lawful and fair. The same cannot be said of a basic 'consent' standard, since such a standard opens the door to *implied* consent—the very doctrine that has rendered American common law privacy so impotent in the workplace.[60] The concern that implied consent could satisfy the first condition in Schedule 2 is reinforced by the analogous provision in Schedule

---

[59] 1998 Act, s. 2.
[60] *Supra*, sect. 4.3.4.2.

3 governing 'sensitive' personal information, which reflects the Directive by requiring the 'explicit consent' of the subject. One can presume that if implied consent were to be unavailable under Schedule 2, then Parliament would have chosen to use an appropriate qualifying word. The glaring omission of the word 'unambiguous' raises concerns that the United Kingdom has failed to implement the Directive fully and properly.

(b) Contract

The second condition in Schedule 2 stipulates that information collection will be lawful and fair if it 'is necessary—(a) for the performance of a contract to which the data subject is a party, or (b) for the taking of steps at the request of the data subject with a view to entering into a contract'. The problem I observed above in relation to the Act's regulation of automatic evaluations arises again here: can an employer justify information collection about employees by arguing that any monitoring and surveillance is aimed at determining whether or not the employees are performing their employment *contracts*? It is clearly possible to interpret the 1998 Act such that the existence of an employment contract permits one of the parties to the contract—the employer—to engage in pervasive monitoring and electronic surveillance so long as the monitoring/surveillance is linked to job performance. Furthermore, one wonders whether the second half of this condition could be interpreted to permit employers to demand that job candidates sign a 'request' for information collection as a condition of participating in the recruiting process (a process that, after all, occurs 'with a view to entering into a contract'). If implied consent is held to be sufficient to render information collection lawful and fair under the first condition in Schedule 2, then it would certainly be consistent to find that coerced 'requests' for information processing satisfy the second condition in the Schedule. In fact, these interpretations of the 1998 Act are consistent with the emphasis that UK labour law has historically placed on freedom of contract and collective *laissez-faire*.

(c) Proportionality balancing

The sixth condition in Schedule 2 is the United Kingdom's effort to codify the balancing test from Article 7(f) of the Directive. This condition states that information processing will be lawful and fair if:

> The processing is necessary for the purposes of legitimate interests pursued by the data controller or by the third party or parties to whom the data are disclosed, except where the processing is *unwarranted* in any particular case by reason of prejudice to the rights and freedoms or legitimate interests of the data subject (emphasis added).[61]

One commentator has written that this condition is 'full of uncertainty and betray[s] the European origins of the Act'.[62] In my view, the condition is problematic in the United Kingdom because it embodies a classic human rights

---

[61] 1998 Act, Sched. 2, condition 6(1).
[62] Ford (1998), 36.

principle of proportionality balancing that the UK has little experience in applying. Of greater concern, however, is the fact that the condition appears to be an
inadequate implementation of the test found in the Directive. The Directive
would render information processing unlawful if the private interests of subjects
outweighed the competing legitimate interests of the data controller (Article
7(f)). The 1998 Act requires that the interests of subjects be sufficient to render
information processing 'unwarranted'. The 'unwarranted' test is, on its face, a
higher standard than the simple balancing test established in the Directive. No
explanation has been offered by the government for this departure from the
terms of the Directive.

10.4.2.3 Interpreting the 1998 Act to Ensure a Protective Regime Governing Information Collection

The basic proposition of the 1998 Act, that information processing is unlawful
and unfair *unless* certain conditions are met, is sound because it places a positive duty on those who collect and use information to justify their actions.
However, in implementing this proposition, the legislative drafters have handed
to employers three 'conditions' which could effectively render the 1998 Act irrelevant in the employment context. Fortunately, the consent, contract, and proportionality balancing conditions found in Schedule 2 are each sufficiently
ambiguous that interpretation will be required to determine their scope. The
responsibility for interpreting and elaborating upon the terms of the 1998 Act in
the employment context will fall in the future upon three bodies: Parliament, the
judiciary, and the Data Protection Commissioner.

  Naturally, Parliament has the option of providing more detailed regulation
relevant to employment through either primary or secondary legislation. For
example, it could choose to regulate specific information-gathering practices
such as video surveillance or e-mail interception in a manner consistent with the
principles of the Directive and the 1998 Act. Alternatively, it could rely on the
new Data Protection Commissioner to consult with workers and employers,
with a view to promulgating codes of practice on particular matters.[63]
Moreover, as I observed above, the Commissioner could assist trade associations and unions to develop their own guidelines and policies on particular
issues.[64] This last approach may be the most consistent with the traditionally
abstentionist bent of United Kingdom labour law, and Parliament may well be
more comfortable encouraging and facilitating the development of workplace
privacy guidelines by employers and unions, as opposed to regulating employer
information-gathering activities either directly, or indirectly through an administrative body. Nevertheless, I would suggest that this approach holds out little
promise at present because of the decline of unionisation in the United

---

[63] 1998 Act, s. 51 empowers the Data Protection Commissioner to consult broadly and develop
and disseminate codes of practice representing 'good practice'.
[64] 1998 Act, s. 51(4).

Kingdom,[65] and the general lack of a tradition of consultation between employers and collective worker representatives. In addition, there is obviously no guarantee that protective guidelines and codes of conduct would emerge from a process of consultation and negotiation.[66]

If neither Parliament nor the Data Protection Commissioner takes action in the area of workplace privacy, then the elaboration of the 1998 Act in the employment sphere will occur on a case-by-case basis through the judicial interpretation of the Data Protection Principles and related conditions embodied in the legislation. The judicial role in expanding upon the terms of the 1998 Act is clearly comprehended by section 13, which permits individuals to seek a civil remedy in the courts for 'any contravention by a data controller of any of the requirements' of the Act. This is a radical expansion of the individual's ability to resort to the courts under the DPA, which was limited to situations in which damages resulted from inaccuracy or unauthorised disclosure of personal information.

Regardless of which institution takes the lead, the Directive itself should be the first interpretive source considered, given the United Kingdom's obligation as a member of the European Union to implement the terms of the directive effectively in domestic law. On this basis, the concept of 'consent' in the first condition of Schedule 2 should be read as 'unambiguous consent' as required by the Directive. Furthermore, regardless of the terminology used in the sixth condition of Schedule 2, the question whether processing is 'unwarranted' should be determined through the application of the simple proportionality balancing test described in the Directive.

The Directive itself can provide only limited assistance in the drafting of employment-specific legislation or codes of conduct, or the interpretation of the 1998 Act in the employment context. I would suggest that the principles I developed in Chapter 7 could provide invaluable assistance, permitting the United Kingdom not only to benefit from the experiences of other countries in the field, but also to develop a highly protective regime of information privacy in employment. In each of the areas of consent, contract, and proportionality balancing, the principles from Chapter 7 are relevant and may serve as a normative guide for determining the standard of protection that should be afforded by the 1998 Act.

(a) Consent Revisited

An interpretation of 'consent' in the first condition of Schedule 2 to the 1998 Act that excludes 'implied consent' would be more in keeping with the analogous terms of the *Directive* ('unambiguous consent'), and would also be supported by *Principle 2, Floor of Rights Application*. In Chapter 7, when writing about this principle, I stated that workplace privacy laws should establish actual standards

---

[65] Deakin and Morris (1995), 42–5.
[66] The problem of resolving workplace privacy issues through negotiations is discussed *supra*, text accompanying nn. 21–4, Chap. 3.

applicable to all employment relationships, and should not permit employers to avoid these standards by acquiring the express or implied consent of candidates/employees. My primary justification for this statement was that the power imbalance existing between employers and candidates/employees made it difficult to identify any consent as genuine and voluntary. In my discussion of genetic testing in Chapter 9, I added a refinement to the issue of consent, by observing that where information collection is for the benefit of candidates'/employees' health, then true consent would be possible. However, a crucial precondition to a finding of true consent in the employment context would be that no adverse employment consequences could result from a refusal on the part of the candidate/employee to provide the information requested.[67]

On this basis, it would be desirable to interpret both the terms 'consent' in Schedule 2 and 'explicit consent' in Schedule 3 (applicable to 'sensitive' personal data) to require a strict test of voluntariness in a situation where an employer is proposing to process personal information about a candidate/employee. In other words, the processing of personal information should only be permissible under the 'consent' provision where the candidates/employees involved are actually free to refuse consent with no adverse employment consequences flowing from the refusal. Such an interpretation should be adopted in light of the peculiar power dynamic existing within employment relationships.

(b) Contract Revisited

At two points in this chapter, in my discussions of automatic performance evaluations under section 12 of the 1998 Act and information collection under the second condition of Schedule 2, I observed that exceptions had been created linked to matters of contract. Hence, employment decisions may be based solely on automatic evaluations where the decisions relate to the entering into or performance of a contract (section 12(6) and (7)). Moreover, personal information may be processed by employers under Schedule 2 if it is necessary for the performance of a contract or for the taking of steps at the request of a data subject to enter into a contract. I fully explained above how these contract exceptions could work in the employment context,[68] and will not repeat that discussion here. The real issue is whether the employment contract should be considered a 'contract' for the purposes of these provisions of the 1998 Act. A strong argument can be mounted that it should not be. First, excluding the employment contract would avoid some absurdity. To illustrate, section 12(1) of the 1998 Act explicitly prohibits automatic evaluation of work performance as the sole basis for employment decisions. As I noted above, this prohibition would be meaningless if it were held that automatic evaluation was nevertheless taken 'in the course of performing' the employment contract, and was therefore permissible so long as employees had the ability 'to make representations' (section 12(7)). Moreover, even if I am correct that 'consent' under Schedule 2 of the 1998 Act

[67] *Supra*, sect. 9.7.2.1.
[68] *Supra*, sects. 10.4.2.1, 10.4.2.2.

requires true voluntariness in the employment sphere, such a protective test would be pointless if employers could require individuals to enter into employment contracts permitting non-consensual information processing. Certainly, employers could argue that the existence of contractual terms permitting or even requiring information processing makes the processing 'necessary for the performance of a contract' (Schedule 2, condition 2(a)). It would, in my view, be absurd to permit such an argument since employers would then be able to contract-out of the consent condition easily through creative provisions of their own employment contracts.

Secondly, a point that I emphasised in section 7.2.1.1 of Chapter 7 is highly relevant here. Employment is a unique contractual relationship for a variety of reasons, including its public nature and the power and control which it grants to employers.[69] The typical employment contract is drafted by the employer with no input from candidates being offered employment. There is, in short, no negotiation regarding employment terms. Even in the collective bargaining context, as I observed in section 3.2 of Chapter 3, the interests of individual members of a bargaining unit may have to give way to the majority position as espoused by the union. As a result, from the perspective of the individual worker, a collective agreement may be no less of an imposition than an employment contract drafted by the employer. In my view, the contract exceptions contained in the 1998 Act make some sense in situations where parties of equal bargaining power agree to terms permitting information processing contrary to the Act, or to terms the performance of which necessitates information processing contrary to the Act. In such situations, the parties involved have a true choice and should be held to their bargain. Employment is not such a situation, however.

If the 1998 Act were interpreted to permit employers to rely on the existence of an employment contract to avoid restrictions on automatic evaluations and information processing, then the protection afforded to candidates/employees would be seriously weakened. Furthermore, if contracting-out of the 1998 Act could be accomplished through the unilateral imposition by employers of contractual terms permitting activities which would otherwise infringe the Data Protection Principle requiring fair and lawful processing, then *Principle 2, Floor of Rights Application* would be further compromised. After all, there can be no legal floor of protection if it is possible under the guise of an employment contract for employers to create conditions under which they are not required to abide by legislated standards.

(c) Proportionality Balancing Revisited

The sixth condition in Schedule 2 to the 1998 Act, which implements a form of proportionality balancing, requires a decision-maker to weigh the legitimate interests of data controllers with the rights and freedoms or legitimate interests

---

[69] *Supra*, text accompanying nn. 30–3, Chap. 7.

of the subjects of data processing. In employment, this condition would prevent the collection of information from candidates/employees if their interests were considered more substantial than the competing interests of employers justifying the collection.[70] At first glance, the condition does not provide much guidance to employers and candidates/employees as to the standard required by the 1998 Act. Extensive elaboration of the condition by the Data Protection Commissioner and by the judiciary will therefore be necessary. Reference to the ideas and principles I outlined in Chapters 2 and 7 would clearly be of assistance in this regard.

The first issue in interpreting the proportionality balancing condition in Schedule 2 concerns the nature of the 'rights and freedoms or legitimate interests' of candidates/employees. What are they? This aspect of the condition should be interpreted as referring first and foremost to the human rights guarantees now incorporated into UK law by the Human Rights Act 1998. Privacy is obviously the most significant of these rights in the data protection context. Although the Human Rights Act, like the European Convention on Human Rights, has direct application only with regard to state action, it would be consistent with *Principle 1, Comprehensive Application Regardless of Status* to conclude that incorporated Convention rights are the 'rights', 'freedoms', or 'interests' referenced in the proportionality balancing condition. In fact, any other interpretation would create tremendous uncertainty since there are no other coherent sources in UK law for rights and freedoms,[71] and the concept of 'interest' is rather nebulous.

The right of privacy, as guaranteed by the Human Rights Act, should therefore be the primary means by which the candidate/employee side of the proportionality balance is measured. The result would be to recognise the full range of private interests protected by the right: territorial, personal/corporeal, and informational.[72] Guaranteeing the right of privacy within the sixth condition of Schedule 2 would also ensure that the interests of candidates/employees are given their due weight in the proportionality balancing exercise, by focusing attention on the justifications underlying the protection of privacy: autonomy, dignity and well-being, health relationships and pluralism.[73] As I observed in Chapter 7, the assertion of the right of privacy involves, at the same time, the assertion of the interests underlying the right. This means that the right of privacy is by its very nature substantial and a pressing matter of public concern. Competing interests must themselves be substantial to overcome the right.[74]

---

[70] As I noted above in sect. 10.4.2.2, the 1998 Act requires information collection to be 'unwarranted in any particular case by reason of prejudice to the rights and freedoms or legitimate interests of the data subject'. My approach to this condition assumes that it embodies the proportionality balancing principle from the Directive.

[71] Ford (1998), 36: 'The [condition] will only work if the courts are prepared to recognise the fundamental importance of human rights, like privacy'.

[72] *Supra*, sect. 2.3.2.

[73] *Supra*, sect. 2.3.3.

[74] *Supra*, sect. 7.2.2.1.

Such a perspective, should it be adopted in UK law, would ensure that the legitimate interests of candidates/employees are taken seriously in the balancing exercise under the sixth condition of Schedule 2. This development would be of crucial importance because the two guiding forces in UK employment law—legal abstentionism and the lack of a human rights tradition—could together have the opposite effect by undermining the protection afforded to candidates/employees in the 1998 Act.

The principles I outlined in Chapter 7 are also of assistance in interpreting the 'legitimate interests' of employers. In fact, *Principle 3, Legitimate and Substantial Limitations* has been explicitly incorporated (in part) into the 1998 Act by the requirement in Schedule 2 that a data controller must assert a 'legitimate interest' to justify data processing. This dictates that an employer's interest must relate to a legitimate management concern to qualify. An employer should not be permitted to act beyond the scope of the employment relationship by, for example, placing itself in the position of the state and attempting to enforce laws or public policies unrelated to employment through data processing. In addition to requiring a substantial link between data processing and legitimate management concerns, interpreters of the 1998 Act should approach employers' economic interests with scepticism, as required by *Principle 5, Insufficiency of Limitations Premised on Economic Interests.* Only in rare circumstances, in my view, will economic interests be sufficiently substantial to outweigh candidates'/employees' private interests.

Consider, for example, a situation in which an employer places video cameras throughout the workplace to monitor employees' job performance and deter abuse of the employment relationship. This form of information collection would be covered by the concept of data 'processing' in the 1998 Act, and its lawfulness could fall to be decided (in the absence of consent and contract considerations) through the application of the proportionality test in Schedule 2. Pervasive monitoring could have a profound impact upon employees' private interests, particularly where it extends to areas of the workplace such as washrooms, staff lounges, parking lots, etc. Therefore, it would be vulnerable to attack under the proportionality test if the employer's interest were solely economic in nature. However, *Principle 4, Sufficiency of Limitations Premised on Third Party Interests* dictates that an employer's interest in protecting the health and safety of employees, consumers, and/or the public would be more likely to overcome the right of privacy. For this reason, video monitoring of employees in a workplace where the maintenance of safety standards is essential, such as a nuclear power plant, would be more likely to pass muster under the proportionality test.

It should also be emphasised that the sixth condition of Schedule 2 stipulates that data processing must be 'necessary for the purposes of legitimate interests pursued by the data controller'. The requirement that information collection be *necessary* for achieving certain interests opens the door to the adoption within the 1998 Act of *Principle 6, Least Restrictive Means.* In outlining this principle in Chapter 7, I observed that it required an analysis of whether an alternative could reasonably accomplish an employer's objective with a reduced impact on privacy. Such an alternative could be a completely different means of achieving the employer's objective, or a more individualised or particularised version of the alternative chosen by the employer. A reasonable interpretation of the proportionality condition in Schedule 2 would hold that the form of processing chosen by an employer is only 'necessary' where it achieves a legitimate interest with the least impact on candidates'/employees' privacy. Hence, to return to the example of a nuclear power plant, a workplace monitoring programme premised on a legitimate interest such as protecting public safety could nevertheless fail the proportionality test as unnecessary. This would occur if it were possible for the employer to achieve its objective while still preserving privacy in areas of the workplace such as washrooms and lounges, or if it were possible to exclude non-safety employees from monitoring.

10.4.2.4 *Information Collection under the 1998 Act*

Through the application of the principles I outlined in Chapter 7 to Schedule 2 to the 1998 Act, it is possible to envisage the development in the United Kingdom of a protective regime governing information collection. The features of such a regime would include severe restrictions on the use of candidate/employee consent and the employment contract to justify information collection which would otherwise infringe the 1998 Act, and a rigorous application of proportionality balancing. In weighing employer interests relative to the competing private interests of candidates/employees, UK law should refuse to give effect to economic motivations for information collection (save in rare cases), and should place a premium on the preservation of as much workplace privacy as possible in any given circumstance. If a regime of this nature were to emerge in the United Kingdom, it would be despite the labour law traditions of the past. However, with the incorporation of the European Convention on Human Rights into UK law, a new human rights tradition could emerge within labour law. A protective regime regulating employment data processing would be consistent with this new tradition, and would advance it further by making the right of privacy a significant new source of regulation in the workplace.

10.5 CONCLUSIONS

In this final chapter, I have considered the impact on United Kingdom workplace privacy law of the incorporation of the European Convention on Human Rights, and the implementation of the European Directive on Data Protection. As a result of these two legal developments, the UK will move from a jurisdiction where the right of privacy has no independent legal existence to one where the right is available to candidates/employees through at least three sources: the

Human Rights Act 1998, unfair dismissal law under the ERA, and the Data Protection Act 1998. Furthermore, the Human Rights Act and the 1998 Act may mark the genesis of a human rights tradition in the United Kingdom which could lead to the development of a common law privacy tort available to candidates/employees, and the enactment of comprehensive workplace privacy legislation by Parliament. However, factors operating against such legal developments include the traditional conservatism of the UK judiciary, and the abstentionist tradition underlying UK labour law.

I close this chapter, and this book, with the observation that there exists a real danger that workplace privacy law will evolve in the United Kingdom in an incoherent manner similar to that of the laws of the United States and Canada. The laws in both North American jurisdictions are a product of the conflict between protecting human rights while at the same time preserving freedom of contract. This conflict could easily emerge in the United Kingdom as well, as legal abstentionism comes to be challenged by new ways of thinking flowing from the Human Rights Act. Judges and other decision-makers may even look to North America for guidance on issues of workplace privacy, thus replicating the problems that have emerged there (consider the issue of consent, for example). However, the UK is presently the legal equivalent of a 'blank slate' in the field of privacy, and the opportunity certainly exists for a comprehensive and protective regime to emerge within employment law. As I have suggested, the legal principles I have developed herein could guide the interpretation and application of the UK's new right of privacy, and the development of future legal reforms. Hence, while my analytical starting point was an analysis of the extant laws of the United States, France, and Canada for the purpose of developing a best practice model for the protection of the right of privacy in the workplace, this same model could be extended directly into United Kingdom law. The United Kingdom could therefore learn from the inadequacies in the laws of other nations, while at the same time patterning its own laws after the most protective and privacy-sensitive aspects of those same foreign laws. Such an approach would ensure that privacy achieves a legal status in the United Kingdom befitting a fundamental human right.

Appendix

Glossary of Terms

Acetylation phenotype: a genetic disorder which results in the production of an enzyme which stuntsthe ability of the liver to detoxify the blood. It has been linked to bladder cancer, and exposure to certain chemical compounds is thought to increase the cancer risk (OTA (1990), 85).

Ataxia telangiectasia: a genetic disorder resulting in neurological, oculocutaneous and immunological complications. Sufferers are predisposed to immune deficiencies and certain cancers. It is thought that exposure to radiation (perhaps from x-rays) could trigger cancer (OTA (1990), 86–7).

Drug use: the limited, controlled consumption of a drug (in terms of frequency and quantity) without significant toxic, adverse physical or psychological consequences to the user (Normand *et al*. (1994), 2).

Drug abuse: a level of drug use that typically leads to adverse consequences (physical or psychological) (Normand *et al*. (1994), 2).

Drug dependence: a level of drug use that has significant adverse physical and psychological consequences. This level of use is characterised by the consumption of toxic doses of the drug that impair the user's ability to function (Normand *et al*. (1994), 2).

Enzyme immunoassay method (EIM): a drug test which employs antibodies to detect the presence of drug metabolites in the subject's urine, and which is capable of detecting the presence of amphetamines, barbiturates, valium, marijuana, cocaine, ethyl alcohol, methadone, opiates (heroin and morphine), quaalude, and phencyclidine (PCP) (OLRC (1992a), 15; Feldthusen (1988), 85).

Gas chromatography: a drug testing method which uses an inert gas, such as nitrogen or helium, to transport a vaporised sample of a drug through a glass column containing a liquid. The drug is identified and qualified by a detector, known as a chromatogram, at the far end of the column (OLRC (1992a), 17–19).

Gas chromatography combined with mass spectrometry: a drug testing method which is said virtually to guarantee the accurate identification of the substances in an individual's urine. After the application of a gas chromatograph, a mass spectrometer subjects each separate component to high energy bombardment. The chemicals fragment into ions, which have a measurable electrical charge. This identifies a unique molecular fingerprint for each drug or metabolite, which can be compared with the 'fingerprints' on record (OLRC (1992a), 17–19).

Linkage analysis: an indirect method of genetic testing involving the identification in an individual of a genetic marker, known as a 'restriction fragment length polymorphism' ('RFLP'), which is linked to a particular genetic mutation. This method is used where it has already been determined that one member of a family suffers from a genetic mutation. By identifying the general location of the mutation in that person (i.e. the marker or RFLP), it is then possible to determine whether other members of the family have the same mutation by looking for the same marker. This method is used to detect genetic disorders such as Huntington's Disease, cystic fibrosis, and Duchenne muscular dystrophy (OTA (1990), 78–9; Hubbard and Wald (1993), 55–7).

Metabolites: the inert, inactive by–products of a drug ingested by an individual. Urinalysis drug testing measures metabolites, while blood testing identifies actual amounts of a given drug in the blood (OLRC (1992a), 14).

Methadone: a drug supplied to heroin addicts which satisfies addictive cravings while being far less damaging to the body.

Monogenic disease: a genetic disease resulting from a defect in a single gene. Monegenic diseases can be subdivided into three categories: (1) autosomal dominant—a condition resulting from a defective gene inherited from either parent (e.g. Huntington's Disease); (2) autosomal recessive—a condition arising only when the defective gene is inherited from both parents (e.g. cystic fibrosis, Tay-Sach's disease); and (3) x-linked—a condition associated with a genetic defect in the x chromosome determining sex, and which only affects male offspring, although females can be carriers (e.g. hæmophilia) (Clarke (1995)).

Nucleotides: chemicals forming DNA. There are four nucleotides: guanine (G), adenine (A), thymine (T), and cytosine (C). A and T are always paired, as are C and G. Hence, DNA is composed of billions of interconnecting AT and CG pairs.

Psychomotor (functional) testing: an employment testing method which concerns the study of movement resulting from mental activity. It assesses the subject's thought processes, and how thoughts are translated into movement. Hand-eye co-ordination and reaction time tests are examples.

Sickle cell anaemia: a genetic condition involving abnormalities in red blood cells, which is thought to be exacerbated by exposure to several chemicals (although this remains controversial) (OTA (1990), 85).

Thalassemias: aA genetic deficiency in the production of hæmoglobin. It has been suggested that exposure to benzene and lead could place individuals at increased risk (OTA (1990), 85).

Thin-layer chromatography: a drug-testing method in which an absorbent material such as silicon gel is applied to a glass plate. This is called the stationary phase. Mixtures of known drug compounds or residues from an extraction of drugs from urine are applied as spots to prepared plates, which are then placed in a closed container with just enough solvent (mobile phase) to wet the bottom of the plate. The solvent then flows across the stationary phase, which causes the substances to separate. These separated substances are then identified by spraying the plate with reagents that produce particular colour reactions. Both the position and the tint of the spots identify the characteristics of the urine (OLRC (1992a), 17–19).

Bibliography

UNCREDITED ARTICLES

Fortune, 'What the Boss Knows About You' (August 1993) 131.

Fresno Bee (5 August 1997) 3.

Human Genome News, 'Fear of Genetic Discrimination Drives Legislative Interest' (Jan.–June 1997), 8, 3.

International Herald-Tribune, 'Marijuana in Driver's Test' (16 July 1997) 22.

Interrights Bulletin (November 1997).

Los Angeles Times, 'Report Questions Value of Employer Drug Programs' (30 November 1993) 2.

New York Times, 'The Many Tests for Drug Abuse' (24 February 1985) 17.

Personal Computer World (April 1997) 232.

The Scotsman(a), Editorial, 'Unsuitable Cases for Treatment' (Tuesday, 23 June 1997) 1.

The Scotsman(b), 'Police Chief Calls for Mandatory Addict Treatment' (Tuesday, 23 June 1997) 1.

Security Management, 'ASIS speaks out on electronic monitoring' (April 1992).

TIME Magazine (25 August 1997) 18.

USA Today (17 October 1996) 1.

ARTICLES AND BOOKS

ACKERMAN (1991), 'A History of Drug Testing', in Coombs and West (eds.), *Drug Testing: Issues and Options* (Oxford: OUP) 3.

ACKOFF (1994), *The Democratic Corporation* (Oxford: OUP).

ADAMS and SINGH (1997), 'Early Experience with NAFTA's Labour Side Accord', 18 *Comp. LLJ* 161.

ADDICTION RESEARCH FOUNDATION (1991), *Workplace Drug and Alcohol Testing: Where to Draw the Line* (Toronto: Addiction Research Foundation).

ADDO (1995), 'The ECHR in English Law', 46 *NILQ* 1.

AIELLO and SVEC (1993), 'Computer-Based Work Monitoring: Electronic Surveillance and its Effects', 23 *J Applied Social Psych.* 499.

ALLISON and STEHLUT (1995), 'DOT, ADA and FMLA: Overlap, Similarities and Differences with Respect to the New Alcohol and Drug Testing Rules', 46 *Labor LJ* 153.

AMERICAN LAW INSTITUTE (ALI)(a) (1958), *Restatement of Agency* (2d) (St. Paul, Min.:).

—— (b) (1972), *Restatement of the Law of Torts* (2d) (St. Paul, Min.:).

AMERICAN MANAGEMENT ASSOCIATION (1993), *1993 Survey of Workplace Drug Testing and Drug Abuse Policies* (New York: AMA).

AMERICAN MEDICAL ASSOCIATION (AMA) (1991), Council on Ethical and Judicial Affairs, 'Use of Genetic Testing by Employers', 266 *JAMA* 1827 (2 October) 1827.

ANDERSON (1996), 'Fundamental Issues in Privacy Law', in B. Markesinis (ed.), *Clifford Chance Lectures, Bridging the Channel* (Oxford: OUP.) 123.

ANDREWS and JAEGER (1991), 'Confidentiality of Genetic Information in the Workplace', 17 *Am. JL & Med.* 75.

ARENDT (1949), 'The Cult of Privacy', 21 *Australian LQ* 69.

ARTHURS *et al.* (1993), *Labour Law and Industrial Relations in Canada* (Toronto: Butterworths).

AXEL (1991), 'Drug Testing in Private Industry', in Coombs and West (eds.), *Drug Testing: Issues and Options* (Oxford: OUP) 148.

BACQUET (1980), 'Réglement intérieur et libertés publiques: Conclusions du Commissaire du Gouvernement', 6 *Dr. Soc.* 310.

BALL (1994), 'Bad Faith Discharge', 39 *McGill LJ* 568–601.

BARKER (1992), 'Constitutional Privacy Rights in the Private Workplace, Under the Federal and California Constitutions', 19 *Hastings Const'l LQ* 1107.

BATES and HOLTON (1995), 'Computerized Performance Monitoring: A Review of Human Resource Issues', 5 *Hum. Res. Mngt. Rev.* 267.

BAUMHART (1992), 'The Employer's Right to Read Employee E-Mail: Protecting Property or Personal Prying', 8 *Labor LJ* 923.

BEAMIS (1989), 'Prohibition of Pencil and Paper Honesty Tests: Is Honesty the Best Policy?', 25 *Williamette LR* 571.

BEANEY(a) (1962), 'The Constitutional Right to Privacy in the Supreme Court', *Sup. Ct. Rev.* 212

—— (b) (1966), 'The Right to Privacy and American Law', 31 *Law and Contemp. Probs.* 253.

BECKWITH (1991), 'The Human Genome Initiative: Genetics Lightning Rod', 17 *Am. J L & Med.* 1.

BEDINGFIELD (1992), 'Privacy or Publicity? The Enduring Confusion Surrounding the American Tort of Invasion of Privacy', 55 *Mod LR* 111.

BENN (1978), 'The Protection and Limitation of Privacy', 52 *Australian LJ* 601, 686.

BENNETT (1992), *Regulating Privacy* (Cornell U Press).

BENSINGER (1982), 'Drugs in the Workplace', 60 *Harv. Bus. Rev.* 48.

BENTHAM (1970), *An Introduction to the Principles of Morals and Legislation* (1789) (eds. Burns and Hart, London: University of London, Athlone Press).

BERLE (1952), 'Constitutional Limitations on Corporate Activity—Protection of Personal Rights from Invasion Through Economic Power', 100 *U Penn. LR* 933.

BERRY (1996), 'The Human Genome Project and the End of Insurance', 7 *U Fl. JLPP* 205.

BERRY and BOLAND (1977), *The Economic Cost of Alcohol Abuse* (New York: Free Press).

BERTRAM *et al.* (1996), *Drug War Politics: The Price of Denial* (Berkeley, Cal.: University of California).

BESNER (1995), 'Employment Legislation for Disabled Individuals: What can France Learn from the *Americans with Disabilities Act*?', 16 *Comp. LLJ* 399.

BILLINGS (1992), 'Discrimination as a Consequence of Genetic Screening', 50 *Am. J Hum. Genetics* 476).

BLACK (1994), 'Personality Screening in Employment', 32 *American Bus. LJ* 69.

BLANPAIN (1993), 'Comparativism in Labour Law and Industrial Relations', in Blanpain and Engels (eds.), *Comparative Labour Law and Industrial Relations in Industrialized Market Economies* (5th edn. (Boston, Mass.: Kluwer Law).

BLAU (1964), *Exchange and Power in Social Life* (New York: Wiley).

BLOUSTEIN(a) (1964), 'Privacy as an Aspect of Human Dignity: An Answer to Dean Prosser', 39 *NYULR* 962.

—— (b) (1968), 'Privacy, Tort Law, and the Constitution: Is Warren & Brandeis Tort Petty and Unconstitutional as Well?', 46 *Texas LR* 611.

BOEHMER (1992), 'Artificial Monitoring and Surveillance of Employees', 41 *DePaul LR* 739.

BOSSU (1994), 'Droits de l'homme et pouvoirs du chef d'entreprise: vers un nouvel équilibre', 9 *Dr. Soc.* 747.

BOWERS and LEWIS (1996), 'Whistleblowing: Freedom of Expression in the Workplace' [1996] *EHRLR* 637.

BOYLE (1995), 'Shaping Priorities in Genetic Medicine', *Hastings Center Rep.* (May–June, supp.) 2.

BRICOLO (1997), 'Italy: Drugs, Prisons, and Treatment' (http:// www.penlex.org. uk).

BRITTAN (1963), 'The Right of Privacy in England and the United States', 37 *Tulane LR* 235.

BROKAW (1990), 'Genetic Screening in the Workplace', 23 *Col. JL & Soc. Probs.* 317.

BROWN and BEATTY (1984), *Canadian Labour Arbitration*, (2nd edn., Aurora: Canada Law Book).

BURNS (1976), 'The Law of Privacy: The Canadian Experience', 54 *Can. Bar. Rev.* 1.

BUY (1993), 'Contrat de Travail' [1993] *Juris Classeur (Travail Traité)* 18–20, para. 31.

CANADIAN BAR ASSOCIATION (1987), *Report of the Canadian Bar Association-Ontario Committee to Study the Implications of Mandatory Drug Testing in the Workplace* (Canadian Bar Association, July).

CANADIAN MEDICAL ASSOCIATION (1992), 'Drug Testing in the Workplace', 146 *CMAJ* 2232A.

CARAYON (1993), 'Effect of Electronic Performance Monitoring on Job Design and Worker Stress', 35 *Human Factors* 383.

CASCIO and THACKER (1994), *Managing Human Resources* (Toronto: McGraw-Hill).

CASEY (1997), 'Primer on Molecular Genetics', United States Department of Energy (Human Genome Project Home Page, http://www.ornl.gov/techresources . . . genome).

CAVICO (1993), 'Invasion of Privacy in the Private Employment Sector', 30 *Houston LR* 1263.

CHAPNIK (1990), 'Workplace Drug Testing', 5 *Admin. LR* 102.

CHARLTON (1994), 'Trade Union Concerns about Substance Abuse in the Workplace', 2 *Can. LLJ* 439.

CHOURAQUAI (1993), 'Legal Flexibility versus Social Cohesion? The Overall Regulatory Complex for the Freedom of Expression of French Employees', 9 *Int. J Comp. LL & IR* 130.

CHRISTIE *et al.* (1993), *Employment Law in Canada* (2nd edn., Toronto: Butterworths,).

CLAPHAM(a) (1993), *Human Rights in the Private Sphere* (Oxford: Clarendon).

—— (b) (1996), 'The Privatisation of Human Rights' [1996] *EHRLR* 20.

CLARKE (1995), 'Professional Norms in the Practice of Medical Genetics', 3 *Health LJ* 131.

CLAYTON and PITT (1997), 'Dress Codes and Freedom of Expression' [1997] *EHRLR* 54.

COLLINS (1987), 'Contre l'abstentionnisme en droit du travail' [1987] 6 *Dr. Soc.* 201.

COHEN (1982), 'Invasion of Privacy: Police and Electronic Surveillance in Canada', 27 *McGill LJ* 619.

COMBES (1995), 'France' in Buxton (ed.), *Employment Law in Europe* (London: Gower) 123.

COMEAU and OUIMET (1995), 'Freedom of Information and Privacy: Quebec's Innovative Role in North America', 80 *Iowa LR* 651.

COMMITTEE ON LABOR & EMPLOYMENT LAW (1988), 'Drug Testing in the Workplace', 43 *ABNYC Record* 447.

CONLON (1996), 'Privacy in the Workplace', 72 *Chi.-Kent LR* 285.

COOLEY(a) (1868), *Treatise on the Constitutional Limitations Which Rest upon the Legislative Power of the States of the American Union* (Boston, Mass.: Little Brown).

—— (b) (1888), *Law of Torts* (2nd edn., Chicago, Ill.: Callaghan).

COOMBS and WEST (1991), *Drug Testing: Issues and Options* (Oxford: OUP).

CORNFIELD (1967), 'The Right to Privacy in Canada', 25 *UT Fac. LR* 103.

COSHAN (1994), 'A Comprehensive Workplace Approach to Substance Abuse: Employee Assistance Programmes and Safety Sensitive Employees', 2 *Can. LLJ* 391.

COX (1947), 'Some Aspects of the Labor-Management Relations Act 1947 (pt. 1)', 61 *Harvard LR* 1.

CRAIG(a) (1997), 'Invasion of Privacy and *Charter* Values: The Common Law Tort Awakens', 42 *McGill LJ* 201.

—— (b) (1998), 'Privacy in the Workplace and the Impact of *European Convention* Incorporation on United Kingdom Labour Law', 19 *Comp. LLJ* 373.

—— and NOLTE (1998), 'Privacy and Free Speech in Germany and Canada: Lessons for an English Privacy Tort' [1998] *EHRLR* 162.

—— and OLIVER (1998), 'The Right to Privacy in the Public Workplace: Should the Private Sector be Concerned?', 27 *ILJ* 49.

CRAIN (1992), 'Rationalizing Inequality: An Anti-Feminist Defense of the 'Free Market'', 61 *George Washington LR* 556.

DADOMO and FARRAN (1997), *French Substantive Law* (London: Sweet & Maxwell).

DAVIES and FREEDLAND (1993), *Labour Legislation and Public Policy* (Oxford: Clarendon).

DEAKIN and MORRIS (1995), *Labour Law* (London: Butterworths).

—— and WILKINSON(a) (1991), *The Economics of Employment Rights* (London, England, Institute of Employment Rights).

—— and —— (b) (1994), 'Rights v. Efficiency? The Economic Case for Transnational Labour Standards', 23 *ILJ* 289.

DECKER(a) (1987), *Employee Privacy Law and Practice* (New York: Wiley & Sons).

—— (b) (1994), *Privacy in the Workplace: Rights, Procedures and Policies* (Horsham, Penn.: LRP Publications).

DE MEYER (1973), 'The Right to Respect for Private and Family Life, Home and Communications in Relations Between Individuals and the Resulting Obligations for State Parties to the Convention', in Robertson (ed.), *Privacy and Human Rights* (Manchester: Manchester U. Press) 255.

DIAMOND (1983), 'Genetic Testing in Employment Situations: A Question of Worker Rights', 4 *J Legal Med.* 231.

DICKSON (1994), *Introduction to French Law* (New York: Longman Group).

DITECCO et al. (1987), *Operator Stress Survey: Report to the Health and Safety Sub-committee on Machine Pacing and Remote Electronic Monitoring* (Toronto: Communications and Electrical Workers of Canada).

DOWD (1993), 'Liberty v. Equality: In Defence of Privileged White Males', 34 *William and Mary LR* 429.

DWORKIN (1965), 'The Common Law Protection of Privacy', 2 *Tasmanian ULR* 418.

EADY (1996), 'A Statutory Right of Privacy' [1996] 3 *EHRLR* 243.

EDELSON (1997), 'Tay Sachs Disease Screening Programs in the US as a Model for the Control of Genetic Disease', 7 *Health Matrix* 125.

EICHBAUM (1979), 'Towards an Autonomy-based Theory of Constitutional Privacy', 14 *Harvard CR-CL LR* 361.

EMERSON (1979), 'Right of Privacy and Freedom of the Press', 14 *Harvard CRCLLR* 329.

ENGLAND(a) (1982), 'Unjust Dismissal in the Federal Jurisdiction: The First Three Years', 12 *Man. LJ* 9.

—— (b) (1995), 'Continuing Tension Between the Rights Paradigm and the Efficiency Paradigm', 20 *Queen's LJ* 557.

EPSTEIN(a) (1983), 'A Common Law for Labor Relations: A Critique of the New Deal Labor Legislation', 92 *Yale LJ* 1357.

—— (b) (1992), *Forbidden Grounds* (Cambridge, Mass.: Harvard U. Press).

—— (c) (1994), 'The Legal Regulation of Genetic Discrimination: Old Responses to New Technology', 74 *Boston ULR* 1.

EWING (1995), 'Democratic Socialism and Labour Law', 24 *ILJ* 103.

FAST (1993), 'Breach of Employee Confidentiality', 142 *U Penn. LR* 431.

FEINBERG (1948), 'Recent Developments in the Law of Privacy', 48 *Col. LR* 713.

FEINMAN (1976), 'The Development of the Employment at Will Rule', 20 *Am. J Legal History* 118.

FELDBAUM (1996), 'Protecting Genetic Privacy', *Chemistry and Industry* (16 Sept.) 704.

FELDMAN (1997), 'The Developing Scope of Article 8 of the *European Convention on Human Rights*' [1997] 3 *EHRLR* 265.

FELDTHUSEN (1988), 'Urinalysis Drug Testing: Just Say No', 5 *CHRYB* 81.

FEYLER (1986), 'The Constitutional Right of Privacy', 14 *NYU Rev. L & Soc. Change* 973.

FIELD (1983), 'Biological Monitoring and Genetic Screening in the Industrial Workplace: A Synopsis and Analysis', 11 *L Med. & Health Care* 125.

FINKIN(a) (1995), *Privacy in Employment Law* (Washington: BNA Books).

—— (b) (1996), 'Employee Privacy, American Values, and the Law', 72 *Chic.-Kent LR* 222.

FLAHERTY (1989), *Protecting Privacy in Surveillance Societies* (University of North Carolina Press).

FLANDERS (1974), 'The Tradition of Voluntarism', 12 *BJIR* 352.

FORD (1998), *Surveillance and Privacy at Work* (London: Institute of Employment Rights).

FOX (1974), *Beyond Contract: Work, Power and Trust Relations* (London: Faber and Faber Ltd.).

FREDMAN (1992), 'The New Rights: Labour Law and Ideology in the Thatcher Years', 12 *OJLS* 24.

—— and MORRIS (1989), *The State as Employer: Labour Law in the Public Services* (London: Mansell).

FRIED(a) (1968), 'Privacy', 77 *Yale LJ* 475.

—— (b) (1984), 'Individual and Collective Rights in Work Relations: Reflections on the Current State of Labour Law and its Prospects', 51 *U of Chicago LR* 1012.

FRIEDMAN (1970), 'The Social Responsibility of Business is to Increase its Profits', *New York Times Magazine* (13 September) 32.

GANTT (1995), 'An Affront to Human Dignity: Electronic Mail Monitoring in the Private Sector Workplace', 8 *Har. J.L & Tech.* 345.

GASTON *et al. (1986)*, 'Prophylaxis with Oral Penicillin in Children With Sickle Cell Anemia', 314 *New Engl. J of Med.* 1593.

GAVISON (1980, 'Privacy and the Limits of the Law', 89 *Yale LJ* 421).

GEDDES (1989), 'The Private Investigator and the Right to Privacy', 27 *Alta. LR* 256.

GERHART(a) (1995), 'Employee Privacy Rights', 17 *Comp. LLJ* 1.

—— (b) (1995), 'Employee Privacy Rights in the United States', 17 *Comp. LLJ* 175.

GLASBEEK(a) (1968), 'Outraged Dignity—Do We Need a New Tort?', 6 *Alta. LR* 77.

—— (b) (1993), 'Agenda for Canadian Labour Law Reform: A Little Liberal Law, Much More Democratic Socialist Politics', 31 *Osgoode Hall LJ* 233.

GLENN(a) (1974), 'Civil Responsibility—the Right to Privacy in Quebec', 52 *Can. Bar. Rev.* 297.

—— (b) (1979), 'Le droit au respect de la vie privée', 39 *R du B* 879.

GOLEMBIEWSKI and MCCONKIE (1975), 'The Centrality of Interpersonal Trust in Group Processes', in Cooper (ed.), *Theories of Group Processes* (New York: Wiley) 131.

GORMLY (1992), 'One Hundred Years of Privacy', 92 *Wisconsin LR* 1335.

GOSTIN (1991), 'Genetic Discrimination: The Use of Genetically Based Diagnostic and Prognostic Tests by Employers and Insurers', 17 *Am. J.L & Med.* 109.

GRINSNIR (1993), 'Les dispositions nouvelles relatives 'au recrutement individuel et aux libertés individuelles' (loi du 31 décembre 1992)' [1993] *Dr. Ouvrier* 237.

GRODIN (1991), 'Constitutional Values in the Private Sector Workplace', 13 *Industrial Rel. LR* 1.

GUAY *et al.* (1992), 'La génétique dans les domaines de l'assurance et de l'emploi', 52 *Rev. du Bar.* 185.

GUFFEY and WEST (1996), 'Employee Privacy: Legal Implications for Managers', 47 *Labor LJ* 735.

GUNTHER (1992), *Individual Rights and Constitutional Law* (5th edn., Westbury, NY: The Foundation Press.).

GUYER and COLLINS (1995), 'How is the Human Genome Project Doing, and What Have We Learned So Far?', 92 *Proc. Nat'l Acad. Sci.* 10841.

HALDANE (1938), *Heredity and Politics* (London: Allen & Unwin).

HARLOW (1980), '"Public" and "Private" Law: Definition Without Distinction' *MLR* 241.

HARRIS and HEFT (1992), 'Alcohol and Drug Use in the Workplace: Issues, Controversies and Directions for Future Research', 18 *J of Mngt.* 239.

HART(a), H. L. A. (1958), 'Separation of Law and Morals', 71 *Harvard LR* 593.

—— (b) (1994), *The Concept of Law* (2nd edn., Oxford: OUP).

HARTLEY, T. C. (1990), *The Foundations of European Community Law* (2nd edn., Oxford: Clarendon).

HARVEY (1991), 'Confidentiality: A Measured Response to the Failure of Privacy', *U Penn. LR* 2385.

HAUCH (1994), 'Protecting Private Facts in France: The Warren & Brandeis Tort is Alive and Well and Flourishing in Paris', 68 *Tulane LR* 1219.

HAYEK (1980), *1980s Unemployment and the Unions* (London: Institute of Economic Affairs).

HENRIKSON (1991), 'The Unconvincing Case for Mandatory Drug Testing', 17 *Can. Pub. Policy* 183.

HELLER and ROBINSON (1991), *Substance Abuse in the Workforce* (Office of the Science Policy Advisor, Ontario Ministry of Labour).

HEPPLE (1995), 'The Future of Labour Law', 24 *ILJ* 303.

HERRMAN (1971), 'Privacy, the Prospective Employee, and Employment Testing', 47 *Wash. LR* 73.

HIRSCH (1978), *Social Limits to Growth* (Cambridge, Mass.: Harvard U Press).

HOBBS and SCRIVNER (1988), 'Farmers, Fixes, Chickens, and Hen Houses: A Case for Limited Mandatory Random Drug Testing of Employees in the Private Sector', 32 *Saint Louis ULJ* 605.

HOEKSTRA (1996), 'Workplace searches: a legal overview', 47 *Labor LJ* 127.

HOLLOWAY (1993), 'The Constitutionalization of Employment Rights: A Comparative View', 14 *Berkeley J Empl't and Labor* L 113.

HOLMES (1997), 'Solving the Insurance/Genetic Fair/Unfair Discrimination Dilemma in Light of the Human Genome Project', 85 *Kentucky LJ* 503.

HORSTINK (1996), 'The Netherlands: Tightening Up of the Cafes Policy', in Dorn, Jepson, and Savon (eds.), *European Drug Policies and Enforcement* (London: St. Martin's Press).

HOSMER (1995), 'Trust: The Connecting Link between Organizational Theory and Philosophical Ethics', 20 *Academy of Mngt. Rev.* 379.

HUBBARD and WALD (1993), *Exploding the Gene Myth* (Boston, Mass.: Beacon Press).

HUNTER (1986), 'Your Urine or Your Job', 19 *Loyola LALR* 1453.

IDS (Income Data Services) (1997), Brief 593 (*Halford* v. *The United Kingdom*).

ILES (1996), 'The Human Genome Project: A Challenge to the Human Rights Framework', 9 *Harv. Hum. Rts. J* 27.

IRVING *et al.* (1986), 'Computerized Performance Monitoring Systems: Use and Abuse', 29 *Communications of the ACM* 794.

ISSACHAROFF (1990), 'Reconstructing Employment', 104 *Harvard LR* 607.

JACOBS and WEIDER (1996), 'The Drug Testing Society', 4 *Euro. J Cr. Crim. L Crim. J* 120.

JACOBY (1982), 'The Duration of Indefinite Employment Contracts in the United States and England: An Historical Analysis', 5 *Comp. LLJ* 85.

JANIS and KAY (1990), *European Human Rights Law* (U of Connecticut).

JOHNSON and HERRING (1989), 'Labor Market Participation Among Young Adults', 21 *Youth and Society* 3.

JOURARD (1966), 'Some Psychological Aspects of Privacy', 31 *Law and Contemp. Probs.* 307.

KADE (1988), 'The Potential of Collective Bargaining in an Era of Economic Restructuring', in Estreicher and Collins (eds.), *Labor Law and Business Change* (New York: Quorum).

KAESTNER(a) (1992), *The Effect of Illicit Drug Use on the Labor Supply of Young Adults* (Cambridge, Mass.: National Bureau of Economic Research).

—— (b) (1990), *The Effect of Illicit Drug Use on the Wages of Young Adults* (Cambridge, Mass.: National Bureau of Economic Research).

KAGEL *et al.* (1980), 'Marihuana and Work Performance: Results from an Experiment', 15 *Journal of Human Resources* 373.

KAHN-FREUND, O.(a) (1959), 'Labour Law', in Ginsberg (ed.), *Law and Opinion in England in the 20th Century* (London: Stevens and Sons Ltd.).

—— (b) (1969), 'Industrial Relations and the Law—Retrospect and Prospect', 7 *BJIR* 301.

—— (c) (1972), *Labour and the Law* (London: Stevens & Sons).

—— (d) (1974), 'On Uses and Misuses of Comparative Law', 37 *MLR* 1.

—— (e) (1983), *Labour and the Law* (3rd edn., London: Stevens & Sons).

KALVEN JR. (1966), 'Privacy in Tort Law—Were Warren & Brandeis Wrong?', 31 *Law and Contemp. Probs.* 326.

KANDEL and DAVIES (1990), 'Labor Force Experiences of a National Sample of Young Adult Men', 21 *Youth and Society* 411.

KANDEL and YAMAGUCHI (1987), 'Job Mobility and Drug Use: An Event History Analysis', 92 *American Journal of Sociology* 836.

KEARNEY (1993), 'Arbitral Practice and Purpose in Employee Off-Duty Misconduct Cases', 69 *Notre Dame LR* 135.

KELLY (1994), 'Romance in the Workplace', 4 *ELLR* 73.

KELSO (1992), 'California's Constitutional Right to Privacy', 19 *Pepperdine LR* 327.

KENNEDY (1982), 'The Status and Decline of the Public/Private Distinction', 130 *U Penn. LR* 1349.

KIM (1996), 'Privacy Rights, Public Policy, and the Employment Relationship', 57 *Ohio State LJ* 671.

KING (1994), 'Privacy Issues in the Private Sector Workplace', 67 *S Cal. LR* 441.

KLARE (1982), 'The Public/Private Distinction in Labour Law', 82 *U Penn. LR* 1358.

KNOPPERS(a) (1991), *Human Dignity and Genetic Heritage* (Ottawa: Law Reform Commission of Canada).

—— (b) (1995), 'Professional Norms: Towards a Canadian Consensus?', 3 *Health LJ* 1.

KRAUSE (1965), 'The Right of Privacy in Germany: Pointers for American Legislation', *Duke LJ* 481.

KONVITZ (1966), 'Privacy and the Law: A Philosophical Prelude', 31 *Law & Contemp. Probs.* 272.

KREIMER (1991), 'Sunlight, Secrets and Scarlett Letters: Privacy and Disclosure', *U Penn. LR* 1 (1991).

LAKE (1986), 'Unrestricted Employee Drug Testing Programs', 23 *Cal. WLR* 72.

LAMARCHE (1996), *Le Régime Québécois de Protection et de Promotion des Droits de la Personne* (Cowansville, PQ: Blais).

LANYON and BLOUN (1992), 'Controlling Drugs in the Workplace and Employee Privacy', 2 *ELLR* 3.

LAPIERRE and KEAN (1994), 'Le droit des travailleurs au respect de leur vie privée', 35 *Cahiers* 709.

LARREMORE (1912), 'Law of Privacy', 12 *Col. LR* 643.

LAURIE (1996), 'The Most Personal Information of All: An Appraisal of Genetic Privacy in the Shadow of the Human Genome Project', 10 *Int'l JLP and Fam.* 74.

LAVAN *et al. (1994)*, 'Litigation of Employer Drug Testing', 45 *Labor LJ* 346.

LAWS, J. (1993), 'Is the High Court the Guardian of Fundamental Constitutional Rights?' [1993] *Public L* 59.

LENAERTS (1991), 'Fundamental Rights to be Included in a Community Catalogue', 16 *European LR* 367.

LENOIR and WALLON (1988), 'Informatique, travail et libertés' [1988] 3 *Dr. Soc.* 213.

LEVINE (1982), 'Industrial Screening Programs for Workers', 24 *Environment* 26.

LEWIS (1979), 'Kahn-Freund and Labour Law: An Outline Critique', 8 *ILJ* 202.

LEWIS and WEIGART (1985), 'Trust as Social Reality', 63 *Social Forces* 967.

LIN (1996), 'Conferring a Federal Property Right in Genetic Material: Stepping into the Future with the Genetic Privacy Act', 22 *Am. J.L and Med.* 109.

LINOWES (1988), *Privacy in America: Is Your Private Life in the Public Eye?* (Urbana: University of Illinois Press).

—— and Spencer (1990), 'Privacy: The Workplace Issue of the '90s', 23 *John Marshall LR* 591.

LUSKY (1972), 'Invasion of Privacy: A Clarification of Legal Concepts', 72 *Col. LR* 693.

Lyon-Caen(a) (1990), 'Labour Law Looking Ahead to 1992: A French Viewpoint', 6 *Int. J Comp. LL & IR* 3.

—— (b) (1992), *Les libertés publiques et l'emploi*, Rapport pour le Ministre du Travail, de l'Emploi, et de la Formation Professionale (Paris: Le Ministre du Travail, de l'Emploi).

—— (c) (1993), *European Employment Glossary: France* (London: Sweet & Maxwell).

Malinowski (1996), 'Globalization of Biotechnology and the Public Health Challenges Accompanying It', 60 *Alb. LR* 119.

—— and Blatt (1997), 'Commercialization of Genetic Testing Services: The FDA, Market Forces, and Biological Tarot Cards', 71 *Tulane LR* 1211.

Maltby (1993), 'Workplace Electronic Monitoring' , 3 *ELLR* 66.

Manfield (1997), 'Imposing Liability on Drug Testing Laboratories for 'False Positives': Getting Around Privity', 64 *U Chic. LR* 287.

Markesinis, B. S.(a) (1994), *The German Law of Torts* (3rd edn., Oxford: Clarendon).

—— (b) (1994), 'A Matter of Style', 110 *LQR* 607.

—— (c) (1992), 'Calcutt Report Must Not Be Forgotten', 55 *MLR* 118.

—— (d) (1990), 'Our Patchy Law of Privacy—Time to do Something About It', 53 *MLR* 802.

Marmor (1992), *Interpretation and Legal Theory* (Oxford: Clarendon Press).

Marshall (1975), 'The Right to Privacy: A Sceptical View' , 21 *McGill LJ* 242.

Mason (1925), *Organized Labour and the Law* (Durham, NC: Duke University Press).

McCourt (1992), 'Performance Testing Makes Sense', *EAP Digest* (January/February) 18.

McEwen (1992), 'Addressing Chemical Dependency-Related Issues in the Workplace' (1992), 2 *Can. LLJ* 421.

McGovern (1987), 'Employee Drug-Testing Legislation: Redrawing the Battlelines in the War on Drugs', 39 *Stanford LR* 1453.

McGuire and Ruhm (1991), 'Workplace Drug Abuse Policy' (Discussion Paper, Series 19) (Boston, Mass.: Boston University Industry Studies).

McVicar *et al.* (1995), *Assessing Costs: Substance Abuse in the Workplace* (Alberta Alcohol and Drug Abuse Commission).

Mead (1965), 'Margaret Mead Re-examines our Right to Privacy', *Redbook* (April) 15.

Mello(a) (1994), 'Prevalent employer discriminatory behaviours toward employees with HIV and the likely impact of the ADA', 45 *Labor LJ* 321.

—— (b) (1995), 'Personality Screening in Employment', 46 *Labor LJ* 662.

Merkett (1996), 'Genetic Diaries: An Analysis of Privacy Protection in DNA Data Banks', 30 *Suffolk ULR* 185.

Meyer (1993), 'Justifications for Permitting Life Insurers to Continue to Underwrite on the Basis of Genetic Information and Genetic Test Results', 27 *Suffolk ULR* 1271.

Meyers (1977), 'The Use of Comparisons of Labor Law', 2 *Comp. LL* 238.

Michael (1994), *Privacy and Human Rights* (Paris: Unesco).

Mill, J. S. (1859), *On Liberty* (Williams (ed.), London: Everyman, 1993).

Miller and Huvos (1994), 'Genetic Blueprints, Employer Cost-cutting, and the ADA', 46 *Admin. LR* 369.

Milunsky (1993), 'The 'New' Genetics: From Research to Reality', 27 *Suffolk ULR* 1307.

Mimo (1993), 'The New Law of Privacy', 143 *New LJ* 1182.

Mole (1990), 'Informatique et libertés du travail: les nouveux enjeux' [1990] 1 *Dr. Soc.* 59.

MORRISON (1973), *Report on the Law of Privacy* (NSW Government Printer).

MOSKOWITZ (1977), 'Hugo Munsterberg: A study in the history of applied psychology', 32 *American Psychologist* 824.

MUCKENBERGER and DEAKIN (1989), 'From Deregulation to a European Floor of Rights: Labour Law, Flexibilisation and the European Labour Market' [1989] *Zeitzschrift für ausländisches und internationales Arbeits- und Sozial Recht* 154.

MYKITIUK and PENNEY (1995), 'Screening for "Deficits": The Legal and Ethical Implications of Genetic Screening and Testing to Reduce Health Care Budgets', 3 *Health LJ* 235.

NAISMITH (1996), 'Photographs, Privacy and Freedom of Expression' [1996] 2 *EHRLR* 150.

NAPIER (1992), 'Computerization and Employment Rights', 21 *ILJ* 1.

NEGLEY (1966), 'Philosophical Views on the Value of Privacy', 31 *Law and Contemp. Probs.* 319.

NEILL (1962), 'Protection of Privacy', 25 *MLR* 393.

NERSON (1971), 'La protection de la vie privée en droit positif français', 23 *Rev. Int. Dr. Comp.* 737.

NORMAND *et al.* (1994), *Under the Influence? Drugs and the American Workforce* (Washington, DC: National Academy Press).

NORWOOD (1994), 'Drug Testing in the Private Sector and its Impact on Employees' Right to Privacy', 45 *Labor LJ* 731.

NOTE(a) (1981), 'Genetic Testing in Employment: Employee Protection or Threat?', 15 *Suffolk UL Rev.* 1187.

—— (b) (1988), 'Lie Detectors in the Workplace: The Need for Civil Actions Against Employers', 101 *Harvard LR* 806.

—— (c) (1989), 'Employee Drug Testing', 103 *Harvard LR* 269.

—— (d) (1990), 'Addressing the New Hazards of the High Technology Workplace', 104 *Harvard LR* 1898.

—— (e) (1995), 'Genetic Testing and Health Care: Points to Consider', 3 *Health LJ* 325.

NUSSBAUM (1986), 'Computer Monitoring: Mismanagement by Remote Control', 56 *Business and Society Rev.* 16.

NUTTING (1957), 'Fifth Amendment and Privacy', 18 *UPHLR* 533.

O'BRIEN (1902), 'Right of Privacy', 2 *Col. LR* 437.

O'MEARA (1994), 'Personality Tests Raise Questions of Legality and Effectiveness', 39 *Hum. R. Magazine* 77.

O'NEILL and QUINN (1993), 'Applications of the Competing Values Framework', 32 *Hum. Res. Mngt.* 1.

ORREN (1991), *Belated Feudalism* (Cambridge: Cambridge University Press).

ORWELL (1949), *Nineteen Eighty-Four*.

OSCAPELLA (1992), 'Drug Testing and Privacy', 2 *Can. LLJ* 325.

PARENT (1983), 'Recent Work on the Concept of Privacy', 20 *American Philosophical Quarterly* 341.

PARKER (1974), 'A Definition of Privacy', 27 *Rutger's LR* 275.

PATEMAN (1983), 'Feminist Critiques of the Public/Private Dichotomy', in Benn and Gaus (eds.), *Public and Private in Social Life* (London: Croom Helm).

PATON-SIMPSON (1995), 'Human interests: Privacy and Free Speech in the Balance', 16 *NZULR* 225.

PEDRICK (1970), 'Publicity and Privacy: Is it Any of Our Business?', *UTLJ* 392.

PEIRCE (1985), 'The Regulation of Genetic Testing in the Workplace—A Legislative Proposal', 46 *Ohio State LJ* 771.

PENNOCK (1930), 'Industrial Research at Hawthorne and Experimental Investigation of Rest Periods, Working Conditions, and Other Influences', 8 *Personnel Journal* 296.

PILLER(a) (1993), 'Bosses With X-ray Eyes', *MacWorld* (July) 120.

—— (b) (1993), 'Privacy in Peril', *MacWorld* (July) 124.

PINCUS and TROTTER (1995), 'The Disparity between Public and Private Sector Employee Privacy: A Call for Legitimate Privacy Rights for Private Sector Workers', 33 *Am. Bus. LJ* 51.

POSNER(a) (1978), 'Right to Privacy', 12 *Ga. LR* 393.

—— (b) (1979), 'Privacy, Secrecy, and Reputation', 28 *Buffalo LR* 1.

POWERS (1996), 'A Cognitive Access Definition of Privacy', 15 *Law & Phil.* 369.

PRATT (1975), 'The Warren and Brandeis Argument for a Right to Privacy' [1975] *Public L* 161.

PROSSER (1960), 'Privacy', 48 *Cal. LR* 383.

QUINN and ROHRBURGH (1983), 'A Spatial Model of Effectiveness Criteria: Towards a Competing Values Approach to Organizational Analysis', 29 *Mngt. Science* 363.

RANKIN (1984), 'Privacy and Technology: A Canadian Perspective', 22 *Alta. LR* 323.

RAVANAS (1989), 'Protection de la vie privée', *Juris-Classeur, Civil*, art. 9, Fasc. 1, 8.

RAY and ROJOT (1996), 'Worker Privacy in France', 17 *Comp. LLJ* 61.

RAZ (1986), *Morality and Freedom* (Oxford: Clarendon Press).

REILLY (1993), 'Public Policy and Legal Issues Raised by Advances in Genetic Screening and Testing', 27 *Suffolk ULR* 1327.

REUTER *et al.* (1993), *Comparing Western European and North American Drug Policies* (Santa Monica, Cal.: Drug Policy Research Center).

RICE and THOMAS (1997), 'Drug Testing in the Workplace', 147 *NLJ* 484.

ROBERTS and GREGOR (1971), 'Privacy: A Cultural View', 13 *Nomos* 199.

ROBERTSON (1993), *Freedom, the Individual and the Law* (7th edn., London: Penguin).

RODRIGUEZ-PINERO (1997), 'Les Droits Sociaux Fondamentaux des Travailleurs et la CIG', unpublished paper presented at the European University Institute, Florence, Italy, 3 March.

—— and CASAS (1997), 'In Support of a European Social Constitution', in Lyon-Caen, Sciarra, Simitis and Davies (eds), *Principles and Perspectives in European Labour Law* (Oxford: Oxford University Press).

ROJOT (1992), 'France', in Wheeler and Rojot (eds.), *Workplace Justice* (Columbia, SC: University of South Carolina Press).

ROMEI and SCIARRA (1995), 'The Protection of Employees' Privacy: A Survey of Italian Legislation and Case Law', 17 *Comp. LLJ* 91.

ROTHSTEIN(a) (1989), *Medical Screening and the Employee Health Cost Crisis* (Washington, DC: Bureau of National Affairs).

—— (b) (1992), 'Genetic Discrimination in Employment and the ADA', 29 *Houston LR* 23.

RUEBHAUSEN and BRIM (1965), 'Privacy and Behavioural Research', 65 *Col. LR* 1184.

RYAN (1973), 'Privacy, Orthodoxy, and Democracy', 51 *Can. Bar Rev.* 84.

SAMAR (1991), *The Right to Privacy* (Philadelphia, Penn.: Temple U Press).

SAMBORN (1994), 'Love Becomes a Labour Law Issue' [1994] *Nat. LJ* 1.

SAVATIER(a) (1990), 'La liberté dans le travail' [1990] *Dr. Soc.* 51.

—— (b) (1991), 'Le licenciement, à raison de ses mœurs, d'un salarié d'une association à caractère réligieux' [1991] 6 *Dr. Soc.* 485.

SAVATIER (c) (1986), 'Secret médical et obligation de discretion de l'employeur' [1986] 5 *Dr. Soc.* 419.

SCHAUER (1982), *Free Speech: A Philosophical Enquiry* (Cambridge: Cambridge University Press).

SCHOTTENFIELD (1989), 'Drug and Alcohol Testing in the Workplace—Objectives, Pitfalls, and Guidelines', 15 *Am. J Drug Alcohol Abuse* 413.

SCIARRA (1996), 'How "Global" is Labour Law? The Perspective of Social Rights in the European Union', Working Paper, European University Institute, Florence.

SEIFERT (1984), 'Monitoring Employees for Genetic Alteration: Is State Regulation Essential?', 15 *Pacific LJ* 349 (1984).

SHARPE (1996), 'Genetic Screening and Testing in Canada: A Model Duty of Care', 4 *Health LJ* 119.

SHAW (1995), 'Drug testing in the workplace and the Bill of Rights' [1995] NZLR 22.

SHILS (1966), 'Privacy: Its Constitution and Vicissitudes', 31 *Law & Contemp. Probs.* 251.

SHILS (1956), *The Torment of Secrecy: The Background and Consequences of American Security Policies* (Glencoe, Ill.: Free Press).

SINGER (1988), 'The Reliance Interest in Property', 40 *Standford LR* 614.

SINGER-CEBAL (1997), 'BRCA-1: To Test or Not to Test, That is the Question', 7 *Health Matrix* 163.

SINGH (1995), 'Privacy and the Unauthorized Publication of Photographs', 139 *Solicitors J* 771.

SIEGEL (1987), 'Toward a New Federal Right to Privacy', 11 *Nova L Rev.* 703.

SKALA (1977), 'Is There a Legal Right to Privacy?', U *Queensland LJ* 127.

Slane (1995), 'The Privacy Implications', *Drug Testing, The Sporting Experience: The Employment Possibility* (Legal Research Foundation, University of Auckland, April) 89.

SMITH (1990), 'Electronic Performance Monitoring and Job Stress in Telecommunications Jobs' (5 October), Madison, Wisc.: University of Wisconsin (Madison), Department of Industrial Engineering and the Communications Workers of America.

SMITH *et al.* (1986), *Motivational, Behavioral, and Psychological Implications of Electronic Monitoring of Worker Performance* (Washington, DC: National Technical Information Service).

SNEIDERMAN (1997), 'Just Say No to the War on Drugs', 24 *Manitoba LJ* 497.

SOLOMON (1985), 'Personal Privacy and the "1984" Syndrome', 7 *WNELR* 753.

STEIN (1977), 'Uses, Misuses—and Nonuses of Comparative Law', 72 *NWULR* 198.

STILLE (1986), 'Drug Testing', 8 *Nat. LJ* 1.

STOKINGER and MOUNTAIN (1963), 'Test for Hypersusceptibility in Hemolytic Chemicals', 6 *Archives Env'l Health* 495.

——and SCHEEL (1973), 'Hypersusceptibility and Genetic Problems in Occupational Medicine—A Consensus Report', 15 *J Occup. Med.* 564.

STONE(a) (1981), 'The Post-War Paradigm in American Labour Law', 90 *Yale LJ* 1509.

——(b) (1991), 'Pre-employment Inquiries: Drug Testing, Alcohol Screening, Physical Exams, Honesty Testing, Genetics Screening—Do They Discriminate? An Empirical Study', 25 *Akron LR* 367.

SWARBRICK and PINSONNEAULT (1995), 'Drug Testing: the Employer's Perspective' [1995] NZLR 82.

SUMMERS (1986), 'The Privatization of Personal Freedoms and Enrichment of Democracy: Some Lessons from Labor Law', U *Ill. LR* 689.

SWINTON (1982), 'Application of the Canadian *Charter of Rights and Freedoms*', in Tarnopolsky and Beaudoin (eds.), *The Canadian Charter of Rights and Freedoms* (Toronto: Carswell) 41.

TAYLOR (1971), 'Privacy and the Public', 34 *MLR* 288.

TERRÉ and FENOUILLET (1996), Droit Civil: Les personnes, la famille, les incapacités (6th edn., Paris: Dalloz).

THOMAS (1992), 'Beyond the Privacy Principle', 92 *Col. LR* 1431.

THOMSON (1975), 'The Right of Privacy', 4 *Philosophy and Public Affairs*.

THORNTON (1995), 'The New International Jurisprudence on the Right to Privacy', 58 *Albany LR* 725.

TISSOT (1995), 'La protection de la vie privée du salarié' [1995] 3 *Dr. Soc.* 222.

TROWERS and HAMLIN (1995), *European Employment Law* (Burr Ridge, IL: Irwin Professional).

UNDERWOOD and CADLE (1985), 'Genetics, Genetic Testing, and the Specter of Discrimination: A Discussion Using Hypothetical Cases', 85 *Kentucky LJ* 665.

UNITED STATES CHAMBER OF COMMERCE (1988), *Employee Benefits 1986* (Washington, DC: USCC).

UPEX (1994), *The Law of Termination of Employment* (Oxford: Clarendon).

VAN DEN HURK (1997), 'The Netherlands: Drugs, Prisons, and Treatment' (http://www.penlex.org.uk).

VAN DIJK and VAN HOOF (1990), *Theory and Practice of the European Convention on Human Rights* (2nd edn., Boston, Mass.: Kluwer Law).

VERDIER and FURON (1990), *Aptitude Physique et Contrat de Travail* (Paris: Editions Liaisons).

VERKERKE (1992), 'Free to Search', 105 *Harvard LR* 2080.

WACKS(a) (1980), *The Protection of Privacy* (Oxford: OUP).

—— (b) (1980), 'Poverty of Privacy', 96 *LQR* 73.

WALDRON (1994), 'Vagueness in Law and Language: Some Philosophical Issues', 82 *California LR* 509.

WALTON (1931), 'The French Law as to the Right of Privacy', 47 *LQR* 219.

WARREN and BRANDEIS (1890), 'The Right to Privacy', 4 *Harvard LR* 193.

WATSON *et al.* (1987), *Molecular Biology of the Gene* (4th edn., Menlo Park, Cal.: Benjamin/Cummings).

WEDGE (1992), 'Limitations on Alcohol and Drug Testing in Collective Bargaining Relationships', 2 *Can. LLJ* 461.

WEILER(a) (1990), *Governing the Workplace: The Future of Labor and Employment Law* (Cambridge, Mass.: Harvard University Press).

—— (b) (1990), 'The *Charter* at Work: Reflections on the Constitutionalizing of Labour and Employment Law', 40 *UTLJ* 117.

WEIR (1994), 'Drug Testing: A Labour Perspective', 2 *Can. LLJ* 451.

WEISNER (1997), 'Clinical Implications of BRCA1 Genetic Testing for Ashkenazi-Jewish Women', 7 *Health Matrix* 3.

WEISS and GECK (1995), 'Worker Privacy in Germany', 17 *Comp. LLJ* 75.

WELLINGTON (1968), *Labour and the Legal Process* (New Haven, Conn.: Yale U Press).

WESTIN(a) (1966), 'Science, Privacy and Freedom', 66 *Col. LR* 1003.

—— (b) (1967), *Privacy and Freedom* (London: Bodley Head).

—— (c) (1972), 'Privacy and Personal Records: A Look at Employee Attitudes', *Civ. Lib. Rev.* 28 (Jan.–Feb.).

WESTIN (d) (1996), 'Privacy in the Workplace: How Well Does American Law Reflect American Values', 72 *Chi.-Kent LR* 271.

WHEELER (1994), 'Employee Rights as Human Rights', 28 *Employee Rights and Industrial Justice* 9.

WHELAN (1984), 'Labor Law and Comparative Law', 63 *Texas LR* 1425.

WHITE *et al.* (1988), 'A Longitudinal Investigation of Drug Use and Work Patterns Among Middle-Class, White Adults', 24 *Journal of Applied Behavioral Science* 455.

WILCOTS (1995), 'Employee Discipline for Off-Duty Conduct', 46 *Labor LJ* 3.

WILKINSON (1994), 'Equality, Efficiency, and Economic Progress: The Case for Universally Applied Equitable Standards for Wages and Conditions of Work', in Sengenberger and Campbell (eds.), *The Role of Labour Standards in Industrial Restructuring* (Geneva: International Institute for Labour Studies).

WILLBORN *et al.* (1993), *Employment Law* (Charlottesville, Vir.: The Michie Co.).

WILLIAMS (1987), 'A Regulatory Model for Genetic Testing in Employment', 40 *Oklahoma LR* 181.

WINFIELD (1931), 'The Right to Privacy', 47 LQR 23.

WISOTSKY (1987), 'The Ideology of Drug Testing', 11 *Nova L Rev.* 763.

WORK (1994), 'Whose Privacy?', 55 *Montana LR* 209.

WORKMAN (1992), 'Privacy and the First Amendment', 29 *Houston LR* 1059.

YANG (1966), 'Privacy: A Comparative Study of English and American Law', 15 *Int. Comp. LQ* 175.

ZIGARELLI (1995), 'Drug Testing Litigation', 5 *Hum. Res. Mngt. Rev.* 245.

ZIMMERMAN (1983), 'Requiem for a Heavyweight: A Farewell to Warren and Brandeis's Privacy Tort', 63 *Cornell LR* 291.

Zwerling (1993), 'Current Practice and Experience in Erug and Alcohol Testing in the Workplace', 45 *Bulletin on Narcotics* 162.

OFFICIAL DOCUMENTS AND REPORTS

CANADIAN DEPARTMENT OF NATIONAL DEFENCE (1992), *Operation Cascade II: An Anonymous Urinalysis Drug Survey Conducted Across the Canadian Forces* (8 December 8).

CANADIAN LABOUR CONGRESS (1990), Submission to the Standing Committee on Transport on Transport Canada's Proposed Programme for Alcohol and Drug Use in the Transportation Industry (10 April).

COMMISSION NATIONALE DE L'INFORMATIQUE ET DES LIBERTÉS (CNIL)(a) (1985), *6e rapport d'activité.*

—— (b) (1985), Déliberation No. 85–44.

—— (c) (1986), *7e rapport d'activité.*

—— (d) (1986), Déliberation No. 86–54.

—— (e) (1988), *9e rapport d'activité.*

—— (f) (1988), *Dix Ans d'Informatiques et Libertés* (Paris: Economica).

—— (g) (1993), *14e rapport d'activité.*

—— (h) (1994), *15e rapport d'activité.*

—— (i) (1994), *Informatique et Libertés.*

—— (j) (1994), Déliberation No. 94–098.

—— (k) (1995), *16e rapport d'activité.*

—— (l) (1996), *17e rapport d'activité*.

—— (m) 1996), Déliberation No. 96–016.

—— (n) (1996), Déliberation No. 96–107.

—— (o) (1996), Déliberation No. 96–108.

COMMITTEE ON PRIVACY (1972), *Report* ('Younger Committee') (London: Home Office).

COMMITTEE ON PRIVACY AND RELATED MATTERS (1990), *Report* ('Calcutt Committee') (London: Home Office).

COUNCIL OF EUROPE (1989), *Protection of Personal Data Used for Employment Purposes*, Recommendation No. R(89)2.

HEALTH AND WELFARE CANADA AND THE NIAGARA INSTITUTE (1988), *A Report of the National Consultation on Substance Abuse and the Workplace*.

HEALTH AND WELFARE CANADA (1990), *Canadian Laboratory Standards for Drugs Screening in the Workplace* (July).

INFORMATION AND PRIVACY COMMISSIONER OF ONTARIO (IPCO) (1993), *Workplace Privacy*.

INTERNATIONAL LABOUR OFFICE (ILO)(1991, 1993a), *Workers' Privacy*, Conditions of Work Digest (1991, Volume 2, Part I) (*Protection of Personal Data in the Workplace* (1)); (1993, Volume 12, Part III) (*Monitoring and Surveillance in the Workplace* (2); *Testing in the Workplace* (3)).

—— (1993b), *Job Stress: The 20th Century Disease*.

—— (1996c), *Drug and Alcohol Testing in the Workplace: Guiding Principles*.

—— (1998d), *World Labour Report*, 1997–98.

—— (1995e), *Draft Code of Practice on the Protection of Workers' Personal Data*.

—— (1995f), *Code of Practice on the Protection of Workers' Personal Data*.

—— (1988g), *Human Rights: A Common Responsibility*, Part I: Report of the Director-General to the 75th Session of the International Labour Conference (Geneva).

JUSTICE (BRITISH SECTION) (1970), *Privacy and the Law*.

LORD CHANCELLOR'S DEPARTMENT/THE SCOTTISH OFFICE (1993), *Infringement of Privacy*, Consultation Paper.

MINISTRY OF LABOUR (FRANCE)(a) (1990), Circulaire DRT 90–13, 9 July.

—— (b) (1993), Circulaire D.R.T. 93–10, 15 March.

NATIONAL HERITAGE SELECT COMMITTEE (1993), 4th Report, *Privacy and Media Intrusion*.

NETHERLANDS, MINISTRY OF SOCIAL AFFAIRS AND EMPLOYMENT (1989), *De electronische schaduw (The electronic shadow)* (The Hague, July).

NIH–DOE WORKING GROUP (1993), (on Ethical, Legal, and Social Implications of Human Genome Research, National Center for Human Genome Research, Genetic Information and Health Insurance), *Report of the Task Force on Genetic Information and Insurance*.

OFFICE OF MANAGEMENT AND BUDGET (OMB) (1987), 'Privacy Act of 1974: Guidelines on the Privacy Act Implications of 'Call Detail' Programs to Manage Employees' Use of the Government's Telecommunications Systems', 52 *Federal Register* 12990.

OHIO TASK FORCE ON GENETIC TESTING (1995), *Final Report*.

ONTARIO COMMISSION ON INFORMATION AND INDIVIDUAL PRIVACY (1980), *Report*, Volume 3.

ONTARIO LAW REFORM COMMISSION (OLRC)(a) (1992), *Report on Drug and Alcohol Testing in the Workplace*.

—— (b) (1992), *Report on Testing for AIDS*.

PARLIAMENT OF CANADA (1992), 'Social Charter' (Constitution Amendment, 1992 ('Charlottetown Accord')).

PRESIDENT'S COMMISSION ON ORGANIZED CRIME (1986), *America's Habit: Drug Abuse, Drug Trafficking and Organized Crime.*

PRIVACY COMMISSIONER OF CANADA (PCC)(a) (1989), *AIDS and the Privacy Act.*

—— (b) (1990), *Drug Testing and Privacy.*

—— (c) (1992), *Genetic Testing and Privacy.*

—— (d) (1993), *Annual Report, 1992–3.*

—— (d) (1995), *Annual Report.*

—— (e) (1995), *Annual Report, 1994–5.*

—— (f) (1991), *Annual Report, 1990–1.*

—— (g) (1992), *Annual Report, 1991–2.*

—— (h) (1993), *Annual Report, 1992–3.*

—— (i) (1994), *Annual Report, 1993–4.*

—— (j) (1995), *Annual Report, 1994–5.*

PRIVACY PROTECTION STUDY COMMISSION (1977), 'Employment Records', Appendix 3 to the *Report of the Privacy Protection Study Commission.*

QUEBEC COMMISSION ON HUMAN RIGHTS (1991), *Annual Report.*

ROYAL COMMISSION ON TRADE UNIONS AND EMPLOYERS ASSOCIATIONS (1968), *Report (Donovan Report) (1965–8).*

TASK FORCE ESTABLISHED BY THE DEPARTMENT OF COMMUNICATIONS/ DEPARTMENT OF JUSTICE (1972), *Report on Privacy and Computers.*

TRANSPORT CANADA, HEFFRING RESEARCH GROUP (1990), *Substance Use in Transportation: Marine, Airports, Aviation, Surface (Bus/Trucking): Overview Report.*

UNITED STATES BUREAU OF THE CENSUS (1995), *Statistical Abstract of the United States.*

UNITED STATES DEPARTMENT OF ENERGY (1998), Office of Energy Research, Human Genome Program Home Page, (http://www.er.doe.gov/production/oher/hug_top. html).

UNITED STATES DEPARTMENT OF LABOR (1996), *An Employer's Guide to Dealing with Substance Abuse.*

UNITED STATES HOUSE OF REPRESENTATIVES COMMITTEE ON EDUCATION AND LABOR (1993), Labor-Management Relations Sub-committee, Hearings on the proposed *Privacy for Consumers and Workers Act*, HR 1900, 30 June 30.

UNITED STATES OFFICE OF TECHNOLOGY ASSESSMENT (OTA) (1990), *Genetic Monitoring and Screening in the Workplace* (United States Congress).

OTHER

CANADIAN STANDARDS ASSOCIATION (1996), *Model Code for the Protection of Personal Information* (CAN/CSA–Q830–1996).

GALLUP ORGANIZATION (1988), *Drug Testing at Work: A Survey of American Corporations.*

INSTITUTE OF PERSONNEL AND DEVELOPMENT (1997), Press Release, 'Sorted for E's, booze, and work?' (24 October).

INSTITUTE OF PUBLIC POLICY RESEARCH (1991), *The Constitution of the United Kingdom*, Ch. 2, Parts I & II.

ROCHE DIAGNOSTIC SYSTEMS (1984), *Abuscreen Radioimmunoassay for Cannabinoids.*

Index